Literacy's Beginnings

Literacy's Beginnings

Supporting Young Readers and Writers

SIXTH EDITION

TOURO COLLEGE LIBRARY
Kings Hwy

Lea M. McGee
The Ohio State University

Donald J. Richgels
Northern Illinois University

Boston   Columbus   Indianapolis   New York   San Francisco   Upper Saddle River
Amsterdam   Cape Town   Dubai   London   Madrid   Milan   Munich   Paris   Montreal   Toronto
Delhi   Mexico City   São Paulo   Sydney   Hong Kong   Seoul   Singapore   Taipei   Tokyo

KH

Vice President, Editor in Chief: *Aurora Martínez Ramos*
Editor: *Erin K. L. Grelak*
Editorial Assistant: *Michelle Hochberg*
Vice President, Director of Marketing: *Margaret Waples*
Marketing Manager: *Krista Clark*
Production Editor: *Mary Beth Finch*
Editorial Production Service: *S4Carlisle Publishing Services*
Manufacturing Buyer: *Megan Cochran*
Electronic Composition: *S4Carlisle Publishing Services*
Cover Coordinator: *Linda Knowles*
Cover Designer: *Jennifer Hart*

Credits and acknowledgments borrowed from other sources and reproduced, with permission, in this textbook appear on appropriate page within text.

Library of Congress Cataloging-in-Publication Data

McGee, Lea M.
  Literacy's beginnings : supporting young readers and writers / Lea M. McGee, Donald J. Richgels. — 6th ed.
      p. cm.
  Includes bibliographical references.
  ISBN-13: 978-0-13-261765-9
  ISBN-10: 0-13-261765-X
  1. Reading (Early childhood)—United States.   2. Language arts (Early childhood)—United States.   3. Literacy—United States.   I. Richgels, Donald J., 1949- II. Title.
  LB1139.5.R43M33 2012
  372.60973—dc22

                                                    2011000807

10 9 8 7 6 5 4 3 2 1   RRD-VA 15 14 13 12 11

www.pearsonhighered.com

ISBN-13: 978-0-13-261765-9
ISBN-10:   0-13-261765-X

3/19/12

About the Authors

Lea M. McGee, the Marie Clay professor of Reading Recovery and Early Literacy at The Ohio State University, is co-author of *Literacy's Beginnings: Supporting Young Readers and Writers* (6th Ed.) and *Designing Early Literacy Programs: Strategies for At-Risk Preschool and Kindergarten Children*. She has published articles in *The Reading Teacher, Language Arts,* and *Reading Research Quarterly*. She has directed two Early Reading First projects and frequently works with teachers in their classrooms.

Donald J. Richgels is Distinguished Research Professor in Literacy Education at Northern Illinois University. He has published three books, numerous book chapters, and many articles in *The Reading Teacher, Reading Research Quarterly,* and *Early Childhood Research Quarterly,* among others. He teaches graduate and undergraduate courses in early childhood education, reading education, and ESL/Bilingual education.

Brief Contents

Contents

Chapter 5 From Six to Eight Years: Conventional Readers and Writers in Early, Transitional, and Self-Generative Phases   117

Chapter 6 Literacy-Rich Classrooms   149

Chapter 7 Supporting Language and Literacy Learning in Preschools   183

Chapter **8** Supporting Literacy Learning in Kindergarten   217

Chapter 9 Supporting Literacy Learning in First Grade   247

Chapter 10 Supporting Literacy Learning in Second through Fourth Grades   279

Chapter 11 Meeting the Needs of English Language Learners   323

Preface

POINT OF VIEW

Literacy's Beginnings: Supporting Young Readers and Writers is intended to help preservice and in-service teachers and other caregivers of young children to be aware of and supportive of children's literacy knowledge as it grows and changes from birth through the elementary school years. Our purpose is to provide readers with a thorough understanding of the long continuum of literacy growth and of how sensitive teachers can guide children as they move along this continuum. We wish to show teachers how to be watchful of children, yet provide learning opportunities and instruction that meet children where they are and take them to the next steps. All instruction that helps children learn to do something new in a joyful way is developmentally appropriate. Teachers who are effective know when to step in and provide more support—even explicit, direct instruction—and when to step back and let children gain independence in accomplishing a task.

We believe that literacy learning is developmental, but not in the sense of proceeding in an irreversible, step-by-step progression. No child's path to conventional reading and writing is exactly the same as another child's. However, literacy learning is developmental in a way that is very commonsensical to anyone who has spent time with children. What a child knows about reading and writing changes dramatically over time.

We also believe that teachers have a critical role to play in young children's literacy learning. Failure to learn to read and write has long-term academic, social, and emotional effects on the lives of children, their families, and society. Teachers make the difference in whether some children, especially children most vulnerable in our society, learn to become effective and motivated readers and writers. We believe that the descriptions of literacy events and instructional practices we describe in this book will help teachers be more careful observers of children so they will be more aware of what children are capable of learning. We hope our instructional suggestions help teachers deliver instruction that has a powerful impact on the learning of their children.

ORGANIZATION OF THE TEXT

Literacy's Beginnings is grouped into two parts. The theme of Part 1 (Chapters 1 through 5) is learners. The first five chapters in the book describe children and how they change as readers and writers. Each of these chapters ends with suggestions for assessing children so that readers of the book can more carefully observe children.

The word *literacy* has many connotations in everyday life. To us, being literate means being able to find meaning in written symbols. This definition includes much territory left out by everyday definitions of literacy; for example, a pretend reading of a favorite storybook qualifies as a literate act by our definition, but it does not usually qualify under the everyday definition. Still, our definition does not include everything that very young children do with books and writing materials.

The terms *beginner, novice, experimenter*, and *conventional* (*early, transitional*, and *critical self-generating*) *reader* and *writer* also demand clarification. We use them as convenient shorthand for the developments described in Chapters 2 through 5, but we do not mean for them to define rigid, irreversible stages. Indeed, we do not call them stages. A child may exhibit many of the knowledges in the cluster of knowledges that we associate with one of those four terms. Furthermore, a child who usually reads or writes like a novice in some situations and with some tasks will also read or write like an experimenter in other situations and with other tasks. The important point is that, over time, children will more often resemble conventional readers and writers.

Part 2 of *Literacy's Beginnings* concerns classrooms and characteristics of school environments and teacher roles that promote children's development from beginners to conventional readers and writers. Chapter 6 is an overview of the elements included in a literacy-rich classroom. Chapter 7 focuses on preschool, Chapter 8 on kindergarten, Chapter 9 on first grade, and Chapter 10 on second, third, and fourth grades. Chapter 11 describes the literacy needs of English language learners. Each of these chapters also includes a section on assessment.

The sixth edition of *Literacy's Beginnings* has several **new features**. This edition

- Includes a description of assessment procedures and tasks in each chapter. This new emphasis on assessment embedded within descriptions of development (Chapters 1 through 5) and instruction (Chapters 6 through 11) captures the assessment-instruction-assessment cycle that drives the most effective instruction. We have added more information about a greater variety of assessments including assessment of writing.
- Describes effective instruction in alphabet recognition, concepts about print, the alphabetic principle, and phonemic awareness in Chapters 7 and 8, which have been considerably revised to reflect the findings of the National Early Literacy Panel and shared through the results of many Early Reading First grants. We have also strengthened in several places descriptions of different kinds of read-aloud techniques to meet the needs of diverse learners. The National Literacy Panel found what it called *shared reading* (reading by adults and shared through extended conversations with children) to be effective in enhancing language development and concepts about print.

- Provides a chapter exclusively focused on English language learners. As these learners have increasingly become evident in nearly all school systems, and because these learners struggle to reach the same levels of performance as their English-speaking peers, teachers need a more systematic approach to their instruction. We continue to discuss differentiating instruction for these learners in every instructional chapter. However, our newly revised Chapter 11 provides a model of effective instruction for English language learners and examples of exemplary teachers using this approach.
- Offers new and research-based information about the importance of response to intervention (RTI) and the use of monitoring and screening assessments to identify children who need more intensive instruction. We have added examples of teachers from PK through the elementary years who use assessments to identify children who struggle and need tier 2 instruction. We have described their differentiated, intense approach to instruction for these struggling readers and writers. Each instructional chapter continues to provide information on differentiating instruction.
- Includes examples of new literacies, which take advantage of today's multimodal methods of communication in classroom activities. Each chapter has a new feature called "Technology Tie-In," which provides information about Web sites for more information related to the chapter topics, Web sites that children can use for reading and writing activities, and free Web sites that allow teachers and children to create podcasts and narrated digital stories.
- Describes new techniques for improving listening comprehension through reading books aloud. More vocabulary activities are included in this edition, and more information about fluency is provided including suggestions on the assessment of fluency and intense teaching of fluency.
- Provides updated case studies of exemplary teachers who teach a wide range of diverse learners in the chapters and at the end of the chapters that allow students to understand the text information through real-life situations.
- Provides updated practice activities at the end of the chapters that allow students to apply the text information in practice formats useful for acquiring a deeper understanding of the material.

Each chapter of *Literacy's Beginnings* again has four sections designed to help readers consolidate and apply what they have learned. First, we list the "Key Concepts" used in the chapter. Applying the information presents a case study on children's interactions with written language similar to the many examples given in the chapter. The reader is asked to apply the chapter's concepts to this example. "Going Beyond the Text" suggests ways for readers to seek out real-life experiences that will test both the chapter's ideas and the readers' understandings. We ask questions and make suggestions to guide readers' planning and reflecting on those experiences. Finally, "References" include a list of all publications cited in the chapter.

MyEducationLab

myeducationlab The power of classroom practice.

In *Preparing Teachers for a Changing World*, Linda Darling-Hammond and her colleagues point out that grounding teacher education in real classrooms—among real teachers and students and among actual examples of students' and teachers' work—is an important, and perhaps even an essential, part of training teachers for the complexities of teaching in today's classrooms. MyEducationLab is an online learning solution that provides contextualized interactive exercises, simulations, and other resources designed to help develop the knowledge and skills teachers need. All of the activities and exercises in MyEducationLab are built around essential learning outcomes for teachers and are mapped to professional teaching standards. Utilizing classroom video, authentic student and teacher artifacts, case studies, and other resources and assessments, the scaffolded learning experiences in MyEducationLab offer preservice teachers and those who teach them a unique and valuable education tool.

For each topic covered in the course, you will find most or all of the following features and resources.

Connection to National Standards

Now it is easier than ever to see how coursework is connected to national standards. Each topic on MyEducationLab lists intended learning outcomes connected to the appropriate national standards. Additionally, all of the activities and exercises in MyEducationLab are mapped to the appropriate national standards and learning outcomes.

Assignments and Activities

Designed to enhance student understanding of concepts covered in class and save instructors preparation and grading time, these assignable exercises show concepts in action (through video, cases, and/or student and teacher artifacts). They help students deepen content knowledge and synthesize and apply concepts and strategies they read about in the book. (Correct answers for these assignments are available to the instructor only under the Instructor Resource tab.)

As part of your access to MyEducationLab.
A+RISE®, developed by three-time Teacher of the Year and administrator, Evelyn Arroyo, gives new teachers in grades K-12 quick, research-based strategies that get to the "how" of targeting their instruction and making content accessible for all students, including English language learners.

A+RISE® Standards2Strategy™ is an innovative and interactive online resource that offers new teachers in grades K-12 just in time, research-based instructional strategies that:

- Meet the linguistic needs of ELLs as they learn content
- Differentiate instruction for all grades and abilities
- Offer reading and writing techniques, cooperative learning, use of linguistic and nonlinguistic representations, scaffolding, teacher modeling, higher order thinking, and alternative classroom ELL assessment
- Provide support to help teachers be effective through the integration of listening, speaking, reading, and writing along with the content curriculum
- Improve student achievement
- Are aligned to Common Core Elementary Language Arts standards (for the literacy strategies) and to English language proficiency standards in WIDA, Texas, California, and Florida.

IRIS Center Resources

The IRIS Center at Vanderbilt University (http://iris.peabody.vanderbilt.edu), which is funded by the U.S. Department of Education's Office of Special Education Programs (OSEP), develops training enhancement materials for preservice and in-service teachers. The Center works with experts from across the country to create challenge-based interactive modules, case study units, and podcasts that provide research-validated information about working with students in inclusive settings. In your MyEducationLab course, we have integrated this content where appropriate.

Course Resources

The Course Resources section on MyEducationLab is designed to help students put together an effective lesson plan, prepare for and begin their career, navigate their first year of teaching, and understand key educational standards, policies, and laws. The Course Resources tab includes the following:

- The **Lesson Plan Builder** is an effective and easy-to-use tool that students can use to create, update, and share quality lesson plans. The software also makes it easy to integrate state content standards into any lesson plan.
- The **Preparing a Portfolio** module provides guidelines for creating a high-quality teaching portfolio.
- **Beginning Your Career** offers tips, advice, and other valuable information on
  - *Resume Writing and Interviewing*: Includes expert advice on how to write impressive resumes and prepare for job interviews.
  - *Your First Year of Teaching*: Provides practical tips to set up a first classroom, manage student behavior, and more easily organize for instruction and assessment.
  - *Law and Public Policies*: Details specific directives and requirements teachers need to understand under the No Child Left Behind Act and the Individuals with Disabilities Education Improvement Act of 2004.

- *Longman Dictionary of Contemporary English Online*. Make use of this online version of the CD-ROM of the *Longman Dictionary of Contemporary English*—the quickest and easiest way to look up any word while you are working on MyEducationLab.

Certification and Licensure

The Certification and Licensure section is designed to help students pass their licensure exam by giving them access to state test requirements, overviews of what tests cover, and sample test items. The Certification and Licensure tab includes the following:

- **State Certification Test Requirements.** Here, students can click on a state and will then be taken to a list of state certification tests.
- Students can click on the **Licensure Exams** they need to take to find
  - Basic information about each test
  - Descriptions of what is covered on each test
  - Sample test questions with explanations of correct answers
- **National Evaluation Series**™ by Pearson. Here, students can see the tests in the NES, learn what is covered on each exam, and access sample test items with descriptions and rationales of correct answers. They can also purchase interactive online tutorials developed by Pearson Evaluation Systems and the Pearson Teacher Education and Development group.
- **ETS Online Praxis Tutorials.** Here, students can purchase interactive online tutorials developed by ETS and by the Pearson Teacher Education and Development group. Tutorials are available for the Praxis I exams and for select Praxis II exams.

Visit www.myeducationlab.com for a demonstration of this exciting new online teaching resource.

The Children and Teachers in This Book

Literacy's Beginnings is based in part on a growing body of research about emerging literacy and in part on our experiences with young children, including our own children. We incorporate many descriptions of those experiences. We wish to add here two important cautions that we will repeat throughout the text. The first is about children's ages. We usually give the age of the children in our examples in order to fully represent the facts. However, we do not intend for those ages to serve as norms against which to compare other children.

Our second caution is about backgrounds. Many, but not all, of the children in our examples have had numerous and varied home experiences with books and writing materials. Their meaningful interactions with written language are often what one would expect of children from such environments. Children with different backgrounds may exhibit different initial orientations toward written language. However, our involvement with teachers whose children come to preschool or elementary school with different backgrounds has shown us that nearly all children can benefit from the informed observation and child-centered, meaning-oriented support described in this book.

The classroom support chapters of this book are based on our own teaching experiences and on our observations of teachers. Just as we have known and observed many literate young children, so also have we known and observed many very sensitive, intelligent, and effective teachers of young children. All the samples of children's reading and writing in this book are authentic cases from our own teaching and research and the research of others cited in the text.

ACKNOWLEDGMENTS

W E OWE A GREAT DEAL to the many children whose experiences with written language were the basis for much of this book. We thank them and their parents for cooperating so generously with us—for supporting us in the extended "literacy event" of writing this book. We thank the teachers who shared their classroom experiences with us: Mary Jane Everett, Candice Jones, Karen Kurr, Roberta McHardy, Nancy Miller, Terry Morel, Kathy Walker, Leigh Courtney, Karen King, Jackie Zickuhr, Carolyn Vaughn, Monette Reyes, Karla Poremba, Diane Roloff, Cindi Chandler, Laurie Coleman, Richard Lomax, Michelle Tran, Michelle Bellamy, Margaret Medders, Linda Rodgers, Kay Armstrong, Litta Norris, Tomasine Lewis, Jade Turk, Ede Wortham, Anna Carlin, Joseph Warren, Andrea Schlomer, Carolyn Palmer, Jan Leopard, Heather Smythe, Juliet Prowell, Victoria Hall, and Annemarie Thomas.

We owe much to the editors and their assistants at Allyn and Bacon, including Aurora Martínez Ramos, Erin Grelak, and Mary Beth Finch. We are also grateful to Norine Strang and the staff at S4Carlisle Publishing Services for their careful handling of the manuscript during editing and production. We thank reviewers Eva L. Davis, Langston University; Gail T. Eichman, Baldwin Wallace College: Lee Freeman, University of Alabama; Margaret C. Hagood, College of Charleston; and Carol Lauritzen, Eastern Oregon University; as well as reviewers of previous editions Lisa Boeglin of Cape Evansville; Sheila G. Cohen, SUNY Cortland; Teunis (Tony) Donk, Hope College; Ann Porter Gifford, Southeast Missouri State University; Margaret Hagood, College of Charleston; and Melissa Stinnett, University of Wisconsin, Oshkosh, for helpful comments and suggestions.

We acknowledge the contributions of our many students. We learned from our discussions with them about literacy's beginnings and from the examples they shared of their interactions with young readers and writers.

CHAPTER 1

Understanding Children's Literacy Development

KEY CONCEPTS

Schema
Feature
Tabula Rasa
Zone of Proximal
   Development
Scaffolding
Pragmatics
Semantics
Syntax
Phonology
Morpheme
Telegraphic Speech
Phonemes
Phonological
   Awareness

Phonemic Awareness
Functions of Written
   Language
Written Language
   Meanings
Contextualized
   Language
Decontextualized
   Language
Written Language Forms
Letter Features
Mock Letters
Metalinguistic
   Awareness
Meaning-Form Links

Alphabetic Principle
Orthography
Phonogram
Beginners
Novices
Experimenters
Conventional Readers
   and Writers
Conventions of Written
   Language
Written Language
   Assessment
Screening Assessments
Monitoring
   Assessments

Language, Thinking, and Learning

IAGET'S (1955) AND VYGOTSKY'S (1978) theories of language and learning make unique contributions to what we understand about young children's literacy development.

Schemas and Learning

An important idea from both Piaget's and Vygotsky's theories is that learning occurs as children acquire new concepts, or **schemas.** A concept or schema is a mental structure in which we organize and store all the information we know about people, places, objects, or activities.

Schemas. We use the concept *book* as an example to explain the nature of schemas. If asked to tell everything that comes to mind when they hear the word *book*, many people will think of a physical object, small enough to be held, carried, and stored on a shelf, with a cover and inked pages that display script that a reader can read. All schemas, such as the schema for *book*, are collections of information called **features.** These features may include *whos, whats, hows,* and *whys,* in this case, *who* uses a book (a reader), *what* constitutes a book (a cover, pages, print), *how* one experiences a book (holding it, carrying it, putting it on a shelf, reading it), and *why* one does so (in order to have easy—portable, storable, readable—access to whatever is encoded by the script).

All concepts or schemas are related to other concepts. For example, our description of the features of the schema for *book* depends on knowing the schemas for *page, script, read,* and *reader.* Other schemas related to *book* include *library, bookstore, bookcase, backpack, paperback, hard cover, textbook, novel, dictionary, travel guide, phonebook,* and even specific titles such as *The Adventures of Huckleberry Finn* or *Catcher in the Rye.*

Any concept or schema, its related concepts or schemas, and their features arise from experience, including the experience of growing up in a certain context and within a particular culture. Many cultures include a notion of *script* that is read left to right (as English script is). However, some scripts, such as Arabic and Hebrew, are read right to left. Furthermore, cultures change and with them the schemas by which they organize and store information. Ancient Romans had a Latin word, *liber,* that translates as "book," but they read script from scrolls, not pages. In traditional Japanese culture, columns of script were read from top to bottom and from right to left (from the bottom of one column to the top of the next column to the left). Yet, modern Japanese script appears in rows and is read from left to right.

However, concept or schema formation is also influenced by personal experiences, needs, and preferences. For some people, the concept *book* includes graphic novels that require reading pictures as much as reading script, e-books that display script on a screen rather than on pages, or audiobooks that are listened to rather than read.

We have schemas for many things, including objects, such as a *computer* or *fire truck;* people, such as a *teacher* or *rock star;* places, such as *home* or *restaurant;* and activities, such as *making a sandwich* or *writing a persuasive essay.* Thinking and learning depend on these many schemas and concepts. Thinking involves calling to mind information from schemas and using that information to perform mental actions such as making inferences, predictions, or generalizations or drawing conclusions. Suppose, for example, that we see someone browsing in the travel section of a bookstore. Later, we are in the checkout line behind this person and we see that she has selected an Italian phrase book and a travel guide for Tuscany. We infer she might be taking a trip to Italy soon.

Similarly, learning involves adding to or changing schemas. Suppose we see for the first time a person lightly passing his hands over the pages of a book that displays not print but rather rows of variously configured embossed dots. We might modify our schema for *script* to include Braille and our schema for *read* to include use of touch as well as sight.

Infants and Schemas.   Children begin life with few concepts—or even none. In this sense, a child's mind might be thought of as a **tabula rasa,** or a blank slate. One of Piaget's greatest insights was his suggestion of how children acquire the knowledge to begin filling in concept schemas, such as a schema for *book*. He suggested that infants are born already knowing how to go about acquiring content knowledge, or knowledge of things. Thus, their minds really are not blank slates; although they may lack concept schemas, they have built-in action schemas for how to acquire concepts.

Piaget's idea was that young humans learn through action. They are born with special schemas for how to act and how to respond to their world. These action schemas bring children in contact with reality (things) in ways that produce knowledge of the world. More action produces more knowledge. As children acquire knowledge and continue to act, changes happen to the things they are in contact with (e.g., milk gets spilled) and changes happen to previous knowledge (e.g., the schema for milk changes to include the idea that milk does not behave like a cracker—it doesn't keep a shape). The action schemas themselves change as active, problem-solving children evolve more effective strategies for making their way in the world.

Two very important conclusions can be drawn from Piaget's theory of how children learn. One is that children create their own knowledge by forming and reforming concepts in their minds. The second conclusion is that children's states of knowledge—or views of the world—can be very different from one time to the next, and especially different from an adult's.

The Relation between Language and Learning

We have already discussed the importance of action to Piaget's idea of learning. Children's actions may physically change objects in the world. While helping to wash the family car, a child may immerse a light, dry, stiff sponge into a bucket of water, changing its appearance and texture as it gets wet. That same action may change the child's concept or schema of a sponge, introducing the features *heavy, wet,* and *squishy,* and it may allow the child to see a connection between the schemas *water* and *sponge.*

But can children change their schema for *sponge* to include the notion that it can be heavy, wet, and squishy without hearing or using those words? How important is it for the child to have the words *sponge, water, heavy, wet,* and *squishy* available as labels for what is experienced in such a situation? Vygotsky stressed the importance of having someone with the child who can supply such language. According to Vygotsky, a parent who says to the child, "Boy that's a wet sponge!" or "The water sure made that sponge heavy!" or "Now that sponge is squishy!" plays a vital role in the child's learning about sponges and water. Vygotsky placed a strong emphasis on the social component of cognitive and language development.

Social Basis for Learning.

Vygotsky argued that all learning first takes place in a social context. In order to build a new concept, children interact with others who provide feedback for their hypotheses or who help them accomplish a task they could not do on their own. Children's or adults' language is an important part of the social context of learning. Suppose that a child's concept of the letter *W* does not include its conventional orientation (upright). This child may write $\Lambda\Lambda$ and call it *W*. Another child who observes this writing may say, "That's not a *W*, that's an *M*." This feedback provides the child with a label for the new concept, *M*, and prompts the child to reconsider the concept of *W* by adding an orientation (upright).

Vygotsky believed that children need to be able to talk about a new problem or a new concept in order to understand it and use it. Adults supply language that fits children's needs at a particular stage or in response to a particular problem. Language can be part of a routinized situation. It can label the situation or parts of the situation, or it can help pose a problem or structure a problem-solving task. As the child gradually internalizes the language that was first supplied by an adult, the language and a routine task that helps in solving the problem become the child's own.

An example of a child's internalizing the language of a routine is how the child learns to use the words *all gone*. The parents of a child might repeatedly hide a favorite toy and then say, "All gone!" Then they reveal the toy and say, "Here it is!" This becomes a game for the child. Eventually, the child may play the game without the adult, using the same language, "All gone" and "Here it is" (Gopnick & Meltzoff, 1986). A young child's ability to play the game of "all gone" alone means that he or she has internalized the actions and language of his or her mother or father. For Vygotsky, all learning involves a movement from doing activities in a social situation with the support of a more knowledgeable other to internalizing the language and actions of the more knowledgeable other and being able to use this knowledge alone.

Zone of Proximal Development.

Vygotsky wrote about a **zone of proximal development,** which is an opportune area for growth but one in which children are dependent on help from others. An adult, or perhaps an older child, must give young children advice if they are to succeed within this zone and if eventually, by internalizing that advice, they are to perform independently.

When children are working in their zones of proximal development, they complete some parts of a task, and adults or older children perform the parts of the task that the younger children cannot yet do alone. In this way, young children can accomplish tasks that are too difficult for them to complete on their own. Adults' or older children's talk is an important part of helping young children—it scaffolds the task. **Scaffolding** is what an adult or an older child does to help a child to do what he or she can do with help but could not do alone. For example, an adult may talk, give advice, direct children's attention, alert them to the sequence of activities, and provide information for completing the task successfully. Gradually, children internalize this talk and use it to direct their own attention, to plan, and to control their activities.

Figure 1.1 presents a letter that five-year-old Kristen and her mother wrote together. After Kristen's second day in kindergarten, she announced, "I'm not going to school tomorrow. I don't like being last in line." Apparently, Kristen rode a different bus from any of the other children in her classroom and the teacher called her last to line up for the buses. When Kristen's mother reminded her of all the things she liked to do in school, Kristen replied, "OK, I'll go [to school], but you tell Mrs. Peters [the teacher] I don't want to be last all the time." Kristen's mother said, "We'll write her a note. You write it and I'll help." Kristen agreed and wrote Mrs. Peter's name as her mother spelled it. Then Kristen said the message she wanted to write ("I always don't want to be the last person in the line"). Her mother said, "The first word is *I*. You can spell that. What letter do you hear?" Kristen wrote the letter *i*, but when her mother began saying the word *always* slowly for Kristen to spell, she refused to spell any more words. So Kristen's mother wrote *always* and then spelled the word *don't* for Kristen to write. She suggested that she write one word and Kristen write one word. As shown in Figure 1.1, the final letter is a combination of Kristen's writing, with invented or incomplete spellings (*t* for *to*, *b* for *be*, *Lst* for *last*, and *pwsn* for *person*) as she listened to her mother say each sound in a word, and her mother's writing. Kristen could not have accomplished the task of writing this letter without her mother's scaffolding.

A year and a half later, Kristen ran into the kitchen where her mother was preparing dinner and handed her the note shown in Figure 1.2. This note reads, "I hate when you brought me to Penny's house" (Penny is Kristen's babysitter). Kristen had written the note in her room by herself after her mother was late picking her up. This note

FIGURE 1.1 Kristen's Letter to Her Teacher

I Hate when you Brot me to prnes house

Kristen's Letter to Her Mother

illustrates the results of scaffolding and working within the zone of proximal development. In kindergarten, Kristen needed her mother's scaffolding to write a letter of protest to her teacher. She needed her mother's support to hear sounds in words, to keep track of what she had written, and to sustain the effort of writing. At the end of first grade, she could write a letter of protest on her own, inventing spellings and reading to keep track of her message as she wrote.

FOUR SYSTEMS OF SPOKEN LANGUAGE

CHILDREN LEARN FROM THE LANGUAGE OF OTHERS. Not only do they learn about the topics of others' talk, but they also learn about language itself. At first they learn about spoken language, but even before they are fully competent speakers and listeners, they also learn about written language—how to read and write.

Spoken language allows speakers to communicate ideas to one another. We communicate and understand through sounds that make up words, through the meaning of words and sentences, and through our understanding of conventions required in conversation (for example, how to take turns so that only one person is talking at a time). Spoken language actually involves four different linguistic systems: pragmatics, semantics, syntax, and phonology.

Pragmatics deals with social and cultural contexts of speaking and conveys the functions or purposes of speech. **Semantics** is related to the system of meaning, including the meaning of words and their combinations. **Syntax** is related to the order and organization of words in sentences. **Phonology** is the system of speech sounds that make up the words of a language.

Pragmatics

An important system of language involves the use of language in everyday life, especially in its most widely experienced expression, conversation. Pragmatics has to do with both the mechanics of conversation (what makes a conversation work, for example, turn taking) and conversational styles (how one person or group converses differently than another person or group, for example, with quicker or shorter passing of turns from one participant to another) (Richgels, 2004). Pragmatics also has to do with the purposes or functions that language serves in everyday life. Children, like the adults around them, use their spoken language in functional ways. Halliday (1975) identified seven functions of spoken language. Table 1.1 summarizes those functions of language, using examples from children's speech.

Semantics

Meaning is at the heart of spoken language (Crystal, 2006). Human experience demands that we communicate messages to one another, and humans are constantly engaged in meaning-making activities through face-to-face conversations. However, meaning sometimes is slippery, requiring that we work at conveying our intentions and getting others'. Messages we construct from conversations are never exact; they always differ in some degree from what was actually spoken. All of us have experienced not being understood; we say, "But, that's not what I meant!" Meaning involves more than just capturing the words others say. It involves interpreting messages.

One aspect of semantics, or the system of meaning, is knowing units of meaning. We usually consider the smallest unit of meaning a word, but units of meaning can actually be smaller than a word. Linguists call the smallest unit of meaning a **morpheme.** The word *start* consists of one morpheme, and the word *restart* has two morphemes: *re* and *start*. *Re* is considered a morpheme because it alters the meaning of the word *start* when it is added to the word. Other morphemes can be added to *start* that will alter meaning by changing the verb tense, such as adding *ed* or *s*. Morphemes can also alter meaning by changing the part of speech, such as when adding *able* to *drink*.

The meaning of words is an important part of the semantic system. We have already discussed how young children begin acquiring word meanings by developing schema or concepts related to words. For example, the meaning of the word *pineapple* may include knowing *spiky, sweet, fruit, yellow, juicy,* and *buy it at the grocery*. We have also stressed that because people have different experiences related to words, they have different meanings associated with them.

Syntax

Syntax is the set of rules for how to produce and comprehend sentences in a language. Syntax draws on order and organization. In some languages, including English, the order of words in sentences is crucial (consider, for example, *The boy kicked the goat* versus *The goat kicked the boy*). In other languages, word order is not important. Instead, word endings are critical for understanding who did what to whom (for example, in Latin, *Lupus agnum portat,* which means, "The wolf carries the lamb," versus *Lupum agnus portat,* which means, "The lamb carries the wolf").

TABLE 1.1 Halliday's Language Functions

Language	Function	Spoken Language Examples	Written Language Examples
Instrumental	Satisfies needs and wants	"Gimme that!" "I want pizza!"	Birthday present wish list, sign-up sheet, grant proposal, petition
Regulatory	Controls others	"Stop that!" "Don't spill!"	List of classroom rules, traffic sign, No Smoking sign, policy handbook
Interactional	Creates interaction with others	"Let's play with the blocks." "Anybody want to paint?"	Party invitation, e-mail to a friend, membership card, "Hello, I'm _____" name tag
Personal	Expresses personal thoughts and opinions	"I like red." "I'm bored."	Letter to the editor, Valentine, journal entry, campaign button
Heuristic	Seeks information	"Are we there yet?" "Why?"	Questionnaire, survey, Internet search entry, insurance claim form, letter of inquiry
Imaginative	Creates imaginary worlds	"This can be our airplane." "You be the robber and I'm the police."	Movie script, short story, novel, poem, label on a play center prop, readers' theater script
Informative	Communicates information	"This is a rectangle." "Today is Wednesday."	Questionnaire results, survey results, Internet site, completed insurance claim form, social studies report, nutrition facts on food package, encyclopedia entry, dictionary entry, class birthday list, school-home newsletter, attendance report, drivers' manual

Source: Adapted from Halliday, 1975.

Changes in syntax are among the hallmarks of language development (Berko-Gleason & Ratner, 2009). Between the ages of fourteen months and eighteen months, children begin putting two and then three words together to communicate what grown-ups would say with a whole sentence. This is called **telegraphic speech.** They use subject-verb "sentences" such as *Daddy come* to mean *Daddy came* or *Daddy is coming* or *I want Daddy to come home.* They use subject-object "sentences" such as *Daddy sock* to mean *Daddy got my sock* or *Daddy dropped his sock,* and verb-object "sentences" such as *put cookie* to mean *Put the cookie here on my plate.* Their questions have the same form as declarative sentences but with rising intonation, such as *We go now?* (with rising tone).

By the time children enter school, they typically use sentences six to eight words in length and sometimes even longer, complex sentences with dependent and independent clauses such as *When we get to Grandma's, I'm going to play on the swing.* At school entry, children's language is so well developed that they can complete sentences by anticipating what words would both be meaningful and fit the grammatical classes indicated in the sentence patterns. For example, when they hear the sentence, *I took a long ride in my mother's _____,* children readily supply the meaningful noun *car* or *truck* to complete the sentence.

When children begin reading in elementary school, their understanding of syntax helps them by allowing them to anticipate words before reading (Clay, 1993; Mansell, Evans, & Hamilton-Hulak, 2005). In fact, children often make mistakes when reading (called miscues) that reveal that they are anticipating words that would make sense and fit the structural or grammatical patterns of sentences. For example, one first grader, when faced with a story about a mother pig and her piglets, made several miscues:

Child: Once upon a time there was a mother pig.

Text: Once there was a mother pig.

Child: She had some little pigs.

Text: She had six little piglets.

Notice that the child added the phrase *upon a time,* which would make sense in the first sentence. In the second sentence, the child substituted the words *some* for *six* and *pigs* for *piglets.* These substitutions make sense and fit the grammatical classes of words expected in the sentence.

Phonology

The phonological system refers to the system of spoken sounds in a language. Each language uses some of the few hundreds of possible speech sounds of human languages. English, for example, uses approximately forty-three speech sounds, or **phonemes** (Table 1.2). Phonemes are the smallest units of sound that are combined and contrasted in a language's words.

Phonemes are the building blocks of words. Consider, for example, the four phonemes /b/, /p/, /i/, and /l/. The last three can be combined to make the word *pill,* and the first two are contrasted when distinguishing the words in the minimal pair *pill* and *bill.* The difference in the pronunciations of /p/ and /b/ is slight. It is only that for /p/ we do not use our voices and for /b/ we do; everything else—how we use our tongues and throats, how we shape our lips, how we part our teeth—is identical. Yet speakers and listeners rely on that very small difference, that contrast; it is all that signals two very different English meanings, a dose of medicine versus a duck's mouth.

Phonemes are also abstractions. For example, when we say "the *p* sound," we reference a set of sounds, slightly different in pronunciation from one another, usually

TABLE 1.2 Common English Phonemes

Consonant Phonemes	Word Examples	Grapheme Examples
/b/	bat, cab, rabbit	B, bb
/ch/	chat, pitcher, match	ch, tch
/d/	dog, hid, opened	d, ed
/f/	fur, bluff, phone, rough, half	f, ff, ph, gh, lf
/g/	goat, dog, burgh	g, gh
/h/	home, wholesome	h, wh
/j/	jump, gem, page, edge	j, g, dge
/k/	cot, kiss, stick, choir	c, k, ck, ch
/l/	like, mill	l, ll
/m/	mop, room, climb, hymn	m, mb, mn
/n/	nose, sun, know, gnash	n, kn, gn
/ng/	sang	ng
/p/	pot, hop, spot	p
/r/	run, write	r, wr
/s/	sat, wipes, mass, scientific, psychiatrist	s, ss, sc, ps
/sh/	shop, rush, champagne, tissue, sugar, pension, social, spacious, motion,	sh, ch, ss, s, c, t
/t/	tip, admit, bottle, stopped	t, tt, ed
/TH/	that, bother, bathing	th
/th/	thick, author, bath	th
/v/	vine, five	v
/w/	water	w
/wh/	when	wh
/y/	yes, opinion	y, i
/z/	zip, buzz, runs, rose, has, xenophobia	z, zz, s, x
/zh/	leisure, azure	s, z

Vowel Phonemes	Word Examples	Grapheme Examples
/A/	take, pain, say, break, hazy, stable, freight, rein, hey	a_e, ai, ay, ea, a, eigh, ei, ey
/a/	sat, giraffe	a
/ar/	car	ar
/aw/	paw, cause, watering, caught, dog, cough, walk	aw, au, a, augh, o, ou, al
/E/	tree, here, be, meat, baby, thief, neither	ee, e_e, e, ea, y, ie, ei
/e/	red, bread	e, ea
/er/	jerk, jury, burr, stir	er, ur, urr, ir
/I/	lime, lie, fry, tight, stifle	i_e, ie, y, igh, i
/i/	pit, myth	i, y
/O/	note, moat, doe, show, oval	o_e, oa, oe, ow, o
/o/	cot, swat, palm	o, a, al
/oi/	soil, toy	oi, oy
/or/	sort	or
/oo/	book, put, should	oo, u, oul
/ow/	out, how	ou, ow
/OO/	boo, duke, glue, stew, suit, group	oo, u_e, ue, ew, ui, ou
/U/	universe, use, cube, few	u, u_e, ew
/u/	rug, blood, rough, ago	u, oo, ou, a

Notes:
- This phoneme list is dialect-sensitive. That is, pronunciations differ from one dialect to another. For example, in some U.S. English dialects, cot and caught are pronounced the same, both with the middle phoneme /o/; there is no separate /aw/ phoneme in those dialects. As another example, in many dialects of U.S. English, the first phonemes of *water* and *when* are identical: /w/; /wh/ is a separate phoneme only in dialects that produce a breathy sound (similar to /h/) before the /w/ in "WH words." As still another example, in some dialects of U.S. English, the first vowel sound in *neither* is /I/, and so *neither* would appear as a word example in the /I/ row of the chart rather than in the /E/ row.
- There is no "C sound"; C usually spells the /k/ phoneme (<u>c</u>at) or the /s/ phoneme (<u>c</u>ity). There is no "X sound"; X usually spells the two phonemes /k/ + /s/ (bo<u>x</u>) or the one phoneme /z/ (<u>x</u>ylophone). There is no "Q sound"; qu usually spells the two phonemes /k/ + /w/.
- Sometimes /r/ after a vowel strongly affects the vowel's pronunciation. With /ar/, /er/, and /or/, this chart shows the /r/ and the vowels it so strongly affects as single vowel phonemes although it can be argued that each of these is really two phonemes. For example, /or/ in *sort* could be represented as the two phonemes /O/ plus /r/; in that case, *sort* would have four phonemes, /s·O·r·t/, rather than three, /s·or·t/.

Source: Adapted from "Common Core Standards in Language Arts," 2010. Retrieved from www.corestandards.org/assets/Appendix_A.pdf, pp. 17, 18, Figures 8 and 9.

depending on the context in which they are pronounced (i.e., what other phonemes precede and follow them) (Crystal, 2006). These differences within a phoneme category do not matter. Language users can ignore them. To appreciate the nature of phoneme categories, notice the difference between /p/ pronunciations in *span* and *pan* (most people do not at first notice this difference, but dangling a piece of paper before their mouths when they say the two words reveals the difference; one pronunciation of /p/ is breathy enough to move the paper, the other is not).

Phonological awareness requires the ability to think and talk about what happens with sounds in spoken language. Children who have phonological awareness notice patterns and groupings of sounds. For example, they can decide if two words rhyme and can clap out syllables in words.

An even more sophisticated level of phonological awareness is called **phonemic awareness.** This is the ability to attend to phonemes—for example, to detect if two words begin with the same sound. Acquiring phonemic awareness is important for literacy development in alphabetic languages, such as English, in which alphabet letters often correspond to phonemes (Adams, 1990; Ehri, Nunes, Willows, Schuster, Yaghoub-Zadeh, & Shanahan, 2001; Verhagen, Aarnoutse, & van Leeuwe, 2009). As we will see later in this book, the ability to segment words into their individual phonemes comes gradually, but it is a crucial part of becoming a reader and writer (National Reading Panel, 2000).

Four Systems of Written Language

BY THE TIME CHILDREN ENTER SCHOOL, they are able unconsciously to control the four language systems—pragmatics, semantics, syntax, and phonology—to communicate with their peers and adults. Children's learning to read and write depends on a solid foundation of spoken language competence, upon which is added knowledge about and skillful use of written language forms and functions (Freeman & Freeman, 2004). Table 1.3 provides information about each of the four language systems in both spoken language and written language.

Written language is similar to but not exactly the same as spoken language. In this part of the chapter, we examine the four systems of written language. Notice that in Table 1.3 the written language system that corresponds with pragmatics is called *functions,* the written language system that corresponds to semantics is called *meanings,* the system related to syntax is called *forms,* and the system corresponding to phonology is called *meaning-form links.* We selected these labels for describing children's concepts about written language to reflect that children are developing writing-specific concepts about language but that those concepts are related to what children know and are learning about the four systems of spoken language.

Functions of Written Language

Because children are acquainted with using spoken language for several purposes, it is not surprising that they learn how to use written language to accomplish a variety of

TABLE 1.3 Systems of Spoken and Written Language

Spoken Language	*Written Language*
Pragmatics System for using language in everyday life, including knowledge of purposes that language serves	*Functions* The purposes written language serves, including establishing identity, recording information, and accumulating knowledge
Semantics System of meaning, including word meanings and morphology	*Meanings* System of meaning, including word meanings, literary language, unusual words; morphology
Syntax System for structuring sentences (English syntax depends heavily on word order)	*Forms* The order of words within sentences; upper- and lowercase alphabet letters (graphemes); spatial directional principles, including left to right, top to bottom; spaces between words; text formats
Phonology System for using sounds, including the combining and contrasting of phonemes in words and the use of intonation (patterns of pause, pitch, and stress) in sentences	*Meaning-Form Links* Phoneme (sound)-grapheme (letter) relationships, including orthographic spelling patterns and phonograms

goals as well. In fact, many of the **functions of written language** are the same as those of spoken language. Table 1.1 also presents several examples of written language that serve each of Halliday's seven functions (1975).

However, written language also serves unique purposes. It is used to establish ownership or identity and to convey authority—often, legal authority. For example, two groups of preschoolers were arguing about the use of a large refrigerator box. One group insisted that the box should be a dollhouse. The other group wanted it to be a fire station. Two boys in the fire station group went to a mother helper and asked her to write the words *fire station*. They copied her writing on a large sheet of paper and taped it to the box. One child pointed to the sign and said, "This is not a house. This is a fire station" (Cochran-Smith, 1984, p. 90). Thus, they established identity and authority.

Written language also has the unique power to make language and thinking permanent and transportable. We can communicate with others over long distances and share information with people we have never met face-to-face. Because information can be recorded and reread, facts can be accumulated and studied critically. New knowledge is built from a critical analysis of accumulated past knowledge. These are just some of the ways by which written language can be distinguished from spoken language (Brockmeier & Olson, 2009). A child who writes *Dear Aunt Peggy, Can I have Harry Potter action figures for my birthday?* is using Halliday's instrumental function, to satisfy his or her wants. But that child is also exercising a written language function, communicating over distance to someone not in his or her here and now. Other written language functions that are not spoken language functions (recording and reminding) are served when Aunt Peggy writes *Harry Potter action figures* on her shopping list.

Meanings in Written Language

Young children come to realize that the written symbols they see around them mean something: Print "says" messages. The printed word *Target* found on the sign outside the familiar department store says "Target" and means a place to shop for toys, clothes, and groceries. Many young preschoolers recognize the circular *Target* logo and find it meaningful. That is, children have an awareness—even before they are actually reading or writing—that printed words convey messages.

Young children's concepts about **written language meanings** are related to their experiences. For example, if children often grocery shop with their parents, when asked what a grocery list might say, they reply "bread, Coke, and candy." Children who have had experiences getting birthday cards, when asked to read one, will reply, "Happy Birthday." Thus, young children's understandings of the meanings of various written texts are related to experiences in which those texts have been used by others but in the children's presence.

Reading and writing, of course, are only two of the ways in which we can communicate meanings. We also communicate meanings through facial expression, gesture, dance, art, conversation, and music. For young children, communicating in spoken language and play is very closely related to communicating in written language (de Haan, 2005; Tsao, 2008).

Unusual Words and Phrases.

However, strategies that are needed to construct meaning in written language are not always needed for spoken language. One difference between spoken and written language is that written language makes more frequent use of unusual words, words that are rarely used in everyday conversation. Words such as *display, exposure, equate, infinite, invariably, literal, luxury, maneuver, participation, provoke,* or *reluctantly* (Cunningham & Stanovich, 1998, p. 10) are found in written stories, newspapers, or textbooks. However, these words are rarely used in daily conversation. Similarly, written language includes *literary language* phrases that are found in literature, such as "once upon a time" and "in the previous section," but that usually are not found in everyday spoken language.

Contextualization.

Another way that written language is different from spoken language is that written language is not exactly talk written down (Cook-Gumperz, 1986). Meaning in spoken language is often augmented by gestures, facial expressions, and voice intonation, which are contextualization clues. Such clues include anything in a specific context that contributes to understanding a message. Much spoken language takes place in a context in which the actual objects discussed can be seen, or between people who know a great deal about each other.

Spoken conversations usually center on recent events and familiar people, whereas novels are about imaginary people in settings never before experienced. That is, spoken conversations usually focus on immediate events (events that occur in the actual world of here and now) and involve the use of **contextualized language.** Contextualized language draws on sources of meaning outside of words. It involves pointing to and looking at people, objects, and activities in a shared context. It uses facial expressions, body language, intonation, and gestures. Written language, in contrast, usually focuses on nonimmediate events (events that have occurred in the past or imagination) and draws on the use of **decontextualized language** (language that draws only on words to communicate meaning and not on real-world context) (Beals, 2001).

An example of a conversation focused on immediate events and using contextualized language follows. A husband and wife are about to return to their jobs after lunching together at a restaurant.

Husband: I took Bruno.

Wife: OK. I'll pick him up.

Husband: It was 9:00 when I dropped him off.

Wife: OK, so 2:00.

Husband: Right.

Wife: Thanks.

There are a few clues embedded in the conversation about its actual meaning, clarifying when someone named Bruno is to be picked up, but most of what is said is not understood without knowing more about the situation, including the two participants, the absent Bruno, and the background experiences of the participants. Here is part of the same conversation, now with the contextualization clues used by the husband and wife made explicit in brackets.

Husband: I took Bruno. [Bruno is the couple's dog, and once a week he goes to doggy day care. Earlier, the husband had taken Bruno there.]

Wife: OK. I'll pick him up. [The husband and wife share responsibilities for dropping off and picking up Bruno.]

Husband: It was 9:00 when I dropped him off.

Wife: OK, so 2:00. [The day care sessions are a maximum of five hours.]

Husband: Right.

Wife: Thanks.

Given these contextualization clues, it is much easier for us to understand what was going on in this conversation. We are now on a more equal footing with the husband and wife. With those clues made explicit, we have now experienced the conversation more as they did, with more of the information that was in the context but not in their spoken words. Suppose the conversation were part of a written story. For it to be meaningful (make sense), the author would have to provide some of those clues in the surrounding text.

Written Language Forms

Written language forms are the visual and spatial aspects of written language such as letters, words, and texts. Knowledge of written language forms includes awareness of visual properties, spatial directional properties, and organizational formats. It is easy to see that words are composed of alphabet letters, sometimes called *graphemes*. Most accomplished readers and writers take for granted a related fact, that alphabet letters are composed of lines and curves, sometimes called **letter features** (Gibson, Gibson, Pick, & Osser, 1962). When learning to read and write, however, children cannot take letter features for granted. Their writing often demonstrates their careful attention to letter features. Figure 1.3 presents one preschooler's printed letters. This writing does include some conventional or nearly conventional alphabet letter forms (*t, r,* and *M*) as well as many letter-like but unconventional symbols. These symbols look like alphabet letters because they include many letter features, such as vertical, diagonal, and curved lines (Yamagata, 2007). Clay (1975) called letters like these **mock letters.**

Words and Sentences. Children also learn about the features of words (Pick, Unze, Brownell, Drozdal, & Hopmann, 1978) and demonstrate this knowledge in their writing (Clay, 1975; Wolter, Wood, & D'zatko, 2009). Figure 1.4 presents a letter that five-year-old Zachery wrote to his Aunt Carol. His writing indicates an awareness of words; he separated words with dashes. Many young children are unsure that a space is enough to mark a boundary between words. Instead, they make boundaries between words very obvious, by using dots or dashes or by circling words. Zachery's writing also demonstrates his strong grasp of the directional principles of written English: he uses left-to-right and top-to-bottom organization.

This letter also demonstrates Zachery's knowledge of the visual features of two other units of written language: sentences and text format. Zachery circled each thought unit, which we call a *sentence,* even though he signaled one sentence boundary with the conventional punctuation mark, a period. His writing also shows a sophisticated

FIGURE 1.3 A Preschooler's Printed Letters

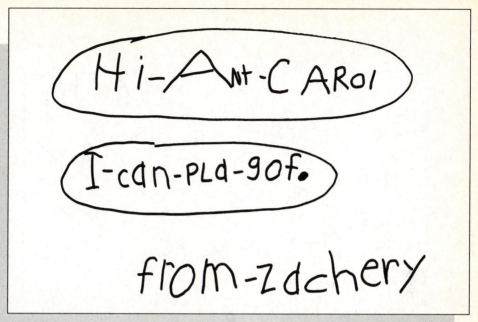

Hi-Ant-C AROl

I-can-PLd-gof.

from-zachery

F**IGURE** 1.4   Zachery's Letter to His Aunt Carol

awareness of how the text of a letter is organized. He begins with a greeting ("Hi Aunt Carol") and ends with a closing ("from Zachery").

Text Formats.   There are many kinds of texts, including poems, recipes, maps, newspapers, dictionaries, books, magazine articles, Web pages, and directions. One thing young children learn about these different text formats is how they look. They may write a pretend grocery list without actual words but with strings of mock letters in a vertical array. Figure 1.5 presents a letter that a first grader wrote to her mom and dad in the early fall. This child's teacher often wrote thank-you letters to classroom visitors and these sample thank-you letters were displayed on the classroom wall. Kaylen had written thank-you letters in her classroom but in this case wrote a letter to her parents. The friendly letter included the salutation (Dear mom and Dad) and the closing (From Kaylen) as well as two sentences. Kaylen took the letter to school to share with her teacher, and the teacher displayed this letter with her own sample letter and letters that many of the other children had brought to school to share.

We have been using words such as *letter*, *word*, *sentence*, and *story*, which make it easy to describe written language. They constitute *language about language*. Children's understanding of and ability to use language about language are a particular kind of knowledge called **metalinguistic awareness** (Wankoff & Cairns, 2009; Zipke, Ehri, & Cairns, 2009). They will learn what a word is, what a sentence is, and what a story is. Experiences in school make these linguistic concepts explicit.

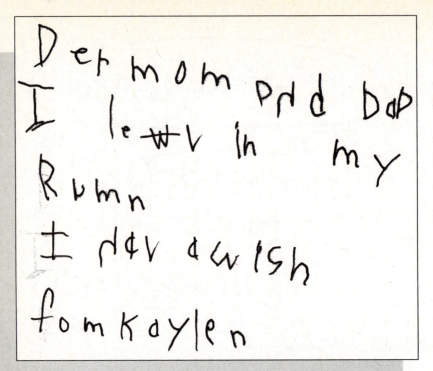

FIGURE 1.5   Kaylen's Letter to Her Mom and Dad

Meaning-Form Links

We use the term **meaning-form links** to refer to the way in which meaning is connected to written forms. The conventional meaning-form link in English is achieved through *sound-letter relationships*. For example, the sound /b/ is related to the letter *b*. When we see the printed word *bat*, we know that the three letters correspond to the three sounds /b/, /a/, and /t/, which blended together produce the spoken word *bat*. However, sound-letter correspondences are complex: A single letter is not always associated with just one speech sound. Some letters are associated with many speech sounds (e.g., the letter *a* with /A/ in *able*, but also with /a/ in *cat*, /o/ in *want*, and /u/ in *about*), and some speech sounds are associated with combinations of letters (e.g., the sound /aw/ with *augh* in *caught*, the sound /A/ with *a_e* in *make* and *ai* in *rain*, and the sound /sh/ with *sh* in *shine*).

Despite these complexities, the **alphabetic principle** does apply to written English and to other alphabetic languages. That is, spoken sounds or phonemes are systematically associated with written letters. Thus, the most noticeable meaning-form link in

English is spelling. Table 1.2 presents the graphemes (spellings) most often associated with each of forty-three common English phonemes. Fortunately, some spellings are nearly always associated with certain pronunciations. **Orthography** is the system in an alphabetic language whereby word parts (individual sounds or larger chunks of spoken words) are associated with individual letters or combinations of letters. **Phonograms** are combinations of letters that are reliably associated with particular pronunciations, especially in the middle and final positions of a word. For example, in all of the rhyming words *ban, can, fan, tan,* and *plan,* the phonogram *-an* is pronounced /an/.

The conventional spelling, or orthography, of a written language embodies the ways that accomplished writers in that language use sound-letter correspondences and meaning-letter correspondences to compose words. Young children take a long time— usually many years—to learn these conventional ways. In the meantime, they have many occasions to attempt to link meaning to their writing. We will describe two of their unconventional attempts in later chapters: scribbling and matching units of print with units of memorized speech. A third way, invented spelling, is closer to conventional spelling than these two ways; it also will be described in a later chapter.

CHILDREN'S CONCEPTS ABOUT WRITTEN LANGUAGE

CHILDREN'S LEARNING ABOUT WRITTEN LANGUAGE includes their acquiring and modifying schemas or concepts for various aspects of written language knowledge. In this part of the chapter, we describe children's concepts about written language.

Ted's Delight: A Case Study of Two Children's Reading and Writing

Ted, who was eight years old, and his sister Carrie, who was three years old, were playing in the corner of the living room. They had set up their card table playhouse. Taped on the playhouse was the sign shown in Figure 1.6.

Ted and Carrie had collected Carrie's plastic play food and doll dishes and put them behind the playhouse. When their father entered the room, he looked at the sign and said, "Oh, I think I need some lunch." The children asked him to visit their restaurant. He entered the playhouse, and Carrie presented him with a menu (Figure 1.7).

Carrie asked, "May I take your order?" Her father read the menu and said, "I'll take pancakes and coffee." Carrie checked off two items on the menu and took it out to Ted, who was behind the playhouse. He pretended to fix pancakes and pour coffee. Ted brought the dishes into the playhouse to his father, who pretended to eat with much relish. When he had finished, he asked, "May I have my check, please?" Carrie picked up a pad of paper and a pencil and wrote a check (Figure 1.8). Her father pretended to pay the check and left the playhouse.

Later that evening, the family discussed the restaurant play. Ted said he had made the sign so that the playhouse could be a restaurant. He had asked Carrie if he could use her toy food and dishes. She had wanted to play, too. Ted said that he and Carrie decided to write on the menu the names of the play food they had. In the middle of his

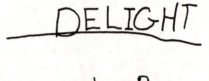

FIGURE 1.6   "Ted's Delight" Sign

FIGURE 1.7   "Ted's Delight" Menu

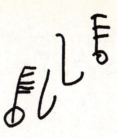

FIGURE 1.8   Carrie's Check

writing the menu, Carrie insisted on helping him. "She wrote the letter that looks like a backward *J* in the middle of the menu," Ted reported. "I had to turn it into the word *Enjoy* to make sense."

Ted's and Carrie's Concepts about Written Language

What do Ted's and Carrie's reading and writing reveal about their concepts of written language? First, both Ted's and Carrie's behaviors indicate that they understand many ways in which written language is used. Carrie knows that a waitperson writes something when a customer orders and when the customer asks for the check. She seems to be learning, just as Ted is, that writing and reading are functional. Ted and Carrie used written language to get their customer into their restaurant (they made a sign), to let their customer know what was available to eat (they made a menu), and to let their customer know how much the meal cost (they wrote a check). They demonstrated written language functions.

Second, the sign and menu Ted wrote suggest that he is learning about written language meanings. His sign communicated a message to his father: a restaurant is open for business. Ted also knows that the messages communicated in written language should be meaningful given the written language context. Ted knew that the "backward *J*" that Carrie had written somehow had to be incorporated into a message that could be communicated on a menu. Random letters on menus do not communicate meaningful messages. Ted made the random letter meaningful by incorporating it into the word *Enjoy*. Carrie also demonstrated that she knows that written language communicates meaning. Even though we cannot read her check, her behavior as she gave it to her father (and her father's reactions to the written check) suggests that her writing communicates a message something like "pay some money for your food."

Third, the sign and menu indicate that Ted is learning about written language forms—what written language looks like. These two writing samples certainly look like a sign and a menu. His menu is written in the form of a list. The content of his menu is organized as a menu is usually organized—drinks and food are grouped and listed separately. Carrie is also learning what at least a few written language forms look like.

CARRIE

FIGURE 1.9 *"Carrie" as Written by Her Preschool Teacher*

The writing on her check looks something like the letters *E* and *J*. Even though Carrie's letters are not yet conventional, they signal that she is paying attention to what letters look like. Although Carrie's *E*s sometimes have too many horizontal lines, she has obviously noticed that horizontal lines are letter features. And, even though Carrie's *J*'s seem to be backward, she does include the curve feature expected at the end of this letter. There is one exception. Carrie put a circle on her letter *E*; most letter *E*s do not include circles. Figure 1.9 (Carrie's name written as her preschool teacher wrote it) suggests why Carrie may have included the circle on her *E*. Her preschool teacher often used what she called "bubble writing," putting small decorative bubbles on each alphabet letter. Carrie noticed that her preschool teacher wrote circles on her letters, so Carrie may have decided to put the same circles on her own letters.

Finally, Ted's and Carrie's writing demonstrates that they are learning a unique system of written language: the manner in which written language conveys meaning. In English, the way written language conveys meaning is that written words map onto spoken words. Letters in written words relate to sounds in speech. Therefore, English is considered an alphabetic language, and learning about sound-letter relationships is an important part of reading and writing. Ted demonstrated his understanding of the relationship between letters and sounds in his spelling errors. Ted's spelling of *pees* for *peas* shows that he knows that the letters *ee* often represent the sound of phoneme /E/.

DEVELOPMENTAL CHANGES IN CHILDREN'S READING AND WRITING

WE HAVE SHOWN THAT CHILDREN have many unconventional concepts about words, alphabet letters, and meaning-form links. Yet all children's concepts become increasingly more conventional. Although the journey to becoming a mature reader and writer is long, what happens during the journey is as valid as the end point. Knowing how children's concepts about written language develop is critical for understanding their reading and writing.

Since the first edition of this book (McGee & Richgels, 1990), we have described four stages of young readers and writers: **beginners, novices, experimenters,** and **conventional readers and writers.** In the intervening years, others have documented similar stages in children's literacy development and have used their own labels for them.

Awareness and Exploration

Even very young children have meaningful experiences with books and writing materials, and these experiences lay the necessary foundations for later literacy development. The children we have called *beginners* are not, of course, readers and writers in the sense of being able to comprehend and create texts on their own. They are dependent on their parents or other readers and writers for their experiences. Other than when sharing books with others, beginners merely observe others as they engage in literacy activities.

In contrast, *novice* readers and writers are aware of print and know that printed text communicates messages. They sometimes write with the intention to communicate their own messages. Novice readers and writers still do not read and write as adults do; their attempts to read and write occur primarily during pretend play. However, they do learn some conventions. **Conventions of written language** are the characteristics of texts and the practices and processes for understanding and producing it that are accepted, expected, and used by accomplished readers and writers in a written language community. For example, one convention that novice readers and writers learn is to recognize and write some alphabet letters. Carrie is an example of a novice reader and writer. She uses what she knows about alphabet letters to write messages.

Most novice readers and writers are three to five years old. Others have characterized reading and writing during this time as the phase of awareness and exploration (International Reading Association & National Association for the Education of Young Children [IRA/NAEYC], 1998) because children become aware of print and explore its properties.

Experimenting Reading and Writing

Children eventually come to recognize that meaning is mapped onto print in a systematic way. The conventional way that meaning is mapped onto printed text is through sound-letter correspondences. Sounds in spoken words correspond to letters in printed words. Children's first attempts to use this correspondence have been characterized as alphabetic reading and writing (Ehri, 2005); they know some alphabet letters and realize that alphabet letters are associated with certain sounds. At this time, their knowledge about letters and sounds is not complete. They cannot completely sound out an unknown word or completely spell a word. Frequently, they recognize a printed word's beginning sound or spell a word with only a few letters for just a few of its sounds. We call these children *experimenters.* They are experimenting with what they can do using the alphabetic principle.

Experimenters use more conventions than novice readers and writers: They learn most of the alphabet letters, and they attempt to spell words using their knowledge of letters and sounds. They memorize short texts and attempt to read by remembering the text and pointing to words. Although they too are not yet conventional readers and writers, they are "almost" to that point. These accomplishments typically emerge in kindergarten and early first grade.

Conventional Reading and Writing

The final phase of learning to read and write is conventional reading and writing. Children we call *conventional readers and writers* have already mastered alphabet recognition and know most letter-sound associations. They can really read and write texts that adults recognize as conventional. They now learn strategies for decoding words, meanings of new vocabulary words, and strategies for comprehending what they read. They compose texts using spelling strategies and known spellings.

One feature that distinguishes conventional readers and writers from experimenters is their attention to larger parts of words than single letters. They come to recognize phonograms and begin to rely on using those patterns of letters to arrive at pronunciations or spellings. For example, even if the word *brand* is unfamiliar to them, they will find in it the phonogram *-and*, which they already know from the words *band*, *hand*, *land*, *sand*, and *stand*.

As they gain experience and through instruction, children learn to understand and compose increasingly complex texts. Eventually, conventional readers and writers know thousands of sight words (words they can read automatically), read a great variety of different kinds of texts, are aware of audience when they write, and monitor their own performances when they read and write. This phase of reading and writing typically emerges in first grade but continues to develop throughout the elementary, middle, and high school years.

TECHNOLOGY TIE-IN

Many researchers and practitioners have identified developmental levels of reading, writing, and spelling that are similar to our beginners, novices, experimenters, and conventional readers and writers (who go through beginning and transitional reading and writing phases in the elementary grades). Visit the following Web sites for more information on developmental levels:

www.myread.org/monitoring_first.htm
http://bankstreet.edu/literacyguide/early
www.sarasota.k12.fl.us/arasota/develstgrd.htm
www.readingrockets.org/article/267
http://mason/gmu.edu/~cwallac7/TAP/TEST/literacy/1.html

Assessment and Phases of Reading and Writing Development

WE HAVE SHOWN THAT CHILDREN generally progress through four broad phases of literacy development. In order for teachers to help children pass through these phases efficiently and effectively, they need to know each child's level of development and how to provide instruction that will encourage that child's growth toward a more advanced phase (Bowman, Donovan, & Burns, 2000). The way that teachers find out about each individual child is through assessment. **Written language assessment** is any activity of teachers to determine students' literacy knowledge, abilities, and understandings (Epstein, Schweinhart, DeBruin-Parecki & Robin, 2004). Assessment can be as simple as observing what a child does, reflecting on the behaviors and talk observed, and making judgments about what this means the child knows and does not know. Assessment also may involve giving children simple tasks to perform, such as asking them to write their names or to identify alphabet letters printed on cards. Assessment may involve a paper-and-pencil test for which children are asked to read paragraphs and to circle answers to multiple choice questions about the paragraphs.

We have found that careful assessment is especially critical when making instructional decisions for children from diverse backgrounds. Children from diverse family, socioeconomic status (SES), ethnic, language, and racial backgrounds will bring to school diverse understandings about the nature of print and its uses. These concepts, like the concepts of all young children, are not likely to be conventional. For example, a preschool teacher observed as Tatie, a bilingual, two-year-old, Haitian child, made the shape of the letter *T* by crossing two fingers. When the teacher asked her what she was doing, Tatie replied, "That's me" (Ballenger, 1999, p. 45). Tatie seemed to recognize the shape of the letter *T*, and though she did not name it, she realized that it represented her name.

Despite the importance of assessment for making instructional decisions for young children, assessing young children is challenging (Pence, 2007). Young children are at early stages of language development and may have difficulty focusing on a task, maintaining attention, or using language to express what they know (Epstein et al., 2004). Thus, assessments of young children may not be highly reliable; the results may not reflect what the children actually know. Therefore, effective and appropriate literacy assessment must be carefully planned, keeping in mind that misinterpretations may arise because of issues of *appropriateness, validity,* and *reliability.* Appropriate assessments are consistent with a child's age and developmental level. Valid assessments are those that actually measure the concept intended to be measured. Reliable assessments are those that give consistent results. Appropriate tests for preschoolers would not involve them in answering questions using a multiple choice format. Valid assessments of reading would not have children writing. A reliable assessment of name writing would yield the same signature on one day as on the next. Teachers will find that in order to meet the various purposes of assessment, they need to employ two kinds of assessments: screening assessments and monitoring assessments.

Screening

One purpose of assessment is for screening children to determine which children are making adequate progress and which children need more intensive instruction in order to make adequate progress. Most but not all children will follow the developmental path that we have laid out in this chapter and about which we will provide further detail in Chapters 2, 3, 4, and 5. Still, teachers will want an indication of who might be at risk for failure. These children might be stuck in a phase of literacy development when most of their peers have moved to considerably higher levels of learning. Thus, teachers in preschool and in the elementary years use **screening assessments** to determine which children might be at risk and need more intense support. Screening assessments are short and are designed to be administered quickly. They contain essential components of reading and writing and are not intended to be a comprehensive assessment of all aspects of literacy learning. Screening assessments that focus on components of early literacy development have been shown to be highly related to later literacy achievement: alphabet knowledge, phonemic awareness, the alphabetic principle, concepts about books and print, and oral listening comprehension (National Institute of Child Health and Human Development [NICHD], 2000; Snow, Burns, & Griffin, 1998). In the elementary years, these foundational concepts continue to be critical as children apply their knowledge to the reading of texts. In those years, five factors are critical for reading success: comprehension, phonics, phonemic awareness, vocabulary, and fluency (NICHD, 2000). Thus, screening assessments would target just the critical components of literacy for particular developmental phases. Chapters 3, 4, and 5 discuss (and Appendix B and C present) examples of assessments that can be used for screening.

Monitoring

The second purpose of an assessment is to monitor whether ongoing classroom instruction and classroom activities are affecting learning in desired ways throughout the year. To achieve this purpose, teachers re-administer some of the screening assessments or similar assessments to determine whether children have actually progressed to expected levels (Morris & Slavin, 2003). The data from **monitoring assessments** allow teachers to identify children whose progress significantly differs from what is expected of them and demonstrated by other children.

Chapter Summary

CHILDREN'S LEARNING IS DEPENDENT on having experiences that lead to the formation of concepts or schemas. Concepts or schemas are mental constructions about objects, people, events or activities, and places. Learning is a matter of acquiring new concepts or adding to and changing old concepts. Language is critical for learning when it provides labels for new concepts and when it is used to scaffold children's attempts at difficult tasks.

Children develop concepts about the functions of written language, including using reading and writing to label and record. Their concepts about written language meanings reflect their experiences with different kinds of texts, such as stories, grocery lists, and traffic signs. They create concepts about written language forms, including learning about letter features, words, sentences, texts, and left-to-right organization. They develop understandings about meaning-form links, including unconventional concepts such as using letter strings and matching spoken units with written units. Later, they acquire the alphabetic principle and begin using more conventional letter-sound matches to spell and decode.

Children's concepts about written language change and grow with their reading and writing experiences. Children begin with unconventional concepts and gradually acquire conventional concepts. Before reading and writing conventionally, they may proceed through phases of awareness and exploration and experimental reading and writing. Teachers use reliable and valid screening and monitoring assessments to discover children's unique understandings about reading and writing.

USING THE INFORMATION

A list of written words follows; the purpose of this exercise is to listen to the words spoken aloud and to segment each word by individual phonemes. This activity is designed to help you learn to hear and say each of the phonemes found in Table 1.2. With three pennies or other coins, move a coin into a box as you say a phoneme in a word. For example, as you segment the word *bat*, you will move a coin into the left-hand box as you say /b/, a second coin into the middle box as you say /a/, and a third coin into the right-hand box as you say /t/. Make a list of those words for which the three boxes are insufficient because the words are composed of more than three phonemes. Which words required only two of the three boxes?

cat	Kate	cot	caught	bought
chug	dug	bed	bead	feed
got	hot	hit	height	Jake
make	win	wing	coat	boy
look	shoot	shout	pat	rat
city	ship	tip	thing	this
cut	cute	vine	wine	yes
zoo	azure	shoe	weigh	

APPLYING THE INFORMATION

Using Figure 1.5, describe what Kaylen's letter reveals about her knowledge of written language (1) meanings, (2) forms, (3) meaning-form links, and (4) functions. Children's writing products are revealing, but they do not tell the whole story. We find out more about children and their understandings about written language when we are present during the creation of those products. Kaylen is one of twenty-two first graders in a school with many English language learners (ELLs), with a high percentage of children on free or reduced lunch, and located in a neighborhood high in crime. However, Kaylen's teacher is recognized throughout this large urban school district for her ability to help most of her children acquire very high levels of success. Write a list of what else you would like to know about the classroom context.

GOING BEYOND THE TEXT

OBSERVE A LITERACY EVENT with at least two children. One way to initiate a literacy event is to prepare for some dramatic play with children. Plan a dramatic play activity that could include reading and writing. For example, plan a restaurant play activity. Bring dramatic play props, such as an apron, dishes, and a tablecloth, as well as reading and writing materials, such as large sheets of paper, small pads of paper, crayons or markers, paper placemats with puzzles, and menus. Suggest to two or three children that they might want to play restaurant and propose that they use the paper and crayons in their play. Observe their actions and talk. Use your observations to find out what the children know about written language meanings, forms, meaning-form links, and functions.

REFERENCES

Adams, M. (1990). *Beginning to read: Thinking and learning about print.* Cambridge, MA: MIT Press.

Ballenger, C. (1999). *Teaching other people's children: Literacy and learning in a bilingual classroom.* New York: Teachers College Press.

Beals, D. (2001). Eating and reading: Links between family conversations with preschoolers and later language and literacy. In D. Dickinson & P. Tabors (Eds.), *Beginning literacy with language: Young children learning at home and school* (pp. 75–92). Baltimore, MD: Brookes Publishing.

Berko-Gleason, J., & Ratner, N. B. (2009). *The development of language* (7th ed.). Boston: Pearson.

Bowman, B. T., Donovan, S., & Burns, M. S. (Eds.). (2000). *Eager to learn: Educating our preschoolers.* Washington, DC: National Academies Press.

Brockmeier, J., & Olson, D. R. (2009). The literacy episteme: From Innis to Derrida. In D. R. Olson & N. Torrance (Eds.), *The Cambridge handbook of literacy* (pp. 3–22). New York: Cambridge University Press.

Clay, M. (1993). *An observation survey of early literacy achievement.* Portsmouth, NH: Heinemann.

Clay, M. M. (1975). *What did I write?* Auckland, New Zealand: Heinemann Educational Books.

Cochran-Smith, M. (1984). *The making of a reader.* Norwood, NJ: Ablex Publishing.

Cook-Gumperz, J. (Ed.). (1986). *The social construction of literacy.* Cambridge, England: Cambridge University Press.

Crystal, D. (2006). *How language works: How babies babble, words change meaning, and languages live or die.* Woodstock, NY: The Overlook Press.

Cunningham, A., & Stanovich, K. (1998). What reading does for the mind. *American Educator, 22,* 8–15.

de Haan, D. (2005). Social pretend play: Potentials and limitations for literacy development. *European Early Childhood Education Research Journal, 13*(1), 41–55.

Ehri, L. C. (2005). Learning to read words: Theory, findings, and issues. *Scientific Studies of Reading, 9*(2), 167–188.

Ehri, L. C., Nunes, S. R., Willows, D. M., Schuster, B. V., Yaghoub-Zadeh, Z., & Shanahan, T. (2001). Phonemic awareness instruction helps children learn to read: Evidence from the National Reading Panel's meta-analysis. *Reading Research Quarterly, 36*(3), 250–287.

Epstein, A. S., Schweinhart, L. J., DeBruin-Parecki, A., & Robin, K. B. (2004). *Preschool assessment: A guide to developing a balanced approach.* New Brunswick, NJ: National Institute for Early Education Research.

Freeman, D. E., & Freeman, Y. S. (2004). *Essential linguistics: What you need to know to teach reading, ESL, spelling, phonics, and grammar.* Portsmouth, NH: Heinemann.

Gibson, E. J., Gibson, J. J., Pick, A. D., & Osser, H. (1962). A developmental study of the discrimination of letter-like forms. *Journal of Comparative Physiological Psychology, 55,* 897–906.

Gopnick, A., & Meltzoff, A. Z. (1986). Relations between semantic and cognitive development in the one-word stage: The specificity hypothesis. *Child Development, 57,* 1040–1053.

Halliday, M. A. K. (1975). *Learning how to mean.* New York: Elsevier.

International Reading Association & National Association for the Education of Young Children. (1998). Learning to read and write: Developmentally appropriate practices for young children. *The Reading Teacher, 52,* 193–216.

Mansell, J., Evans, M. A., & Hamilton-Hulak, L. (2005). Developmental changes in parents' use of miscue feedback during shared book reading. *Reading Research Quarterly, 40*(3), 294–317.

McGee, L. M., & Richgels, D. J. (1990). *Literacy's beginnings: Supporting young readers and writers.* Boston: Allyn & Bacon.

Morris, D., & Slavin, R. E. (2003). *Every child reading.* Boston: Allyn & Bacon.

National Institute of Child Health and Human Development (NICHD). (2000). *Report of the National Reading Panel: Teaching children to read.* Washington, DC: National Institutes of Health.

National Reading Panel. (2000). *Report of the National Reading Panel.* Washington, DC: National Institutes of Health.

Pence, K. L. (2007). *Assessment in emergent literacy: A volume in the emergent and early literacy series.* San Diego: Plural Publishing.

Piaget, J. (1955). *The language and thought of the child.* Cleveland: World.

Pick, A. D., Unze, M. G., Brownell, C. A., Drozdal, J. G. Jr., & Hopmann, M. R. (1978). Young children's knowledge of word structure. *Child Development, 49,* 669–680.

Richgels, D. J. (2004). Theory and research into practice: Paying attention to language. *Reading Research Quarterly, 39,* 470–477.

Snow, C., Burns, S. M., & Griffin, P. (1998). *Preventing reading difficulties in young children.* Washington, DC : National Academies Press.

Tsao, Y.-L. (2008). Using guided play to enhance children's conversation, creativity and competence in literacy. *Education, 128*(3), 515–520.

Verhagen, W. G. M., Aarnoutse, C. A. J., & van Leeuwe, J. F. J. (2009). The predictive power of phonemic awareness and naming speed for early Dutch word recognition. *Educational Research and Evaluation, 15*(1), 93–116.

Vygotsky, L. S. (1978). *Mind in society. The development of higher psychological processes* (Michael Cole, Trans.). Cambridge, MA: Harvard University Press.

Wankoff, L. S., & Cairns, H. S. (2009). Why ambiguity detection is a predictor of early reading skill. *Communication Disorders Quarterly, 30*(3), 183–192.

Wolter, J. A., Wood, A., & D'zatko, K. W. (2009). The influence of morphological awareness on the literacy development of first-grade children. *Language, Speech, and Hearing Services in Schools, 40*(3), 286–298.

Yamagata, K. (2007). Differential emergence of representational systems: Drawings, letters, and numerals. *Cognitive Development, 22*(2), 244–257.

Zipke, M., Ehri, L. C., & Cairns, H. S. (2009). Using semantic ambiguity instruction to improve third graders' metalinguistic awareness and reading comprehension: An experimental study. *Reading Research Quarterly, 44*(3), 300–321.

PEARSON myeducationlab

Go to the topics Phonemic Awareness and Phonics and Assessment in the MyEducationLab (www.myeducationlab .com) for your course, where you can:

- Find learning outcomes for Phonemic Awareness and Phonics and Assessment along with the national standards that connect to these outcomes.
- Complete Assignments and Activities that can help you more deeply understand the chapter content.
- Examine challenging situations and cases presented in the IRIS Center Resources.

A+RISE

Go to the Topic A+RISE in the MyEducationLab (www.myeducationlab.com) for your course. A+RISE® Standards2Strategy™ is an innovative and interactive online resource that offers new teachers in grades K–12 just-in-time, research-based instructional strategies that:

- Meet the linguistic needs of ELLs as they learn content
- Differentiate instruction for all grades and abilities
- Offer reading and writing techniques, cooperative learning, use of linguistic and nonlinguistic representations, scaffolding, teacher modeling, higher order thinking, and alternative classroom ELL assessment
- Provide support to help teachers be effective through the integration of listening, speaking, reading, and writing along with the content curriculum
- Improve student achievement
- Are aligned to Common Core Elementary Language Arts standards (for the literacy strategies) and to English language proficiency standards in WIDA, Texas, California, and Florida.

CHAPTER

2

Birth to Three Years

THE FOUNDATIONS OF LITERACY DEVELOPMENT

KEY CONCEPTS

Booksharing Routines

Bookhandling Skills

Scribbling

Interactive Bookreading

Story Grammar

Concept of Story

Environmental Print

Decontextualized
    Language

Telegraphic Speech

Formulaic Speech

THE BEGINNINGS OF LITERACY

MANY CHILDREN, but not all, have literacy experiences with their families as infants and toddlers, and by three years of age, most children have participated in many literacy experiences. They may share books with parents and other caregivers, they may be invited to use markers and crayons, and they are likely to notice the print found in their environment. These early experiences with books and print allow children to acquire concepts that form the foundation for later reading and writing.

Kristen's Early Literacy Experiences

As an example of the rich literacy experiences that are available to some children, we present a case study of Kristen from her birth until she turned three years old. During this time, she was primarily in the stage of beginning reading and writing. She observed literacy, for example, as her mother and father read books aloud to her. She practiced drawing but did not intend for her drawing to be considered "writing."

Literacy Experiences from Birth to One.
Early in the first few months of her life, Kristen's mother and father would actively engage her in language activities especially during daily routines. For example, her father would talk with Kristen when he changed her diaper. As Kristen lay on the changing table, her father would say, "I am going to put on a nice dry diaper." Kristen would coo and gurgle, and her father would reply, "I know you like that, don't you?" Kristen would wiggle, and her father would continue, "I agree. Dry diapers are the best."

Kristen received her first books when she was just a few months old. Many of these were sturdy cardboard books such as *A Goodnight Hug* (Roth, 1986). They were kept in her toy basket along with her rattles. Her mother and father read to her while she sat in their laps. When Kristen could sit up, she began grabbing her books, picking them up, and holding them. She did not look at the pictures in her books; instead, she made insistent attempts to turn the pages. Her books were some of her favorite toys. She would pull books out of a basket and dump them on her blanket, grab for books, turn pages, and try to chew on the pages. Her mother and father engaged her in active games with books. When they read a book with nursery rhymes, they would hold Kristen and use actions to engage her attention. As they recited a nursery rhyme, they would hold her close and rock her back and forth. They would hold her arms and hands and help her clap or take her body and gently pretend to fall.

Some months before her first birthday, Kristen could recognize books by their names. Her father would say, "Let's read the Humpty Dumpty book." Kristen would crawl to the book basket and select her "Humpty Dumpty book," *The Real Mother Goose* (Wright, 1916). She would turn to the page that had the Humpty Dumpty rhyme and sway her body as her father recited the rhyme.

Literacy Experiences from One to Two.
By her first birthday, Kristen would hold a book right side up and turn the pages from front to back. Sometimes she smiled and patted

the pictures or turned pages over from one side to the next, intently checking the pictures on each side of the page.

A few months after her first birthday, Kristen began to point to things around her, saying "dat?" with a rising intonation. She would also point to and ask "dat?" about animals and people pictured in her books. Her mother or father would obligingly name the animals and people. Kristen's mother often requested that she locate animals or people in her books. She would ask, "Where's the kitten?" and Kristen would point to it.

Kristen received crayons as a Christmas present when she was fifteen months old. Her first attempts at drawing were rapid back-and-forth swipes at paper (Figure 2.1). She would quickly make a few marks and push the paper on the floor, indicating that she wanted another sheet of paper.

When Kristen was about sixteen months old, she began interrupting bookreading by jumping off her father's lap to seek a toy or object in the house. She did this only when she saw certain pictures in her books. Each time Kristen saw a picture of crayons, for example, she would get up and find *her* crayons.

When she was twenty-one months old, Kristen began making round-and-round lines and dots. Her mother and father began drawing to entertain her. They drew people, houses, flowers, cats, dogs, and other familiar objects.

Literacy Experiences from Two to Three.   By the time Kristen turned two years old, she could recite some of the text in her books. In *Hop on Pop* (Seuss, 1963), Kristen said, "No. No. No sit," after her mother read, "No, Pat, No. Don't sit on that." As her father read the text of *Goodnight Moon* (Brown, 1947), he would pause for Kristen to fill in part of the rhyme. Kristen began recognizing McDonald's and Burger King signs. She would say "DeDonald's" or "Bugar King" each time she saw the signs. Kristen also pointed to her favorite cereals and cookies in the grocery store, saying "Aisin Ban" and "Oeos."

FIGURE 2.1   Back-and-Forth Lines

Drawing continued to be a favorite activity. She began to control her drawing and could make jagged lines, straight lines, and dots. When asked to tell about her drawing, she often replied, "dots." She frequently initiated drawing activities with her parents. She would take paper and crayons to her mother and command, "Draw little girl," or "Draw little boy." After drawing a little girl, her mother would say, "That's Kristen. Now I'll write Kristen," and she would write her name next to the picture. After drawing a little boy, her mother would say, "That's daddy. I'll write daddy, too."

At twenty-seven months of age, Kristen made concentrated efforts to control her marks. She would slowly draw a continuous line all around the edges of her paper. It seemed as if she were pushing the crayon around the paper and watching its progress. She began making circular shapes of just a single line or a few lines (Figure 2.2).

Although Kristen continued to thoroughly enjoy drawing, she resisted her mother's attempts to invite her to label her drawings. When asked to tell about her drawings, she would often shrug. However, just before Kristen turned three years old, her mother noticed a change in Kristen's drawings. Now Kristen seemed more intentional about her drawings. She made round shapes and carefully added some straight lines and dots. Though her drawings still looked like scribbles, her mother could tell she was trying to draw something, rather than just make marks. One day, when her mother encouraged her to draw a picture of herself, Kristen announced, "I can't draw that." Another day, Kristen's mother convinced her to draw by saying, "Just do some lines and dots and circles." Kristen selected a blue marker and made several quick line strokes down her page. After making several of these marks, she cried, "Look at the rain." She made several

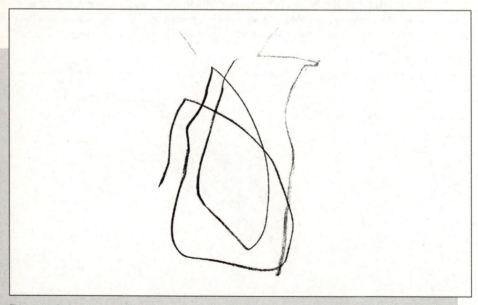

FIGURE 2.2 Circular Shapes

more marks, saying, "More rain. Look at the rain, Mommy." Then she began making dots, saying, "Look at all these raindrops" (Figure 2.3).

By the time Kristen was three years old, she was drawing people (Figure 2.4). She would draw a circle, add two lines for arms, two lines for legs, and some dots for eyes. After drawing the person in Figure 2.4, Kristen said, "This is a picture of Daddy."

FIGURE 2.3   "Rain" and "Raindrops"

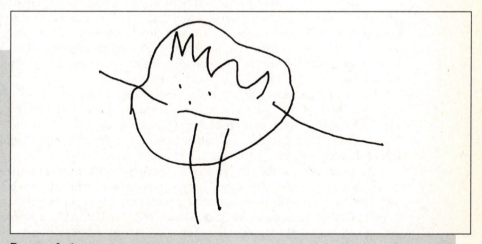

FIGURE 2.4   "This is a picture of Daddy"

At three years of age, Kristen participated in book and familiar print reading in many ways. She made comments about characters and actions depicted in her books. Pointing to the picture of the wolf in *Walt Disney's Peter and the Wolf* (Walt Disney Productions Staff, 1974), she said, "He needs to be good." She commented about the predicament of Wully-Wully in *Babar and the Wully-Wully* (de Brunhoff, 1975), saying "He's in the cage" and "He got out" as she pointed to the pictures of Wully-Wully captured and rescued.

Concepts about Literacy Acquired from Early Book and Drawing Experiences

As part of these experiences interacting with her parents as they read books with her and using crayons and markers, Kristen acquired four foundational concepts about literacy.

1. *Literacy activities are pleasurable.* Perhaps one of the most important concepts that children can learn at the beginning of their literacy experiences is that reading is a pleasurable activity. When children are read to early in their lives, they play with books as a preferred and frequent activity (Bus, 2001). Bookreading is one of the closest activities parents and children share.

   Children also enjoy drawing and writing. Adult observers sense children's intense concentration as they hold tightly to both markers and paper and watch intently the shapes they create (Taylor & Dorsey-Gaines, 1988; Vandermaas-Peeler, Nelson, Bumpass, & Sassine, 2009).

2. *Literacy activities occur in predictable routines and other social interactions embedded in cultural practices.* From a sociocultural view of literacy (Hammerberg, 2004), perceiving how children are enculturated into particular literacy practices requires examining three factors: the act of reading, the identities of participants, and the text. For Kristen, the *act of reading* consisted of drawing on personal experiences in order to understand a text's meaning, when that meaning was assumed to be "in" the text's words. Kristen's parents took pride in her remembering words from the text. In other homes, reading might consist of deciding the meaning of a Bible passage, problem solving how to come up with the money to pay a bill, or playing a video game.

   The second factor in a sociocultural view of literacy is the *identities of the participants.* Children and parents take on particular identities in literacy events. Clearly, Kristen's parents expected her to take on the identity of "a reader" rather than "a listener," and "a drawer" rather than "a scribbler." In other homes, preschool children are expected to "listen and not be heard."

   The third factor is the *text.* Kristen's experiences of texts were of personally owned quality pieces of literature. Literacy in her home included print literacy of high academic value. In other homes, a greater proportion of printed texts might be printed advertising flyers, but those homes might also provide numerous experiences with such oral and visual texts as spoken stories and television daytime talk shows, or the discussion of family finances and the video game we mentioned in connection with different acts of reading. These are the texts of *multimodal literacies,* that is, literacies that involve reading not just print but also nonprint sources of meaning.

Frequently, reading acts, participants, and texts come together in the context of social routines (Carter, Chard, & Pool, 2009). Toddlers and their parents learn ways of interacting with each other while reading books. They develop **booksharing routines,** that is, familiar, expected actions and language that accompany their book reading. Kristen learned how to initiate and participate in bookreading sessions. She frequently selected a book and backed into a lap. She clearly signaled that she wanted to share a book. Once her mother or father began sharing a book, Kristen located characters when asked to do so and solicited comments from her mother or father by pointing to something in the picture or making comments and asking questions. She learned to answer questions. Gradually, she learned to listen to more of the story her mother or father was reading.

Booksharing routines make it possible for children to show parents what they are learning (Garton & Pratt, 2009). Parents respond by giving children opportunities to use their new abilities and expecting children to use them. Kristen and her parents demonstrated this in their playing of a routine known as the *naming game* (Ninio & Bruner, 1978; Takaya, 2008). It begins with an adult's pointing to and naming pictured animals, people, and objects; it progresses as adults ask questions; and it ends with children's pointing to and labeling pictures on their own.

3. *Literacy materials are handled in special ways.* One of the outcomes of reading routines is that children learn **bookhandling skills,** ways of handling and looking at books. Kristen learned how to hold books right side up and how to turn pages. She also discovered that books are for viewing and reading and not just for turning pages.

Literacy routines are not limited to reading. They also lay foundations for later writing skills (Robins & Treiman, 2009). Writing acts, participants, and writing materials (paper, pencils, crayons, markers, dry-erase boards) come together in writing routines. Children learn to make as many as twenty basic scribbles, which become the building blocks of art and writing (Kellogg, 1969).

4. *Literacy involves the use of symbols and the communication of meanings.* Illustrations in books are symbols—they represent or symbolize real objects or people. At first, children treat books as objects. They consider books as interesting objects to manipulate and explore with all their senses. Only gradually do children learn to look at the pictures in books as representations rather than interesting colors, shapes, and lines (Wu, 2009). Kristen demonstrated her awareness that book illustrations are symbols, or representations, when she sought out her box of crayons after she saw a picture of crayons in a favorite book.

Kristen took longer to understand that her drawings could also be symbols. At first, her drawing consisted of **scribbling**—uncontrolled marks made on a page without any intention of drawing a particular object or person. Then she recognized her mother's and father's drawing as symbols for people. It was not until she was nearly three years old that Kristen created her first representational drawing— a symbol for her father. *Representational drawings* are planned and look something like the object or person the child-drawer intends to create. For example, children who intend to draw a person often announce their intentions as they draw, saying, "I am drawing a picture of my daddy."

Such intentionality is evidence that children appreciate the meaning making that is at the core of language, both spoken and written. Children learn that books and other print materials communicate meaning—they tell a message. Learning to "mean" (Halliday, 2002), to understand what others say and do, is involved in nearly every activity, not only in literacy activities. It is the great undertaking of life—we constantly try to understand the messages that bombard us and to send messages to others. We use many clues to help us understand others and to help others understand us. We use the situation we are in and its clues to meaning (characteristics of the location or people's clothing), as well as spoken language and its clues to meaning (words, stress, and intonation). These are called *contextualization clues.*

This book is primarily about how children achieve literacy in the sense of reading and writing printed texts. Nonetheless, the notion of reading nonprinted texts is not as unusual as it may at first seem. Most people are familiar with the terms *reading some-one's expression,* for the act of determining someone's emotional state from the look on his or her face, or *reading the sky,* for the act of predicting the weather based on how the sky looks. The same notion of *to read* applies when someone in a highly oral culture is adept at making meaning not only from what storytellers say but also from how they move, how they use their voices, and how they manipulate elements of their culture's story structures for didactic and entertainment value. Such a person is a good reader of the text of a spoken story. Similarly, someone who knows well the art and craft of moviemaking is adept at reading a movie, that is, getting meanings from what is shown on the screen. Such a person notices a director's choices of camera angles, a film editor's style of cutting, and set builders' and costumers' choices of production values. Such highly informed movie viewing results in a better "read" of a movie than what the average movie viewer gets.

Children grow up in many different contexts, with different effects on their reading and writing. Some children, like Kristen, have experiences with home literacies that are very much like the literacies they will experience in school (Heath, 1983; Leseman & van Tuijl, 2005). In other communities, home literacy experiences are not school-like; instead, they are about getting the daily business of life accomplished (Perez, 2004). This means that nearly all children grow up experiencing many kinds of language in their home communities, especially instrumental and social language (see Halliday's instrumental and interactional uses of language in Table 1.1), but some children have far fewer experiences than other children with academic forms of spoken and written language like those they will experience in school.

Effective teachers recognize that all children come to school with rich language experiences. For example, African American children are likely to grow up in homes that value oral storytelling sometimes communicated through music (Dyson, 2003; Smith, 2004). These children are likely to have advanced abilities to entertain their peers with lively stories. However, for teachers who are familiar only with middle-class and school-like literacies, such as those that Kristen, Ted, and Carrie (see Chapter 1) experienced in their homes, other linguistic strengths, such as oral storytelling, might be missed. Teachers should be open to all the varieties of home language that children bring to school. For example, they may want to step back as African American children share information in oral reports or show-and-tell situations. As teachers notice the different ways children convey main points and make connections in those oral language contexts, they will come to expect and appreciate children's different styles of engagement in reading and writing (Michaels, 1981; Michaels, O'Connor, & Resnick, 2008).

HOME INFLUENCES ON LITERACY LEARNING: LEARNING IN SOCIAL AND CULTURAL CONTEXTS

AS WE HAVE SHOWN, literacy learning begins in the home. Children's first experiences with literacy are mediated by the ways in which parents and other caregivers use reading and writing in their lives (Purcell-Gates, 1996; Rodriguez, Tamis-LeMonda, Spellmann, Pan, Raikes, Lugo-Gil, & Luze, 2009). One way in which mainstream parents invite very young children to participate in literacy activities is to read storybooks aloud. In fact, one predictor of children's reading achievement in school is the number of hours they are read to as preschoolers (Wells, 1986). We also know that preschoolers who interact more with their parents as they read aloud have larger vocabularies and better story understanding as five-year-olds than do children who contribute less during storybook readings (Leseman & de Jong, 1998). Clearly, reading aloud with young children is an important vehicle through which they acquire literacy concepts.

It is not surprising that children who have home experiences with books are more likely to have larger vocabularies and better understanding of stories than children who have few home book experiences. Reading storybooks aloud to preschoolers gives them practice in the very activity they will be expected to master in kindergarten: listening to the teacher read storybooks aloud.

Parent-Child Interactive Bookreading

We describe the interactions between two children and their parents as they share books together. These interactions demonstrate the strategies used by parents and other caregivers to support young children's interest in and construction of meaning. They also show how children's abilities to understand books expand as a result of participating in **interactive bookreading.**

Interactive bookreading is a booksharing experience by a child and a more knowledgeable other person, usually an adult, to which both contribute. Parents read, comment, ask questions, and point to the illustrations. Children point, make comments, and answer questions. We share these examples of interactive bookreading to highlight what children can learn to do and how adults can support that learning.

Elizabeth and Her Mother Share Where's Spot?   A portion of the interaction between Elizabeth (twenty-six months) and her mother as they shared *Where's Spot?* (Hill, 1980) is presented in Figure 2.5. Elizabeth took charge of the interaction by turning the pages and making comments. She labeled objects in the pictures ("There's a doggy there") and answered her mother's questions.

Elizabeth's mother used many strategies for expanding and supporting Elizabeth's participation in this booksharing event. First, she featured an important narrative element (action and character motivation) by telling Elizabeth that the mother dog was looking for her puppy. She continually used this as a context for helping Elizabeth understand why the dog was looking behind doors and under beds. She matched her reading style to Elizabeth's ability to participate in the bookreading by interweaving her talk with reading the text (Martin, 1998). She helped Elizabeth find meaning from

FIGURE 2.5   Elizabeth and Her Mother Share *Where's Spot?* (Hill, 1980)

Paraphrased text is underlined. Brackets indicate portions of the dialogue that occurred simultaneously.

⌈ M: We are looking for Spot. Let's turn the page. He's a little tiny puppy. Can
⎪   you see if you can find him <u>behind the door.</u> Is he there?
⌊ E: (turns to next page)

 M: No?—What's inside the clock? Is he in there?

 E: He's in there.

 M: That's a snake. That's not a little dog.

 E: Let me read it.

 M: Okay.

 E: It's a snake.

⌈ M: Turn the page. Where's Spot? Let's see if we can find the puppy. Is he—
⌊ E: (turns back to look at snake again)

 M: Let's see what's behind the next page. We need to find Spot. Is he in there?
       (points to piano)

 E: There's a doggy there. (points to Mother Dog, Sally)

 M: He's looking for another doggy. Spot's not there.

 E: There? (points to Sally on next page)

 M: Yes. That's a doggy. He's looking for another doggy, a puppy. Is there a
       puppy <u>in the piano</u>?

 E: No.

the words of the text by using her explanations and expansions of the story as a support for meaning construction. In addition, she asked Elizabeth questions that called for labeling ("What's inside the clock?") and provided feedback to her daughter's answers (correcting Elizabeth when she mistook the mother dog for the puppy).

Jon-Marc and His Father Share The Story of Ferdinand.   Figure 2.6 presents part of a booksharing interaction between Jon-Marc, a three-year-old, and his father. Jon-Marc listened carefully and looked intently at each illustration as his father read *The Story of Ferdinand* (Leaf, 1936). One strategy Jon-Marc used to make meaning was to apply his understanding of events in the real world to make inferences about story events. Jon-Marc asked if Ferdinand would go home "And . . . and . . . and love

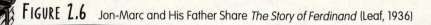

FIGURE 2.6   Jon-Marc and His Father Share *The Story of Ferdinand* (Leaf, 1936)

Text is presented in all capital letters.

Illustration: Ferdinand in a small cart going over the mountain. A bull ring is the
                background.

Father: SO THEY HAD TO TAKE FERDINAND HOME.

Jon-Marc: Why?

Father: Because he wouldn't fight. He just wouldn't fight. He didn't like to fight.
          He just wanted to smell the flowers. (Note, this is a paraphrase of the text
          that had just been read on the previous pages.)

Jon-Marc: Is that why they wanted to . . . to . . . to fight in the drid?

Father: In Madrid? Yeah, they wanted . . . they wanted him to fight in Madrid.
          Madrid's the name of a city. They wanted him to fight the matador. But he
          didn't. He just wanted to go home and smell the flowers.

Jon-Marc: And . . . and . . . and love her mother cow?

Father: Yeah, and . . . and love his mother.

Jon-Marc: Where's her mother cow?

Father: Well, she's back in the book a little bit.

her mother cow?" This question reveals that Jon-Marc used inferences to predict story events (after going home, Ferdinand would love his mother). It also illustrates that he used his own life as a frame of reference for understanding the story. Jon-Marc probably went home to love his mother, so he inferred that Ferdinand would be going home to love his mother.

Jon-Marc's father was skillful at adapting the booksharing event to his child's abilities. He expanded on information from the text and related to Jon-Marc's concerns (he explained that Madrid is a city), and he provided more adult models of language ("And love his mother"). He repeated information from the story text to answer Jon-Marc's question and, therefore, made explicit the causal relations among events in the story ("They wanted him to fight the matador. But he didn't. He just wanted to go home and smell the flowers."). All of his talk was contingent on Jon-Marc's talk; that is, it was in response to Jon-Marc's questions and comments.

Participation in Interactive Bookreading

We carefully selected the interactions of Elizabeth and her mother and Jon-Marc and his father to illustrate how children's participation in and parents' support during interactive read-alouds shift as children gain more language and literacy experience.

TECHNOLOGY TIE-IN

Web sites directed toward parents provide some very good information about how and why to read aloud to babies and toddlers.

www.kidshealth.org/parent/positive provides lots of pull-down menus that include information all about reading aloud. They have three specific pull-downs: reading to babies, toddler reading time, and storytime for preschoolers. At each of these sites is a short, information-packed article that parents can click and the information is read aloud to them. What a great support for parents with low literacy skills! www.readtoyourbaby.com has a pull-down menu to explain why and how to read aloud to babies. This site has *excellent* photographs of a diverse group of moms and dads reading aloud to babies and toddlers, which show the different ways parents and children cuddle into books.

Use the search string "read to your baby" (and *CBS News*) and you will find several sites presenting a video clip of a special interview at CBS headquarters with an editor of a parenting magazine. This clip provides information about how and why reading aloud even in the first few weeks of a baby's life influences brain and language development.

At first, parents seem to focus on gaining their children's attention and getting them actively involved. During these interactions, parents are not concerned about the story (Martin, 1998); books most parents read at this age are merely a series of interesting pictures (for example, of babies eating, playing, or sleeping) rather than stories. At this age, parents cuddle children closely on their laps, let children hold the book and turn pages, and use motivating and attention-getting strategies such as pointing and saying, "Look here at this baby." They encourage their children to point and label pictures by asking, "Look, what's that?" as they point to details in an illustration (Bus, 2001). They make comments that connect book ideas to their children by saying, "Look. That blanket is yellow just like yours." Parents follow children's leads by letting them turn the book's pages or close the book, signaling that this book is finished.

As children develop a deep sense of enjoyment about books and gain confidence in their role as participants, parents begin taking a more active role in directing children's attention to characters and events in storybooks or to ideas in informational books (Martin, 1998). Now parents seem more concerned with helping children understand the basic sequence of events in a story although they still expect their children to answer questions, make comments, and label pictures. These strategies actively engage children and call for them to use thinking at relatively low levels of cognitive demand. Activities that call on low levels of cognitive demand focus on word-level recall of ideas, mostly on the *what* of a message.

As children get older, parents intuitively select books with more complex stories or information. These books trigger opportunities for talking about challenging vocabulary and clarifying character traits and motivations. Now parents shift from using

FIGURE 2.7 Strategies Parents Use to Support Children's Active Engagement during Interactive Bookreading

Attention Getting and Sustaining Strategies

allowing child to hold book and turn pages

pointing to and labeling or commenting on details in illustrations

helping child imitate or asking child to make gestures or sounds

asking for child to point out details in illustrations

asking for child to label details in illustrations

adjusting language of text for child (may not read text, but talk about illustrations)

answering and responding to child's questions and comments

Low Cognitive Demand Strategies

reading text and pausing for child to supply word

asking child who, what, and where questions calling for recall of information in text

High Cognitive Demand Strategies

asking child why questions calling for inferences (I wonder why . . . ?)

asking child questions calling for making connections between ideas in text and child's personal experience (What does this remind you of . . . ?)

prompting child to predict (What do you think will happen next?)

prompting child to clarify or elaborate

elaborating on child's comments or text

explaining vocabulary word or connections between ideas

commenting on character traits or motivations

strategies that focus on lower cognitive demand related to understanding the *what* of stories and information books to using strategies that call on high levels of cognitive demand related to understanding the *why* and *how* of stories (Dickinson & Smith, 1994). Figure 2.7 presents a summary of the range of attention-getting, low-cognitive-demand, and high-cognitive-demand strategies that parents use to elicit their children's participation in interactive bookreading experiences (adapted from Dickinson & Smith, 1994; and Martin, 1998).

Concept of Story

As parents and teachers begin reading stories to their children and directing their attention to characters and story events, children develop an awareness of the elements found in typical literary stories (Naughton, 2008). Most stories have a main character and several supporting characters. The events of the story are set in motion when the main character recognizes a problem or decides to achieve a goal. The plot of the story consists of a series of events in which the main character actively tries to solve the problem or achieve the goal. The story ends as the character solves the problem or achieves the goal (the happily ever after of most fairy tales). A **story grammar** describes all the components that are included in an ideal story (Mandler & Johnson, 1977; Zipprich, Grace, & Grote-Garcia, 2009). Table 2.1 presents the narrative elements of a story grammar and an example of an ideal story (based on Stein & Glenn, 1979). Most adults are at least intuitively aware of the elements included in this story grammar.

Children's awareness of the story elements included in a story grammar is called their **concept of story** (Applebee, 1978). Most preschoolers have undeveloped concepts of stories. When asked to tell stories, they may list the names of their friends or describe the actions of a favorite pet. Some children have better developed concepts of stories; they may tell stories with imaginary characters but rely on their knowledge of everyday actions to invent story events. They are not likely to include problems or goals.

TABLE 2.1 Story Grammar

Narrative Elements	*Story Example* **A Smart Dog**
Main characters (animals or people)	An old man, his grandson Jim, and their sheepdog
Setting (description of location)	Shep lived on a mountainside.
Action or event (introduction of problem)	One dewy morning, while Jim was watching the sheep, Grandpa took Shep and set out to look for wild berries. Grandpa slipped on the wet grass and broke his leg.
Goal (formulation of a goal)	He decided to send Shep for help.
Attempt (actions to solve the problem)	Grandpa tied his scarf around Shep's neck and sent him to find the sheep.
Resolution (outcome of actions)	When Jim saw the scarf around Shep's neck, he knew that Grandpa was in trouble. He left Shep to watch the sheep and followed Shep's tracks in the dewy grass toward where Grandpa lay. Soon he heard Grandpa's calling. Jim helped his grandfather back to their house where they could call a doctor.
Reaction (character's feelings about outcome)	Grandpa and Jim were glad that they had such a smart sheep dog.

Environmental Print

Whereas sharing books may not occur in every family, nearly all children have experiences with print in their environment. In fact, research has shown that, especially for African American children, experiences with **environmental print** (print found on signs and in logos) often are the first and most important form of early literacy experience (Craig & Washington, 2004). As children eat breakfast, they see a box of Rice Krispies and they hear talk about eating the Rice Krispies. They observe and listen in the grocery store as their parents look for Rice Krispies. As children acquire language, they learn to talk about "Rice Krispies."

Many toddlers and two-year-olds do not notice or pay much attention to the print on their cereal boxes or cookie packages; nonetheless, the print is there. The print on the packages becomes part of what children know about those objects. Later, children will recognize just the print and stylized picture or logo without the object's being there.

Children learn about other print in their environment as they participate in a variety of everyday literacy events (Neumann, Hood, & Neumann, 2009). They are included in shopping trips for which parents read lists, clip coupons, or write checks. They observe as parents write reminder notes or help older children with homework. Children whose homes include more frequent literacy events (such as parents' reading of magazines and books and writing letters or lists) know more about how reading and writing are used (Purcell-Gates, 1996).

SPOKEN LANGUAGE DEVELOPMENT AND ITS RELATIONSHIP TO LITERACY DEVELOPMENT

AS WE HAVE SEEN in the examples of Elizabeth and Jon-Marc, children's spoken language provides a pathway into literacy. Spoken language development supports and provides a foundation for written language development.

Spoken Language Development

Literacy instruction that is founded on children's abilities and skills with spoken language requires knowing about the workings of spoken language (Crystal, 2005). These include both formal and nonformal aspects of language. The formal aspects are the characteristics of and interplay among sounds (phonology), the structures of sentences (syntax), the architecture of words and word parts (morphology), and what words mean and how their meanings interact when used in sentences (semantics). Nonformal aspects of language include—to name just a few—what children know about concept of story, the functions of language, and the mechanics of conversation.

Children are born with unconscious phonemic knowledge; as young as a few weeks old, for example, they can distinguish between /s/ and /z/ (Eimas, Siqueland, Jusczyk, & Vigorito, 1971). Later, they will use that knowledge to recognize and produce spoken words. Raising such knowledge to the level of consciousness, that is, to phonemic *awareness*, is necessary for reading and writing. Effective teachers recognize their students' levels of phonemic awareness and implement instructional strategies for supporting the development of phonemic awareness to the level that children can use it in phonics for reading and spelling.

Effective teachers also support students' attention to phonology at the largest scale, that is, to intonation. Spoken language is rich in intonation. Even very young children can use intonation to distinguish, for example, questions from statements. Questions have end-rising intonation, whether worded as questions or not: *Is Grandma coming? Grandma's coming?* Statements have end-falling intonation: *Grandma's coming.*

As shown by these examples of statements and questions, intonation involves not just sounds but also sentence structures. In other words, phonology interacts with syntax. Of course, sentence structures include more than just statements and questions. Effective teachers scaffold the use of difficult and late-developing sentence structures. For example, children master the passive sentence structure (e.g., *The car was bumped by the bus*) later than the active sentence structure (e.g., *The bus bumped the car*) (Bever, 1970), and complex sentences (e.g., *Fido barked when the mailman rang the doorbell*) later than compound sentences (e.g., *The mailman rang the doorbell and Fido barked*). Written language typically uses more complex sentence structures than does spoken language (Halliday, 1987).

Morphology and semantics are about the role of meanings in producing and understanding language. Children's early spoken language development includes their gaining competence with morphemes such as the following word endings (remember: we are talking about spoken language, so these are pronunciations, not spellings): *-ing* to show present progressive (e.g., *I am playing* versus *I play*), *-ed* to show past tense (e.g., *I played* versus *I play*), or *-s* to show number of both nouns and verbs (e.g., *toys* versus *toy* and *plays* versus *play*). Literacy learning is helped by raising such knowledge to a conscious level (morphological awareness) so that morphemes can be associated with spellings (Carlisle, 2004).

Semantics, like morphology, is concerned with meaning, but on a larger scale. It is concerned with word meanings, including how words mean together. Vocabulary development is one of the most important and visible aspects of children's language acquisition. Vocabulary size is a barometer of children's linguistic health and a factor in their ability to use language in varied contexts and for multiple purposes. Numerous studies identify vocabulary knowledge as a predictor of success in learning to read (Biemiller, 2006; Sènèchal, Ouellette, & Rodney, 2006; Wagner, Muse, & Tannenbaum, 2007).

As we saw with Elizabeth and Jon-Marc, an especially powerful context for children's explorations of meanings is story reading and storytelling. Children can engage in extended discourse—often much longer than most other language experiences, including their usually brief conversations—when they tell stories. They use and develop their concept of story. Effective teachers create opportunities for storytelling and pretend play that incorporate written language (Neuman & Roskos, 1992; Paley, 1990; Pickett, 2005). They equally value and encourage different styles of storytelling, not just the topic-focused style that schools have traditionally privileged (Gee, 2008).

Teachers who pay attention to functions of language (see Table 1.1) note the purposes of children's talk, create opportunities for exercising neglected functions, and facilitate written language's serving not just Halliday's seven functions but also those additional functions that are unique to written language, such as communicating over distance and time, record keeping, and self-reminding (Pinnell, 1985).

The heart and soul of everyday language use is conversation. Children's conversational skills can appear limited. Their conversations may be brief or may veer from topic to topic (Newkirk & McLure, 1992). Nonetheless, many young children know much about how a conversation works, for example, how to open a conversation (e.g., *Guess what?*), how to take turns (they seldom interrupt during two-party conversation), and how to fill pauses (*um*) in order to keep a turn (Garvey, 1984). Thus, effective teachers provide frequent occasions for true conversation (not contrived question and answer) and scaffold the use of **decontextualized language** and unusual vocabulary, that is, vocabulary not usually found in children's everyday talk.

English Language Learners

The examples that we have just given are of English language speakers and their emergence as language users in English-speaking communities. The principles of language learning, developmental sequences and components of language that must be acquired, apply across all languages. So, children learning Spanish, Dutch, Korean, or any other language must all gradually acquire the ability to form sounds, words, and sentences in ways that are culturally acceptable in their language communities.

However, when young children whose home language is not English enter English-speaking day cares or preschools, they begin a different language-learning pathway than what they had begun at home as first language learners (Tabors, 1997). Not all English language learners (ELLs) learn English as a second language in precisely the same way; however, four characteristics of language learning in the early years can be expected: a nonverbal phase of listening, using telegraphic speech, using formulaic speech, and growing fluency in English.

During the nonverbal period, children use gestures, facial expressions, giving and taking objects, and other physical movements to gain attention, to request help or actions, to protest the actions of others, and to have fun with others. The limitations of nonverbal communications are great; without a sympathetic and perceptive listener, children often fail to communicate. Thus, the teacher's most important role is to become that sympathetic and perceptive listener.

Children use two strategies to begin to learn to communicate in English: (1) they watch and listen intently while involved in group activities, and (2) they privately rehearse. As ELLs watch and listen, for example, in the block area, they overhear what English language speakers say. As part of watching and listening, ELLs may rehearse; they quietly repeat sounds, words, and phrases. Eventually, as they become more confident, they begin talking with other children in English. At first, children use *telegraphic* and *formulaic speech*. **Telegraphic speech** is the use of just a few words to communicate meanings that an adult would say with complete sentences. **Formulaic speech** is words or phrases that occur repeatedly and predictably in routine social situations. Children use the phrases of formulaic speech as single meaning units rather than as syntactic structures that build meaning by combining individually meaningful words. For example, a child may use *Me first* as a formula for getting ahead of his or her classmates without knowing the individual meanings of *me* and *first* or being able to use those separate words meaningfully in other contexts. Other examples of formulaic speech are *Okay?*, *Uh-oh*, *Look*, *What's that?*, *Bye-bye*, and *Wanna play?* More about the development of English for speakers of other languages is presented in Chapter 11.

ASSESSING LITERACY BEGINNERS

T EACHERS OF INFANTS, TODDLERS, AND TWO-YEAR-OLDS more often broadly assess language, cognitive, social, emotional, and physical development rather than assessing the more specific area of literacy development. Yet, for three-year-olds, such assessments are of growing importance. Many three-year-olds are included in publicly funded preschool programs that require valid and reliable assessments of language, literacy, and numeracy development. Head Start, for example, requires that children be assessed in language and literacy as well as in all other areas of development (U.S. Department of Health and Human Services, 2003). Thus, many teachers will need to combine a systematic approach to observation with other reliable and valid assessments.

In order to serve assessment needs, observations must be systematic. *Systematic observations* are planned and result in written notes. In this chapter, we have shown that beginners participate with adults in bookreading events by attending to the illustrations, pointing to objects in illustrations upon request, naming objects in illustrations, and answering questions at both low and high cognitive levels. Beginners also pay attention to environmental print in familiar contexts and can name it. They begin to tell stories that have some of the components of ideal story grammars. Thus, teachers' planned, systematic literacy observations of beginners can include watching for these behaviors.

As children participate in bookreading and environmental print reading events and tell stories, teachers write what they observe children doing and saying. Teachers capture as much information about the events as they can in their written notes, which are called *anecdotal notes* (Rhodes & Nathenson-Mejia, 1992). Anecdotal notes do not include judgments of how well children are performing. Instead, they are descriptions of actions and talk. Later, teachers will reflect on the actions and talk and write statements about what the child knows and can do. These statements are added to anecdotal notes as written *reflections*. Figure 2.8 presents an anecdotal note (Figure 2.8a) and reflection (Figure 2.8b) about four-year-old Danielle, a developmentally delayed child, as she worked in her preschool art center. The figure also includes two samples of drawings that Danielle made as the teacher observed. Notice that the anecdotal note carefully describes Danielle's actions and her words, and the reflection is the teacher's judgment about what Danielle has learned to do in this activity.

Anecdotal notes taken across time will reflect children's growing literacy knowledge, so notes and reflections should be written frequently—at least once a month. One method of keeping track of anecdotal notes, reflections, and samples of children's work is to have an assessment notebook. Assessment notebooks are notebooks in which teachers keep all of their anecdotal notes and analyses. Teachers can use dividers to make a separate section for each child in the classroom. Teachers place their anecdotal notes in the assessment notebook immediately in order not to misplace them. Most teachers write anecdotal notes on dated sticky notes during observations and then later tape these sticky notes to pages in their assessment notebooks. Once or twice each week, they analyze observations taped in their notebooks. They quickly read through the current notes and the previous month's observations for a child and jot down a few insights about the significance of what they observed most recently. Thus, assessment notebooks help teachers keep track of change over time in literacy learning.

FIGURE 2.8a   Danielle's Round and Round Drawing

Anecdotal Note: Danielle was drawing at the art center. When asked what she was doing said, "I make round and round." I said it looked like a head with lots of curly hair. I asked where the eyes would be and she pointed inside her drawing. I suggested she put dots in to make a face. She made two scribble marks. I said I would add legs and I drew two lines down. Danielle got out another paper and said: "I make a head, too." Her drawing included head, eyes, legs, and maybe a mouth.

FIGURE 2.8b   Danielle's Person

Reflection: This is the first time Danielle has made a representational drawing. 4/23/05

CHAPTER SUMMARY

THIS CHAPTER DESCRIBES THE FIRST PHASE OF LITERACY DEVELOPMENT: the beginnings of reading and writing. Very young children begin their literacy learning when they interact with their parents and other caring adults as they share books or other kinds of print items. Young children who have opportunities to draw and to talk about their drawing are also on their way to knowing about literacy. Infants, toddlers, and two- and three-year-olds typically are not yet literate (as we describe *literate* in the preface of this book), but they do have many literacy behaviors and they do know something about literacy. They find reading and writing activities pleasurable, and they have bookhandling skills and participate in booksharing routines. Young children gain control over their arms, hands, and fingers as they develop motor schemes for creating shapes they have in mind. They know that the shapes they draw and the pictures they view can be named, are symbols or representations of reality, and communicate meaning.

Young children's home experiences have a powerful influence on their literacy learning. Children acquire literacy concepts through booksharing, through other literacy activities (including interactions with environmental print and drawing), and in conversations in which they are coached in using decontextualized oral language.

As children share books with their parents and other caregivers, they acquire meaning-making strategies and a concept of story. Parents support children's meaning making through storybook reading that is responsive and interactive. They also support children as they interact with environmental print.

Teachers can play an important role in very young children's literacy learning. They can make literacy materials available, offer literacy experiences, and respond to children's literacy attempts. They use systematic observations, anecdotal notes, and reflections collected in an assessment notebook to track children's literacy development over time. Figure 2.9 presents a summary of what literacy beginners know about written language meanings, forms, meaning-form links, and functions.

FIGURE 2.9   Summary: What Literacy Beginners Know about Written Language

Meaning
know booksharing routines
learn meaning-making strategies
use decontextualized language
develop concepts about stories

Forms
develop motor schemes
recognize the alphabet as a special set of
    written signs

Meaning-Form Links
make symbols

Functions
draw and share books as pleasurable
    activities
use books and drawing to gain the
    attention of others

USING THE INFORMATION

When visiting a Head Start classroom of three-year-olds, we invited several children to "tell us a story." Some of the stories the children told us are repeated here. Consider each story and compare its elements to the elements included in the story grammar presented in Table 2.1. Discuss which elements are included in the children's stories and which are omitted.

De'Brean: Me and my sister and my mother and my mother's boyfriend and my grandma and my little brother.

Keveon: Bunny seen a grandmother and gived her a flower. The grandmother dancing.

Rayshawn: There once was a little boy. He walk to the store and buy some potato chips. He walk to the store and buy milk. He walk to the store and buy some junk food.

Stanika: Girl goin home. Boy goin to sleep. The sister eatin. The mama takin a bath. The daddy washing the car.

Amber: Once upon a time there was a little girl. Her mama spank her, and then she cry.

Tyreke: Once there was a little boy. He lives in a tent. Then the little boy go up a beanstalk. There was a big giant. He ate the little boy. Then the boy go down the beanstalk and go home. The giant go down and was dead.

APPLYING THE INFORMATION

Soowon is a three-year-old in a classroom that supports recently immigrated children in a large urban school system. She has been in the classroom for six months and is beginning to produce some English. Her teacher has read *The Seven Chinese Sisters* (Tucker & Lin, 2003) several times during the year and it is Soowon's favorite book. Her teacher wrote this anecdotal note: 2/24. Soowon went to the reading center and got out 7 Chinese Sisters. She hugged the book and looked through the pages acting out the parts for the sisters (karate, barking like a dog, riding a motorbike). As she turned pages she said, "Help, help. Come on. Go, go. Help, help. You safe. Home go." Soowon then went to the art center and drew the picture in Figure 2.10. She asked her teacher to write "The Seven Sisters" on her paper. Describe Soowon's language and literacy knowledge.

FIGURE 2.10   The Seven Sisters

GOING BEYOND THE TEXT

MAKE AN AUDIO RECORDING OF A CONVERSATION between a three-year-old and an adult. Compare the adult's and the child's uses of phonology, morphology, semantics, and syntax. What makes the conversation work (mechanics of conversation)? What phonemes, if any, has the child not yet mastered in his or her pronunciations? In what ways does the adult support the child's participation, that is, make up for the child's less developed vocabulary and less complete knowledge of morphology, semantics, syntax, and conventions of conversation? What functions of language does the child express? What contextual clues were available to the adult and child that supported this conversation?

REFERENCES

Applebee, A. N. (1978). *The child's concept of story.* Chicago: University of Chicago Press.

Bever, T. G. (1970). The cognitive basis for linguistic structure. In J. R. Hayes (Ed.), *Cognition and the development of language* (pp. 279–362). New York: Wiley.

Biemiller, A. (2006). Vocabulary development and instruction: A prerequisite for school learning. In D. Dickinson & S. B. Neuman (Eds.), *Handbook of early literacy research, Vol. 2* (pp. 41–51). New York: Guilford Press.

Brown, M. W. (1947). *Goodnight moon.* New York: Harper & Row.

de Brunhoff, L. (1975). *Babar and the Wully-Wully.* New York: Random House.

Bus, A. (2001). Joint caregiver-child storybook reading: A route to literacy development. In S. Neuman & D. Dickinson (Eds.), *Handbook of early literacy research* (pp. 179–191).

Carlisle, J. F. (2004). Morphological processes that influence learning to read. In C. A. Stone, E. R. Silliman, B. J. Ehren, & K. Apel (Eds.), *Handbook of language and literacy: Development and disorders* (pp. 318–339). New York: Guilford Press.

Carter, D. R., Chard, D. J., & Pool, J. L. (2009). A family strengths approach to early language and literacy development. *Early Childhood Education Journal, 36*(6), 519–526.

Craig, H., & Washington, J. (2004). Language variation and literacy learning. In C. Stone, E. Silliman, B. Ehren, & K. Apel (Eds.), *Handbook of language and literacy: Development and disorders* (pp. 228–247). New York: Guilford Press.

Crystal, D. (2005). *How language works.* Woodstock, NY: The Overlook Press.

Dickinson, D., & Smith, M. (1994). Long-term effects of preschool teachers' book readings on low-income children's vocabulary and story comprehension. *Reading Research Quarterly, 29,* 105–122.

Dyson, A. H. (2003). *The brothers and sisters learn to write: Popular literacies in childhood and school cultures.* New York: Teachers College Press.

Eimas, P. D., Siqueland, E. R., Jusczyk, P., & Vigorito, J. (1971). Speech perception in infants. *Science, 171,* 303–306.

Garton, A. F., & Pratt, C. (2009). Cultural and developmental predispositions to literacy. In D. R. Olson & N. Torrance (Eds.), *The Cambridge handbook of literacy* (pp. 501–517). New York: Cambridge University Press.

Garvey, C. (1984). *Children's talk.* Cambridge, MA: Harvard University Press.

Gee, J. P. (2008). *Social linguistics and literacies: Ideology in discourses* (3rd ed.). London: Routledge.

Halliday, M. A. K. (1987). Spoken and written modes of meaning. In R. Horowitz & S. J. Samuels

(Eds.), *Comprehending oral and written language* (pp. 55–82). San Diego: Academic Press.

Halliday, M. A. K. (2002). Relevant models of language. In B. M. Power & R. S. Hubbard (Eds.), *Language development: A reader for teachers* (2nd ed., pp. 49–53). Upper Saddle River, NJ: Merrill.

Hammerberg, D. (2004). Comprehension instruction for socioculturally diverse classrooms: A review of what we know. *The Reading Teacher, 57,* 648–658.

Heath, S. B. (1983). *Ways with words: Language, life, and work in communities and classrooms.* New York: Cambridge University Press.

Hill, E. (1980). *Where's Spot?* New York: Putnam.

Kellogg, R. (1969). *Analyzing children's art.* Palo Alto, CA: National Press Books.

Leaf, M. (1936). *The story of Ferdinand.* New York: Viking Press.

Leseman, P., & de Jong, P. (1998). Home literacy: Opportunity, instruction, cooperation and social-emotional quality predicting early reading achievement. *Reading Research Quarterly, 33*(3), 294–318.

Leseman, P., & van Tuijl, C. (2005). Cultural diversity in early literacy: Findings in Dutch studies. In D. K. Dickinson & S. B. Neuman (Eds.), *Handbook of early literacy research, Vol. 2* (pp. 211–228). New York: Guilford Press.

Mandler, L., & Johnson, N. (1977). Remembrance of things parsed: Story structure and recall. *Cognitive Psychology, 9,* 11–51.

Martin, L. (1998). Early book reading: How mothers deviate from printed text for young children. *Reading Research and Instruction, 37,* 137–160.

Michaels, S. (1981). "Sharing time": Children's narrative styles and differential access to literacy. *Language in Society, 10,* 423–442.

Michaels, S., O'Connor, C., & Resnick, L. B. (2008). Deliberative discourse idealized and realized: Accountable talk in the classroom and in civic life. *Studies in Philosophy and Education, 27*(4), 283–297.

Naughton, V. M. (2008). Picture it! *The Reading Teacher, 62*(1), 65–68.

Neuman, S. B., & Roskos, K. (1992). Literacy objects as cultural tools: Effects on children's behaviors in play. *Reading Research Quarterly, 27,* 202–225.

Neumann, M. M., Hood, M., & Neumann, D. L. (2009). The scaffolding of emergent literacy skills in the home environment: A case study. *Early Childhood Education Journal, 36*(4), 313–319.

Newkirk, T., & McLure, P. (1992). *Listening in: Children talk about books (and other things).* Portsmouth, NH: Heinemann.

Ninio, A., & Bruner, J. (1978). Antecedents of the achievements of labeling. *Journal of Child Language, 5,* 1–15.

Paley, V. G. (1990). *The boy who would be a helicopter: The uses of storytelling in the classroom.* Cambridge, MA: Harvard University Press.

Perez, B. (2004). Language, literacy, and biliteracy. In B. Perez (Ed.), *Sociocultural contexts of language and literacy* (2nd ed., pp. 25–56). Mahwah, NJ: Lawrence Erlbaum Associates.

Pickett, L. (2005). Potential for play in a primary literacy curriculum. *Journal of Early Childhood Teacher Education, 25*(3), 267–274.

Pinnell, G. S. (1985). Ways to look at the functions of children's language. In A. Jaggar & M. T. Smith-Burke (Eds.), *Observing the language learner* (pp. 57–72). Newark, DE: International Reading Association.

Purcell-Gates, V. (1996). Stories, coupons, and the "TV Guide": Relationships between home literacy experiences and emergent literacy knowledge. *Reading Research Quarterly, 31,* 406–428.

Rhodes, L., & Nathenson-Mejia, S. (1992). Anecdotal records: A powerful tool for ongoing literacy assessment. *The Reading Teacher, 45,* 502–509.

Robins, S., & Treiman, R. (2009). Talking about writing: What we can learn from conversations between parents and their young children. *Applied Psycholinguistics, 30*(3), 463–484.

Rodriguez, E. T., Tamis-LeMonda, C. S., Spellmann, M. E., Pan, B. A., Raikes, H., Lugo-Gil, J., & Luze, G. (2009). The formative role of home literacy experiences across the first three years of life in children from low-income families. *Journal of Applied Developmental Psychology, 30*(6), 677–694.

Roth, H. (1986). *A goodnight hug.* New York: Grosset & Dunlap.

Sènèchal, M., Ouellette, G., & Rodney, D. (2006). The misunderstood giant: On the predictive role of early vocabulary to future reading. In D. Dickinson & S. B. Neuman (Eds.), *Handbook of early literacy research, Vol. 2* (pp. 173–182). New York: Guilford Press.

Seuss, Dr. (Theodor Geisel). (1963). *Hop on pop.* New York: Random House.

Smith, H. (2004). Literacy and instruction in African American communities: Shall we overcome? In

B. Perez (Ed.), *Sociocultural contexts of language and literacy* (2nd ed., pp. 207–245). Mahwah, NJ: Lawrence Erlbaum Associates.

Stein, N., & Glenn, C. (1979). An analysis of story comprehension in elementary children. In R. Freedle (Ed.), *Advances in discourse processes: Vol 2. New directions in discourse processing* (pp. 53–120). Norwood, NJ: Ablex Publishing.

Tabors, P. (1997). *One child, two languages: A guide for preschool educators of children learning English as a second language.* Baltimore, MD: Brookes Publishing.

Takaya, K. (2008). Jerome Bruner's theory of education: From early Bruner to later Bruner. *Interchange: A Quarterly Review of Education, 39*(1), 1–19.

Taylor, D., & Dorsey-Gaines, C. (1988). *Growing up literate: Learning from inner-city families.* Portsmouth, NH: Heinemann.

Tucker, K., & Lin, G. (2003). *The seven Chinese sisters.* Morton Grove, IL: Albert Whitman & Company.

U.S. Department of Health and Human Services. (2003). The national reporting system: What is it and how will it work? *Head Start Bulletin, 76.*

Vandermaas-Peeler, M., Nelson, J., Bumpass, C., & Sassine, B. (2009). Social contexts of development: Parent-child interactions during reading and play. *Journal of Early Childhood Literacy, 9*(3), 295–317.

Wagner, R. K., Muse, A. E., & Tannenbaum, K. R. (Eds.). (2007). *Vocabulary acquisiton: Implications for reading comprehension.* New York: Guilford Press.

Walt Disney Productions Staff. (1974). *Walt Disney's Peter and the wolf.* New York: Random House.

Wells, G. (1986). *The meaning makers.* Portsmouth, NH: Heinemann.

Wright, B. F. (Illustrator). (1916). *The real Mother Goose.* New York: Rand McNally.

Wu, L.-Y. (2009). Children's graphical representations and emergent writing: Evidence from children's drawings. *Early Child Development and Care, 179*(1), 69–79.

Zipprich, M. A., Grace, M., & Grote-Garcia, S. A. (2009). Building story schema: Using patterned books as a means of instruction for students with disabilities. *Intervention in School and Clinic, 44*(5), 294–299.

PEARSON myeducationlab

Go to the topics Oral Language Development and Family Literacy in the MyEducationLab (www.myeducationlab.com) for your course, where you can:

- Find learning outcomes for Oral Language Development and Family Literacy along with the national standards that connect to these outcomes.
- Complete Assignments and Activities that can help you more deeply understand the chapter content.
- Examine challenging situations and cases presented in the IRIS Center Resources.

A+RISE

Go to the Topic A+RISE in the MyEducationLab (www.myeducationlab.com) for your course. A+RISE® Standards2Strategy™ is an innovative and interactive online resource that offers new teachers in grades K–12 just-in-time, research-based instructional strategies that:

- Meet the linguistic needs of ELLs as they learn content
- Differentiate instruction for all grades and abilities
- Offer reading and writing techniques, cooperative learning, use of linguistic and nonlinguistic representations, scaffolding, teacher modeling, higher order thinking, and alternative classroom ELL assessment
- Provide support to help teachers be effective through the integration of listening, speaking, reading, and writing along with the content curriculum
- Improve student achievement
- Are aligned to Common Core Elementary Language Arts standards (for the literacy strategies) and to English language proficiency standards in WIDA, Texas, California, and Florida.

CHAPTER 3

Three to Five Years

Novice Readers and Writers in the Phase of Awareness and Exploration

KEY CONCEPTS

Mock Letters

Analytic Talk

Pretend Reading

Concepts about Print (CAP)

Book Orientation Concepts

Directionality Concepts

Mock Cursive

Text Formats

Alphabetic Principle

Contextual Dependency

Sign Concept

Phonological Awareness

Phonemic Awareness

Basic Interpersonal Communication Skills (BICS)

Cognitive Academic Language Proficiency (CALP)

Retelling Checklist

WHO ARE NOVICE READERS AND WRITERS?

IN THIS CHAPTER, we examine the literacy learning of many preschoolers and kindergartners who are in the phase of awareness and exploration (International Reading Association & National Association for the Education of Young Children [IRA/NAEYC], 1998). We draw on examples from children in a variety of preschool and kindergarten settings. We intentionally include children from diverse SES, ethnic, and language backgrounds. We call the children who are discussed in this chapter *novice readers and writers*, whereas we called the children we described in Chapter 2 *beginners*. Our decision to use the word *novice* to describe children's interactions with literacy events in this chapter and the word *beginner* to describe children's interactions with literacy events in Chapter 2 is intentional and we believe important in differentiating what young children discover in the phase of awareness and exploration. At first, when young children are beginners, they are included in literacy events, and their parents or caregivers help them participate at their level of development. Babies and toddlers learn to point to pictures in books. Two-year-olds learn to control crayons and markers and engage in simple symbolic play (e.g., pretending to feed a baby doll). They discover how to use drawing to construct symbols—usually making representational drawings of familiar people. However, novice readers and writers demonstrate several new competencies as literacy users.

Written Language Communicates Messages: Novice Readers' and Writers' New Insights

The first new competency that novice readers and writers demonstrate is what we call *intentionality*. Around the age of three or four, preschoolers are not yet able to read and write in a conventional way, but they demonstrate an intention to communicate a message with their marks rather than merely to draw. Figure 3.1 presents scribble-like writing that four-year-old Javaris made as he played in the housekeeping center. At first glance, we would assume this writing was merely a scribble drawing. However, when asked what he had written, Javaris replied, "This is my grocery list. It says here bread, lettuce, tomatoes, eggs, and cheese." Although Javaris's writing looks like a scribble, *he acted and talked as if the scribble were actually a written message*—he even called it a grocery list. His teacher responded to the scribble *as if it were actually writing*—she asked him what it said. When asked what his writing said, Javaris was able to construct a plausible list of food that could be expected on a grocery list. He acted as a novice writer because he intentionally created a written symbol, his scribble, with the purpose of communicating a message, the food on a grocery list. He did not intend to draw a picture, nor did he treat his written marking as a picture. He intended his mark to be writing and treated it as if it said something.

A second new competency that novice readers and writers demonstrate is awareness of print. Children demonstrate this new awareness as they explore environmental print's role in communicating messages. Novice readers may recognize "Cheerios," "Target," or "Pepsi" on the familiar cereal box, department store sign, or drink can.

However, they go beyond simple recognition of meaning in familiar items or contexts that happen to include printed symbols and words. *Novices react to the meaning communicated in printed signs and labels even when they are not located on the items they represent or in the context in which they are usually found.* They recognize the Cheerios and Target logos even when the actual object (the box of cereal) is not present or when the familiar context (the department store building) is not available. When they see an unfamiliar environmental print sign, novice readers are likely to ask, "What does that say?" signaling their awareness that print in the environment is intended to communicate messages.

These new insights about literacy allow children sometimes to engage with literacy in new ways. However, it is important to keep in mind that novice readers and writers do not always use their new insights. Children often draw, scribble, and even write whole pages of letter-like forms without intending to do anything other than "draw" or "write." *Sometimes* being willing to use scribbles or letter-like forms to construct a message and at other times being unwilling to do so is to be expected. Across a variety of tasks or activities, children display *repertoires of literacy knowledge* (Schickedanz, 1999). This means that sometimes—for example, when pretending to be

FIGURE 3.1   *Javaris's Grocery List: Bread, Lettuce, Tomatoes, Eggs, and Cheese*

a waitress in a preschool restaurant dramatic play center—they will write with the intention of communicating a message. At other times—for example, when drawing at a preschool art center—they will create marks just for the experience of seeing what they can create.

An Example of Novice Writing and Reading

Quadaravious is four years old. He has had many experiences sharing books with his Head Start teacher, and he enjoys drawing and writing with his classmates. One day, his teacher invited a small group of children to draw pictures of themselves. As the children finished their drawings, the teacher reminded them to write their names on their pictures. Quadaravious immediately wrote four **mock letters** (Figure 3.2). Three of the letters were circles with a long vertical line that began inside the circle and extended down from it. The fourth letter consisted of a vertical line. When he was finished writing, he read what he wrote. He said to his teacher, "I wrote my name." His teacher noticed that Quadaravious used several mock letter Qs to write his name.

Quadaravious is a novice. His behaviors and talk indicate that he finds written symbols meaningful. He wrote his name using his special symbol, a mock letter Q. It is

F IGURE 3.2   Quadaravious's Signature and Self-Portrait

significant that he constructed meaning from written symbols that he created on his own but within a supportive activity. He wrote his name to signal ownership or identity of his self-portrait when his teacher invited him to write his name.

Would we call this really writing and reading? This is an important question, one that has created controversy. Some define *writing* as the ability to write identifiable words in isolation or in simple stories. Similarly, they define *reading* as the ability to identify words printed in isolation or in simple stories. The study of children's literacy development took a historic leap forward when, after careful observation of children, researchers such as Baghban (1984); Goodman (1980); and Harste, Woodward, and Burke (1984) argued for a new definition of "reading and writing": Anytime children produce print or look at print with the intention that it be meaningful, with awareness that print "says" messages, they are readers and writers. They are not yet conventional readers and writers, but they have made their own leap forward with their intentional, meaningful creation of and interaction with print. That is what qualifies them, in our terms, as *novices*.

MEANING

THOUGH THEY DO NOT READ AND WRITE CONVENTIONALLY, novice readers and writers attend to an ever-increasing variety of texts, including menus, computer programs, telephone books, grocery lists, coupons, and, especially, stories. Novice writers make meaning by creating an increasing variety of written symbols.

Constructing the Meaning of Environmental Print

By the age of two-and-a-half or three, many young children find some environmental print symbols meaningful (Hiebert, 1978). Novice readers do not really read the words on environmental print. Unlike beginners, however, they do pay attention to the print on environmental print objects. Whereas beginners respond to such objects as wholes, which include print, novices focus on the print; they point to it. They know that the print is an important part of the object, that somehow it conveys meanings appropriate to the object.

Children expect many kinds of print items to be meaningful. For example, four-year-old Takesha was asked to read a handwritten grocery list. She said, "Green beans, coffee, and bread." She also offered to read a telephone book and said, "Takesha, 75983." Although Takesha did not really read the grocery list or the telephone book, she knew the kinds of messages associated with these kinds of print and used this knowledge to pretend to read.

Constructing Meaning While Listening to Story and Information Book Read-Alouds

In order to understand a story being read to them, children must listen to the words of the story. Of course, most books for children include pictures that provide clues for understanding the stories. Eventually, however, children must learn to rely only on the text and not on picture context to understand stories that they read (Dickinson, 2001).

Most children's early experiences with constructing story meanings are highly personalized; they capitalize on the children's experiences with particular stories. Novices begin also to use knowledge of stories in general, that is, how stories work, especially the use of sequence and causation. They learn that events in stories often occur in a familiar order and that some events in stories cause other events to occur. We have called children's awareness of elements of story their *concept of story,* or *story schema* (see Chapter 2).

As children approach school age—preschool or kindergarten—their storybook experiences often include many-to-one situations. In group story-sharing situations, children are not as close to the pictures as they are in one-to-one story-sharing situations. Thus, they have to rely more on the teacher's reading of the words of the text to construct story meaning than on extensive viewing of pictures (McGee & Schickedanz, 2007).

Children's Meaning-Making Strategies.

Mrs. Jones is a preschool teacher who is skilled at sharing books with her class of low-income four-year-olds. Figure 3.3 presents a portion of the interaction among nine four-year-olds and Mrs. Jones as she shared *There's a Nightmare in My Closet* (Mayer, 1968).

The children's comments and questions demonstrate that they understood much of the *literal meaning* of the story, facts stated in the text or shown in the illustrations. Obviously, the children understood that there was a nightmare in the closet; they knew that the character needed protection. Their comments and questions demonstrate that they also made many inferences about *implied meanings* in the story. They made *inferences* about motivations for the character's actions (he shut the door "Cause he doesn't want the nightmare to come out"); about the character's traits ("He's a scaredy cat"); and about reasons for the character's feelings (he was afraid "cause the wind blow"). Inferences are children's deductions of information not stated. The children also made predictions; they made guesses about upcoming story events. Just before Mrs. Jones turned to the last page of the story, which contains an illustration of a second nightmare peeking out of the closet, one child predicted, "There's gonna be another one."

In addition, the children paid attention to each other's comments. When one child commented about an action of the character ("Cause he's scared"), another one agreed ("He's a scaredy cat"). Similarly, when one child noted that "the wind blow," another child added, "Yeah, the curtain's out."

This brief story interaction illustrates that four-year-olds in group story-sharing can construct many kinds of meanings (Hindman, Connor, Jewkes, & Morrison, 2008). They understand what the author says—the *literal meaning.* They also understand what the author implies—*implied meaning.*

Preschoolers and kindergartners also listen as their teachers read nonfiction or informational books aloud and participate actively in trying to understand the ideas presented in these kinds of texts. Novice readers use many of the same strategies to understand informational texts as they use with story texts (Leung, 2008). They may predict and speculate on behavior of animals or people in the book based on their own experiences, or they may ask questions and make inferences (Tower, 2002). For

FIGURE 3.3   A Portion of the Interaction as Mrs. Jones and Her Prekindergartners Share *There's a Nightmare in My Closet* (Mayer, 1968)

Brackets indicate portions of the dialogue that occurred simultaneously.

Mrs. J: (shows cover of book, invites children to talk about nightmares, reads title and author, and reads first page of text stating the character's belief that a nightmare once lived inside his bedroom closet)

Child 1:   He got toys and a gun on his bed.

Mrs. J: Umm, I wonder why?

Child 2:   So he can protect him.

Mrs. J: Protect him. Umm. (reads text about closing the door to the closet)

Child 1:   Cause he's scared.

⌈ Child 3:   He's a scaredy cat.

⌊ Child 1:   My momma take the light off, I'm not scared.

Child 4:   He might lock it.

Mrs. J: Why would he lock it?

Child 4:   Cause he doesn't want the nightmare to come out.

Mrs. J: (reads text about character being afraid to even look in the closet)

Child 1:   Cause the wind blow.

Mrs. J: The wind blows?

⌈ Child 3:   Yeah, the curtain's out.

⌊ Child 2:   It's blowing.

Mrs. J: It must have been a dark, windy night. (continues reading text, making comments, and asking questions)

Children: (continue making comments and asking questions)

Mrs. J: (reads text about character deciding to get rid of the nightmare)

Child 1:   I guess he ain't cause that's not a real gun.

Mrs. J: (turns page to illustration of the nightmare coming out of the closet and walking toward the boy in the bed)

⌈ Child 1:   There he is.

⌊ Child 5:   Why he's awake?

Mrs. J: Well what did it say? He was going to try to get rid of his nightmare, so he stayed awake waiting for his nightmare.

example, as a teacher was reading *Let's Find Out about Ice Cream* (Reid, 1996), a book about the process of making ice cream, a teacher and three children had this discussion about an illustration of a man working in an ice cream freezer:

Teacher: He has a freezer suit on.

Kenny: Why?

Althea: Cause he won't, cause he can't get cold.

Kenny: Cause he won't catch a cold.

Jason: Yeah, and not get a cough. (Tower, 2002, p. 72)

Teachers' Roles in Helping Children Understand Interactive Read-Alouds.   Figure 3.3 presented only a small portion of the interactive read-aloud of *There's a Nightmare in My Closet*. In this read-aloud, Mrs. Jones read with expression and used three different voices: one for the narrator, one for the little boy, and one for the monster. She was so familiar with this story that she frequently turned to look at the children as she read portions of the story so they could see her facial expressions. She pointed to specific places in the pictures as she read, and she paused for dramatic effect.

Mrs. Jones's reading invites a great deal of participation from the children (Smolkin & Donovan, 2002). She reads the story, but she also encourages the children to comment and ask questions. She demands a high *level of cognitive engagement.* That is, she helps children use higher-level thinking by making inferences about character traits and their motives. She helps children make connections between events in the story so that they can understand what causes characters to act as they do. She helps children understand the meaning of words and connects events in books to children's experiences. This style of reading helps children engage in **analytic talk** (Dickinson, 2001) in which they are analyzing characters and events rather than merely recalling what happened.

Teachers play many of the same roles when sharing informational books as we have seen when they share storybooks. They connect children's comments and questions to the technical vocabulary used in the books and describe the actions and objects in illustrations (Smolkin & Donovan, 2002). For example, while discussing the book about making ice cream, one four-year-old pointed to a picture of sugar cane stalks and asked, "And what are—snakes?" Her teacher clarified, "These are called sugar cane plants" (Tower, 2002, p. 67).

Constructing Meaning in Pretend Reading and Retelling

Novices also use their concept of story when they attempt to retell stories. A special kind of retelling is when children look at favorite picture books—ones they have shared many times with their parents or teacher—and attempt to reread them on their own. These retellings or rereadings are called **pretend readings** (Pappas, 1993).

However, during the preschool and kindergarten years, children listen to more than just stories. They enjoy poems, songs, and information books. Just as they gain a growing awareness of the characteristics of storybooks and the organizational patterns in stories, children learn the organization of information books (Duke, 2004, 2007;

TABLE 3.1 Components of Stories and Information Books Children Typically Include in Their Pretend Readings

Story	Information Book
Past Tense: "Once there was a woodpecker."	**Timeless Present Tense:** "Squirrels have furry bodies."
Particular Character: "The woodpecker"	**General Class of Things:** "Squirrels"
Sequence of Events: "The woodpecker flew to a tree and began pecking at the tree."	**Defining Characteristics of the Class:** "Squirrels have nice furry ears. Squirrels put up their ears to keep them warm."
Problems: "The tree was so hard, the woodpecker couldn't make a hole."	**Typical Activities:** "Squirrels search for nuts and dig in the ground."

Pappas, 2006), that is, the particular components that make up informational accounts. Table 3.1 presents the components that preschoolers usually include in their pretend readings of stories and information books (Pappas, 1991, 1993).

Writing Meaningful Messages

Novices have a new interest in participating in writing messages. Much of novice writers' message making is a part of playful activity. They pretend to read and write in their dramatic play (Roskos, Christie, Widman, & Holding, 2010).

In order to prompt this kind of reading and writing, teachers provide many hands-on activities in preschool and take advantage of making field trips around the school building and playground and in the community. For example, one preschool teacher, Ms. Varelas, prepared for a field trip to the school kitchen where the children's food was prepared every day. She knew the children would be interested in the very large stove and oven; the oversized pots, pans, and utensils; and the walk-in freezer. She visited the kitchen and took a tour led by the head cook and learned about the double-deck, full-size oven that could hold six racks of food; the special slicer they used; the fryer with its two fry baskets, and the huge mixer, which had a 105-quart capacity. She and the cook prepared a field trip in which children saw these appliances in action making french fries, sliced cheese for grilled cheese and tomato sandwiches with carrot strips, and chocolate cake. The teacher prompted the cook to repeat the names of the appliances and utensils that children would see in action. Also, the teacher wanted the cook to stress the sequence of steps in preparing the food (first readying the fryer, then getting the french fries out of the freezer, and then frying them at the last minute as children entered the cafeteria).

To prepare children for the field trip, Ms. Varelas wrote directions for home activities for parents on her Web site and alerted her ESL assistant, who called two parents. She sent e-mail messages to parents alerting them to the look at the directions on the Web page. She called three parents she knew might not see the e-mail messages. At home, children were to look at their stove and find out how many burners it had. They were to look at the pots their mothers and fathers used for cooking and find a skillet and a cooking pot. They were to look at three utensils parents used during cooking and talk about how they were used. Finally, they were to look inside the refrigerator and describe at least three parts (e.g., freezer, drawer, shelves, ice maker).

During the field trip, children compared and contrasted the school kitchen appliances and utensils with those in their homes. After the field trip, children were invited to draw and write about what they had seen. Anita drew a picture of a spoon her mother used, then wrote a string of three mock letters (Figure 3.4a). Ms. Varelas said, "Tell me about this, Anita," and Anita said, "It's my mother's spoon." Anita pointed to her picture, then said, "spoon" pointing to the mock letters (indicating this was her writing). Then Anita said, "Now, I'm going to write about the spoon in the school kitchen." She drew a much larger picture and said in a very large, exaggerated voice, "SPOON." This writing appears in Figure 3.4b.

Anita knows that writing can be used to label drawings, and the meanings she constructs are conveyed in both the writing and the drawing. She is not yet using the conventional meaning-form link of actually attempting to spell but, rather, is connecting her written forms with her drawn symbols in a systematic way (if a spoon is big, it is written and spoken big, too).

Technology Tie-In

There are many history museums, art museums, and zoos that provide virtual tours. Use a browsing tool and a search string such as "virtual tours of Smithsonian" or "virtual tours of zoos" and you will have several choices. We watched a tour of a snake exhibit and took a tour around an Asian environment to view the various animals living there.

A good site to start with is a virtual tour of Mount Vernon at www.mountvernon.org. Check out the time line of George Washington's life, and many videos will play explaining myths and truths about his life.

http://australian-animal.net is another idea for a virtual tour. Click on one of the unusual native animals and learn more about it.

An unusual virtual tour can be taken at http://cybersmart.org/Africa/storytelling/gallery. Here are digital stories filmed and narrated by African youth about the village they live in.

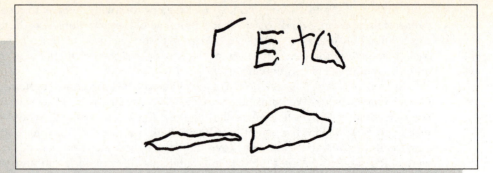

FIGURE 3.4a   "spoon"

FIGURE 3.4b   "SPOON"

WRITTEN LANGUAGE FORMS

WHILE THEY ARE DEVELOPING NEW INSIGHTS about written language meanings, novices also demonstrate new awarenesses about written language forms. They notice the print on environmental print items and in books, they acquire notions of how print looks and how it is organized, and they begin to display these notions in their own writing.

Concepts about Print

Children's **concepts about print (CAP)** are understandings that they have about how print is visually organized and read. They learn that alphabet letters are a special category of visual symbols, that print "says," and that print is read rather than the pictures. In Chapter 2, we described several concepts about print called *bookhandling skills* that very young children learn; books are held right side up (children know which is the top and bottom of a book), and their pages are turned one by one from the front of the book to the back. These **book orientation concepts** form the foundation for later discovering **directionality concepts.** Directionality concepts involve children's awareness that print is written and read from left to right, line by line. Later, we will show that novice writers display awareness of directionality in their writing. Novice readers begin this process when they pretend to read a favorite book. They may point to the print as they read, sweeping their hands across the print. Novice readers are not able to point to each word of a book one by one (this will come later), but they do display awareness that books are read in a systematic fashion.

From Scribbles to Alphabet Letters

Children's awareness of print and their developing concepts about print influence the kinds of marks they make in their writing. Novice writers attempt to create marks that look like print and are organized on a page like writing. However, children's early writing attempts, called *scribble writing* (Schickedanz, 1999), have virtually none of the features we would expect of alphabet writing. They do not include alphabet letters or even forms that somewhat resemble letters. Earlier, we presented Javaris's grocery list (see Figure 3.1) and his writing as an example of scribble writing. Most of the marks he made were uncontrolled, round-and-round scribbles. A more sophisticated form of writing is called *linear scribble writing* (Bloodgood, 1999; Hildreth, 1936) and consists of horizontally arranged, wavy lines. Linear scribble writing is sometimes called **mock cursive,** because the continuous lines of up-and-down scribbling resemble cursive writing. Figure 3.5 presents an example of mock cursive. Three-year-old Kendrel wrote this at his Head Start writing center and announced to his teacher that he had written his name. Notice his writing's linearity.

Eventually, children's writing begins to include separate units or symbols although the units may not look very much like alphabet letters. For example, many children's writing attempts consist of a series of circles resembling the letter *O.* Other children

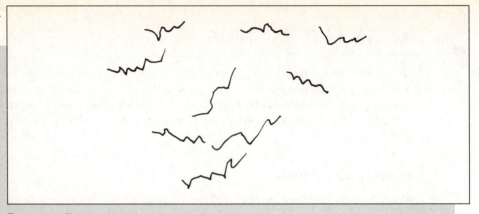

FIGURE 3.5   Kendrel Writes His Name

may compose symbols using lines and curves along with circle shapes. Figure 3.6 presents an example of writing that consists of separate units presented in a nonlinear arrangement.

As children gain awareness of alphabet letters, their writing includes a mixture of *letter-like forms*, symbols, numbers, and even conventionally formed alphabet letters. Children seem to enjoy both writing the same form repeatedly in their writing and changing forms to see what new forms they can create (Clay, 1975). Writing with a mixture of letters, numbers, other symbols, and letter-like shapes is sometimes called *symbol salad writing* (Bear, Invernizzi, Templeton, & Johnston, 2008). Figure 3.7 presents an example of symbol salad writing in which the writer drew on his awareness of both linearity and directionality; he wrote from left to right.

Of course, children frequently draw and write on a single sheet of paper. However, even when they draw and write, children as young as three demonstrate that they

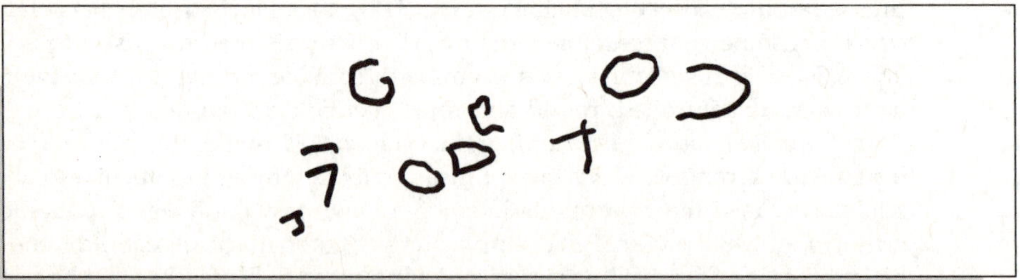

FIGURE 3.6   Writing with Separate Units

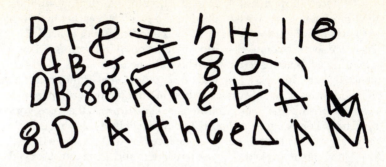

FIGURE 3.7   Symbol Salad

differentiate between drawing and writing. Figure 3.2 presented a picture Quadaravious drew of himself and his signature. Although his name consists only of four letter-like forms, three of which resemble the alphabet letter *Q*, his writing is clearly differentiated from his drawing. Often, the initial letter in a child's name is the first letter he or she can recognize and write (Schickedanz, 1999).

Alphabet Letters

Novices demonstrate in many ways their understanding of the importance of letters of the alphabet. They do not yet know what the role of alphabet letters is (to represent the fundamental units of spoken language, sounds called phonemes). However, before they learn to name any alphabet letters or to write recognizable letter formations, children discover a great deal about alphabet letters (McGee & Richgels, 1989). One thing they learn is to call this special category of written symbols *the alphabet* or *letters.* They learn that alphabet letters are related to or associated with important people, places, or objects. Kristen thought that *Special K* cereal and *Kmart* were *her* cereal and *her* store. In one preschool classroom, Jean-Marc always wrote his name with *J* for *Jean-Marc, E* for *Emmanuel, A* for *Andre, N* for *Natalie*—and then he stopped writing because he did not know anyone whose name began with *M* (Ballenger, 1999, p. 45).

Eventually, preschoolers learn the names of the alphabet letters and how to write them (Piasta & Wagner, 2010). In order to do this, they need a clear visual image of the letter and control over motor schemes to make the lines that they visualize (Schickedanz, 1999). Children build up strong visual images of letters as they experiment with *letter features,* the special lines and shapes that make up letters.

The letter *T* is made up of a horizontal and a vertical line; the letter *O* is made up of an enclosed, continuous curved line; and the letter *N* is made up of two vertical lines and a diagonal line. Children must learn to pay attention to letter features in order to distinguish between letters (for example, between the letters *w* and *v* or *l* and *i*).

Children show that they pay attention to letter features in their writing through their mock letters. As we described in Chapter 1 and earlier in this chapter, *mock letters* are letter-like shapes with many of the same features of conventional alphabet letters. There are several examples of mock letters found in Figure 3.7. This writer seems to be exploring whether the letter *H* can become the letter *I* or *A*. Mock letters are often constructed as children play with letter orientation. That is, they rotate letters so they seem to lie sideways or upside down. Letters are frequently written in mirror-image form. It is not surprising that young children are slow to grasp the correct orientation of alphabet letters. For example, a chair is a chair whether it faces left or right. But lowercase *b* and *d* are different letters because one faces left and one faces right.

Many three-year-olds know a few letters and some four-year-olds know nearly all the alphabet letters. Large studies of young children show that on average a four-year-old knows nine to fourteen alphabet letters (Bloodgood, 1999; Smith & Dixon, 1995). Such studies show that children from low-income families know fewer alphabet letters but learn quickly when they are provided alphabet learning activities in preschool (Roberts & Neal, 2004).

Signatures

Just as children learn to name and write alphabet letters and acquire concepts about what alphabet letters are, they also learn to write their names and acquire concepts about what written names are. Children's ability to write recognizable signatures develops in an identifiable pattern (Hildreth, 1936). Their ability depends on their growing motor control, awareness of letter features, and knowledge of letters as discrete units. Figure 3.8 presents Nah'Kiyah's name-writing attempts over a nine-month period while she was in a prekindergarten program for low-income four-year-olds. The first example of her signature, produced in early August, consisted of some recognizable letters (*N, H, K,* and *Y*) and some mock letters (that also look like *N, H, K,* and *Y*). The letters are all in uppercase form, although she was being taught to write her name in uppercase *and* lowercase letters in her preschool. In October, Nah'Kiyah's signature still has mostly uppercase letters; however, a lowercase *h* and the special printed form of the lowercase *a* have appeared. In November, Nah'Kiyah would only write part of her name, but notice how the letters are smaller and look more like conventional letters showing her growing motor control over writing. In February, Nah'Kiyah's signature includes every letter except the final *a* (with a little bit of ordering difficulty). By April, she has achieved a conventional signature although the apostrophe is still omitted.

As children learn to recognize and write their names, their concepts about signatures are quite different from those of adults. Ferreiro (1986) described Mariana, who claimed that she could write her name. She wrote five capital letters (*PSQIA*) as she said "Mariana" several times. When asked, "What does it say here?" about the letters *PS*, she replied, "Two Mariana." When asked, "What does it say here?" about the letters *QIA,* she replied, "Three Mariana" (Ferreiro, p. 37). Her answers reflect that Mariana believed each letter she wrote would say her name. Mariana's comments about her name illustrate that some children do not conceive of signatures as words composed of letters that represent sounds.

FIGURE 3.8   Nah'Kiyah's Signatures: August, October, November, February, and April

Texts

Novice readers and writers learn a great deal about different kinds of writing, and they use this knowledge to create a variety of texts, especially story texts. Novices come to know a variety of text formats that are used in special contexts and for particular functions. They become aware of and use text features (such as "Dear ___ " at the beginning of a letter). Additionally, their concept of story and concept of information book organization develop (Duke & Hays, 1998).

Novice writers produce many different **text formats.** For example, Javaris wrote a grocery list (see Figure 3.1). Later in this chapter, we will describe Jeremy's "Book of Poems." Included in such texts are words that writers say as they write and words that describe the contexts of their writing. When we look only at Javaris's writing, it does not appear to be a text. It is only apparent that it is a text when we pay attention to the context of his writing, including his talk and his actions.

MEANING–FORM LINKS

THE CONVENTIONAL WAY THAT MEANING (the messages writers intend) is linked to *forms* (words that writers use) is that words are comprised of alphabet letters and alphabet letters are related to phonemes in spoken words. This phoneme-letter relationship is often referenced as the **alphabetic principle.** This term suggests a regularity and precision—even a simplicity—that is not really the case (Strauss, 2005). Letters do not stand for one and only one sound (for example, *c* stands for /s/ and /k/: *city* and *cat*); and sounds are not represented by one and only one letter (for example, /s/ is represented by *s* and by *c*: *sit* and *city*). Nonetheless, this principle often works well enough to point readers in the right direction. For example, knowing that *c* sometimes represents /k/, *a* sometimes represents /a/, *t* usually represents /t/, and *p* usually represents /p/ can help children to read *cat* and *cap* correctly. As fluent readers, we are not often consciously aware of the alphabetic principle because we do not draw on it very often. Instead, we immediately recognize most of the words we read (these are called *sight words* because we recognize them by sight) without having to look at their letters and "sound out" words letter by letter. Novice readers and writers may recognize letters and, as we will see, may actually be able to isolate and say a phoneme, but they do not understand the relationship between letters and sounds. Instead, they use another method for making their writing meaningful—*contextual dependency*.

Contextual Dependency

Contextual dependency means that written forms convey meaning only through children's talk about their writing or their drawing. All of the examples given so far in this chapter have a common characteristic: the use of contextual dependency to link written forms to meanings. If we did not know what the children said about their writing, or could not look at their drawings, we would not be able to determine the messages that the child writers intended to communicate. We can only know the messages that novice writers convey when we listen to what they say about their writing or when we know about their drawing. Clay (1975) called children's dependency on context to link meaning and form the **sign concept.** For example, the two written words in Figure 3.4 (*spoon* and *SPOON*) use contextual dependency in order to convey the meanings and demonstrate the sign concept (written symbols are signs that signify an intended meaning).

Matching Print to Spoken Language: More Than Contextual Dependency

Although novice readers and writers depend primarily on the context in which their writing is produced to link meaning and form, many researchers have found that children's concepts about the relations between meaning and form change as they gain experience using written language (Dyson, 1982; Ferreiro & Teberosky, 1982). Children's knowledge of meaning-form links is very complex.

Figure 3.9 presents John's writing and story: "I have a dog. He is big. He is my best friend." As John read the story, he swept his finger from left to right across each line of text as he said each sentence. He demonstrated contextual dependency in making meaning from his own writing. But, in addition, John noticed that printed text must be matched somehow to the oral message; he matched a line of text with a spoken sentence. Although not yet conventional, this matching of the text with the oral message is a precursor to a later, more-developed kind of meaning-form linking, that is, matching one spoken sound (or phoneme) with one letter (or grapheme).

Phonological Awareness

As novice readers and writers, young children have many experiences that allow them to develop **phonological awareness.** For example, the rhythm created in nursery rhymes highlights and segments speech sounds in a way that conversation does not. The syllables *PE ter PE ter PUMP kin EAT er* are naturally separated by the stress in the rhyme. This natural play with language sounds invites children to enjoy the music of language. Children who have listened to nursery rhymes and other writing that uses language play soon begin to play with speech sounds themselves. While four-year-old James was playing with a toy typewriter in his preschool room, he muttered "James, Fames, Wames" to himself. It is not clear whether James realized that he was making up rhyming words. However, once children do consciously attend to sounds in words apart from words' meanings, then they have phonological awareness.

A special kind of phonological awareness, known as **phonemic awareness,** requires children consciously to attend to single phonemes in words. Some novice readers and writers, for example, intentionally create rhyming words by isolating initial phonemes and substituting other phonemes for them, especially when their parents, caregivers, or teachers share books that contain many words with alliteration,

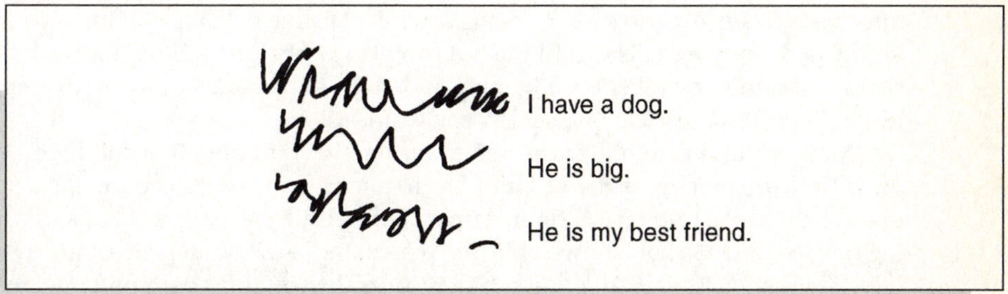

I have a dog.

He is big.

He is my best friend.

FIGURE 3.9   John's Story

such as the book *Some Smug Slug* (Duncan, 1996), and books with rhymes, such as the book *Dog Days: Rhymes around the Year* (Prelutsky & Wolcott, 2001).

Using Symbols: The Connections among Dramatic Play, Writing, and Computer Use

Play is a critical component of the preschool years (McNamee, 2005). Children's approach to writing during these years is closely connected to their play. Careful observers will notice that preschoolers most often write during dramatic play. They will take a phone message when they are pretending to be a mother with a sick baby or take notes on a patient chart when they are pretending to be a doctor. Children's pretend writing is very much like their symbolic use of objects in imaginary play. For example, they may create a symbol of a thermometer as they pretend to take a baby's temperature using a spoon to be the thermometer. Children's activities on the computer are also playful and involve the use of symbols (Labbo, 1996; Turbill & Murray, 2006). They create symbols using drawing and stamping tools and then transform them into pictures. For example, one child created a picture of his sister using a stamp of an ice cream cone to represent or symbolize her nose.

Children's ability to use complex and abstract symbols in dramatic play seems to precede their acquisition of more conventional literacy skills. Perhaps such experiences with abstract symbols during play and exploration on the computer provide a foundation for later being able to use the even more abstract symbols of letters for phonemes.

WRITTEN LANGUAGE FUNCTIONS

DURING THE PRESCHOOL AND KINDERGARTEN YEARS, young children still are socialized into their families' ways of using literacy although they will also be socialized into their school literacy culture (Dyson, 2003; Gee, 2001; Purcell-Gates, 1996). Many families use literacy in a variety of ways, such as for entertainment (reading novels), for information (surfing the Web for deals on cheap airline tickets), and for accomplishing family tasks (paying bills and filling out forms to apply for loans). Children observe the ways that family members use literacy and want to be included as they do in all family activities (Gee, 2001; Taylor & Dorsey-Gaines, 1988).

Many children from literacy-rich homes go beyond merely using literacy in their play. They use literacy as themes for play. In one Head Start classroom, the teacher was in week three of a unit on building. As part of this unit, she had read books about building houses, and she had shown children her examples of a blueprint made by an architect. She demonstrated drawing a blueprint of her own home on a large chart sheet using a blue pencil. The teacher then placed smaller "blueprint" sheets on a clipboard in the block center along with a cup with blue pencils. The children often drew blueprints for houses as part of their block play.

In contrast to the pretend making of blueprints, Tom used literacy in more functional ways. When Tom was four, he became angry because his mother would not buy

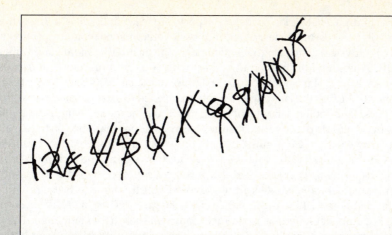

FIGURE 3.10   Tom's Calendar

him a new toy. His mother said that she would be paid in three weeks and that Tom could have a toy then. Tom asked how many days were in three weeks and went to his room. He made the calendar (a portion of which is presented in Figure 3.10) with a number for each of the twenty-one days remaining until he could get a new toy. Every day as his father read him a story at bedtime, Tom crossed off a day on his calendar, and on the twenty-first day, his mother bought him his new toy.

English Language Learners as Novice Readers and Writers

AS WE DISCUSSED IN CHAPTER 2, when children whose home language is not English enter a preschool or kindergarten in which the language of instruction is English, they face special challenges not faced by English-speaking children. Learning English is only one of these challenges. Others include learning how to fit in socially with children from different cultural backgrounds and learning the special ways of "doing school" that may be radically different from any experience these children have had previously. In English-dominant preschool and kindergarten classrooms, children will be expected not only to acquire English quickly but also to begin learning foundational literacy concepts in English.

Although many preschool and kindergarten children may enter native language or bilingual programs in which other children and the teacher and assistant speak their home language, many children enter classrooms in which teachers, even when they can speak the children's native language, are expected to teach in English. In this situation, children will be expected to learn not only basic interpersonal communication skills, but also cognitive academic language proficiency. **Basic interpersonal communication skills (BICS)** are the skills needed to interact with and communicate with friends and others in social and play situations. On the other hand, **cognitive academic language proficiency (CALP)** is the language competence needed to learn science, social studies, mathematics, and other school subjects. Cognitive academic language generally includes many words that refer to abstract concepts rather than the concrete words in everyday conversation (Cummins, 2000). In preschool and kindergarten, children will be expected to learn to use the academic vocabulary of reading and writing instruction, including the terms *alphabet letter, sound, word, uppercase, lowercase, spell, write,* and *read*.

As preschoolers and kindergartners, most English language learners will have been exposed to the written forms of their home language. They may have been taught to recognize alphabet letters or write their names in their home language. They may have found meaning in many environmental print signs and logos in their home language and may have listened to stories read from home-language picture books. Thus, children will already be learning about the unique features that make up alphabet letters in their home language as well as the concepts about print that govern reading and writing in that language.

The greater the similarity of a child's home written language to written English, the easier it will be for that child to learn to read and write in English (Cummins, 1989). For example, it is easier for Spanish-speaking children than for Chinese-speaking children to learn concepts about print in English (Barone, Mallette, & Xu, 2005). This is because written Spanish, like written English, is alphabetic (alphabet letters correspond roughly to spoken phonemes), while written Chinese is nonalphabetic (characters represent whole syllables).

Less radical are form differences from one alphabetic language to another. These differences typically are at the level of features of individual letters. Although many written languages, such as Spanish use an alphabet that is the same as or very similar to the alphabet used to write English, other languages, such as Hebrew, use letters composed of other feaures than English's straight lines and curves, horizontals, verticals, and diagonals. Still, both written English and written Hebrew depend on the systematic use of letter-sound correspondences. That is, both are alphabetic languages.

Whatever the nature of their home language's writing system, children who share reading and writing experiences with other people in their homes and communities begin to learn about written language forms. Some will learn letter features; others will learn features of characters.

ASSESSING NOVICE READERS AND WRITERS

MANY CHILDREN IN PRESCHOOL AND KINDERGARTEN are novice readers and writers. Because their literacy behaviors and knowledge are still unconventional, teachers will want to continue to document their development through systematic observation accompanied by written anecdotes and reflection. Observing children as they attempt to read and write is a critical component of a systematic approach to assessment for all young children (see suggestions for writing anecdotal notes and reflections in Chapter 2).

However, novice readers and writers do make progress in learning some conventions including alphabet knowledge, concepts about print, phonological and phonemic awareness, vocabulary, and oral comprehension. Because these concepts are critical to children's success in later becoming effective readers and writers, teachers monitor children's progress in acquiring them. In fact, in more and more preschools, teachers are required to screen children when they first enter in order to determine what they already know, and to administer frequent assessments to monitor children's progress. Early Reading First, a portion of recent legislation in the United States, the No Child Left Behind Act of 2001 (U.S. Congress, 2001), provides grants for preschools to create "centers of preschool excellence," in which teachers are required to screen and monitor children's language and literacy development. Similarly, Head Start teachers are required to assess children's language and literacy development, as well as their development in other domains.

One way of assessing children's literacy development is to collect work samples on a systematic basis. Work samples are children's actual writing products. A work sample might be a picture with a label that a child wrote at the writing center, a digital photograph of a shared writing step-up chart on which the child has copied some letters, or an audiotaped retelling of a favorite story told during center time. Teachers select samples of children's writing and retellings that provide insight into their continuing literacy development.

Another way of assessing children's literacy development is to give children *assessment tasks* in the critical areas of literacy foundational concepts. Assessment tasks are activities that teachers ask children to perform, while teachers score whether children can do the task or not. For example, a teacher might show children some alphabet letters and ask children to name them. Teachers would record which letters were named and which were not. At the beginnings of the phase of awareness and exploration, typical novice readers and writers demonstrate few, if any, conventional concepts on assessment tasks. However, as children move through preschool and kindergarten, they make progress in acquiring many of these foundational concepts and show their competence on many assessment tasks. If teachers administer these assessment tasks two or three times a year and regularly gather work samples and write anecdotal notes and reflections based on careful observations, then, across the preschool and kindergarten years, they can create an evolving picture of children's emergence into more conventional reading and writing.

Assessing Alphabet Knowledge and Signature Writing

Alphabet knowledge involves several different skills. *Alphabet recognition* is the ability to look at an alphabet letter and immediately say its name. Appendix B presents an uppercase and lowercase alphabet recognition task score sheet and directions for making an administration sheet to use with children. To prepare the uppercase alphabet administration sheet, teachers type, in a large font, five rows of six uppercase letters in the order presented on the score sheet. For younger preschool children, teachers may make individual letter cards or type letters in a single row on an index card (using twenty-six cards in the case of one letter per card, or five cards in the case of typing six letters in a row on each card). Kindergarten children may be shown all twenty-six letters typed on one sheet of paper. Each child is shown the uppercase administration cards or sheet, and the teacher points to each letter for the child to name. Teachers copy the score sheet found in Appendix B for each child and circle or check the letters each child correctly names. For children who know several uppercase letters, teachers can also assess children's recognition of lowercase letters. Again, teachers would construct an administration sheet with the lowercase letters typed in the order presented on the score sheet.

To assess how many letters children know how to write, teachers can give children paper and ask them to write particular letters. Teachers we know ask children to write uppercase letters in the order they are presented on the uppercase alphabet recognition score sheet. (Children are not shown this list of letters but, rather, write letters from memory.) After children write, teachers can score the alphabet writing task sheet by marking which letters children have written in recognizable form, keeping in mind that it is acceptable for preschoolers to have orientation difficulties (e.g., backward letters) and that they are not likely to use the "correct" formation that is expected in later elementary grades.

All children should also be asked to write their names. Teachers can expect preschool and kindergarten children's signature writing to progress from level 0 to level 6 (based on Bloodgood, 1999) as follows: (0) uncontrolled scribbling; (1) controlled scribbles, such as mock cursive; (2) separate marks that do not resemble letters; (3) a signature with several marks but only one or two recognizable letters; (4) a signature with nearly all letters in recognizable form but possibly having orientation difficulties; (5) a recognizable and correct signature with few orientation difficulties; (6) a first and last name signature with mostly correct letter formation.

Assessing Concepts about Print

Novice readers and writers also begin acquiring concepts about print. These are understandings about how texts work, how they are configured, and how a reader approaches them (Clay, 2005). Appendix B presents directions for administering and scoring a concepts about print task that assesses children's bookhandling skills, knowledge about directionality, and concepts about letters and words.

Assessing Phonological and Phonemic Awareness

Teachers can assess children's awareness of rhyming by asking children to generate rhyming words. The teacher says a word and has children say other words that rhyme with it. Appendix B presents directions for administering and scoring a rhyming word assessment. Teachers can assess novice readers' and writers' phonemic awareness by asking them to say the beginning sounds of words that are spoken aloud. The isolating beginning phoneme task in Appendix B includes ten words that teachers pronounce and then ask children to say the beginning sounds. The directions for administering and scoring this task are presented in the appendix.

Assessing Vocabulary and Oral Comprehension

Children expand their vocabularies and oral comprehension. *Vocabulary* refers to children's understandings about the meanings of words and their ability to use words effectively in speech. *Oral comprehension* is their ability to understand books and other texts read aloud to them (that is, they can answer literal and inferential questions or retell the story). We recommend that teachers assess children's oral comprehension and their use of sophisticated vocabulary using a **retelling checklist,** which is a list of the important events in a story and its important and sophisticated vocabulary. Appendix B presents directions for administering and scoring a retelling checklist for the book *Owl Moon* (Yolen & Schoenherr, 1987). Teachers read the book aloud to a group of children two or three times and then individually ask children to retell what they remember. As a child retells the book, the teacher makes a check mark on the checklist shown in Appendix B for any event the child tells about and circles any listed vocabulary the child uses. Most children do not use the exact words of the storybook, so teachers check the retelling checklist for when children mention the gist of the story.

Analyzing Assessment Data

The preschool and kindergarten assessment tasks that we have described in this chapter are useful for screening and monitoring what individual children know and can do. In Table 3.2, we present three children's scores on these tasks. All three children

TABLE 3.2   Beginning-of-the-Year Kindergarten Scores on Monitoring Assessment Tasks

	Zyderrious	Imani	Kambrisha
Upper alphabet recognition (26)	25	25	1
Lower alphabet recognition (26)	24	21	5
Writing alphabet letters (15)	14	14	1
Level of name writing (6)	4	5	3
Concepts about print (15)	5	10	3
Generating rhyming words	3	0	0
Isolating beginning sounds (10)	0	10	0
Oral retelling, ideas (44)	7	17	4
Oral retelling, vocabulary (12)	0	4	0

attended Head Start and are entering kindergarten in a school that primarily serves low-income children (98 percent of the children qualify for free or reduced lunch). Two children know most alphabet letters, but one of these children is still more advanced and has begun to develop phonemic awareness. Imani can isolate beginning sounds in spoken words, whereas Zyderrious cannot. Zyderrious also lacks any concepts about print except for basic bookhandling; he recalls few ideas from books read aloud to him; and he does not yet include sophisticated vocabulary from books in his meager retellings. In contrast, Imani knows bookhandling, has most directionality concepts in place, and is developing letter and word concepts. She has a strong recall of books and even incorporates a good deal of the sophisticated language from books in her retellings. The third child, Kambrisha, has very little conventional knowledge at the beginning of kindergarten although she is beginning to learn the alphabet. She was served in Head Start by the language specialist for language delays and still struggles to recall ideas from books read aloud.

These children are typical of entering kindergarten children in most locations. Some children, like Imani, have a great deal of conventional knowledge; some children, like Zyderrious, have knowledge in some areas but not in others; and other children, like Kambrisha, have very little conventional knowledge. Effective teachers will carefully observe children in classroom activities in order to acquire further information about their language and literacy development.

It is important to keep in mind that two of the children in Table 3.2 are at the end of the phase of novice reading and writing. Therefore, they have acquired many conventional concepts. If we had assessed them as three-year-olds when they began Head Start, we likely would have found them unable to do any of the conventional tasks we describe in this chapter. Instead, we likely would have seen them engaging in many pretend reading and writing activities, such as pretending to read environmental print and pretending to write telephone messages. These pretend behaviors, though unconventional, are just as much a part of literacy as being able to correctly identify alphabet letters. All children begin with unconventional notions about print, reading, and writing and gradually acquire the conventional understandings that are displayed in Table 3.2. That is why it is critical that teachers combine careful observation with preschool and kindergarten monitoring tasks.

Chapter Summary

NOVICE READERS AND WRITERS approach reading and writing in unconventional but systematic ways. They expect written language to be meaningful, and the meanings they associate with particular kinds of texts (such as environmental print, grocery lists, and stories) reflect their growing awareness of the language associated with these texts. Novice readers and writers find environmental print meaningful. The contextualized nature of this type of print initially supports children's meaning-making efforts, but novice readers respond to environmental print even when it is not in contexts that provide clues to its meaning. Novice readers make strides in understanding the decontextualized print in stories that are read aloud to them. They learn to construct "stories as wholes." They learn that stories are more than individual pictures, that stories are formed by a causally related series of events. They learn to make inferences and evaluations about characters and events.

Novice writers often intend to communicate a meaning in their writing, and the meaning they communicate reflects how they expect to use their written products (e.g., as a grocery list or a story). Novice readers and writers gradually begin to learn names for alphabet letters and to form conventional letters and signatures. Their concepts of letters and signatures differ from those of adults. Their learning to write many kinds of texts reflects knowledge of text features, and their talk about texts reveals an awareness of the content associated with different kinds of texts. In particular, novice readers and writers develop more complex understandings of the content, language, and organization of stories and information books.

Novices rely on stylized print and pictures to read the logos in environmental print, and they depend on the context of their writing and talk to assign meanings to their writing. They use reading and writing for a variety of purposes, including playing, interacting with others, and conducting the business of daily living in their families and communities. The kinds of reading and writing activities in which children participate may vary, and what children learn about written language functions may differ accordingly. English language learners also learn about the alphabet and concepts about print of their home language. They may also begin to acquire these concepts in English. Teachers can best capture all children's development, including that of ELLs, by combining observation and assessment tasks. Assessment tasks include screening and monitoring children's alphabet recognition, phonemic awareness, concepts about print, and oral listening vocabulary and comprehension.

Figure 3.11 provides a summary of the concepts presented in this chapter. It is important to keep in mind that a concept may appear in more than one section of the figure. For example, children's concept of story is an important part of their knowledge of written language forms. However, concept of story is also an important part of novice readers' and writers' knowledge about written language meanings. They use their concept of story as they construct meanings of the stories read aloud to them and as they compose the content of their own stories. Children's reading and writing ultimately reflect the interdependence of meaning, form, and function.

FIGURE 3.11   Summary: What Novice Readers and Writers Know about Written Language

Meaning Making

intend to communicate meaning in writing

assign meaning to environmental print

assign meaning to a variety of texts, pretend to read, by applying knowledge of the content and language used in those texts

apply concept of story in constructing the meaning of stories read aloud, retelling stories, and pretend reading of stories especially using sequence and causality

construct literal meaning

construct inferential meaning

use some literary language in retelling and pretend reading

Forms

recognize alphabet letters as a special set of graphic symbols

learn alphabet letter names and formations

learn letter features (and may write mock letters)

write own signature

use a variety of text features to construct different kinds of texts

Meaning-Form Links

use contextual dependency

differentiate pictures from print (but sometimes think pictures are read)

pay attention to print (and sometimes know that print is read)

go beyond contextual dependency by matching segments of the printed text with segments of the spoken text (sometimes matching lines to spoken sentences, segments of text to spoken words, or letters to syllables)

develop the beginnings of phonological awareness (by constructing rhyming words and identifying beginning phonemes)

Functions

use reading and writing in play

use reading and writing across time to regulate the behavior of self and others

use reading and writing as part of family and community activities (such as to complete daily-living routines)

USING THE INFORMATION

The following is a list of some behaviors of novice readers and writers. This listing is based on Figure 3.11, which summarizes what novice readers and writers are learning about written language. Find a figure or a vignette from this chapter that demonstrates each of these behaviors of novice readers and writers and tell why.

1. communicating meaning in writing (for example, Figure 3.1 demonstrates that Javaris intended to communicate "bread, lettuce, tomatoes, eggs, and cheese" in his scribble—be sure to find at least one more example)

2. finding meaning in (reading) environmental print (for example, Kristen recognized the Kmart sign and believed it was her special place—be sure to find at least one more example)

3. finding meaning in (pretending to read) a variety of texts such as grocery lists, telephone books, and familiar stories

4. finding literal meaning and inferential meaning

5. naming and forming alphabet letters

6. writing signatures

7. creating texts with distinctive features, such as writing grocery lists in a vertical list format and stories using horizontal lines of writing

8. demonstrating contextual dependency to convey meaning in writing by telling a teacher, friend, or parent the message

9. going beyond contextual dependency by trying to match up what is written with the spoken message, such as by reading one word for each line of text

10. demonstrating phonological awareness, such as by making up rhyming words

11. reading and writing in dramatic pretend play

APPLYING THE INFORMATION

The following vignette took place in the housekeeping area and the post office dramatic play center found in a Head Start classroom serving four-year-olds. Discuss what this event reveals about Nah'Kiyah's understandings about written language meanings, forms, functions, and meaning-form links. Use the concepts listed in Figure 3.11 to guide your discussion.

Nah'Kiyah was playing with three other children in the housekeeping center. They were planning a party that they wanted to have and discussing people to invite. The teacher casually dropped in at the center and suggested that the children might want to write invitations. She went to the writing center and returned with several envelopes for the children to use. The children found markers in a special basket that is used to keep different kinds of writing implements and notepads. They sat at the kitchen table and began writing. Nah'Kiyah said, "I'm going to invite my mother, and I know how to write her name. Teresa. Yes, and we live in Greenville, Alabama." She finished her envelope quickly and said, "Now I'm fixing to go on over to that post office and mail this off." She grabbed a purse and a baby doll and headed over to the other center where children were pretending to be postal workers, mail carriers, and customers. Nah'Kiyah stepped up to the counter and asked for a stamp. The worker took out a date stamp (that has no ink) and stamped the envelope. He threw it in a special crate used to keep mail and said, "It'll be delivered tomorrow." Nah'Kiyah left the post office, returned to the housekeeping area, and wrote five more envelopes and mailed each one before it was time for cleanup. Figure 3.12 presents the envelope Nah'Kiyah addressed to her mother.

FIGURE 3.12   Nah'Kiyah's Envelope: "Teresa Greenville, AL."

Going Beyond the Text

ARRANGE TO VISIT WITH A FAMILY that has a preschooler, or visit a preschool or kindergarten. Take a children's storybook and be prepared to tape-record your interaction as you share the story with the preschooler or kindergartner. Take some paper and markers or crayons and invite the child to draw and write about the story. Record what the child says while drawing and writing. Ask the child to write his or her name. Administer the alphabet recognition task, concepts about print task, phonemic awareness task, or retelling checklist. Describe the child's knowledge of written language meanings, forms, meaning-form links, and functions.

References

Baghban, M. (1984). *Our daughter learns to read and write.* Newark, DE: International Reading Association.

Ballenger, C. (1999). *Teaching other people's children: Literacy and learning in a bilingual classroom.* New York: Teachers College Press.

Barone, D., Mallette, M., & Xu, S. (2005). *Teaching early literacy: Development, assessment, and instruction.* New York: Guilford Press.

Bear, D., Invernizzi, M., Templeton, S., & Johnston, F. (2008). *Words their way: Word study for phonics, vocabulary, and spelling instruction* (4th ed.). Boston: Allyn & Bacon.

Bloodgood, J. (1999). What's in a name? Children's name writing and name acquisition. *Reading Research Quarterly, 34,* 342–367.

Clay, M. M. (1975). *What did I write?* Auckland, New Zealand: Heinemann Educational Books.

Clay, M. M. (2005). *An observation survey of early literacy achievement.* Auckland, New Zealand: Heinemann Educational Books.

Cummins, J. (1989). *Empowering minority students.* Sacramento: California Association for Bilingual Education.

Cummins, J. (2000). *Language, power, and pedagogy: Bilingual children in the crossfire.* Clevedon, England/Buffalo, NY: Multilingual Matters.

Dickinson, D. (2001). Book reading in preschool classrooms: Is recommended practice common? In D. Dickinson & P. Tabors (Eds.), *Beginning literacy with language: Young children learning at home and school* (pp. 149–174). Baltimore, MD: Brookes Publishing.

Duke, N. (2004). The case for information text. *Education Leadership, 61*(6), 40.

Duke, N. K. (2007). Let's look in a book: Using nonfiction reference materials with young children. *Young Children, 62*(3), 12–16.

Duke, N. K., & Hays, J. (1998). "Can I say 'Once upon a time'?": Kindergarten children developing knowledge of informational book language. *Early Childhood Research Quarterly, 13,* 295–318.

Duncan, P. (1996). *Some smug slug.* New York: HarperTrophy.

Dyson, A. H. (1982). The emergence of visible language: Interrelationships between drawing and early writing. *Visible Language, 16,* 360–381.

Dyson, A. H. (2003). *The brothers and sisters learn to write: Popular literacies in childhood and school cultures.* New York: Teachers College Press.

Ferreiro, E. (1986). The interplay between information and assimilation in beginning literacy. In W. H. Teale & E. Sulzby (Eds.), *Emergent literacy: Writing and reading* (pp. 15–49). Norwood, NJ: Ablex Publishing.

Ferreiro, E., & Teberosky, A. (1982). *Literacy before schooling.* Exeter, NH: Heinemann.

Gee, J. (2001). A sociocultural perspective on early literacy development. In S. Neuman &

D. Dickinson (Eds.), *Handbook of early literacy research* (pp. 30–42). New York: Guilford Press.

Goodman, Y. (1980). The roots of literacy. In M. Douglass (Ed.), *Claremont reading conference, 44th yearbook* (pp. 1–32). Claremont, CA: Claremont Graduate School.

Harste, J. C., Woodward, V. A., & Burke, C. L. (1984). *Language stories and literacy lessons.* Portsmouth, NH: Heinemann.

Hiebert, E. H. (1978). Preschool children's understanding of written language. *Child Development, 49,* 1231–1234.

Hildreth, G. (1936). Developmental sequences in name writing. *Child Development, 7,* 291–302.

Hindman, A. H., Connor, C. M., Jewkes, A. M., & Morrison, F. J. (2008). Untangling the effects of shared book reading: Multiple factors and their associations with preschool literacy outcomes. *Early Childhood Research Quarterly, 23*(3), 330–350.

International Reading Association & National Association for the Education of Young Children (IRA/NAEYC). (1998). Learning to read and write: Developmentally appropriate practices for young children. *The Reading Teacher, 53,* 193–216.

Labbo, L. (1996). A semiotic analysis of young children's symbol making in a classroom computer center. *Reading Research Quarterly, 31,* 353–385.

Leung, C. B. (2008). Preschoolers' acquisition of scientific vocabulary through repeated read-aloud events, retellings, and hands-on science activities. *Reading Psychology, 29*(2), 165–193.

Mayer, M. (1968). *There's a nightmare in my closet.* New York: Dial Press.

McGee, L., & Richgels, D. (1989). "K is Kristen's": Learning the alphabet from a child's perspective. *The Reading Teacher, 43,* 216–225.

McGee, L. M., & Schickedanz, J. A. (2007). Repeated interactive read-alouds in preschool and kindergarten. *The Reading Teacher, 60*(8), 742–751.

McNamee, G. D. (2005). "The one who gathers children": The work of Vivian Gussin Paley and current debates about how we educate young children. *Journal of Early Childhood Teacher Education, 25*(3), 275–296.

Pappas, C. (1993). Is narrative "primary"? Some insights from kindergartners' pretend readings of stories and information books. *Journal of Reading Behavior, 25,* 97–129.

Pappas, C. C. (1991). Fostering full access to literacy by including informational books. *Language Arts, 68,* 449–462.

Pappas, C. C. (2006). The information book genre: Its role in integrated science literacy research and practice. *Reading Research Quarterly, 41,* 226–250.

Piasta, S. B., & Wagner, R. K. (2010). Developing early literacy skills: A meta-analysis of alphabet learning and instruction. *Reading Research Quarterly, 45*(1), 8–38.

Prelutsky, J., & Wolcott, D. (2001). *Dog days: Rhymes around the year.* New York: Dragonfly Books.

Purcell-Gates, V. (1996). Stories, coupons, and the "TV Guide": Relationships between home literacy experiences and emergent literacy knowledge. *Reading Research Quarterly, 31,* 406–428.

Reid, M. (1996). *Let's find out about ice cream.* New York: Scholastic.

Roberts, T., & Neal H. (2004). Relationships among preschool English language learner's oral proficiency in English, instructional experience and literacy development. *Contemporary Educational Psychology, 29,* 283–311.

Roskos, K. A., Christie, J. F., Widman, S., & Holding, A. (2010). Three decades in: Priming for meta-analysis in play-literacy research. *Journal of Early Childhood Literacy, 10*(1), 55–96.

Schickedanz, J. (1999). *Much more than the ABCs: The early stages of reading and writing.* Washington, DC: National Association for the Education of Young Children.

Smith, S., & Dixon, R. (1995). Literacy concepts of low- and middle-class four-year-olds entering preschool. *Journal of Educational Research, 88,* 243–253.

Smolkin, L., & Donovan, C. (2002). "Oh excellent, excellent question!": Developmental differences and comprehension acquisition. In C. Block & M. Pressley (Eds.), *Comprehension instruction: Research-based best practices* (pp. 140–157). New York: Guilford Press.

Strauss, S. L. (2005). *The linguistics, neurology, and politics of phonics: Silent "E" speaks out.* Mahwah, NJ: Lawrence Erlbaum Associates.

Taylor, D., & Dorsey-Gaines, C. (1988). *Growing up literate: Learning from inner-city families.* Portsmouth, NH: Heinemann.

Tower, C. (2002). "It's a snake, you guys!": The power of text characteristics on children's responses to informational books. *Research in the Teaching of English, 37,* 55–88.

Turbill, J., & Murray, J. (2006). Early literacy and new technologies in Australian schools: Policy, research, and practice. In M. C. McKenna, L. D. Labbo, R. D. Kieffer, & D. Reinking (Eds.), *International handbook of literacy and technology, Vol. II* (pp. 93–108). Mahwah, NJ: Lawrence Erlbaum Associates.

U.S. Congress. (2001). *No child left behind act of 2001. Public Law 107-110. 107th Congress.* Washington, DC: U.S. Government Printing Office.

Yolen, J., & Schoenherr, J. (1987). *Owl moon.* New York: Philomel Books.

PEARSON myeducationlab

Go to the topics Phonemic Awareness and Phonics, Writing Development, English Language Learners, and Assessment in the MyEducationLab (www.myeducationlab.com) for your course, where you can:

- Find learning outcomes for Phonemic Awareness and Phonics, Writing Development, English Language Learners, and Assessment along with the national standards that connect to these outcomes.
- Complete Assignments and Activities that can help you more deeply understand the chapter content.
- Examine challenging situations and cases presented in the IRIS Center Resources.

A+RISE

Go to the Topic A+RISE in the MyEducationLab (www.myeducationlab.com) for your course. A+RISE® Standards2Strategy™ is an innovative and interactive online resource that offers new teachers in grades K–12 just-in-time, research-based instructional strategies that:

- Meet the linguistic needs of ELLs as they learn content
- Differentiate instruction for all grades and abilities
- Offer reading and writing techniques, cooperative learning, use of linguistic and nonlinguistic representations, scaffolding, teacher modeling, higher order thinking, and alternative classroom ELL assessment
- Provide support to help teachers be effective through the integration of listening, speaking, reading, and writing along with the content curriculum
- Improve student achievement
- Are aligned to Common Core Elementary Language Arts standards (for the literacy strategies) and to English language proficiency standards in WIDA, Texas, California, and Florida.

CHAPTER 4

From Five to Seven Years

Experimenting Readers and Writers

KEY CONCEPTS

Experimenters
Phonemes
Alphabetic Principle
Phonics
Invented Spelling
Situated Literacy
   Perspective
School Literacy
   Perspective

Metalinguistic
   Awareness
Concept of Written Word
Concept of Word
   Boundaries
Mock Cursive
Sounding Literate
Being Precise
Finger-Point Reading

Phonemic
   Awareness
Onset
Rime
Phonogram
Phoneme
   Repertoire
Multiple Literacies
Message Concept

Who are Experimenters?

EXPERIMENTERS ARE CHILDREN MAKING THE TRANSITION from what we described as novice reading and writing to conventional reading and writing. They are at a unique place in their literacy development when they will make, on their own and through the careful instruction of teachers, many critical discoveries about print, written language, letters, words, stories, phonemes, and the functions of reading and writing. We call this unique phase of literacy development experimenting reading and writing. We call it this because children are experimenting with what they know about print as they try to make sense of it. Throughout this chapter, we will demonstrate how children experiment with many components of literacy.

Many children's home and community experiences of literacy propel them into experimenting reading and writing. These children are usually in homes in which mothers and fathers own books, read to their children frequently, and invite them to write and participate in events that include reading (such as reading favorite children's books) and writing (such as writing postcards, thank-you notes, and grocery lists). Through these activities, children actually receive as many as 1,000 hours of personalized guidance in reading and writing.

Other children begin to gain insights about the conventions of reading and writing because their preschool and kindergarten teachers surround them with reading and writing that is meaningful to them. Most children enter and move through the period we call experimenting reading and writing through a combination of their experiences in homes and communities and in classrooms. Teachers can expect many preschoolers and most kindergartners to begin the experimenting phase of reading and writing. Many first graders begin the year with this kind of awareness.

All children who eventually will become conventional readers and writers must first navigate this critical experimenting period of literacy development. They must move from the pretend reading and writing of novices to realizing that print is read in a particular way. Most children require time to acquire this understanding. For example, just one aspect of their accomplishment is working out how letters in written words relate to sounds in spoken words (Ehri & Roberts, 2006). Children approach even this aspect of reading and writing in different and unconventional ways.

The New Understandings and Awareness of Experimenting Readers and Writers

Four new understandings and behaviors mark experimenting readers and writers:

- thoughtful attitude toward and awareness of print
- discovery of words
- discovery of a relation between sounds and letters
- ability to focus on only one or a few aspects of conventional reading and writing at a time

Whereas novices are aware of print, look at it, and attempt to write it and read it, experimenters demonstrate an awareness that print works in a special way. Unlike novice readers and writers, who are sure they can read and write and do so in their pretend play, experimenters often are convinced they cannot. One of the first indications that children have entered this new print-focused phase of awareness is their suddenly refusing to read and write when before, as novice readers and writers, they had been eager to join in these activities. Now, however, children are aware that pretending to read and write is not "really" reading and writing as adults or older children do. It takes a sensitive adult to help children get past their feelings of *I can't* in order to use what they do know. For example, children can be helped to read environmental print and copy words from this print as a way to demonstrate to them they can read and can write. Throughout this chapter (and in Chapter 8), we describe other ways to overcome children's reluctance to read and write that is to be expected in this phase.

Another shift that occurs during experimenting reading and writing is that children now attend to words. Because children come to the phase of experimenting already knowing most letters (having learned them as novices), they begin to discover a new form of written language: a word. They realize that readers read words, that writers write words, and that words are composed of letters. Gradually, they come to accept that words are separated by spaces.

A third shift is when experimenting readers and writers notice that **phonemes** in spoken words are related, albeit not always in a straightforward manner, to letters in written words. Recall that in Chapter 3 we used the term **alphabetic principle** to reference this imperfect but helpful relation. Experimenters eventually discover that the English written language system is an alphabetic writing system. One of three systems for linking written forms with meanings that children learn in order to read and write English is **phonics,** the linking of letters and combinations of letters with sounds and combinations of sounds. (We will describe the other two systems in Chapter 5.)

Examples of Experimenters

Here are two examples of experimenters:

> Three-year-old Sophie listens to her uncle read a storybook. She directs his reading, "Read that. . . . Read that." She always points first to the left-hand page and then to the right-hand page. When they finish the book, Sophie begins pointing to individual words on a page and again says, "Read that. . . . Read that," this time for each word she points to. This pointing proceeds right to left, word by word, until Sophie's uncle has identified every word in a line.

> Five-year-old Bashir uses magnetic letters to label a picture of a bench in a picture book. He says, "B-ench" and chooses a *B* from an array of magnetic letters. He places the *B* on a magnetized strip below the picture. He then says, "B-ench-en-en" and places an *N* on the strip. Then he says, "B-en—sh—that might be an *H*" and chooses an *H*. His spelling of *bench* is *BNH.*

Sophie knows left-to-right directionality for pages. More important, although she does not know left-to-right directionality for word reading, her careful pointing to words shows that she is able to identify word boundaries. She has a concept of written word. She explores the power of written words, the combinations of letters bordered by spaces, to evoke particular spoken words from a reader. Compared with novices, who may point to whole lines of text as representations of anything from a sentence to a word, Sophie has a much more precise understanding of word-by-word, speech-to-print matching.

Bashir's writing shows that he knows something about letter names and sounds in words. Compared with novices, who do not know about phonics, Bashir has a very mature understanding of how writing works. Although his spelling is not conventional, he systematically pairs letters with sounds: Both /b/ and the name of the letter *B* ("bee") start with the phoneme /b/; /en/ is the name of the letter *N*; and /sh/ is close to the sound at the end of the name of the letter *H* ("aitch"). Bashir's invented spellings show his working out aspects of the alphabetic principle. **Invented spelling** is children's systematic but not conventional matching of sounds in words with letters.

Experimenters often focus on what might be called the mechanics of reading and writing, for example, on the important relation between sounds in speech and letters in print. It is important, however, that parents and teachers who guide experimenters avoid the misconception that literacy learning is only about the mechanics of spelling, sound-letter relationships, or concepts about print. One of the most important contributions of teachers is to plan many events in which reading and writing are used for purposes that make sense to children. We view learning to read and write more from a situated literacy perspective than from a school literacy perspective. From the **situated literacy perspective,** reading and writing are activities taking place in the real world for the purpose of achieving real-life goals. Reading and writing become meaningful in the lives of young children when they serve children's need to explore the real world and their desire to connect with the power of play. In contrast, from the **school literacy perspective,** "reading and writing are viewed as a compilation of skills that can be taught 'for school'" (Powell & Davidson, 2005, p. 249). Reading and writing are considered ends in themselves, skills to be learned, rather than tools for genuine communication.

EXPERIMENTING WITH MEANING

THE MEANING MAKING OF EXPERIMENTERS is only slightly more complex than that of novices. Novices and experimenters share a basic understanding of the power and meaning found in written language. Both write in order to communicate a message, and both engage in interactive storybook reading using sophisticated strategies for constructing meaning. Experimenters continue to use the meaning-making strategies they devised as novices (see Chapter 3).

For example, experimenters are likely to have a fully developed concept of story or story schema (see Chapter 2). They are more likely to attend to problems in stories. Later in this chapter, we will describe experimenters' new attention to the literary properties of informational texts. They have learned that written stories and informational books have certain language forms and word orders not found in spoken language. Experimenters are likely to use literary language when composing and recalling stories, for example, "Away we went to grandmother's house."

Experimenting with Forms

EXPERIMENTERS HAVE CONSIDERABLE KNOWLEDGE about letters; they can recognize most letters, write most letters with conventional formations, and recite the alphabet. Experimenters also have **metalinguistic awareness** of letters; that is, they can talk and think about the names and properties of letters. Sarah, a kindergartner, wanted to write the *M* in *snowman*. Her classmate Jason told her, "M." She asked, "Is that the up-down, up-down one?" Experimenters also show their concept of word in their reading and writing. They create a variety of texts using a variety of writing strategies.

Concept of Word and Word Boundaries

A fully developed **concept of written word** includes knowledge that words are composed of combinations of letters, that words are bounded by the spaces between them, and that the sounds within them are related to alphabet letters (Mesmer & Lake, 2010; Roberts, 1996). Experimenters acquire bits and pieces of this concept as they move forward in learning to read and write.

One way children show their interest in words is by attempting to write words. Figure 4.1 shows some writing that Kathy produced one day as she sat by herself in her room. When her mother asked her to read her writing, she replied, "It's just words." Notice that Kathy's writing is much like a novice's—we could not know the meaning

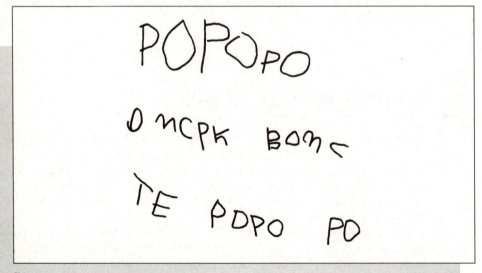

FIGURE 4.1   Kathy's Invented Words

Kathy intended to communicate unless we listened to Kathy read her writing (and, in this case, Kathy did not seem to intend to communicate a message).

However, three aspects of Kathy's attempts to write words are typical of experimenters. First, she is experimenting with letter combinations to produce writing that she calls words. Second, she is experimenting with using spaces between letter combinations to signal boundaries between her words. Third, Kathy seems to be paying attention to only one aspect of written language—words and how they look—and ignoring other aspects of written language, such as meaning.

As children become aware that words in spoken and written language can be segmented, they develop a **concept of word boundaries.** In conventional writing, we use spaces to show boundaries between individually printed words. Experimenters begin to respond to individual words in environmental print and in books, and they experiment with ways to show the boundaries between words in their own writing. Children show their awareness of word boundaries in many ways. Paul used dots between words, for example: *PAULZ • HOS • PLANF • ELD • VRMAT* (Paul's house, Plainfield, Vermont) (Bissex, 1980, p. 22). Other children circle words, put them in vertical arrangements, or even separate them with carefully drawn and blackened squares (Harste, Burke, & Woodward, 1983; Temple, Nathan, Temple, & Burris, 1993).

Figure 4.2 presents a list Erin composed while playing in her kindergarten housekeeping center. She wrote her name and other words she knows how to spell: *cat, MOM, DAD,* and *ADAM* (her brother's name). She emphasized her words by circling all but her brother's name.

FIGURE 4.2   Erin's Dramatic Play Writing with Circles around Words

Texts

In Chapter 3, we showed that novices are aware of several text formats when they play with writing in different contexts for various purposes. Chapter 3 included examples of novices' lists and stories. Experimenters continue to be interested in a variety of text forms, but they use more strategies to produce sophisticated texts.

The texts that experimenters create usually look more conventional than those produced by novices. Experimenters generate a greater variety of texts as well. There are several reasons for the differences between these two types of writers. Experimenters are more likely to ask for an adult's assistance in constructing their messages because they are aware that they cannot yet produce a readable message on their own.

Eventually, most experimenters can be encouraged to try writing a story or other type of text, especially if they know that teachers will be satisfied even with their unconventional attempts. Two composing strategies of experimenters are making **mock cursive** and writing letter strings. They tell a story as they write or when they are invited to tell about their writing. Mock cursive is wavy lines that look like cursive writing. Letter strings are lines of letters that do not seem to include words and certainly are not attempts to invent spellings. Figure 4.3 presents a story Marianne wrote about seeing a zebra at the zoo. Marianne attended a preschool for low-income four-year-olds in which the teacher modeled writing for children daily on large charts. Figure 4.3 also includes the story Marianne told when she was invited to tell about her writing. Though we would expect novices also to write using mock cursive or letter strings, the story that Marianne told is the product of an experimenter. With its consistent use of past tense, its literary language (*Once upon a time* and *the end*), and its coherent characters, events, and dialogue, it is more sophisticated than we might expect of novices.

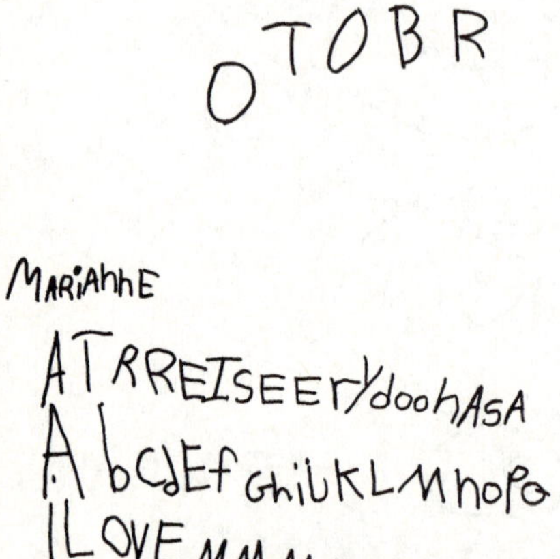

Once upon a time I went to the zoo and saw a zebra. Then I yelled, "Yeah," because I never saw a zebra before. He licked me on the hand. Then I said, "Mom and Dad, look. Sister, look." Then we went home. The end.

FIGURE 4.3   Marianne's Story

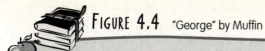

FIGURE 4.4   "George" by Muffin

This is a story about George. She is a girl. She got a father, but her mom died. She still miss her. She saw one snowflake and soon it would be Christmas. Her father and her went and got a Christmas tree. Then they decorated the tree. They went to bed, and Santa Claus came that night. When she woke up, she saw a lot of stuff. She asked her daddy if she could go out and play and he said, "Yes." When she got outside she made a beautify heart snowman for her mama. The End.

Figure 4.4 shows another way that experimenters compose, by dictation. Dictation is a child's slowly speaking a message or telling a story as a teacher or other adult writes it, usually for later reading by the adult and child. The text in Figure 4.4 is a story that Muffin, a four-year-old, told her day care teacher. The language of the story reflects her home dialect. The elements that mark this as the work of an experimenter are the same as in Marianne's story: its unity (it is about events in a special day of a main character, George), its consistent use of past tense (for those events beginning with *She saw*), and its use of the literary closing *The End*.

Children sometimes dictate literary texts other than stories. Jeffrey dictated a poem to his mother as he ran back and forth across his patio.

The Running Poem
Bubble gun boppers,
Candy heart sneakers,
Sparky love.
Buster slimers,
Booger man,
Barbecue pit.
Blue ribbons win.
The end.

Whereas the content of Jeffrey's poem relates to what he was doing (running) and seeing (his sneakers, the barbecue pit, and the family dog, Sparky), it also shows Jeffrey's understandings of the conventions of poetry forms. His poem consisted of phrases rather than sentences, and he used alliteration—five lines of his poem start with words beginning with the sound /b/. Alliteration is the use of the same sound at the beginning of two or more words. It is interesting that Jeffrey ended his poem with "The end," which is the formulaic ending for a story rather than a poem. Still, his poem demonstrates Jeffrey's experimentation with language forms associated with poetry.

The third way experimenters compose is by copying, especially copying of familiar texts such as informational texts on topics that especially interest them. Richgels (2003) documented kindergartners' painstaking but enthusiastic copying from books about dinosaurs and books about chick development and hatching. Experimenters' careful, time-consuming copying demonstrates their willingness to concentrate on literacy tasks and devote considerable energy to their constructions.

The fourth way experimenters compose is by writing words with invented spellings. Invented spelling is the process of listening carefully to the sounds (phonemes) in words and selecting and sequencing letters to spell those sounds, as Bashir did when he wrote *BNH* for *bench*. Invented spelling is not misspelling. It is not that experimenting writers have learned but choose to disregard conventional spellings. Rather, by systematically using sound-letter correspondences, they are creating genuine, though nonconventional, spellings. Often, they cannot read their invented spellings a short time after writing them. With more experience of text and with instruction, their spellings become more conventional. Composing with nearly complete and more conventional spellings and being able later to read those spellings is a sign that children are leaving experimenting reading and writing behind and entering the phase of conventional reading and writing.

It is important to keep in mind that experimenters use some of the same conventions as more conventional readers and writers. We tend to think of children at this stage as not yet being very knowledgeable about written language. Even when we are accepting and supportive, what usually catches our attention in children's experimental products is their mistakes. However, there is much that is correct in their products, even by conventional standards. Bashir's spelling of *bench*, for example, looks wrong: *BNH*. However, he used two conventional sound-letter correspondences (/b/–*B* and /n/–*N*), and he arranged the letters in conventional left-to-right order.

EXPERIMENTING WITH MEANING–FORM LINKS

ISCOVERING THE ESSENTIALS of how meanings and forms are linked in an alphabetic writing system is the main work of experimenters. It is the achievement that most clearly sets them apart from novices and puts them on the path to conventional reading and writing. In Chapter 3, we saw that novices' ways of linking form and meaning often are limited by their dependence on context, and that novices lack understanding of sound-letter relations. Experimenters' attention to print is much more purposeful than is that of novices. Not only do they know that print is important, but they begin to discover how it works—that sound-letter correspondences are at the core of the relation between print and meaning.

In their writing, experimenters develop two important kinds of awareness: awareness that their written messages are permanent and stable (they and others can return to them to retrieve their meanings) and awareness of phonemes, the units of sound from which words are built and to which letters are matched. They move from writing by dictating stories, using booklike language, to writing with invented spelling.

Experimenters' writing and reading discoveries interact. For example, phonemic awareness practiced and enhanced during invented spelling is put to use in reading.

Sounding Literate

A new accomplishment of experimenters is to sound literate when they pretend to read and write. **Sounding literate** means that as children look at books and retell a book's story to themselves or friends, they know to use literary language like *once upon a time* or *the end*. They use sophisticated words and word order such as *up the hill they went, leading the lovely princess*. They even use intonation that sounds like reading a text rather than conversation. Experimenters sound literate especially when pretending to read a favorite storybook they have heard read aloud many times (Sulzby, 1985; Cox, Fang, & Otto, 1997).

In contrast, novices' pretend readings of books are very simple: They label parts of illustrations or tell a story to match the illustrations. When experimenters pretend to read a favorite storybook, the words they use often quite closely resemble the actual words of the book. Eventually, experimenters can retell a favorite book word for word.

Developmental Changes in Pretend Reading. Research has documented that children go through various phases in pretend reading that show they are getting closer and closer to conventional reading (Sulzby, 1985). Table 4.1 presents three major phases of pretend storybook reading. Actually, the first phase is what novices do; they label pictures or tell stories. Their pretend readings do not sound literate and therefore are

TABLE 4.1 Types of Storybook Reading

Influenced by Illustrations

- Oral-language-like (beginners and novices)
  - Collections of labels and comments (e.g., "House. Flowers. He's the baby.")
  - Everyday storytelling (e.g., "There was three bears and . . . and . . . and . . .")
- Written-language-like (but not paying attention to the print)
  - Reading in a manner similar to the original story text (experimenters) (see Figure 4.5)
  - Verbatim recreation of the text (experimenters)

Influenced by Text

- All are written-language-like and come from paying attention to the print.
- Attempts at reading the text using finger-point reading, attempting to sound out words, or reading known sight words
- Conventional reading

Source: Adapted from Sulzby (1985).

called oral-language-like because they sound more like conversation about a story than reading of a text.

The second phase of pretend reading is written-language-like; children in this phase sound literate. At first, experimenters tell a story similar to what is in the book using more of their spoken language; then they begin to include words from the actual text; and finally they tell the text word for word. The third phase of pretend reading is beyond experimenters. It is more sophisticated because children are really attempting to read conventionally.

Figure 4.5 presents Hamza's pretend reading of *Caps for Sale: A Tale of a Peddler, Some Monkeys and Their Monkey Business* (Slobodkina, 1940). In this story, a peddler places the caps he has to sell, one on top of the other, on his head. One day, he fails to sell any caps and takes a nap under a tree. When he awakens, he finds that some monkeys have taken the hats and climbed up high in a tree where the peddler cannot reach them. Hamza's pretend reading is of the first page where the peddler tries to make the monkeys bring the hats back. He retells much of the information about the story and uses some but not all of the words in the text. Instead of putting some of the text into words, he uses actions (shaking his finger), turning the decontextualized language of the story into the contextualized use of gestures.

Sounding Literate in Writing. We have seen that experimenters write by making letter strings or mock cursive and telling about them during and after composing, by dictating, by copying, and by inventing spellings. The tellings, which accompany their composing and their reading what they have already composed, sound literate just as their readings of others' texts do. They use reading intonation, literary language, and characters' dialogue. Recall Marianne's story about the zoo presented in Figure 4.3 and Muffin's dictated story about Christmas day in Figure 4.4. They included the narrative closing *The End* and such dialogue markers as *I said* and *he said*.

FIGURE 4.5 Hamza's Pretend Reading of *Caps for Sale: A Tale of a Peddler, Some Monkeys and Their Monkey Business* (Slobodkina, 1940)

Text*	Hamza's Pretend Reading
"You monkeys, you," He said, Shaking a finger at them,	"You monkeys" (he shakes his finger at the monkeys in the illustration)
"you give me back my caps."	"Give me my hats."

* From the page in which the peddler shakes his finger at the monkeys because they have taken his caps and run up a tree.

Being Precise

Another new characteristic of experimenters is their awareness of the need to be precise when reading and writing. **Being precise** is reading a text the same way across multiple readings because of using the exact words of the author. Further, these words are spoken at just the right times (when looking at the correct page of a storybook, for example). Being precise goes even further when children begin to track print in books and say words as they point carefully but not always correctly at certain words.

Novices notice print, but experimenters are more aware that print consists of words that are actually read. Experimenters do not read many words, but they use what skills they have, which is to remember texts of favorite stories and attempt to point to words in the text. Teachers will notice that experimenters put their fingers on the text of books as they pretend to read. At first, experimenters merely sweep their hands across lines of text without trying to match up what they are saying with the actual words. Eventually, they deliberately point to each word and try to say just a word. They make many miscalculations in their attempts—for example, saying a syllable while pointing to a whole word or saying a phrase while pointing to a single word. Finally, experimenters learn to slow down, point word by word, and say word-by-word favorite memorized texts (Morris, Bloodgood, Lomax, & Perney, 2003).

When experimenters put their fingers on parts of text as they pretend to read, they are **finger-point reading** (Mesmer & Lake, 2010; Morris, 1993). This is not conventional reading, but it is critical for eventually learning to read conventionally. With finger-point reading, children experiment with where words begin and end in print. For example, a child may point one by one, from left to right to the three written words of the text *Little Miss Muffet* while saying three syllables, "Lit-tle Miss" and perhaps stop there or perhaps continue with "Muf-fet" while pointing to the first two words of the next line of text. Finger-point reading is developmental. Eventually, the child will correctly match saying the three words of the first line of the nursery rhyme with pointing to the three written words and saying the four words of the second line with pointing to the four written words.

Children may also demonstrate being precise in writing. They reveal this by the way they attempt to reread their own writing. Figure 4.6 presents a Father's Day card that four-year-old Brooke composed. On the front of her card, she drew a bird and some flowers. On the inside, she wrote nine letters: *R, A, Y, g, P, G, O, G,* and *I*. Afterward, she

FIGURE 4.6 Brooke's Father's Day Card

read her writing to her mother, pointing to the first five letters one at a time: "I/ love/ you/ dad/ dy." Then she paused for a few moments and pointed at the remaining four letters one at a time, reading, "ver/ y/ much/ too." Brooke is being precise by carefully matching each letter of her writing with a segment of her spoken message (in this case, a syllable).

Using Sound-Letter Relationships

Experimenters can link meaning with written form through the use of sound-letter relationships in their spellings and pretend readings. For example, a child whose teacher frequently reads a book of nursery rhymes may notice that both *Jack* and *Jill* start with the letter *J* and that both words and the letter's name ("jay") start with /j/ (see Table 1.2 for phoneme symbols). When the child comments about this and the parent acknowledges and confirms this, the child is gaining phonics knowledge.

A System Based on Phonemic Awareness

In order to spell, writers need a system: they need a rather precise, analytic understanding of the relationship between spoken and written language; they need the ability to examine words one sound unit at a time; and they need an awareness of some kind of relationship between spoken sounds and letters. What this means is that young writers must first be able to segment their spoken message into its component parts—words. Then spellers must further segment words into smaller parts—eventually, into phonemes.

Early inventive spellers do not usually separately pronounce every phoneme in a word, one at a time; this is a later-developing ability. Instead, they may pronounce only the first part, that is, the first phoneme. Then spellers must decide which letter to use to represent that phoneme. This is a long and complicated process that involves a great deal of conscious attention.

The process of attending to phonemes is part of the phonological awareness we described in Chapter 3. Phonological awareness includes attention to all aspects of the sounds of a language. Attention to phonemes, **phonemic awareness,** is most developed when a person can segment a word into each and every one of its phonemes, for example, segmenting the word *tan* into /t/, /a/, and /n/. This most developed kind of phonemic awareness only gradually emerges and signals that children have moved to a higher level of reading and writing than experimenting.

Invented spelling is phonemic awareness in action (Richgels, 2001). Kristen Marie's first spellings provide a case in point. She announced that she could spell and looked around the room for things to spell. She said, "I can spell phone," and repeated the word to herself, saying it slowly, stretching out the initial /f/, "Ffffone, phone. I know—it's spelled V." Then she looked around again and said, "I can spell window, too." Again, she slowly repeated the word, stretching out the initial /w/, "Wwwwindow. Window is Y."

Kristen Marie's spellings are not conventional, but they have the characteristics of true spelling; they are systematic, and they demonstrate phonemic awareness. Using only one letter to spell each word is consistent with not pronouncing each phoneme of a word one at a time. She pronounced a whole word and paid attention to the first phoneme in that word. She was not doing the complete phoneme-by-phoneme analysis that demonstrates the most developed form of phonemic awareness, but her attention to each word was at the level of the phoneme.

Ways of Relating Sounds and Letters

While attending to the phonemes at the beginnings of *phone* and *window,* Kristen Marie used two clues for choosing an appropriate letter for spelling: manner of articulation and identity of sound. *Manner of articulation* is the placement of the mouth, tongue, and teeth when speaking. Kristen Marie noticed that her upper teeth were touching her lower lip both when she started to say the word *phone* and when she started to say the name of the letter *V.*

With *window* and *Y,* there is another possible explanation of Kristen Marie's spelling. She may have used identity of sound. Both *window* and the name of the letter *Y* start with /w/ (the letter name *Y* is made up of two phonemes /w/ and /I/). Inventive spellers associate phonemes in letter names with phonemes in the spoken words they wish to spell.

Figure 4.7 shows the story writing of two classmates on March 23 of their kindergarten year. They wrote in story folders, which are manila file folders that open to show a picture and beneath it the words *Once upon a time* and a space for writing a story to go with the picture. The story folders are laminated, and kindergartners write with erasable marker pens. The teacher makes photocopies of students' stories for them to

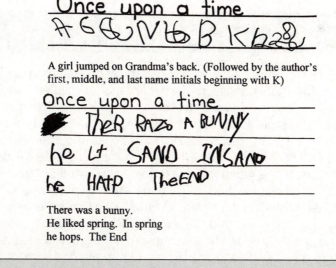

A girl jumped on Grandma's back. (Followed by the author's first, middle, and last name initials beginning with K)

There was a bunny.
He liked spring. In spring
he hops. The End

FIGURE 4.7 Story Folder Writing by Two Kindergartners

keep and then wipes the folders clean so they can be reused by other kindergarten authors. The first story was written to accompany a picture of a girl hugging a woman and the second story to accompany a picture of a rabbit. Both stories are within the range of writing products we would expect of kindergartners two-thirds of the way through the school year. Both authors used invented spelling. However, there are noticeable differences in the spelling strategies that these kindergartners employed.

The first story (*A G G N G B* for *A girl jumped on Grandma's back*) is composed of one letter per word. The author's spelling choices are systematic. She uses the letter-name strategy for the first word, pronounced "aye" like the name of the letter she chooses. Many of her choices are governed by identity of the target sound and a sound in the name of a letter: a letter *G* for the word *jumped* (the name of the letter *G* and the word *jump* both start with /j/), an *N* for the word *in*, and a *B* for the word *back*. She uses *G* for /g/ in the words *girl* and *Grandma*, although that sound is not in that letter's name; she knows the conventional /g/-*G* sound-letter correspondence.

The second story (TheR RAZS A BUNNy / he Lt SAND INSAND / he HAtP TheEND for *There was a bunny. He liked spring. In spring he hops. The end*) has discernible spaces between words, except between the two words for *in spring* and the two words for *The end*. The author uses at least two letters per word. He knows that some words require even more letters; the familiar word *and* seems to be a filler for word parts that he cannot spell. The spelling for *bunny* was given to him. He routinely uses knowledge of sound-letter correspondences for many other spellings, notably the endings of *there* (TheR), *was* (RAZS), *liked* (Lt), and *hop* (HAtP) (though his spelling omits the final sound of the word as he reads it, "hops"). He uses correct vowel letters for words that are familiar to him: *he, the,* and *end*.

TECHNOLOGY TIE-IN

Visit www.Meddybemps.com. This is Chateau Meddybemps, a site for children's interactive play. There are dozens of sites like this for children and their parents (or for school use). However, this site has some of the nicest graphics of all the sites we have visited. In addition, its creators include an expert in Early Childhood Education. It has many different learning activities including stories about camouflage with games to play and pictures to color. But best of all, it has several different locations to learn about letters. Locate the Alphabet Soup Café in the Fun and Games section. Here you can learn about different fonts of letters, and there is a spider who writes letters while you watch (demonstrating the strokes in order). Don't miss the Young Writer's Workshop section under the Fun and Games folder. There are some lovely graphics and text for story starters. Plus, there are examples of writing from four-, five-, and six-year-olds that you can view. Spend lots of time at this site and think of all the learning opportunities this holds for children. We liked the wonderful on-site photographs of flowers and animals.

Stages of Spelling Development

We can conclude from the spellings in Figure 4.7 that although neither of these kindergarten authors is a conventional speller, both spell systematically. They know what spelling is supposed to accomplish, that it is an alphabetic code that matches sounds with letters with the goal of enabling readers to retrieve writers' words. A second conclusion is that invented spelling seems to progress through stages, with the end point being conventional spelling.

Research supports these hypotheses, documenting stages of spelling development, from invented to conventional (Templeton & Morris, 2000; Templeton, 2003). Table 4.2 describes four stages in that progression. The progression is based on a similar scheme described by Bear, Invernizzi, Templeton, and Johnston (2008), who in turn built on the earlier work of Read (1971) and of Henderson and his students (e.g., Beers & Henderson, 1977; Gentry, 1978; Morris, 1981; Zutell, 1978). The four stages are labeled nonspelling (because it may not even involve letters and is random, not systematic), emergent spelling, early letter-name or early alphabetic spelling, and middle letter-name or middle alphabetic spelling (for later stages, beginning with late letter-name or late alphabetic spelling, see Chapter 5).

The first stage, nonspelling, is what novices do. They do not actually spell. Individual letters in their writing are not even representative of beginning sounds in the words of their intended messages.

The second, third, and fourth stages represent the kinds of spelling we expect from experimenters. In these three stages, experimenters use letters to make words based on analyses of sound units in words and knowledge of sound-letter correspondences. They progress from only partial encoding (initial or initial and final sounds) to nearly complete encoding of word sounds, and from representing only consonant sounds to representing consonants and vowels.

Emergent spelling is characterized by children's use of at least one letter to represent a phoneme in a word although the letter selected by the child may not be conventional. For example, children might spell using letters that have sounds in their names that are like sounds in the words, as Kristen Marie did when she wrote the word *phone* with the letter *V* and the word *window* with the letter *Y*. Slightly more sophisticated is the phase of *early letter-name spelling* or *early alphabetic spelling*. Children begin using the whole letter name to spell a segment of a word or a phoneme. For example, spelling the word *feet* as *FET*, with the name of the letter *E* as its middle sound; or the word *deep* as *DP*, with the name of the letter *D* as its beginning and middle sounds. In this phase, spellings routinely include sound-letter correspondences. Sometimes those include middle and ending sounds. In the *middle letter-name spelling* or *middle alphabetic spelling* phase, children nearly always represent the beginning and ending sounds of words and a vowel sound in their spellings although these spellings are still not conventional. (Note: middle here refers to the developmental sequence, early, middle, and late, not to the middle of words.)

These stages are intended to clarify the direction of change in children's spelling development. They do not represent a rigid sequence. Children may spell like emergent spellers in a particular context, including particular purposes and assistance, and spell like early or middle letter-name spellers in other contexts with other purposes and kinds of assistance.

TABLE 4.2 Stages of Spelling Development

Nonspelling
- Consistent with Bear, Invernizzi, Templeton, and Johnston's (2008) early emergent spelling and middle emergent spelling (see Figure 3.2 for an example)
- Uses drawing and writing together, at first interchangeably, later distinguishing between drawing and writing
- Arranges marks horizontally
- Uses letter-like forms

Emergent Spelling
- Consistent with Bear et al.'s (2008) late emergent spelling
- Consistently uses left-to-right directionality
- Demonstrates concept of word but may not always use spaces between words
- Writes some letters of the alphabet
- Occasionally uses sound-letter correspondences or memorized spellings of common words
  Example (from McGee & Richgels, 2003): MfRETfR - TZRDEfR - KHCDR for *My favorite ride is the roller coaster.*

Early Letter-Name or Early Alphabetic Spelling[*]
- Writes most letters of the alphabet
- Routinely uses sound-letter correspondences (e.g., *MZM* for *museum, FET* for *feet*)
- Routinely represents beginning consonants (e.g., *T* for *telephone, L* for *ladder*)
- Represents some ending consonants (e.g., *n* for *in, Tr* for *tiger, SK* for *sock, BD* for *bird, Ht* for *hot*)
- Only partially represents consonant blends and digraphs (e.g., *BEG* for *bridge, PN* for *playing, pat* for *plant, SID* for *slide, CKS* for *chicks*)
- Occasionally represents short vowel sounds using similar articulation of vowel's letter name (e.g., *BEG* for *bridge*)
- Occasionally represents long vowel sounds using the letter whose name is the same as the vowel sound (e.g., *FET* for *feet, SID* for *slide, NOZ* for *nose, Her* for *here*)

Middle Letter-Name or Middle Alphabetic Spelling[*]
- Routinely represents both beginning and ending consonant sounds (e.g., *Hct* for *hatched, WZ* for *was*)
- Routinely represents short vowel sounds, sometimes using similar articulation of vowel's letter name (e.g., *RiCS* for *rocks*), sometimes using conventional spellings, especially in high-frequency words (e.g., *BAtmAN* for *Bat Man, HOT* for *hot, BIG* for *big*)
- Routinely represents long vowel sounds using the letter whose name is the same as the vowel sound (e.g., *PnNO* for *piano, PePL* for *people, ONIE* for *only, AWAK* for *awake*)

[*] Adapted from Bear, Invernizzi, Templeton, and Johnston's (2008) stages with the same names. Examples from research conducted by the authors.

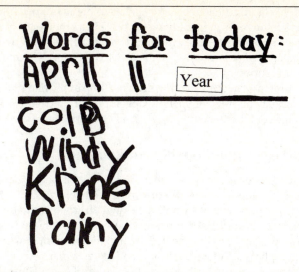

FIGURE 4.8   Zack's Words for Today

Figure 4.8 shows Zack's writing when he was the student helper for the Words for Today routine in his kindergarten classroom (Richgels, 2003). His classmates suggested words for him to write. He wrote *windy* and *rainy* by copying them from the class's weather report chart. His teacher and classmates helped him to hear the sounds, choose the letters, and write the letters for ColD and Krme (*crummy*). For example, his teacher said, "What do you hear in the beginning of *c-c-crummy*?" and Zack answered, "K", and wrote *K* without help. But when she asked, "Crrrrrrr—hear that rrrrr?" she had to prompt Zack with the letter and direct his attention to a model for writing it: "That's an *R*. An *R*. It's the first letter of *rainy*." She also had to tell Zack that *M* spells the next sound, but he decided on his own that the letter *E* spells the last sound in *crummy*.

On the very same day, Zack's teacher asked him to spell six words without help. Zack's spellings were *A* for *apple, D* for *ladder, T* for *tiger, P* for *porcupine, e* for *telephone*, and *P* for *piano*. Just a month earlier, during free play time, Zack was the clerk at a pretend pizza restaurant. With a pencil in hand and a slip of paper on a clipboard, he took a customer's order for "large, thick crust, with pepperoni and black olives." He wrote four wavy lines of mock cursive writing, one for each element of the order: *large, thick crust, pepperoni, black olives* (Richgels, 2003).

At what stage is Zack's spelling? Is he a nonspeller, as his wavy-line, pizza-store writing might suggest? Is he the early letter-name speller that his invented spelling assessment performance indicates? Or is he the middle letter-name speller that ColD and Krme suggest? Answers to these questions depend on the context and the level of support that is available (Richgels, 2008). Zack's literacy-related pretend play does not require spelling. Independently, he seems to be an early letter-name speller. With help, he can spell like a middle letter-name speller. What is important in responding to Zack's invented spellings is not identifying his place in a scheme like the one shown in Table 4.2 but, rather, supporting his continued development so that over time, his spellings resemble later stages more often than earlier stages (see Chapter 8 for extensive discussion of such support).

Children's growth in spelling does not stop at the end of the middle letter-name or middle alphabetic stage of spelling development. In Chapter 5, we will describe additional stages of invented spelling that are beyond what experimenters do.

Sound-Letter Relationships in Reading

Children's awareness of systematic (but unconventional) relations between letters and spoken language influences their reading (Richgels, 1995). Children's reading of environmental print, storybooks, and their own writing gradually reflects their awareness of written words and the relationships between letters in written words and sounds in spoken language. For example, Jeffrey, a kindergartner, looked at the *F* page in a word book (an alphabet picture book that had several pictures on a page depicting objects and actions associated with a particular letter). He called out to his mother, "Do you want to hear me read this page?" Jeffrey's mother knew that he could not really read, but she was willing to be an audience as he pretended to read this favorite book. Jeffrey pointed to the word *fence* and said "fence." He pointed to each of the words or phrases *fruit tree, flag, funny face,* and *four fish* and said the appropriate word or phrase. Then he paused as he scanned the picture of a farmer driving a tractor. The words accompanying this picture were *front wheels* and *fertilizer.* Finally, Jeffrey said, "I'm looking for the word *tractor* because this is a tractor. But I can't find it. All of these words have *F*'s. But *tractor* shouldn't be *F*. Where is it, Mom? Can you find the word for 'tractor'?"

Another way that children use sound-letter relationships is by reading and writing new words from the patterns they discover in families of rhyming words, that is, groups of words that rhyme. Together, rhyming word families represent hundreds of words to which children gain access by learning a relatively small number of prototypes. As children learn only a few of the words in a rhyming word family, they notice that the rime remains the same and the onset changes. The **onset** is the initial consonant, consonant blend, or consonant digraph of a syllable; the **rime** is the part of a syllable from its vowel through its end. They can recognize in reading and spell in writing many new words by recognizing the rime as a written unit—a **phonogram**—and applying their sound-letter knowledge to decoding or encoding the onsets. For example, Ebony's kindergarten teacher had presented the familiar words *me* and *beet* on chart paper because the sound-letter correspondences introduced in her class's instructional materials include long vowel sounds (in this case, /E/) and consonant sounds. The teacher then demonstrated making the rhyming words *we* and *feet* and encouraged her students to write other words. Ebony wrote *Meet.*

English Language Learners and Invented Spelling

Like other experimenters, those who are also English language learners listen for sounds in spoken words and associate them with letters in written words. In bilingual programs, ELLs will spell in their home language; however, in other programs, they are expected to learn to spell in English. Their spelling success depends in part on how the **phoneme repertoires** of their native languages compare to those of English. They are likely to find it especially difficult to spell phonemes of English that are not phonemes of their home languages. For example, /th/ is not a phoneme of either Spanish or Chinese. The sounds /b/ and /v/ are separate phonemes in English but are only variants of a single phoneme in Spanish. That sound difference can be the sole contrast between two English words (e.g., *bat* and *vat*) but never is the sole contrast between two Spanish words (Barone, Mallette, & Xu, 2005). ELLs have difficulty hearing sounds that are not phonemes in their home languages and are likely to substitute sounds that resemble those in their home languages.

Because Spanish speakers are such a large proportion of ELLs, teachers must be especially informed about the similarities and differences of the sound systems of English and Spanish (Helman, 2004). Both languages include the consonant phonemes /b/, /d/, /f/, /g/, /k/, /l/, /m/, /n/, /p/, /s/, /t/, /w/, /y/, and /ch/ (Goldstein, 2001). It is appropriate to include those in phonemic awareness and sound-letter instruction and to encourage children to use them in their invented spellings. Other English consonant phonemes are not phonemes of Spanish, and children are likely to make substitutions for them. For example, /j/ is not a phoneme of Spanish; therefore, Spanish-speaking experimenters are likely to substitute /ch/ for it. Similarly, /s/ will be substituted for /z/, /t/, or /d/ for /th/, and /ch/ for /sh/. Spanish-speaking children's spellings likely will be influenced by these substitutions. They might spell *them* as DEM or *shed* as CHED (Helman, 2004).

EXPERIMENTING WITH FUNCTIONS OF WRITTEN LANGUAGE

YOUNG EXPERIMENTERS continue what they began as novices; they continue to use written language to communicate for a variety of purposes. Experimenters do, however, cover some new ground in the domain of written language functions. They read and write with the two new purposes of learning to read and write and of preserving specific messages.

In this chapter are many examples of experimenters' devoting considerable energy to reading and writing, to experimenting with how written language works. Experimenters learn by doing, even when the doing is at times painstaking. Their appearing to work hard is the result of the careful analysis, the concentrated thinking, and the reasoned trying out that is the essence of experimentation and invention.

Another kind of experimenting that young experimenting readers and writers do is with **multiple literacies.** These include the ways in which children read and write and construct new meanings using new technologies such as the Internet; multimodal publication software such as *Kid Pix Delux;* text messaging, instant messaging, hypertext, and other information and communication technologies (ICT) just now emerging (Karchmer, Mallette, & Leu, 2003). When considering that preschool and kindergarten-age children are the fastest growing group of Internet users—a jump from 6 to 35 percent between 2000 and 2002 (Fitzgerald, 2003), it is not surprising that many children are experimenting with new concepts about print, text formats, and methods of making meaning. Children using the Internet find new ways to jump from page to page, ignore top-to-bottom orientation, and read multiple signs and symbols. Children using *Kid Pix Delux* experiment with ways to manipulate symbols in the program to extend their dramatic play (Barone et al., 2005). They also use such software to integrate digital photographs and symbols they have created with icon stamps (Labbo, Eakle, & Montero, 2004; Turbill, 2004). Children write captions for photographs and label parts of photographs. (See Labbo and colleagues at www.readingonline.org/electronic/labbo2/index.html for examples of children's experimenting with multiple literacies.)

Experimenters, unlike novices, understand that written messages, whether their own or others', are stable and permanent. Meagan (who wrote in her kindergarten journal chicks r ranein for *Chicks are running*) and two kindergarten story folder authors (see Figure 4.7) knew that by writing a journal entry or a story, they rendered their messages readable. Meagan wanted to record the activities of the chicks that had hatched in her classroom; and the story folder authors wanted to take home photocopies of the stories they had created about the folders' pictures. All three of these children could achieve those goals by writing. They had accomplished the most significant function-related conceptual change of the experimental stage, the discovery that written language can preserve a writer's message exactly. This is known as the **message concept** (Clay, 1975).

ASSESSING EXPERIMENTING READERS AND WRITERS IN KINDERGARTEN AND FIRST GRADE

CHILDREN WHO ARE JUST SHOWING SIGNS of being experimenters are able to perform most of the preschool and kindergarten assessment tasks presented in Chapter 3 and Appendix B. They are able to identify many alphabet letters, know several concepts about print, and have some ability to isolate beginning phonemes. Four additional assessments can be used to track children as they enter and move through experimenting reading and writing:

- sound-letter relationships
- finger-point reading and locating words
- invented spelling
- reading and writing familiar rhyming words

These assessments evaluate children's new awareness of how the alphabetic principle works through their identification of sound-letter correspondences, their tracking print and making one-to-one matches of oral language to written language, their application of sound-letter knowledge to their writing, and their use of known words to discover similarly constructed words. Teachers continue to assess children's vocabulary and oral comprehension development using retelling assessments such as those presented in Chapter 3.

Assessing Phonemic Awareness and Sound-Letter Knowledge

Assessing children's phonemic awareness at a more advanced level than merely segmenting a beginning phoneme (see Chapter 3 and Appendix B) may use the Yopp-Singer Test of Phonemic Segmentation. This free assessment is found on many school Web sites, including http://teams.lacoe.edu/reading/assessments/yopp.html. These sites give directions for administration and scoring of this assessment. Assessing children's knowledge of sound-letter relationships can be accomplished simply by pointing to each consonant letter on the uppercase letter recognition administration sheet and asking children to say the sound of each letter. Experimenters are not expected to know the vowel sounds; that will be assessed later in their development. Teachers can use the Uppercase Alphabet Recognition administration sheet and score sheet presented in Appendix B.

Assessing Concepts about Print

To assess children's ability to match one-to-one spoken words with written words, a critical concept about print that must be developed right at the emergence of reading, teachers can use the finger-point reading assessment. A teacher should prepare a small booklet of a favorite nursery rhyme with four pages of text. Each page should have two lines of print. Appendix C presents the text of the rhyme "I'm a Little Teapot" with large font and extra large word spaces that can be used to create a finger-point reading assessment. To administer the assessment, the teacher first teaches all children the nursery rhyme so that each child can say it verbatim from memory. Then the teacher uses the Teapot book with individual children, saying, "Here is a book with the teapot rhyme in it. Watch as I say it and point to each word." The teacher says the rhyme and points to each word. Then the teacher invites the child to read along, "This time I'll help you point to the words as you say the rhyme." The teacher prompts the child so that he or she successfully says each word as the child points to that word. Then the teacher invites the child to do finger-point reading independently, saying, "Now you point to the words and say the rhyme." The child earns a point for each line of text for which he or she correctly points to each word while saying that exact word.

   The next part of the finger-point reading assessment is for the child to use one-to-one matching in finger-point reading to locate words. The teacher demonstrates: "I can find the word *little*, like this." The teacher demonstrates one-to-one finger-point reading of the first line of the text, then says, "Here is the word *little*." The teacher continues: "This poem has the word *teapot*. Can you show me which word is *teapot*?" The child is asked to find seven words: *teapot, short, I, up, shout, tip,* and *me.* Teachers can use the score sheet for finger-point reading and locating words presented in Appendix C.

Assessing Alphabetic Principle

To assess the alphabetic principle, children are asked to invent spellings for five words. Teachers demonstrate listening to sounds in a word before writing. They say, "We're going to listen to sounds in words and then spell them. Like the word *tea.*

I like hot tea in the winter and iced tea in the summer. I'm going to listen to the sounds in the word *tea*: /t/. I know that sound is spelled *T*. Let me listen again: /t/ /E/. I hear *E*. Now it's your turn. I'll say some words, and you spell them by listening to the sounds." Appendix C presents five words. Teachers analyze what children know by first considering whether children attempt to spell beginning consonants, beginning and ending consonants, blends, long vowels, and short vowels. At the beginning of experimenting, children likely only spell some sounds—usually beginning consonants. Even with experience, most experimenters do not spell with correct vowels or blends but eventually spell with expected beginning and ending consonants. After analyzing children's spellings, teachers can use Table 4.2 to determine the phase of spelling development of each child. Chapter 8 presents dictation sentences (based on Clay, 2005) that can also be used to screen and monitor children's emerging alphabetic principle.

Finally, teachers want to assess whether children can use their growing awareness of letter-sound associations to read and spell new words composed from onsets and rimes of familiar rhyming words. For example, a teacher might introduce the familiar word *bat* printed on a small whiteboard, telling a child, "This is the word *bat*. Now I am going to wipe off the letter *b* and make another word. I'll put on an *f*. Now the word is *fat*. Now let me wipe off the letter *f* and make another word. I'll put on an *r*. Now the word is *rat*. Now it's your turn. I'll put on some new letters and you read the words." The teacher creates the words *hat, mat, sat, vat,* and *cat*. Next, he or she writes the word *big* and says, "This word is *big*. I want you to wipe off a letter and write the word *dig*. What would you wipe off to make *big* into *dig*?" The teacher then asks children to spell *fig, jig, wig,* and *zig*. The score sheet for reading and writing new rhyming words is presented in Appendix C.

Developing an Assessment Plan

Once teachers have selected screening and monitoring assessments, they schedule times to administer them (usually early fall for screening and then three times throughout the year for monitoring). Teachers may select all or only a subset of the screening measures to use on particular monitoring occasions. For example, assessments of alphabet knowledge and phonemic awareness are useful at the end of first and second quarters in kindergarten whereas assessments of sound-letter knowledge and the alphabetic principle are useful at the end of second and third quarters.

Finally, teachers make a schedule that allows systematic observation of all children (such as observing each child closely for five to eight minutes twice a month) as they participate in a variety of classroom activities. One plan is to schedule observations on Mondays and Thursdays. The first week of the month, the teacher designates three or four children for observation on Monday and three or four additional children on Thursday. During center or workstation time, outside play, and mealtimes, the teacher observes each of the designated children for a few minutes and makes anecdotal notes. During the second, third, and fourth Mondays and Thursdays of the month, other children are observed. Once all the children have been observed, the cycle of observation repeats. Chapter 8 presents a systematic plan one kindergarten teacher used to keep track of the learning of her students.

Keeping Records

Teachers must keep track of the results of screening and monitoring assessments as well as the work samples and records of classroom observations for each child and for the classroom as a whole.

Assessment notebooks should also have a class profile of the results of the screening and monitoring assessments for all children in the classroom (see Appendixes B and C for class profiles). While analyzing anecdotal notes, teachers can see with a glance at these profiles how well individual children performed on the profiled assessments.

Chapter Summary

EXPERIMENTERS ARE AWARE that there is a system of written language that they only partly understand. The meaning making that experimenters do is similar to what they did as novices. They continue writing in order to present a message, and they continue using sophisticated strategies for interacting with books.

Some of the most striking new achievements of experimenters are related to their greater control over form and meaning-form links. They acquire a concept of spoken and written words, and they devise means for showing word boundaries in their writing. In addition to knowing what physical arrangements are appropriate for different text forms, they know what special language is appropriate.

Experimenters' reading and writing are increasingly print governed. They achieve phonemic awareness and use it in alphabetic reading and invented spelling. They carefully analyze speech sounds in almost any word they want to write, and match those sounds with letters. Experimenters also show new knowledge of meaning-form links by sounding literate and being precise. Often, they are aware that written language is more precise than spoken language and that what readers say depends on what writers write.

As with novices, written language serves a variety of functions for experimenters. A new purpose for their reading and writing is simply to experiment. Another is to preserve readable messages. Teachers can use four additional assessments to track the growing development of experimenters: sound-letter recognition, finger-point reading and identifying words, invented spelling, and reading and writing new rhyming words. They continue to gather work samples, especially of children's writing, and to systematically observe children.

A summary of what experimenters know about written language meanings, forms, meaning-form links, and functions is presented in Figure 4.9.

FIGURE 4.9 Summary: What Experimenting Readers and Writers Know about Written Language Meanings, Forms, Meaning-Form Links, and Functions

Meaning Making

assign meaning to text by applying knowledge of specialized literary language (such as literary syntax and alliteration)

Forms

know nearly all alphabet letter names and formations

have metalinguistic awareness of letters

develop concept of spoken words

develop concept of written words

develop concept of word boundaries

use specialized literary knowledge to construct a wide variety of texts

use a variety of strategies to produce conventional texts (including copying, asking for spellings, dictating, and spelling)

Meaning-Form Links

sound literate when assigning meaning to storybooks and compositions

are precise when assigning meaning to storybooks and compositions

develop phonemic awareness

use manner of articulation to associate sounds and letters in spellings

use letter names to associate sounds and letters in spellings

use identity of sounds to associate sounds and letters in spellings

spell at the levels of emergent, early letter-name, and middle letter-name spelling

use knowledge of sound-letter relationships to monitor emergent reading

use finger-point reading

can use familiar rhyming words to learn some sight words

Functions

read and write to experiment with written language

understand that written language is readable (develop the message concept)

Using the Information

Go back to three figures in this chapter and describe the elements of meaning making, forms, meaning-form links, and functions (use Figure 4.9) that can be inferred from them. For example, Figure 4.6 is Brooke's Father's Day card. Brooke has expressed a powerfully felt message—"I love you, Daddy. Very much, too." She shows control of writing alphabet letters, although she adds little dots at end points and intersections of the lines and curves that make up the letters. Perhaps she is imitating the decorative writing of a teacher, as Carrie did (see Figures 1.8 and 1.9). She has not written words; her composition is a single string of letters with no spaces. Still, her finger-point reading of her message shows that she is aware of words in speech and intends a correspondence between those words and the individual symbols that she has written (letters). In this way, she is being precise in her reading of her own composition. Brooke's writing clearly has the purpose of expressing her feelings on the important occasion of Father's Day. Her written message is an extension of, an elaboration of, the happy feelings suggested by the picture of a bird and flowers that she drew on the cover of her card. Brooke's writing sample demonstrates many of the accomplishments listed in Figure 4.9.

Applying the Information

Eric's teacher was in the midst of monitoring children's progress in acquiring the alphabetic principle. When it was his turn to be assessed, she asked him to spell six words. He wrote A for *apple,* L for *ladder,* T for *tiger,* P for *porcupine,* T for *telephone,* and P for *piano.* Two weeks later, his teacher was observing Eric at the writing center. His class earlier had viewed the inside of a fertilized chick egg by shining a powerful light through it. Now with the help of an adult helper in the classroom, he was writing in a journal about what he saw. His journal entry is shown in Figure 4.10. His message was *A black eye. Veins bring food.* The helper supplied the spelling for the first word, and Eric copied *black* from a black crayon. When the adult helper asked, "Do you have any ideas about how to write *eye*?" Eric answered, "Just an *I.*" The helper asked, "What would *vvein*—" and before even hearing the end of the word, Eric answered, "*V!*" And when the helper asked, "Do you want to write any other letters for *veinzzzz*?" Eric answered, "Z." What can you say about Eric's writing and spelling during the monitoring assessment and during journal writing? Which spelling was the most sophisticated and why? How was Eric able to achieve this level of spelling? What does this suggest about instruction that would strengthen Eric as a speller and writer?

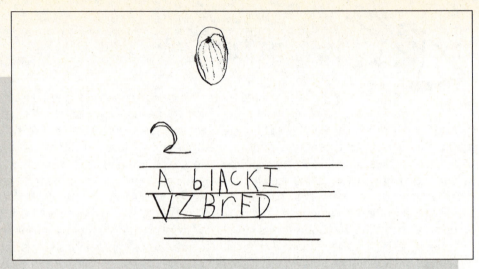

FIGURE 4.10 Eric's Assisted Journal Entry

GOING BEYOND THE TEXT

VISIT A KINDERGARTEN CLASSROOM. Join the children who are writing. Notice what their writing activities are. What experimenting behaviors do you observe? What text forms are the children using? How many of them are spellers? Begin your own writing activity (writing a letter, a story, a list of some kind, a reminder to yourself, or a poem). Talk about it with the children. How many of them take up your activity and attempt similar pieces? Does the character of their writing change from what it was for their own activities? Is there more or less invented spelling, more or less word writing, more or less scribbling?

Ask the teacher if children have favorite storybooks. If so, invite children to read their favorites to you. How do they interpret that invitation? If they would rather you read to them, how willing are they to supply parts of the reading? What parts do they know best? What parts do they like best?

REFERENCES

Barone, D., Mallette, M., & Xu, S. (2005). *Teaching early literacy: Development, assessment, and instruction.* New York: Guilford Press.

Bear, D. R., Invernizzi, M., Templeton, S., & Johnston, F. (2008). *Words their way: Word study for phonics, vocabulary, and spelling instruction* (4th ed.). Boston: Allyn & Bacon.

Beers, J. W., & Henderson, E. H. (1977). A study of developing orthographic concepts among first grade children. *Research in the Teaching of English, 11*, 133–148.

Bissex, G. L. (1980). *GNYS AT WRK. A child learns to write and read.* Cambridge, MA: Harvard University Press.

Clay, M. M. (1975). *What did I write? Beginning writing behavior.* Exeter, NH: Heinemann.

Clay, M. M. (2005). *Literacy lessons designed for individuals: Part two, teaching procedures.* Portsmouth, NH: Heinemann.

Cox, B., Fang, Z., & Otto, B. (1997). Preschoolers' developing ownership of the literate register. *Reading Research Quarterly, 32*, 34–53.

Ehri, L. C., & Roberts, T. (2006). The roots of learning to read and write: Acquisition of letters and phonemic awareness. In D. K. Dickinson & S. B. Neuman (Eds.), *Handbook of early literacy research, Vol. 2* (pp. 113–132). New York: Guilford Press.

Fitzgerald, T. (2003). Meet the first Internet babies. *Media Life Magazine.* www.media lifemagazine.com/news2003/mar03/mar24/4_thurs/news1thursday.html.

Gentry, J. R. (1978). Early spelling strategies. *Elementary School Journal, 79*, 88–92.

Goldstein, B. (2001). Transcription of Spanish and Spanish-influenced English. *Communication Disorders Quarterly, 23*, 54–60.

Harste, J. C., Burke, C. L., & Woodward, V. A. (1983). *Young child as writer-reader, and informant* (Final report project NIE-G-80–0121). Bloomington, IN: Language Education Departments, Indiana University.

Helman, L. (2004). Building on the sound system of Spanish: Insights from the alphabetic spellings of English-language learners. *The Reading Teacher, 57*, 452–460.

Karchmer, R., Mallette, M., & Leu, D. (2003). Early literacy in a digital age: Moving from a singular book literacy to the multiple literacies of networked information and communication technologies. In D. Barone & L. Morrow (Eds.), *Literacy and young children: Research-based practices* (pp. 175–194). New York: Guilford Press.

Labbo, L., Eakle, A. J., & Montero, M. (2004). Digital language experience approach: Using digital photographs and software as a language experience approach innovation. *Reading Online.* www.readingonline.org/electronic/labbo2/index.html.

McGee, L. M., & Richgels, D. J. (2003). *Designing early literacy programs: Strategies for at-risk preschool and kindergarten children.* New York: Guilford Press.

Mesmer, H. A. E., & Lake, K. (2010). The role of syllable awareness and syllable-controlled text in the development of finger-point reading. *Reading Psychology, 31*(2), 176–201.

Morris, D. (1981). Concept of word: A developmental phenomenon in the beginning reading and writing processes. *Language Arts, 58*, 659–668.

Morris, D. (1993). The relationship between children's concept of word in text and phoneme awareness in learning to read: A longitudinal study. *Research in the Teaching of English, 27*, 133–154.

Morris, D., Bloodgood, J. W., Lomax, R. G., & Perney, J. (2003). Developmental steps in learning to read: A longitudinal study in kindergarten and first grade. *Reading Research Quarterly, 38*, 302–328.

Powell, R., & Davidson, N. (2005). The donut house: Real world literacy in an urban kindergarten class. *Language Arts, 82*, 248–256.

Read, C. (1971). Pre-school children's knowledge of English phonology. *Harvard Educational Review, 41*, 1–34.

Richgels, D. (1995). Invented spelling ability and printed word learning in kindergarten. *Reading Research Quarterly, 30*, 96–109.

Richgels, D. J. (2001). Invented spelling, phonemic awareness, and reading and writing instruction. In S. B. Neuman & D. K. Dickinson (Eds.), *Handbook of early literacy research* (pp. 142–155). New York: Guilford Press.

Richgels, D. J. (2003). *Going to kindergarten: A year with an outstanding teacher.* Lanham, MD: Scarecrow.

Richgels, D. J. (2008). Practice to theory: Invented spelling. In A. DeBruin-Parecki (Ed.), *Effective early literacy practice: Here's how, here's why* (pp. 39–51). Baltimore, MD: Brookes Publishing.

Roberts, B. (1996). Spelling and the growth of concept of word as first graders write. *Reading Psychology, 17*(3), 229–252.

Slobodkina, E. (1940). *Caps for sale: A tale of a peddler, some monkeys and their monkey business.* New York: William R. Scott.

Sulzby, E. (1985). Children's emergent reading of favorite storybooks: A developmental study. *Reading Research Quarterly, 20*, 458–481.

Temple, C., Nathan, R., Temple, F., & Burris, N. (1993). *The beginnings of writing* (3rd ed.). Boston: Allyn & Bacon.

Templeton, S. (2003). Spelling. In J. Flood, D. Lapp, J. R. Squire, & J. M. Jensen (Eds.), *Handbook of research on teaching the English language arts* (2nd ed., pp. 738–751). Mahwah, NJ: Lawrence Erlbaum Associates.

Templeton, S., & Morris, D. (2000). Spelling. In M. L. Kamil, P. B. Mosenthal, P. D. Pearson, & R. Barr (Eds.), *Handbook of reading research,* *Vol. 3* (pp. 525–543). Mahwah, NJ: Lawrence Erlbaum Associates.

Turbill, J. (2004). Exploring the potential of the digital language experience approach in Australian classrooms. *Reading Online.* www.readingonline.org/international/turbill7.

Zutell, J. (1978). Some psycholinguistic perspectives on children's spelling. *Language Arts, 55,* 844–850.

Go to the topics Phonemic Awareness and Phonics, Word Study, and Writing Development in the MyEducationLab (www.myeducationlab.com) for your course, where you can:

- Find learning outcomes for Phonemic Awareness and Phonics, Word Study, and Writing Development along with the national standards that connect to these outcomes.
- Complete Assignments and Activities that can help you more deeply understand the chapter content.
- Examine challenging situations and cases presented in the IRIS Center Resources.

A+RISE

Go to the Topic A+RISE in the MyEducationLab (www.myeducationlab.com) for your course. A+RISE® Standards2Strategy™ is an innovative and interactive online resource that offers new teachers in grades K–12 just-in-time, research-based instructional strategies that:

- Meet the linguistic needs of ELLs as they learn content
- Differentiate instruction for all grades and abilities
- Offer reading and writing techniques, cooperative learning, use of linguistic and nonlinguistic representations, scaffolding, teacher modeling, higher order thinking, and alternative classroom ELL assessment
- Provide support to help teachers be effective through the integration of listening, speaking, reading, and writing along with the content curriculum
- Improve student achievement
- Are aligned to Common Core Elementary Language Arts standards (for the literacy strategies) and to English language proficiency standards in WIDA, Texas, California, and Florida.

CHAPTER 5

From Six to Eight Years

CONVENTIONAL READERS AND WRITERS IN EARLY, TRANSITIONAL, AND SELF-GENERATIVE PHASES

KEY CONCEPTS

Conventional Readers
   and Writers

Early Readers and
   Writers

Transitional Readers
   and Writers

Self-Generative Readers
   and Writers

High-Frequency Words

Sight Words

Grapho-Semantics

Grapho-Syntax

Phonics

Orchestration

Writing Workshop

Vowel Markers

Metacognitive
   Awareness

Literary Interpretation

Transaction

Critical Interpretations

Referential Dimension

Exposition

Morpheme

Morphological
   Awareness

Compound Sentences

Complex Sentences

Story Grammar

Approximations

Elements of
   Informational Texts

Decoding

Orthographic
   Reading

Speech Emergence

Intermediate Fluency

Instructional Reading
   Level

Independent Reading
   Level

Running Record

Individualized Reading
   Inventory

Miscue Analysis

Developmental Spelling
   Inventory

WHO ARE CONVENTIONAL READERS AND WRITERS?

LEARNING ABOUT READING AND WRITING is a gradual process. It is not possible to identify the exact moment when a child becomes a reader or writer in a conventional sense. Nonetheless, children do become **conventional readers and writers** who are able to read texts on their own and write texts that they and others can read. In this chapter, we can provide only a few of the most critical insights that children gain as they go through three phases of conventional reading and writing.

Three Phases of Conventional Literacy Development

The National Association for the Education of Young Children and the International Reading Association, two professional organizations for teachers of young children, suggest that children's conventional reading and writing emerge through three phases, which they call early, transitional, and self-generative reading and writing (NAEYC/IRA, 1998). **Early readers and writers,** who are reading within the first-grade level, differ from experimenting readers in that they can read accurately both their own writing and simple texts composed by others, including simple storybooks. They are often called *beginning readers and writers.* **Transitional readers and writers,** reading on the second- through fourth- or fifth-grade level, have moved beyond the earliest forms of conventional reading and writing although they still need good teaching. *Critical readers and writers,* who are sometimes called **self-generative readers and writers,** are reading at the sixth- or seventh-grade level and above. They are critical self-learners, although they still need the support of effective and caring teachers to point them in the right directions for academic success.

Early readers are able to read simple texts on their own. This is helped by the fact that the texts contain many **high-frequency words,** such as *the, is, were, she, and, of, from,* and *with.* Children with even a few years of experience looking at and being read storybooks and information books will have encountered these words many times; they appear in almost any text that is more than a few sentences in length. From instruction, experience, or both, early readers know them as **sight words,** that is, words they can read immediately upon seeing them, automatically, and without sounding them out. Early readers are also helped to read simple texts by having learned an increasing number of strategies for identifying words that they cannot read by sight. Among these decoding strategies is the use of phonics or knowledge of sound-letter relationships to link letters or combinations of letters with pronunciations.

Transitional readers are able to read more complex text that includes longer sentences and fewer high-frequency words, and they acquire many sight words. They can read more fluently and comprehend more complicated stories and informational texts. They make the transition to reading silently and enjoy simple chapter books, although picture books continue to be an important part of their reading diet. They use more sophisticated decoding strategies that go beyond merely blending individual letters and phonemes. These include using grapho-semantics and using grapho-syntax. **Graphosemantics** is the application of vocabulary knowledge and knowledge of morphemes to the process of decoding. Transitional readers who know the meanings of *the, run, -er,* *cross, -ed,* and *finish line* and can immediately identify *the, runner,* and *finish line* but at first are stumped by the appearance of *crossed* can nonetheless use grapho-semantics to read the sentence *The runner crossed the finish line.* They know how words and word parts and their meanings interact. They compute that interaction something like this: What do runners do with finish lines? They cross them. What does *-ed* do for a verb? It makes it past tense. So the third word in that sentence must be the past tense form of *cross,* which is pronounced /k r aw s t/. Notice that this is actually more efficient than using phonics, which likely would produce a meaningless pronunciation, /k r ah s uh d/.

Grapho-syntax is the application of sentence structure knowledge to the process of decoding. In the example just given of *The runner crossed the finish line,* the reader knows the meaning of *cross* and can use it in speech but is at first stumped by the appearance of *crossed* in print. We saw that knowledge of the meanings of several other words and word parts help to dispel the confusion about *crossed.* But that is not all; the reader is also helped by knowledge of how English sentences work. He or she knows that a sentence needs a verb, that *The runner* and *the finish line* are not verbs, and so the unfamiliar grapheme *crossed* must be a verb. That is why the first question in the computation described in the previous paragraph is about *doing*—What do runners do with finish lines?—and why the second question is about *verbs*—What does *-ed* do for a verb? Thus, grapho-semantics and grapho-syntax almost always work together. Of course, they also work with **phonics.** Knowing how to pronounce the *cr* consonant blend at the beginning of *crossed* helps the reader— almost as much as do the meanings of *runner, -ed,* and *finish line*—to close in on the verb *crossed.*

Transitional readers develop more complex comprehension strategies. They recognize parts of words, make multiple predictions, monitor their understanding, and draw inferences. Transitional spellers know how to spell many words conventionally, and they learn how to use a variety of strategies for spelling words that they do not yet know how to spell conventionally. They write in several different genres including personal narratives (recounts of events in their own lives), stories, poems, and science reports (Wollman-Bonilla, 2000). Many children become transitional readers and writers sometime during second grade and continue in this phase of development through fourth, fifth, or sixth grade.

Later, students will enter an even more sophisticated phase of literacy development. Critical readers are becoming highly skilled readers who can control many strategies for reading complex texts, learning from text, and acquiring new vocabulary. Critical writers are increasingly able to revise their own writing to communicate for a wide variety of purposes and audiences.

Examples of Early and Transitional Readers and Writers

Conventional readers and writers are able to orchestrate many different parts of the reading and writing process. **Orchestration** is readers' and writers' ability to do some reading processes unconsciously so they are freed up to concentrate on other processes. For example, early readers and writers are already fluent at the process of reading from left to right and matching one-on-one spoken words with written words. They do not have to think about these processes—they can accomplish them unconsciously.

However, these early reading processes must also be orchestrated with other processes such as reading words by sight, decoding words, comprehending, and monitoring the meaning of what they read.

In order to demonstrate how readers and writers are better able to orchestrate more complex strategies and texts, we present a glimpse into one child's reading and writing as she enters the phases of early and transitional reading and writing. Kristen entered first grade in the experimenting phase of reading and writing. She could not read on her own yet, although she could blend many consonants into word parts such as *at* to create and read new words such as *bat, cat, fat,* and *hat*. She could invent spellings, and Figure 5.1 presents an example of a message that she wrote to her mother at the classroom writing table. Later, when asked to read her message, Kristen said, "I love you" even though her message spelling suggested that she wrote, "I like you."

Kristen entered the phase of early reading and writing midyear in first grade. Figure 5.2 presents an example of the kinds of text she could read with support at that time. *Go, Dog. Go!* (Eastman, 1961) is considered a primer level text (text that is read during the mid part of first grade). One year later, Kristen became a transitional reader; she was able to read *Frog and Toad Together* (Lobel, 1971), which is considered a second-grade text and indicates the beginning of transitional reading. Midyear in third grade, Kristen could read the chapter book titled *The Chocolate Touch* (Catling, 1952), which is considered a third-grade text. Though she was reading on grade level at this time, Kristen had difficulty comprehending complex stories without instructional support. She would not yet be considered a self-generative reader.

The texts presented in Figure 5.2 highlight the striking differences in idea complexity, number of words, complexity of sentence structure, and level of vocabulary found in texts children read in the first, second, and third grades. As children move through the primary grades, they are expected to make rapid growth, as Kristen did, in their ability to read increasingly difficult texts with fluency and comprehension.

Kristen made similar strides in writing development during the same time period. Figure 5.3 presents three samples of Kristen's writing collected midyear in first, second, and third grades. She wrote the first sample ("Do not come in here") on a rainy day when a classmate came to play (see grade 1). Kristen's mother found the note taped to her bedroom door. Earlier, she had interrupted the girls' play twice when they were too noisy and engaged in rowdy play. Later, Kristen told her mother she had written the note so that she and her friend could "have some privacy." The writing on the

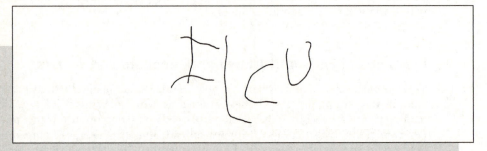

FIGURE 5.1   Kristen's Message: "I Like You"

FIGURE 5.2   Page 18 from Books Kristen Read with Instructional Support at Midyear in the First, Second, and Third Grades

Grade	Title	Sample Text
1	*Go, Dog. Go!* (Eastman, 1961)	The green dog is up. The yellow dog is down (p. 18).
2	*Frog and Toad Together* (Lobel, 1971)	Frog was in his garden. Toad came walking by. "What a fine garden you have, Frog," he said. "Yes," said Frog. "It is very nice, but it was hard work." "I wish I had a garden," said Toad. "Here are some flower seeds. Plant them in the ground," said Frog (p. 18).
3	*The Chocolate Touch* (Catling, 1952)	A few seconds after the bedroom door had closed behind his mother, John leaped to the floor, got down on his hands and knees, and felt under the bed for the candy box. He soon had it on the pillow and set to work unfastening it. First he took off the thin outer sheet of cellophane. Then he lifted off the lid. Then he removed a sheet of cardboard. Then he pulled off a square of heavy tinfoil. Then he took out a layer of shredded paper. As the wrappings piled up around him, John became rather anxious (paragraph included on p. 18).

note demonstrates that although Kristen did not use conventional vowels in her spellings (*iw* for *o* in *do, i* for *o* in *come,* and *i* for *e* in *here*), she does have an increasing awareness of the need to use vowels as well as knowledge of some conventional spellings (*not* and *in*).

Kristen wrote the second sample presented in Figure 5.3 during **writing workshop** in her second-grade classroom, a specific time during the day when children are expected to use the writing process of drafting, revising, and sharing (see more about the writing workshop approach in Chapter 10). This sample was a first draft (see grade 2). It demonstrates a dramatic increase in the number of words that Kristen knows how to spell conventionally, control over word spacing and handwriting, and text composition. Her spelling of vowels has shifted from the one-vowel, one-letter strategy she used in first grade to now using **vowel markers.** Vowel markers are the extra vowels

FIGURE 5.3 Writing Samples Composed by Kristen Midyear in the First, Second, and Third Grades

Grade	Sample	Translation
1	Diwhoɤcitm i ḥ iʳ	do not come in here
2	my room I have a room Fild with lose of toys. I ts os em. You will not bleve Youer eiys. I have a bed and a dresr. Iv got a desch and a sefve to put all the toys in.	my room I have a room filled with lots of toys. It's awesome. You will not believe your eyes. I have a bed and a dresser. I've got a desk and a shelf to put all the toys in.
3	In the winter Caty Cat sleeps on the warm bed Pur In the spring Caty Cat sleeps on the window lege, Pur In the saummer Caty Cat sleeps on tile Pur In the fall Caty Cat sleeps anywere at all	

In the winter Catty Cat sleeps on the warm bed, Purr.
In the spring Catty Cat sleeps on the widow ledge, Purr.
In the summer Catty Cat sleeps on the tile, Purr.
In the fall Catty Cat sleeps anywhere at all.

that are used to indicate a long vowel or other non-short-vowel phoneme. For example, some long vowels are spelled with a "silent *e*" at the end of the word to mark the vowel in the middle of the word as long (as in the words *cake, bike,* and *stove*) and other long vowels are spelled with two or more letters together (such as *ai* in the word *wait, eigh* in the word *height,* and *oa* in the word *boat*). Kristen did not yet use vowel markers conventionally in second grade, but she demonstrated awareness of this spelling concept when she spelled *bleve* for the word *believe, eiys* for *eyes,* and *sefve* for *shelf.*

The third writing sample, collected during third grade, was also created as a part of writing workshop; however, it is a second rather than a first draft. Kristen shared her first draft with and got feedback from the other children and her teacher. Based on these comments, she produced the second draft of the poem. Nearly all words are spelled correctly, with a shift in attention from merely writing a message to writing with attention to literary qualities, such as rhythm and repetition.

Meaning Construction

THE CHILDREN DESCRIBED IN THIS CHAPTER are able to construct meaning from what they read by themselves and in what they write for someone else. They develop many strategies for understanding the different kinds of texts they read.

Meaning Making in Reading: Using Strategies

One of the first and most important strategies that children use to understand what they read is to monitor whether what they are reading makes sense (is meaningful), sounds like language (has acceptable syntax), and looks right (has the sequences of letters that they expect). Children show that they are monitoring by rereading a portion of the text when what they have read does not make sense or by rereading to correct a word that does not fit the text.

Eventually, readers are able to use several different reading strategies to help them understand or comprehend what they read (Paris, Wasik, & Turner, 1991). For example, readers pause to connect what they are reading with what they already know. If they are reading a story about a cat, readers draw on their prior knowledge (Pressley, 2002) of cats—what they do, what they eat, where they live, and how they interact with people. *Prior knowledge* is what a reader knows about a topic before reading about it (see discussion about *schema* in Chapter 1). Using information from the story and their prior knowledge allows readers to predict what will happen; as they read, they look for information to confirm or disconfirm their predictions. They visualize scenes in stories and summarize to themselves what has happened so far. Sometimes readers remember events in their own lives or people they know that are like the events and characters in stories, or they think about characters from other stories.

At first, readers use simple strategies of sounding out words, skipping confusing parts of stories, and then rereading. Even these simple strategies may be used deliberately by beginning readers (Freppon, 1991). This conscious use of strategies is called **metacognitive awareness.** Later, children develop *fix-up strategies,* that is, they correct problems they notice while reading (Sinatra, Brown, & Reynolds, 2002). Readers may reread a portion of a story when they realize that something does not make sense or that they have missed one of the elements of story form that they know to expect. They may skip a word they do not know if they are aware that they are still able to understand the story. They may adjust their pace or change their level of engagement, looking for main ideas and a developing gist or noting finer details.

Sophisticated comprehension includes building literary and critical interpretations of a story. A **literary interpretation** is an attempt to understand the story at a more abstract level, using the story to understand one's self or the world (Sipe, 2007). As they read a story or listen to it being read to them, children can construct their own personal understandings and, sometimes, interpretations of that text, partly based on their unique background experiences. This unique interaction between the text and the reader is called a **transaction** (Rosenblatt, 1978). For example, a group of inner-city first graders discussed the story *Hey, Al* (Yorinks, 1986), in which Al, a janitor who is dissatisfied with his life, is enticed by a strange bird to fly to an island in the sky that the bird describes as a paradise. When he reaches the island, Al begins to turn into a bird himself, but he flies home before he completely loses his identity in this false paradise. One child interpreted the last illustration, "They [Al and his dog] painted it [his old dingy room] yellow like the place [the island]. He was happy then" (Tompkins & McGee, 1993). This child recognized that the color of the paint was a symbol for the happiness that Al and his dog were feeling after their narrow escape from the island in the sky.

Critical interpretations go beyond literary interpretations. **Critical interpretations** involve asking questions such as *Whose story is this? Who benefits from this story?* and *Whose voices are not being heard?* (Leland, Harste, & Huber, 2005). For example, one first-grade teacher had been reading aloud many picture books that focused on troubling social issues in which some characters were marginalized by past or present systems of power. The children in her class responded to *The Other Side* (Woodson, 2001), a story about a black girl and a white girl who lived on opposite sides of a fence that the black girl was not allowed to cross because it was not safe. One child commented, "When they knock the fence down, the black and white people can play together and their moms can meet each other and they can give their phone number and they will have a lot of fun" (Leland et al., p. 266). This child clearly recognized that the fence stands for all obstacles to communication between races.

Meaning Making in Writing

Conventional writers draw on many strategies for writing. Rachel wrote the story presented in Figure 5.4 when she was in second grade. Several elements of this story are noteworthy. Although Rachel uses knowledge of everyday activities (such as hide-and-go-seek) and familiar others (such as her friends) in her compositions, she clearly uses these elements to construct a believable and consistent, but imaginary, story world. Conventional writers are able to go beyond the personal and immediate—what is happening or just recently happened—to the abstract—what has not yet happened or might never really happen. The relation of the writer with the subject matter (from immediate to abstract) is called the **referential dimension** of writing (Moffett, 1968). Rachel is in a special urban school that serves a variety of ELLs with a strong writing program.

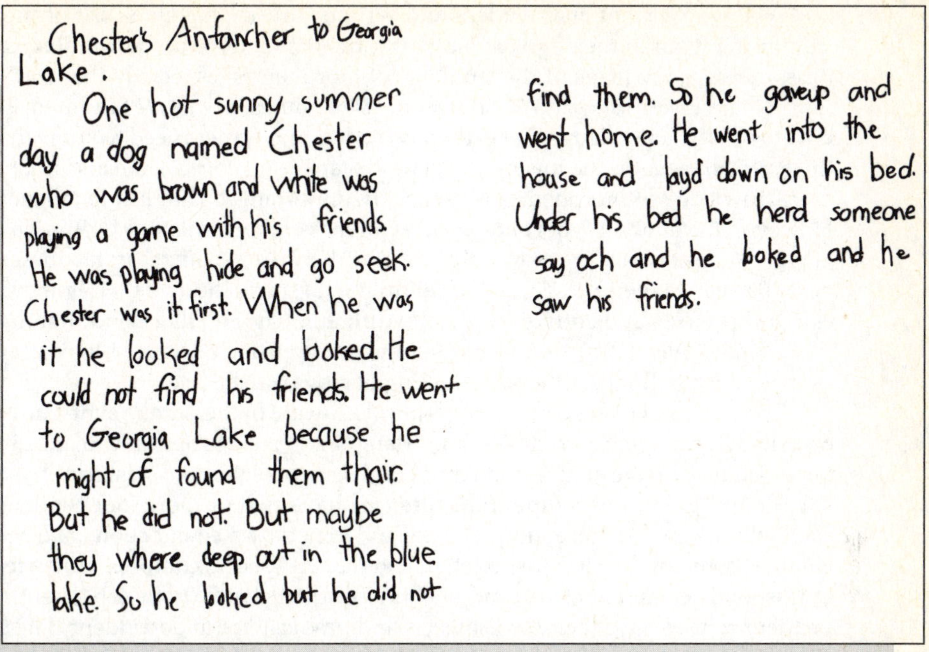

> Chester's Anfancher to Georgia Lake.
>
> One hot sunny summer day a dog named Chester who was brown and white was playing a game with his friends. He was playing hide and go seek. Chester was it first. When he was it he looked and boked. He could not find his friends. He went to Georgia Lake because he might of found them thair. But he did not. But maybe they where deep out in the blue lake. So he boked but he did not find them. So he gaveup and went home. He went into the house and layd down on his bed. Under his bed he herd someone say och and he boked and he saw his friends.

FIGURE 5.4   Chester's Adventure to Georgia Lake

WRITTEN LANGUAGE FORMS

AS THEY BECOME CONVENTIONAL READERS AND WRITERS, children gain knowledge of the fine points of form at the word level in English writing. Children's writing begins to show their achievement of a fully conventional concept of word. They also start to use narrative form in their writing, and their knowledge of a different category of text form, **exposition,** grows. Expositions are nonfictional, nonnarrative texts sometimes called *informational texts.* Among these are explanatory, persuasive, and instructional pieces; essays; how-to texts; and biographies.

Morphological Awareness and Grammar

Conventional readers and writers know how morphemes work in written language (Carlisle, 2004). A **morpheme** is the smallest unit of meaning in a language. Conventional readers and writers learn that morphemes may be written as individual words, such as the articles *a, an,* and *the,* or they may be written as word parts, such as *-ed, -ing,* and *-s.* Thus, the word *boys* has two morphemes, *boy* and *s.*

Whereas conventional readers and writers already have a sense of morphemes from using them in their spoken language, they must develop **morphological aware-ness,** that is, knowledge of the language of morphemes, especially the words *prefixes, suffixes,* and *base words* (Kuo & Anderson, 2006; Nunes, Bryant, & Bindman, 2006), and how to use that knowledge. For example, readers and writers need to know that adding the prefix *un* negates the meaning of a base word (e.g., *unhappy* means "not happy").

Knowledge of morphemes is especially important for English language learners. However, the effects of morphological awareness on reading and writing in a second language are complex. For example, because there are no affixes in Japanese and Chinese (Barone, Mallette, & Xu, 2005), children who speak these as their home languages can find prefixes and suffixes especially difficult. On the other hand, Ramirez, Chen, Geva, and Kiefer (2010) found cross-linguistic transfer of morphological awareness from Spanish to English but not from English to Spanish.

Conventional readers and writers are also aware of the unique syntactic properties of written language (Scott, 2004). Native language speakers naturally make uses of syntax when they create simple and compound sentences. Simple sentences have a single subject and predicate; **compound sentences** have two or more independent clauses, each with its own subject and predicate and joined by a conjunction (*and, or, but*). But complex sentences occur more often in text than in speech; **complex sentences** include at least one dependent clause and one independent clause (both dependent and independent clauses have their own subjects and predicates, but dependent clauses are not able to stand alone—they must be associated with an independent clause). *Because Clarence took an umbrella, he stayed dry* is a complex sentence, with the dependent clause *Because Clarence took an umbrella.* ELLs may need even more experience with complex sentences than do native English speakers.

Composing Stories and Expositions

During elementary school, children learn a great deal about how to write many different types of texts including stories, poems, and informational texts. They learn about the kinds of information or elements that are included in these different text genres and also how to organize that information. In general, the number of elements children include in their compositions increases, the organization of their texts gets more complex, and they demonstrate a growing awareness of audience (Wollman-Bonilla, 2001).

Narrative Elements.   Before we examine children's story compositions, we review the elements identified in a **story grammar** (see Table 2.1 in Chapter 2): Characters are introduced in a setting, an initiating event introduces a problem, and the main character sets a goal to try to solve a problem. The initiating event sets in place a chain of causally related attempts and outcomes in which the main character acts to achieve the goal or solve the problem. Complex stories have a series of attempts and outcomes as the main character must overcome several obstacles before achieving the goal. The story ends as the main character reacts to having achieved the goal.

Stories may also be appreciated for their use of the additional literary elements of point of view, style, mood, and theme (Lukens, 1995). *Point of view* is the perspective from which the story is told. Point of view is particularly important because it positions the reader inside or outside the story. When point of view allows readers inside the story, they know all the characters' thoughts and feelings. *Style* is the way the author uses language, including use of imagery (descriptions that appeal to the senses, such as sight, sound, or touch), word choice, and figurative language (such as the use of simile or metaphor). *Mood* is the emotional tone of a story (humorous, somber, lighthearted, mysterious, frightening). *Theme* is the abstract statement about life or humanity revealed by the story as a whole. Through theme, stories achieve a consistency at an abstract level.

The structure of narratives, both spoken and written, is also influenced by their creators' oral language knowledge and by cultural norms for storytelling. Curenton and Lucas (2007) measured the syntactic complexity of children's stories in terms of the average number of words in a subject-predicate phrase; and, in contrast to linearly sequenced European monologue narratives, they described African, Asian, Latino, and European styles. African styles, for example, include a circular temporal pattern and multiple narrators. Asian stories are concise in deference to a cultural preference for brevity and disapproval of verbosity. "Children are not encouraged to narrate elaborate or detailed descriptions in their stories because it is the listener's responsibility to infer these details" (Curenton & Lucas, p. 402). Latino traditions include a large number of characters, greater importance of overall theme than of linear temporal sequence, evaluative comments, and characters' internal state talk.

Developmental Trends in Children's Story Writing.   What kinds of literary elements might we expect to find in primary schoolchildren's compositions? Return to Rachel's story presented in Figure 5.4. It includes a main character, Chester, the brown and white dog. It also includes Chester's friends (who act as playful antagonists in the game of hide-and-seek and in the story). Rachel implied one of Chester's character traits: he is persistent (he looked and looked for his hidden friends). Tension arises naturally from the conflict of searching; the friends are very difficult to find! The story is told consistently from the third-person point of view with a narrator speaking directly to the reader about how clever Chester was for searching for his friends at Georgia Lake. Rachel's literary style includes the use of repetition (looked and looked). The mood is playful, beginning with the title ("Chester's Adventure to Georgia Lake") and continuing through to the climax when "och" reveals Chester's friends hiding under his bed. This story has most of the literary elements of narratives.

Thus, we can conclude that children do use many literary elements of narratives in their stories but not necessarily all elements—nor are the elements always well developed. We understand that primary schoolchildren's stories may lack plot complexity and descriptive detail. We might expect that young conventional writers' stories would gradually acquire overall story consistency, believability, and detail; but much of this development occurs after the primary grades.

In fact, most first graders do not write stories that include all the elements that would actually qualify their compositions to be called stories (Donovan, 2001). It is not until second and third grade that a majority of children write stories with most of the basic story grammar elements—and, therefore, would qualify to be called *stories*. Instead, most young children's story compositions are in emergent or approximate forms. As with their **approximations** in other areas of emergent literacy—for example, with their mock letter writing, invented spelling, and finger-point reading—children's approximations when writing a story are not as fully realized as an adult's product would be. Their attempts to write stories almost never contain all seven of the literary elements of a well-crafted story. Their stories only approximate the ideal story, with its setting, character, plot, point of view, style, mood, and theme. Figure 5.5 presents approximate forms of children's story writing (adapted from Donovan). When children are asked to write or dictate a story, these are the kinds of forms their stories take. We present their stories, in order from simple to more complex, without invented spellings to emphasize their form. These narratives were collected from pre-K through fourth-grade children in a Title I school.

Expository Texts. Not all texts are stories. Some texts are expository or informational texts. They inform or explain, rather than relate a story. **Elements of informational texts** include topic presentation in which the topic of exposition is introduced (e.g., "Zebras

Figure 5.5   Approximate Forms of Children's Story Writing

Label

present tense, word or phrase

This is David. This is Lisa. This is Casey and Wynell and Willima. This is Travis.

Statement

past tense, sentence about an event

Once upon a time there was a witch who lived in the forest. (Donovan, 2001, p. 418)

No Structure

story opener, past tense, lacks sequence and sustained character

Once there was a boy and a dog. The grandmother was dancing. The bunny gave the grandmother a flower.

Action Sequence

past tense, sequence of events, sustained character, no goal

There once was a little boy. He went to the store and bought potato chips. He went to the store and bought milk. He went to the store and bought some junk food. The end.

Reactive Sequence

past tense, causally related sequence of events, no goal

There was an elephant. He climbed up and he fell and bumped his head. The gorilla kissed his head.

Simple Goal Directed

past tense, causally related sequence of events toward resolution of goal

A lady went into a castle. She saw some jewels and she took some. The giant chased her. She put it on and went home. She wore it to bed.

Complex Goal Directed

past tense, causally related sequence of events toward resolution of goal, obstacles and complications

(see Figure 5.4, Chester's Adventure to Georgia Lake)

Source: Adapted from Donovan, 2001.

are intelligent animals,"; Donovan, 2001, p. 426), description of attributes in which the topic is described (e.g., "Zebras are very strong," p. 426), characteristic events in which typical activities related to the topic are described (e.g., "They eat grass and leaves. They live in packs," p. 426), category comparison in which the topic is compared to another similar topic (e.g., "Zebras are smarter than work horses," p. 426), and final summary in which all the information presented about the topic is stated in a more general way (e.g., "Zebras are wild animals and shall remain in the wild forever," p. 426). Expositions may not include all of these elements; however, all informational texts must include a topic presentation and at least one or more additional informational text elements.

Expositions may also be appreciated for their use of consistency, ordered relationships, and hierarchical relationships (Newkirk, 1987). For a text to have consistency, all its ideas must be related to one another. Ordered relationships are ideas that are related in some order. For example, two ideas might be related because one idea is an example of or illustrates another idea. Causes and effects, problems and solutions, comparisons, and sequences are all ideas that are ordered—they are related to one another in specific ways. Hierarchical relationships result from the fact that expository texts are complex and can be broken into one or more main topics. These topics, in turn, can be broken down into subtopics, forming a hierarchy.

Developmental Trends in Children's Expositions.   Most young children attempt to write expository texts; however, it is not until second grade that many children include more than one or two elements of informational texts in their expositions (Donovan, 2001). In addition, most children do not include ordered relationships in their informational text writing. Instead, most young children's expositions, like their story compositions, are only approximations. They can be considered in emergent or intermediate forms. Figure 5.6 presents approximate forms of informational text writing (adapted from Donovan). When children are asked to write or dictate an informational text, these are the kinds of forms their expositions take. They are arranged from simple to more complex form.

Again, these samples were collected from a Title I school with a small population of ELLs and over 80 percent of children on free lunch. We have used correct spellings.

Figure 5.6 does not include the most complex forms of expository writing that children are expected to write by the end of elementary school and into the middle school years. Instead, it presents the kinds of expositions we would expect from children through fourth or fifth grade. Even so, most third graders and many fourth graders do not yet have control over the most complex structures presented in this figure.

Meaning-Form Links

EARLY AND TRANSITIONAL READERS AND WRITERS acquire many strategies for decoding and spelling, including using alphabetic and orthographic understandings.

Decoding

Decoding is a term usually applied to what readers do when they try to figure out a word that they do not recognize by sight. Early readers are alphabetic decoders, at first

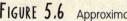

FIGURE 5.6 Approximate Forms of Children's Expositions

Label
present tense, words or phrases

My dog, you, and me

Statement
present tense, sentence, may introduce
topic

I know about rabbits

Simple Couplet
present tense, two related statements,
second statement describes or extends
first statement

The reptiles are snakes and the reptiles
are in the zoo

Attribute List
present tense, random list of two or
more facts related to topic

Cats get on the couch when it is tired.
When it's sleepy, it goes in its bed. When it
doesn't want to be by you, it would scratch. And
it would hurt you if you hurt it.

Complex Couplet
present tense, attribute list in which
two or more statements are related
to one another

Dogs
Dogs are very furry. They are also a mammal. Most
dogs bark and hear. If dogs can't bark that's
because their voice box is not working very well.
If dogs can't hear that's because when they were
born they were born deaf or they have a real bad
ear infection. Dogs can have an ear infection.
Dogs are a lot like humans.

Hierarchical Attribute List
present tense, two or more basic
attribute lists that introduce
subtopics

Basketball
Basketball is a sport that you play with a ball and
someone to play against. Usually it is played on a
wooden floor or concrete. You shoot the ball into
a basketball net that is held up by a long metal
post. The post has a flat piece of wood with a
square shape in the middle of the wood. If you
take more than three steps it is called traveling
and it is the other team's ball. There are four
types of shooting the ball. The first one is a set
shot. The second is a jump shot. Then a granny
shot and lay up shot. I think there are four
quarters in a game. In between each quarter is a
break that is called halftime. There is an
announcer that talks about the game.

Source: Adapted from Donovan, 2001.

using only initial letters to attempt to decode a word rather than using all of the word's letters. This ability emerges from experimenters' discovery of letter-sound relationships as well as from teachers' instruction.

Moving beyond this level of decoding depends on knowing where to look beyond the first letter. For example, consonant digraphs are comprised of two letters but represent only one phoneme (e.g., *th, sh, sch,* and *ng*). Similarly, most long vowels (such as the sound represented by *ay* in the word *way*) and many other vowels (such as the sound represented by *oo* in the word *foot*) are spelled with two letters. As they decode, children must quickly scan a word from left to right and determine which letters and letter combinations to pay attention to. The ability to sound out all of a word's letters into phonemes is called *fully phonemic decoding.*

Transitional readers move beyond merely noticing letters or letter combinations. They use familiar word parts to pronounce unknown words. Using known word parts to decode an unfamiliar word is called **orthographic reading** (Castles & Nation, 2008). This is based on an awareness of spelling principles, that certain letter patterns are always associated with particular pronunciations (Pressley, 2002). For example, knowing the word *sand* allows readers to use the word part *and* along with its pronunciation to decode many words including *stand, standard,* and *stranded,* among others. As children near the end of transitional reading, they have enough sight words to use dozens and even hundreds of familiar word parts to decode, in turn, hundreds of unfamiliar and fairly rare words seemingly automatically (Share, 1995). Thus, they are on their way to becoming self-generative readers who are able to learn more about decoding merely by reading. Still, self-generative readers do benefit from instruction (especially in spelling) about prefixes, suffixes, and other advanced level word characteristics. They are orthographic decoders and intuitively decide which groups of letters should be pronounced and blended to identify an unknown word.

Spelling

Conventional writers learn new invented spelling strategies, especially visual ones, that contribute to their becoming conventional spellers. As experimenters, they may have spelled the word *weight* as *yt* or *wt*. As early writers, they may spell *weight* as *wat*; as transitional writers, they may spell it *wayt* or *wate* before finally spelling the word conventionally. We have seen that experimenters' spellings are influenced merely by sound. Early readers and writers are also influenced by sound, especially as they achieve fully phonemic spelling (where an invented spelling includes a letter for nearly every phoneme in a word), but the hallmark of conventional writing is beginning to use new, more visual strategies for spelling.

Transitional writers' spellings are influenced by four visual factors: (1) knowledge of the standardized spellings of certain morphemes (*jumped* is spelled with an *ed* even though it sounds like *jumpt*); (2) an expectation of certain letters in certain contexts (for example, the *ight* sequence in *sight, might,* and *fight*)—the similar words that give rise to the expectation described in this second factor are called word families; (3) knowledge of spelling patterns for long vowel and other vowel pairs (*meat* is spelled with *ea,* whereas *meet* is spelled with *ee*); and (4) knowledge of consonant doubling (*stopping* includes the doubled *p*) and adding affixes (*re*start and place*ment*).

We now turn to three additional stages of invented spelling: later letter-name or later alphabetic spelling, within-a-word spelling, and syllable juncture spelling (Bear, Invernizzi, Templeton, & Johnston, 2008). These stages are presented in Table 5.1 (and follow the stages presented in Table 4.2 in Chapter 4). These stages of spelling continue considerably beyond the primary years we address in this book; however, we would expect a few second graders and some third and fourth graders to exhibit some of the characteristics of syllables-and-affix spelling.

TABLE 5.1   Stages of Spelling Development

Later Letter-Name or Later Alphabetic Spelling*

- Routinely represents one-to-one all salient sounds in a word (also called fully phonemic spelling) (e.g., *LadR* for *ladder*)
- Occasionally to routinely spells consonant blends and digraphs conventionally (e.g., *BREG* for *bridge*, *Thr* for *there*)
- Routinely uses word spaces
- Occasionally differentiates spellings of homophones, words that are pronounced the same but spelled differently (e.g., *to* and *two*, *for* and *four*)
- Routinely includes vowels

Within-a-Word Spelling*

- Routinely spells single-syllable short vowel words conventionally
- Occasionally to routinely spells *r*-controlled vowels conventionally in common single-syllable words (e.g., *star*, *her*)
- Routinely represents long vowel sounds and other vowel sounds using vowel markers (e.g., *GRATE* for *great*, *TEE* for *tea*, *TOOB* for *tube*) sometimes using conventional spellings
- Routinely spells nasals (e.g., *jump*) conventionally
- Routinely spells common morphemes (e.g., *ed, ing, s*) conventionally

Syllable Juncture Spelling*

- Occasionally to routinely uses consonant doubling at syllable junctures (e.g., *battle, riddle*)
- Occasionally to routinely uses consonant doubling when adding a suffix (e.g., *STOPPING* for *stopping*)
- Occasionally to routinely spells common prefixes and suffixes (e.g., *PICHER* for *pitcher*, *MOSHUN* for *motion*)
- Occasionally to routinely drops *e* when adding suffixes (e.g., *RIDDING* for *riding*)

*Adapted from Bear, Invernizzi, Templeton, and Johnston's (2008) stages with the same names.

Later Letter–Name or Later Alphabetic Spelling. Later letter-name or later alphabetic spelling marks the end of children's sole reliance on listening to sounds in words as a spelling strategy. In this stage, early writers can hear most salient phonemes in a word and assign a letter to spell that sound—they use fully phonemic spellings. Many of the spellings found in Figure 5.3 (grade 1) are representative of the later letter-name or later alphabetic spelling stage. The spelling of *come* (*cim*), for example, includes one letter for each of the three phonemes found in the word. All of the spellings include vowels, and two short vowel single-syllable words are spelled conventionally (*not* and *in*) as would also be expected at this stage. However, the spelling of the word *do* as *Diw* heralds the next spelling stage.

Within-a-Word Spelling. Within-a-word spelling is influenced by transitional writers' awareness of visual spelling patterns (how spellings look) as well as by their increasing store of known spellings. By now, nearly all single-syllable short vowel words are spelled conventionally as are consonant blends and digraphs. At this stage, children are aware that most long vowels and some other vowels require more than one vowel letter in their spelling. Thus, Kristen's spelling (in Figure 5.3) of the word *do* as *Diw* demonstrates her growing awareness of possible vowel spelling patterns. Many of Kristen's spellings in Figure 5.3 (grade 2) have characteristics representative of the within-a-word spelling stage. Her spelling of the words *eyes* (as *eiys*) and *shelf* (as *sefve*) reflects a use of a visual spelling strategy. That is, Kristen realizes that the word *eyes* has a *y* in it, so she first spells the long *i* phoneme with the letters *ei* and then adds the *y*. Similarly, Kristen is aware that the word *shelves* includes the letter *v*, so she spells the /f/ phoneme with the letter *f* and then adds the *v*. Notice her use of the final *e* visual pattern in the words *believe* (*bleve*) and *shelf* (*sefve*).

Syllable Juncture Spelling. Later in the transitional phase, writers begin to learn how consonant and vowel patterns work in multisyllabic words (words with more than one syllable) and what occurs when syllables join (Bear et al., 2008). At this stage of syllable juncture spelling, children learn how to join prefixes and suffixes to base words as well as spelling rules associated with adding suffixes to words (for example, when to drop an *e* or double a consonant). During the early parts of this stage, children confuse rules for adding suffixes; however, their spelling errors reveal their awareness of these spelling patterns.

FUNCTIONS

CONVENTIONAL READERS AND WRITERS have a keen awareness of audience. They have a more constant and pervasive realization that literacy involves creating meaning with someone else in mind, whether it is the author whose book they are reading, the intended reader of their writing, or the listener to whom they are reading. They understand that such meaning making is the single most important element of reading and writing.

One indication of children's increasing identification of themselves as authors who communicate with others is their willingness to use information and communication technologies (ICT), such as text messaging and instant messaging. They enjoy reading and writing during Internet projects such as those shown on the Internet Projects

Registry at www.globalschoolnet.org/gsh/pr/. These projects involve hundreds of children from around the world who complete a common task and register their results on a single Web site so that all children who participate can see all the results. Recently, elementary students have discovered electronic magazines or *e-zines* (Cohen & Meyer, 2004). For example, a group of second graders each wrote a zine on a topic of his or her choice and included a cover *dear reader* letter, poem, fiction story, nonfiction piece, word search, or picture search. The zines were published on the school Web site.

English Language Learners

In Chapter 3, we introduced early phases of oral language development of children acquiring a second language: preproduction when they are not yet speaking in English and early production when they rely on telegraphic speech and formulaic language (Hadaway, Vardell, & Young, 2002). Of course, children's ages at these stages depend on when they begin to acquire their second language. Nonetheless, in this chapter we describe the last two stages of English language acquisition because they represent a level of competence one might be more likely to encounter with the older children who are the focus of this chapter than with the younger children we focused on in earlier chapters.

Speech Emergence.   In the stage of **speech emergence,** children continue to acquire vocabulary, and they develop a wider range of sentence structures. As they learn more syntax during this phase of development, they may overgeneralize these syntactic rules, and so their use of grammatically incorrect sentences is to be expected. It is important to keep in mind that in order to make gains in English competence, children still need face-to-face interactions that include visual clues to meanings.

TECHNOLOGY TIE-IN

Following you will find some sites where children have produced stories or informational pieces in podcasts. Podcasts are audio recordings that can be posted to Web sites. Depending on how podcasts are made, they can be accompanied by text on the screen, by photographs or scanned-in pictures, or by video (see Technology Tie-In for Chapter 9 on how to make podcasts with children). The sites we have listed give good examples of how children read, write, and speak at a variety of grade levels during the early and transitional phases of conventional reading and writing. The last site presents several teachers in kindergarten and first grade who use podcasting daily with their children to support instruction.

http://secondgrade.podomatic.com
http://b-7bobcats.wikispaces.com
http://bobsprankle.com
http://conner.podbean.com
www.shambles.net/pages/learning/infolit/studentpod

Intermediate Fluency. The last stage of second language acquisition is **intermediate fluency.** This is the stage of language proficiency that native English-speaking children have when they enter kindergarten. Native English speakers at the age of five have acquired sufficient vocabulary and fluency with a variety of sentence structures that they are ready to acquire academic concepts in reading, writing, math, and science. In contrast, English language learners can spend nine months in the stage of preproduction, six months in early production, and up to one year in speech emergence before reaching the stage of intermediate fluency (Hadaway et al., 2002). Therefore, ELLs who learn English at home or in preschool have a head start over their peers who begin learning English only when they enter kindergarten.

Phonemic Awareness, Phonics, Vocabulary, Comprehension, and Fluency

Throughout this book, we use the categories *form, meaning, meaning-form links,* and *functions* to characterize young readers' and writers' understandings and competence. These categories are consistent with the National Reading Panel's (2000) identification of five elements of early reading achievement: phonemic awareness, phonics, vocabulary, comprehension, and fluency. We have demonstrated in Chapters 1 through 5 that

- Children acquire phonemic awareness.
- Children who have phonemic awareness learn to read, in part, due to such awareness.
- Children who have phonemic awareness learn to spell.
- Children learn phonics, a method for matching phonemes (sounds in spoken language) with graphemes (letters in written language).
- Children who know and use phonics principles pass through more advanced phases of reading and writing.
- Phonics is needed by all children of all social economic statuses and by English language learners.
- Phonemic awareness and phonics are critical during the experimenting, early, and transitional phases of reading and writing.
- Without phonemic awareness and phonics knowledge, children cannot enter into the experimenting phase of reading and will be hampered in rapid development as effective readers and writers.
- Phonemic awareness and phonics are not the only elements of reading and writing children need to know in order to move quickly and effectively through the phases of reading and writing development.
- Children's vocabulary increases and plays a critical role in language comprehension, both spoken and written.
- Children's metacognitive understandings about morphemes and grammar increase and play a critical role in reading and writing.
- Children gain fluency as they learn to monitor their reading and apply fix-up strategies.
- Children gain conscious awareness of reading and writing strategies that enhance their comprehension and composition of increasingly more complex text.

Thus, in Chapters 1 through 5, we have carefully focused on children and what they can learn to do when they are immersed in reading and writing in their homes and communities and when they are taught well. In the remainder of this book, we focus on the qualities of effective instruction that allow all children to develop the high levels of reading and writing described so far.

Assessing Children's Ability to Read Texts of Increasing Difficulty

ONE OF THE MOST IMPORTANT ASSESSMENTS that teachers can make as children enter the conventional reading phase is to monitor their progress reading and writing texts at increasingly more difficult levels with sufficient fluency and comprehension (Chapters 9 and 10 provide more information on a systematic approach to assessment in grade 1 and in grades 2 to 4). The first step in monitoring whether children are able to read text of increasing levels of difficulty is to determine children's instructional and independent reading levels. **Instructional reading level** is the level of text that children can read with support from their teacher. They can read most words (90 to 95 percent) correctly and, when asked questions, can answer most (70 to 90 percent) correctly. However, these texts are still challenging enough that teachers guide children as they read. **Independent reading level** is the level of text that children can read on their own. They read all or nearly all of the words (96 to 100 percent) correctly and, when asked questions, answer nearly all correctly (91 to 100 percent).

Over time, children's instructional and independent reading levels should increase. Traditionally, the progression of levels of difficulty at first grade included preprimer, primer, and then first grade, second grade, and so on. More recent concepts of levels of text difficulty have arisen from levels used in Reading Recovery instruction (Peterson, 1991). Reading Recovery includes many levels of difficulty; by the end of third grade, proficient readers would have progressed from level 1 to level 38, with levels 1 through 16 to 18 considered first-grade texts. Other leveling schemes use alphabet letters to indicate increasing difficulty (Fountas & Pinnell, 2010) and include levels A through Z, with levels A through I considered first-grade texts. Another way to level books is to use Lexile book measures. A Lexile book measure is a metric that takes into account the difficulty of a passage using measures of word frequency and sentence length. First-grade books are considered to be from 200 to 400 Lexile (200L to 400L).

Using Running Records to Determine Reading Levels

A **running record** is used to analyze children's reading; it provides information about children's use of strategic actions that children use on a particular level of text. Making a running record involves several steps. To begin, the teacher selects a text at a particular known difficulty level. For example, the teacher can select a short book on one of the Reading Recovery levels. One commercial assessment, *Developmental Reading Assessment 2* (Beaver, 2009), provides books at levels 1, 2, 3, 4, 6, 8, 10, 12, 14, 16, 18, 20, 24, 28, 30, 34, and 38. Or, teachers may select texts from a basal reading series at a particular difficulty level. Another alternative is to use texts found in an **individualized reading inventory,** a commercial assessment consisting of a collection of texts written at preprimer through middle school or even high school levels of difficulty.

Next, children read the text that has been selected. The teacher starts with a level of text that he or she believes a child can read with ease. As the child reads aloud, the teacher records miscues (or actions that children make as they read, usually substituting, rereading, omitting, inserting, or self-correcting). As the child reads, the teacher records all the student's actions either by marking on a copy of the text or by using checks and other symbols on a separate sheet of paper.

Figure 5.7 presents a copy of a text that Charlie read, *The Three Little Pigs.* This figure shows the teacher's marks on the text that indicate words that Charlie omitted—they are crossed out in text; words that he inserted—they are added above the text; words that he substituted—words substituted are written over the correct word in the text; and words that he self-corrected—*SC* is written beside a substitution over the correct word. The figure also shows the teacher's running record, which captures Charlie's omissions, insertions, substitutions, and self-corrections using marks on a blank sheet of paper.

Teachers then determine the child's accuracy rate, the percentage of words read correctly, by counting the total number of miscues or errors not including miscues that were self-corrected. The total number of miscues is subtracted from the total number of words in the passage to find the number of words read correctly. Finally, the number of words read correctly is divided by the total number of words in the passage. For example, Charlie read *The Three Little Pigs* passage with fourteen miscues including three self-corrected miscues for a total of eleven miscues. This number (11) is subtracted from the total number of words in the passage (181) to determine the number of words read correctly (170). The number of words read correctly is divided by the total number of words to reach the percentage of words read correctly—the accuracy rate. The accuracy rate for Charlie's reading of *The Three Little Pigs* is 93 percent. The accuracy rate is used to determine whether the text is on the independent, instructional, or frustrational reading level. Charlie's accuracy rate indicates that the passage *The Three Little Pigs* is at his instructional level.

The level of the text determines children's instructional reading level. For example, *The Three Little Pigs* text is approximately a first-grade level text (Level 13 to 14). Thus, Charlie's instructional reading level is first grade as far as word accuracy is concerned. The teacher would need to ask questions to determine whether Charlie comprehended the text at the instructional level as well and would have Charlie read even easier text to determine his independent reading level.

Using Questions to Analyze Comprehension and Vocabulary

Teachers need to assess children's comprehension and their understanding of vocabulary as a part of their determining a child's instructional or independent reading level. To assess a child's comprehension of a particular text, a teacher could ask questions. The questions can probe children's literal and inferential understanding of the text as well as their understanding of vocabulary meanings within the context of the text. Teachers can construct their own questions being sure to include those that can be answered with information directly stated in the text (literal) and those that require inferences (inferential) as well as those that ask for the meanings of words. When children

FIGURE 5.7 Running Record for *The Three Little Pigs*

TEXT: The Three Little Pigs

Once upon a time there were three pigs. Mother pig sent the
three^{sc} ... *said*^{sc} | sent

three little pigs out to make their way in the world. The first
the ... T

pig made a house of straw. The second pig made a house of
sticks

sticks. The third pig made a house of bricks. A wolf came to

the first pig's house and said, "I'll huff and puff and blow your

house down." The wolf blew the house down and the little pig ran
little

away fast. The wolf came to the second pig's house and said,

"I'll huff and puff and blow your house down." The wolf blew the
fast

house down but the little pig ran away faster. The wolf came to

the third pig's house and said, "I'll huff and puff and blow your
did ... *down*

house down." He blew and blew but could not blow down the house.
s T

He tried to sneak down the chimney but the pig put a big pot of

water on the fire. The wolf came down the chimney and burned his
fast^{sc}

tail. He ran away the fastest of all.

EXAMPLES:

child matches text	✓	
child substitutes	$\frac{child}{text}$	
child omits	$\frac{\bullet}{text}$	
child inserts	$\frac{child}{\bullet}$	
child repeats	⌐text	
child self-corrects	sc	
teacher prompts	T	

RUNNING RECORD

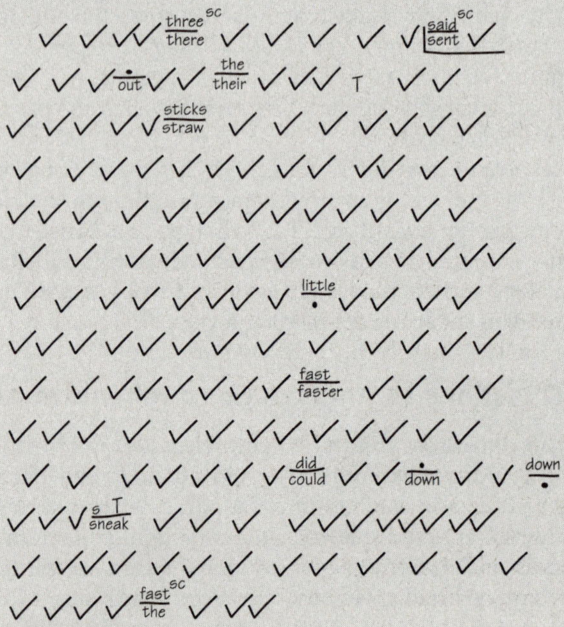

✓ ✓ ✓ $\frac{three}{there}$^{sc} ✓ ✓ ✓ ✓ ✓ $\frac{said}{sent}$^{sc} ✓

✓ ✓ ✓ $\frac{\bullet}{out}$ ✓ ✓ $\frac{the}{their}$ ✓ ✓ ✓ T ✓ ✓

✓ ✓ ✓ ✓ ✓ $\frac{sticks}{straw}$ ✓ ✓ ✓ ✓ ✓ ✓ ✓

✓ ✓ ✓ ✓ ✓ ✓ ✓ ✓ ✓ ✓ ✓ ✓ ✓

✓ ✓ ✓ ✓ ✓ ✓ ✓ ✓ ✓ ✓ ✓ ✓ ✓

✓ ✓ ✓ ✓ ✓ ✓ ✓ ✓ ✓ ✓ ✓ ✓

✓ ✓ ✓ ✓ ✓ ✓ $\frac{little}{\bullet}$ ✓ ✓ ✓ ✓

✓ ✓ ✓ ✓ ✓ ✓ ✓ ✓ ✓ ✓ ✓ ✓

✓ ✓ ✓ ✓ ✓ ✓ $\frac{fast}{faster}$ ✓ ✓ ✓

✓ ✓ ✓ ✓ ✓ ✓ ✓ ✓ ✓ ✓ ✓

✓ ✓ ✓ ✓ ✓ $\frac{did}{could}$ ✓ ✓ $\frac{\bullet}{down}$ ✓ ✓ $\frac{down}{\bullet}$

✓ ✓ ✓ $\frac{s\ T}{sneak}$ ✓ ✓ ✓ ✓ ✓ ✓ ✓ ✓ ✓

✓ ✓ ✓ ✓ ✓ ✓ ✓ ✓ ✓

✓ ✓ ✓ ✓ $\frac{fast}{the}$^{sc} ✓ ✓ ✓

can answer 70 to 90 percent of questions correctly, the passage is at their instructional level. When they can answer 91 percent or more of the questions correctly, the passage is at their independent level. For example, two questions at the literal level and two questions for the inferential level and a question about vocabulary for *The Three Little Pigs* passage are

- What did the three pigs use to make their houses? Straw, sticks, and bricks
- Why did the wolf run away from the third pig's house? He burned his tail
- Why did the wolf blow down the houses of the first two pigs? (He wanted to eat them, he wanted to get them)
- Why couldn't the wolf blow down the house of the third pig? (It was made of bricks and that made the house too strong)
- What does the word *sneak* mean? How is the word *sneak* used in the story? (try to do something that no one knows about, the wolf tried to get up on the roof without the third pig knowing about it so he could get in the house through the chimney)

Miscue Analysis

A **miscue analysis** provides information about children's use of the semantic cuing system (semantics), the syntactic cuing system (syntax), and the grapho-phonic cuing system (Goodman & Burke, 1972). To assist in a miscue analysis, teachers construct a miscue analysis chart. Figure 5.8 displays the miscue analysis for Charlie's reading of *The Three*

FIGURE 5.8 Miscue Analysis Chart for *The Three Little Pigs*

Child/Text	Semantically Acceptable	Syntactically Acceptable	Graphophonically same as B	M	E	Self-Corrects	Comments
three/there			✔			✔	*
said/sent			✔			✔	*
the/their		✔	✔				
sticks/straw		✔	✔				
fast/faster	✔		✔	✔			
did/could	✔	✔			✔		
fast/the						✔	*
s/sneak			✔				
	2/8	3/8	6/8	1/8	1/8	3/8	

*Sentence makes sense up to point of miscue.

Little Pigs. The teacher analyzes only substitutions to determine whether they are semantically acceptable (miscue has a meaning similar to that of the text word), syntactically acceptable (miscue is syntactically acceptable in the sentence and usually the same
part of speech), or graphophonically acceptable (miscue visually matches the text word
at the beginning, middle, or end). The teacher also records whether the miscue was self-
corrected.

According to the miscue analysis presented in Figure 5.8, one-fourth of Charlie's
miscues were semantically acceptable, and Charlie self-corrected three miscues. Three-
eighths of his miscues were syntactically acceptable. All the miscues except two had the
same beginning letters as the text word. According to this analysis, when Charlie has
difficulty, he attends especially to beginning letters, but also to semantics and syntax.

Using Running Records to Analyze Fluency and Strategy Use

Running records and miscue analyses can also be used to assess children's strategy
use (whether they are paying attention to meaning along with monitoring the letters in words, for example), their fluency, and their use of alphabetic or orthographic decoding skills. Slow, word-by-word reading indicates children are paying
too much attention to individual words rather than focusing on the meaning of
what they are reading. Fluent reading emerges when children know most of the
words they are reading by sight, when they can rapidly employ orthographic decoding strategies to identify unknown words quickly, and when their understanding is sufficient to allow them to read with intonation and phrasing that expresses
the meaning of the text.

Analyzing Children's Decoding Strategies

Children's miscues, or errors, in running records provide excellent resources for determining their knowledge and use of alphabetic and orthographic principles in decoding
(knowledge of sound-letter relationships, prefixes, suffixes, and familiar word parts).
Teachers examine children's miscues to conduct a decoding analysis. Here are Charlie's
errors in reading *The Three Little Pigs* passage.

Text	*Child*
three	there
said	sent
sticks	straw
fast	faster
did	could
fast	the
s-	sneak

In a decoding analysis of Charlie's miscues, his teacher noticed he nearly always
substituted a word with the same first consonant, blend, or digraph. However, he usually first guessed a word he knew with those letters rather than looking beyond those

letters into the middle or end of words or combining his letter sense with the evolving meaning. He did self-correct using meaning and structure.

Analyzing Spelling

To assess strategies in spelling, teachers can examine children's spellings in first draft compositions looking for emergent spellings, letter-name or alphabetic spellings, within-a-word spellings, and syllable juncture spellings (see Tables 4.2 and 5.1). Teachers can have children look at wordless books and write a story to accompany the illustrations. A more systematic approach is to use a **developmental spelling inventory.** A developmental spelling inventory is a list of words children are asked to spell. The list is purposefully designed so that many different spelling patterns are included. For example, one list (Johnston, Invernizzi, & Juel, 1998) intended for first graders includes ten words (*van, pet, rug, sad, plum, chip, shine, skate, float,* and *treat*) that have initial and final consonants, short vowels, blends and digraphs, and long vowel markers (p. 49). We recommend using the *Elementary Spelling Inventory* (Bear et al., 2008) and its accompanying *Feature Guide.* The *Feature Guide* allows teachers to record which spelling patterns children use correctly or misspell. Teachers can determine whether children consistently use, use but sometimes confuse, or do not use particular spelling patterns.

CHAPTER SUMMARY

THERE ARE THREE PHASES of conventional reading and writing: early, transitional, and self-generative. Conventional readers and writers are able to orchestrate several processes and control several strategies in extended episodes of writing or reading. They are aware of how well or how poorly their reading is going; they monitor their reading and use fix-up strategies when it goes poorly. Conventional readers' meaning making extends to being able to make interpretations and understand abstract literary elements, including point of view, symbol, and theme. They know the fine points of form at the word level in English; they have a conventional concept of word. They acquire sophisticated awareness of story form that comprises knowledge about setting, characters, plot, point of view, style, mood, and theme.

These children also gain a greater knowledge of text structure than they had as experimenters, especially knowledge of expository text. However, before writing fully developed stories or expositions, they produce approximations.

Conventional readers and writers have many new spelling strategies. They build on their previous understandings of what spelling is all about by adding multiple strategies for representing words in print, some using their earlier knowledge of sound-letter correspondences and some using visual information in new ways.

Conventional writers move through three stages of spelling: later letter-name or later alphabetic spelling, within-a-word spelling, and syllable juncture spelling.

It is critical that teachers monitor conventional readers' ability to read text of increasing difficulty. Teachers use grade-leveled texts selected from leveled text sets, assessment kits, or basal readers. Children read these aloud as teachers take running records, and then teachers ask questions about the texts. Later, teachers do miscue analyses and determine word-reading accuracy rates and levels of comprehension to know which texts are on children's independent and instructional reading levels. Teachers can analyze the kinds of decoding errors children make in running records and examine their information writing for expository text forms. Teachers also make assessments of children's spelling by examining their writing or using a developmental spelling assessment.

Figure 5.9 summarizes what conventional readers and writers know about written language meanings, forms, meaning-form links, and functions.

FIGURE 5.9 Summary: What Conventional Readers and Writers Know about Written Language Meanings, Forms, Meaning-Form Links, and Functions

Meaning Making
use metacognitive strategies to focus on meaning while reading, including monitoring that reading makes sense
use strategies for generating ideas during composing, including knowing the expectations of their audience
interpret literature and move toward interpretations at the abstract level, including point of view, theme, and symbol
use knowledge of abstract literary elements and style to compose stories and other literary texts

Forms
have fully developed concept of word
understand morphemes
develop an ever-increasing stock of sight words
know conventional spellings of an ever-increasing stock of words
use knowledge of literary elements in narratives to compose stories that include settings, characters, and some plot elements and that signal growing control over point of view, mood, and style
develop knowledge of how exposition is organized, using consistency, ordered relationships, and hierarchical relationships to compose gradually more organized expository texts

Meaning-Form Links
develop conventional spelling ability, including learning alternative spelling patterns, phonograms, and morphemes
use orthographic concepts to spell and to decode words in reading (decoding by analogy)

Functions
read and write to meet a variety of personal needs
read and write to join the classroom literate community

USING THE INFORMATION

Figure 5.10 presents a graphic organizer prepared to summarize the accomplishments of children in the conventional phases of early reading and writing and transitional reading and writing, with transitional further divided into earlier transitional and later transitional. Here is a set of terms that can be used to fill in this organizer. Place the terms on the graphic organizer under the appropriate phases of conventional reading and writing.

Uses alphabetic decoding	Reads preprimer- to end-of-first-grade level texts
Monitors, summarizes, and interprets	Uses orthographic decoding (syllables, affixes)
Predicts, confirms, and recalls literal ideas	Reads third-grade level texts or higher
Knows 300–400 high-frequency sight words	Is a later letter-name or later alphabetic speller
Makes high-level text approximations	Is a syllable juncture speller
Knows 400–2,000 sight words	Uses beginning orthographic decoding (word parts)
Reads second- to third-grade level texts	Infers abstract themes and uses strategies for fix-ups
Knows thousands of sight words	Writes with within-a-word spelling
Makes low-level text approximations	Makes moderate-level text approximations

FIGURE 5.10   Graphic Organizer for Conventional Reading and Writing

	Early Readers and Writers	*Earlier Transitional Readers and Writers*	*Later Transitional Readers and Writers*
Level of Text Read			
Sight Words			
Level of Decoding			
Comprehension Strategies			
Level of Narrative and Exposition Compositions			
Level of Spelling			

Applying the Information

In the following literacy event, a first grader writes a story and shares it with his classmates. Discuss what this event shows about understandings of written language meanings, forms, meaning-form links, and functions. Pay particular attention to his spellings and his narrative form.

Figure 5.11 displays Zachary's "whale story." He wrote this as a first draft on six sheets of paper. Later, he read his story aloud to his classmates as part of an author's circle (a gathering of students who listen to others read their compositions, give compliments, and ask questions): "Made and illustrated by Zachary. To my mom and dad. Once upon a time there were two whales. They liked to play. One day when the whales were playing, a hammerhead came along. They fought for a time. Finally it was finished and the whales won. And they lived happily ever after."

After Zachary read his composition, his classmates asked him several questions, including "What kind of whales are they?" "Where do they live—what ocean?" and "How did they win the fight?"

After listening to his classmates' questions, Zachary announced, "I am going to change my story by saying they lived in the Atlantic Ocean and they won the fight because they were bigger than the hammerhead and used their tails to defeat him."

Going Beyond the Text

Visit a third-grade classroom. Observe the class during a time devoted to reading or writing. Try to identify two children whose behaviors suggest conventional reading or writing. Interview them. Ask them what they do when they begin a new writing piece. What do they do to make a piece better? Ask how they choose a book to read for enjoyment. How do they begin a reading assignment for social studies or science class? Ask them if they would be willing to show you something they have written lately. Ask if they would read part of a book or tell about part of a book they are reading. Make a running record of the children's reading and analyze their writing samples.

FIGURE 5.11   Zachary's "Whale Story"

REFERENCES

Barone, D., Mallette, M., & Xu, S. (2005). *Teaching early literacy: Development, assessment and instruction*. New York: Guilford Press.

Bear, D. R., Invernizzi, M., Templeton, S., & Johnston, F. (2008). *Words their way: Word study for phonics, vocabulary, and spelling instruction* (4th ed.). Boston: Allyn & Bacon.

Beaver, J. (2009). *Developmental reading assessment 2*. Boston: Pearson.

Carlisle, J. F. (2004). Morphological processes that influence learning to read. In C. A. Stone, E. R. Silliman, B. J. Ehren, & K. Apel (Eds.), *Handbook of language and literacy: Development and disorders* (pp. 318–339). New York: Guilford Press.

Castles, A., & Nation, K. (2008). Learning to be a good orthographic reader. *Journal of Research in Reading, 31*(1), 1–7.

Catling, P. (1952). *The chocolate touch*. New York: William Morrow.

Cohen, B., & Meyer, R. (2004). The zine project: Writing with a personal perspective. *Language Arts, 82*, 129–138.

Curenton, S. M., & Lucas, T. D. (2007). Assessing young children's oral narrative skills: The story pyramid framework. In K. L. Pence (Ed.), *Assessment in emergent literacy* (pp. 377–427). San Diego, CA: Plural Publishing.

Donovan, C. (2001). Children's development and control of written story and informational genres: Insights from one elementary school. *Research in the Teaching of English, 35*, 394–447.

Eastman, P. (1961). *Go, dog. Go!* New York: Random House.

Fountas, I. C., & Pinnell, G. S. (2010). *The continuum of literacy learning, grades PreK-2: A guide to teaching*. Portsmouth, NH: Heinemann.

Freppon, P. (1991). Children's concepts of the nature and purpose of reading in different instructional settings. *Journal of Reading Behavior, 23*, 139–163.

Goodman, Y., & Burke, C. (1972). *The reading miscue inventory*. New York: Macmillan.

Hadaway, N. L., Vardell, S. M., & Young, T. A. (2002). *Literature-based instruction with English language learners, K–12*. Boston: Allyn & Bacon.

Johnston, F. R., Invernizzi, M., & Juel, C. (1998). *Book buddies: Guidelines for volunteer tutors of emergent and early readers*. New York: Guilford Press.

Kuo, L., & Anderson, R. C. (2006). Morphological awareness and learning to read: A cross-language perspective. *Educational Psychologist, 41*, 161–180.

Leland, C., Harste, J., & Huber, K. (2005). Out of the box: Critical literacy in a first-grade classroom. *Language Arts, 82*, 257–268.

Lobel, A. (1971). *Frog and Toad together*. New York: HarperCollins.

Lukens, R. (1995). *A critical handbook of children's literature* (5th ed.). Glenview, IL: Scott, Foresman/Little, Brown.

Moffett, J. (1968). *Teaching the universe of discourse*. Boston: Houghton Mifflin.

National Association for the Education of Young Children & International Reading Association (NAEYC/IRA). (1998). Learning to read and write: Developmentally appropriate practices for young children. *Young Children, 53*, 30–46.

National Reading Panel. (2000). *Teaching children to read: An evidence-based assessment of the scientific research literature on reading and its implications for reading instruction*. Reports of the subgroups. Washington, DC: National Institute of Child Health and Human Development.

Newkirk, T. (1987). The non-narrative writing of young children. *Research in the Teaching of English, 21*, 121–144.

Nunes, T., Bryant, P., & Bindman, M. (2006). The effects of learning to spell on children's awareness of morphology. *Reading and Writing: An Interdisciplinary Journal, 19*(7), 767–787.

Paris, S., Wasik, B., & Turner, J. (1991). The development of strategic readers. In R. Barr, M. Kamil, P. Mosenthal, & P. Pearson (Eds.), *Handbook of reading research* (2nd ed., pp. 609–640). New York: Longman.

Peterson, B. (1991). Selecting books for beginning readers. In D. DeFord, C. Lyons, & G. Pinnell (Eds.), *Bridges to literacy: Learning from Reading Recovery* (pp. 119–147). Portsmouth, NH: Heinemann.

Pressley, M. (2002). Comprehension strategies instruction: A turn-of-the-century status report. In C. Block & M. Pressley (Eds.), *Comprehension instruction: Research-based best practices* (pp. 11–27). New York: Guilford Press.

Ramirez, G., Chen, X., Geva, E., & Kiefer, H. (2010). Morphological awareness in Spanish-speaking English language learners: Within and cross-language effects on word reading. *Reading and Writing: An Interdisciplinary Journal, 23*(3–4), 337–358.

Rosenblatt, L. (1978). *The reader, the text, the poem: The transactional theory of the literary work.* Carbondale: Southern Illinois University Press.

Scott, C. M. (2004). Syntactic contributions to literacy learning. In C. A. Stone, E. R. Silliman, B. J. Ehren, & K. Apel (Eds.), *Handbook of language and literacy: Development and disorders* (pp. 340–362). New York: Guilford Press.

Share, D. (1995). Phonological recoding and self-teaching: Sine qua non of reading acquisition. *Cognition, 55,* 151–218.

Sinatra, G., Brown, K., & Reynolds, R. (2002). Implications of cognitive resource allocation for comprehension strategies instruction. In C. Block & M. Pressley (Eds.), *Comprehension instruction: Research-based best practices* (pp. 62–76). New York: Guilford Press.

Sipe, L. R. (2007). *Storytime: Young children's literary understanding in the classroom.* New York: Teachers College Press.

Tompkins, G., & McGee, L. M. (1993). *Teaching reading with literature: Case studies to action plans.* New York: Merrill/Macmillan.

Wollman-Bonilla, J. (2000). Teaching science writing to first graders: Genre learning and recontextualization. *Research in the Teaching of English, 35,* 35–65.

Wollman-Bonilla, J. (2001). Can first-grade writers demonstrate audience awareness? *Reading Research Quarterly, 36,* 184–201.

Woodson, J. (2001). *The other side.* New York: Putnam.

Yorinks, A. (1986). *Hey, Al.* New York: Farrar, Straus & Giroux.

PEARSON myeducationlab

Go to the topics Phonemic Awareness and Phonics, Writing Development, and Comprehension in the MyEducationLab (www.myeducationlab.com) for your course, where you can:

- Find learning outcomes for Phonemic Awareness and Phonics, Writing Development, and Comprehension along with the national standards that connect to these outcomes.
- Complete Assignments and Activities that can help you more deeply understand the chapter content.
- Examine challenging situations and cases presented in the IRIS Center Resources.

A+RISE

Go to the Topic A+RISE in the MyEducationLab (www.myeducationlab.com) for your course. A+RISE® Standards2Strategy™ is an innovative and interactive online resource that offers new teachers in grades K–12 just-in-time, research-based instructional strategies that:

- Meet the linguistic needs of ELLs as they learn content
- Differentiate instruction for all grades and abilities
- Offer reading and writing techniques, cooperative learning, use of linguistic and nonlinguistic representations, scaffolding, teacher modeling, higher order thinking, and alternative classroom ELL assessment
- Provide support to help teachers be effective through the integration of listening, speaking, reading, and writing along with the content curriculum
- Improve student achievement
- Are aligned to Common Core Elementary Language Arts standards (for the literacy strategies) and to English language proficiency standards in WIDA, Texas, California, and Florida.

CHAPTER

6

Literacy-Rich Classrooms

KEY CONCEPTS

Analytic Talk
Shared Reading
Modeled Writing
Shared Writing
Interactive Writing
Guided Reading
Dynamic Ability
    Grouping
Authentic Materials
Leveled Books

Curriculum
Multicultural Literature
Culturally Authentic
    Literature
Curriculum Integration
Literacy and Language
    Environmental
    Rating Scales
Indirect Instruction
Direct Instruction

Explicit Instruction
Gradual Release of
    Responsibility
Culturally Responsive
    Instruction
Screening Assessments
Monitoring
    Assessments
Response to
    Intervention (RTI)

Components of Language- and Literacy-Rich Classrooms

AN OLD ADAGE SUGGESTS THAT THE CLASSROOM is like a second teacher. A well-arranged classroom, where children know how to find materials they need and are responsible for caring for those materials and where teachers can put their fingertips on just the right books, magnetic letters, and whiteboards for the lesson at hand, supports optimal learning opportunities. But classroom environments are more than mere arrangements of furniture, collections of materials, and displays. Good classroom environments include a strong and supportive emotional climate along with high-quality instruction. Thus, the classroom environment includes a physical component (the arrangement of furniture, displays, and materials); a temporal component (the routine scheduling of various activities); and a social-interactive component (patterns of teacher-student and student-student interaction) (Reutzel & Jones, 2010). In this chapter, we describe classroom environments that research suggests accelerate children's language and literacy development. We call these environments *language- and print-rich classrooms* (Wolfersberger, Reutzel, Sudweeks, & Fawson, 2004).

One way to consider classroom environments is to describe the learners they produce. We argue that language- and literacy-rich classrooms will produce children who are reflective and motivated readers and writers who use literacy to learn more about themselves and the world in which they live. For example, four-year-olds who listen to their teacher read about the differences between tortoises and turtles to help identify the animal that one of them brought to school are reflective, motivated readers who use reading to find out more about their world.

Being reflective means that children are thinkers; they construct meanings for themselves and can use the thinking of others to modify those meanings. Reflective readers construct personal understandings from information books, poems, and stories. Their initial understandings are usually tentative and unfocused. Sharing such undeveloped understandings requires great risk taking. Reflective thinkers often modify their understandings given additional information from other books or from talking with their friends or teachers. Similarly, reflective writers compose personally meaningful stories, expositions, and poems, but they also take into account the needs and interests of their audience.

Being motivated means that children are self-directed, self-motivated (Guthrie, Wigfield, & Von Secker, 2000), and self-regulated (Perry, Hutchinson, & Thauberger, 2007). Many children, especially in the elementary grades, are expected to participate in reading and writing activities because the teacher tells them to, but motivated learners also participate in many activities because they choose to. Motivating activities have three characteristics (Morrow & Gambrell, 1998):

- They allow children some choices in materials and activities.
- They provide challenges but call on strategies previously modeled by the teacher.
- They require social collaboration.

Activities that create self-regulated learners add three more characteristics (Parsons, 2008):

- They require tasks that are authentic (are completed by people in their lives at home and work).
- They have a culminating end product.
- They require sustained work over several days.

Classrooms like these do not merely happen. They are well planned, and even when teachers do not have access to the latest materials or technology, when furniture is not optimal, and when funds are sadly lacking, creative teachers find a way to make classrooms fit the learning needs of their students. Good classroom environments begin as teachers consider the kinds of learning activities that will occur and the materials and spaces that are needed for these activities. As teachers consider these activities, the physical classroom environment is planned along with the daily schedule.

PLANNING FOR THE PHYSICAL ARRANGEMENT OF CLASSROOM AND DAILY SCHEDULE

THE PHYSICAL ENVIRONMENT OF A CLASSROOM matters and sets the stage for all learning that will occur in that space. Classrooms that are cluttered and dirty suggest that no one cares about what happens in them. Children and teachers are not likely to be motivated or energized in such settings. Classrooms arranged with desks in straight lines facing the front; with commercial materials on bulletin boards; and with displays of routine, fill-in-the-blank work by children are likely to be places where children have little choice, where all children are treated the same, and where teaching is viewed as merely telling children what to do. Students may be well managed in such classrooms, but neither they nor their teachers are likely to be reflective decision makers (Miller, 2008).

We suggest that teachers consider the following questions about the kinds of activities they will use when planning the physical arrangement of the classroom:

- Will I need a whole-group space? What will the children and I be doing in the whole-group space? Can the space double for another activity when it is not in use for the whole group?
- Will I need space to teach small groups or for small groups of children to meet? What will the children and I be doing in small-group lessons? How many children will routinely be using this space in one lesson?
- How will I provide tables or desks for individual children? Where will they keep their individual materials, books, and supplies? Will I be able to use these tables for other purposes at other times during the day? What will children be doing at their individual spaces and how do I want them to interact together?
- Will I need spaces for centers or workstations, where groups of children will be interacting with materials independently for a variety of purposes? How many will I need and for what purposes?

- Will I need a separate space for a classroom library, a writing center, or a computer center? Will I need a separate space for math, social studies, or science materials?

Teachers in preschool or in the elementary school may answer these questions very differently; thus, their classrooms would be arranged differently. One way to begin making decisions about the classroom spaces, materials, displays, and schedule is to divide a paper into three columns. In the first column, write down all the whole-group activities that you anticipate will occur in your classroom. In the second column, write all the small-group activities; and in the third, write the kinds of things children will be doing individually or in pairs. For example, a Head Start teacher brainstormed the whole-group activities she thought she would use during the year (reading aloud a variety of books, big books, and charts of poems or songs; engaging in drama; doing movement and music activities; creating shared writing charts; talking with children about issues and providing new information; and playing games to reinforce concepts about letters, words, or sounds). She brainstormed two small-group activities: language and literacy lessons, and math and science lessons, which might include art and cooking. Finally, she knew her children would self-select center activities. In contrast, a third-grade teacher decided she would be reading aloud, conducting mini-lessons, and teaching lessons in whole group. She would have a large variety of small groups that would be directed sometimes by her and sometimes by children: reading groups, book clubs, revision and editing groups, inquiry groups exploring science and social studies topics, and spelling groups. Children would work independently or in pairs on practice activities and assigned individual work.

Whole-Class Literacy Routines

Whole-class instruction builds a sense of community and is intended to introduce all children to new strategies and information. At least five instructional activities occur routinely during whole-class instruction in language- and literacy-rich classrooms.

Reading Aloud. Reading aloud daily to children accelerates their literacy development (Mol, Bus, & de Jong, 2009). Children are more motivated to read on their own and have better vocabularies and comprehension when they are in classrooms in which teachers frequently read aloud, model good comprehension strategies, and draw attention to sophisticated vocabulary (Dickinson, 2001). The effects of read-alouds on children's vocabulary development is especially pronounced for children who enter preschools with low levels of vocabulary (Connor, Morrison, Slominski, 2006). The most effective read-alouds are those that prompt children to engage in analytic talk (Dickinson & Smith, 1994; Sipe, 2002). **Analytic talk** occurs when children and the teacher discuss events that go beyond the literal meaning presented in the text or illustrations. For example, analytic talk occurs when children infer character traits and motivations, elaborate on problems, connect events across parts of a book, detect cause-and-effect relationships, and construct explanations for why characters act as they do. In the elementary grades, children's analytic thinking is used as they search for the "big ideas" that are evolving and highly abstract statements of theme (Miller, 2008).

Six characteristics of effective read-alouds maximize children's use of analytic talk and discovery of the big ideas (adapted from McGee & Schickedanz, 2007).

- Before reading, teachers provide short introductions that either identify a storybook's main character and hint about the problem that character will encounter or introduce information about a book's topic and organizational scheme. These introductions allow children to call to mind prior knowledge related to the book they will listen to.
- While they read, teachers make comments that model analytic thinking or demonstrate how they made an inference, or are beginning to have a hypothesis about what this book is really about. These demonstrations provide examples for children about how they should think.
- While they read, teachers ask a few questions that help children to recall what has happened so far and then to think analytically. These questions promote discussion that includes extended analytic talk and focuses attention on inferences, elaborations, and hypotheses.
- While they read, teachers highlight the meaning of a few sophisticated vocabulary words by slipping in short defining phrases. These definitions help children comprehend the story more fully.
- After they read, teachers ask broad, open-ended questions that call for rich explanation.
- Teachers read some books at least three times. As a book becomes more familiar, even shy children are more willing to make comments, and other children notice details they missed during a first read.

Teachers can also tell stories and help children to dramatize and tell stories using storytelling props (McGee, 2003). Among the many kinds of literature props that teachers can use to dramatize a story are line drawings of characters' faces copied on cardstock. Each child can hold the character he or she will be dramatizing (such as the troll or little billy goat) as the whole group dramatizes the story. Children have many creative ideas for constructing their own drama and retelling props. First graders used a green pipe cleaner for a caterpillar and punched holes in construction paper food cutouts to retell *The Very Hungry Caterpillar* (Carle, 1979). As they retold the story, they slipped each food cutout onto the green, pipe-cleaner caterpillar. Third graders worked together to decide the number and content of pictures needed to retell *Nine-in-One. Grr! Grr!* (Xiong, 1989). As they retold the story, children clipped their pictures on a story clothesline (a clothesline strung between two chairs).

It is important that teachers select information books for reading aloud to children (Richgels, 2002). Many teachers do not choose information books, and they are not as plentiful in most elementary classrooms (Duke, 2000; Yopp & Yopp, 2006) and preschools (Pentimonti, Zucker, Justice, & Kaderavek, 2010). However, many children prefer information books over storybooks (Chapman, Filipenko, McTavish, & Shapiro, 2007), and discussions of information books can be especially lively and thought provoking (Smolkin, McTigue, & Donovan, 2008). Even preschoolers use more abstract thinking and more sophisticated vocabulary when talking about nonfiction books as they are read aloud (Price, van Kleeck, & Huberty, 2009).

Shared Reading.　**Shared reading** is a form of reading aloud in which children chant the words along with the teacher (they share the reading) as they view enlarged text. This style of reading has a dual focus: for enjoyment and teaching concepts about print (Parkes, 2000) or other skills such as using context to determine the meaning of a vocabulary word or reading to discover character traits. During shared reading, teachers read from *big books,* which are large versions of published children's books, or from texts written on chart paper or projected onto a screen. Books, poems, and texts used in shared reading in preschool and kindergarten are usually very easy to understand and frequently use repetition. Children naturally catch on to the repeated language and spontaneously begin reading along with teachers.

For older children, teachers may share a portion of a longer, more complex text, using an overhead projector or projection on a Smart Board. As they read the text aloud, teachers might help children to make inferences about character motivation and character traits by stopping and asking, "What do you think this character is thinking right now? What gives us a clue?"

Modeled Writing, Shared Writing, and Interactive Writing.　**Modeled writing** occurs when teachers compose a text as children watch. The teacher first thinks aloud about what he or she might write, then talks through the composition process of selecting the words to write. The teacher then thinks aloud while rereading and revising the text. Thus, modeled writing demonstrates for children the processes writers use before, during, and after writing. Teachers also use modeled writing to introduce children to the characteristics of text genres. For example, a teacher might demonstrate writing a *shape poem,* that is, a poem whose shape is a critical feature, for example, a poem about birds whose words are arranged in the shape of a bird.

Shared writing occurs when the teacher invites children to contribute to the ideas to be written. For example, after reading many versions of *Henny Penny,* a group of children compose their own version. The teacher asks children to contribute their ideas for the text as the teacher writes. Later, this text can be reread and revised and finally typed so each child can make an illustration for it. The children's work can be bound as a book for the classroom library.

Interactive writing occurs when the teacher goes beyond shared writing by inviting children not only to contribute ideas but also to take the pen or marker and form letters, words, phrases, or sentences. Interactive writing provides practice deciding which words to use while composing, applying letter-sound knowledge, and using spelling patterns.

Letter-Word-Sound Workshop or Word Work.　Preschoolers receive instruction in recognizing the alphabet and developing phonemic awareness. Kindergarten and primary-grade students receive daily instruction that focuses on decoding and spelling words. Older elementary schoolchildren continue to learn about abstract spelling patterns such as recognizing prefixes and suffixes. All these activities occur during small-group instruction targeted at specific needs of children. However, teachers may also provide a daily letter-sound-word workshop or word work as part of whole-class instruction (Cunningham, 2004). For example, in preschool, children might play the Mystery Letter game with their teacher (Schickedanz, 2003). The teacher writes the first stroke of a particular alphabet letter, such as the vertical line used to write the capital letter *L.*

The children take turns guessing which letter it could be until someone guesses the correct letter. In kindergarten, the teacher might use magnetic letters to spell a familiar rhyming word on a magnetic board. Children are invited to step up to the board and select letters to spell a new word. In second grade, children might be asked to step up to an overhead projector that displays words with the letters *ea*, some with a short *e* sound (e.g., *bread*) and some with a long *e* sound (e.g., *team*); they are asked to circle the long-*e* words. In fourth grade, students might practice adding *ing* to words in which the final consonant is doubled or the final *e* is dropped.

Small-Group Literacy Instruction

One of the most important daily literacy routines is small-group instruction in reading (Pinnell & Fountas, 1996). All children need daily small-group reading instruction tailored to their levels of development. Small-group instruction is when teachers help children learn at their very cutting edge of performance. Even in preschool, small-group instruction is critical. Children learn more about the foundational concepts of literacy—alphabet letter recognition, phonemic awareness, and the alphabetic principle—when they are included in small-group lessons (Connor et al., 2006). Beginning in kindergarten, children are grouped—and regrouped as the pace of their growth demands—with other children who are at similar points in their literacy development (Diller, 2007). Therefore, small-group instruction provides all learners, even struggling readers and writers, with just the right support they need to take next steps in learning (Allington, 2008).

As children begin formal reading instruction, small-group reading instruction often includes guided reading. **Guided reading** occurs when teachers select a particular text that is moderately challenging for a particular group of children to read, then guide and support children as they read that text (Schulman & Payne, 2000). With guidance, children gradually read more difficult texts.

Children selected for guided-reading groups are usually called *small, dynamic ability groups* (Fountas & Pinnell, 1996). In **dynamic ability grouping,** a small number of children who have similar reading abilities are selected to read together. Texts are carefully selected to match the needs of the small group of readers. Teachers read twenty to thirty minutes with the small group of readers at least four times per week. However, many teachers meet twice daily with some small groups of children who are struggling to make progress.

Independent Practice

All children need extended practice reading and writing (Allington, 2005). Practice activities are not merely to keep children busy so that the teacher can meet with small groups for instruction. Rather, they are carefully considered to provide children with extensive opportunities to explore new materials or to consolidate strategies and skills that have just been taught. In preschool, centers (small partitioned areas of the classroom devoted to specific types of play such as the blocks center) can provide children with valuable learning opportunities such as engaging in extended conversations with other children and the teacher to solve problems and to negotiate new roles. Highly effective preschool teachers also place materials they have recently used in small-group instruction in centers and invite children to use those materials. This provides opportunities for children to practice newly learned skills alone or with other children and for teachers to provide additional feedback and support (Casbergue, McGee, & Bedford, 2008).

Daily independent practice reading and writing allows students to maximize the volume of their reading and writing (Allington, 2005). Volume of reading and writing can be determined either by calculating the amount of text read or written in a day or by counting the number of minutes in a day spent reading and writing continuous texts (not working with words, filling in work sheets, or answering questions). In elementary school, good readers spend more than an hour reading at school and home daily. Poor readers spend less than ten minutes a day reading at home and probably no more than that amount in school (Taylor, Frye, & Maruyama, 1990). A good rule of thumb is that all elementary students should read texts for thirty minutes in school and thirty minutes at home. A summary of whole-group, small-group, and independent activities is provided in Figure 6.1.

FIGURE 6.1 Summary of Whole-Group, Small-Group, and Independent-Practice Activities

Whole-Group Activities	Read aloud	Teacher reads picture storybook or nonfiction aloud to children, interspersing questions or demonstrating how to think.
	Shared reading	Teacher reads from a big book or a chart with enlarged print inviting children to read aloud often in choral reading.
	Drama	The children dramatize a favorite, well-known story by saying a character's part. More than one child may say each character's part, and they speak in unison.
	Movement and music	The children chant poems or sing songs often presented on charts and often accompanied by movement (these reinforce concepts such as rhyme or letter names and sounds).
	Mini-lessons	Teachers provide direct instruction in a strategy in reading or writing such as how a character is revealed by what they say or how writers use vivid verbs.

FIGURE 6.1 continued

	Letters/words/ sounds (word work)	Teachers provide instruction in alphabet letter names or sounds, in concepts about print, or phonics or spelling patterns and their use.
	Shared writing	Preschool and kindergarten children provide suggestions for content to write in short lists, graphic organizers, or other text forms on large chart paper. Sometimes children can write portions of the message on the chart in interactive writing.
	Modeled writing	Teachers model how to write particular text genre, select words for effect, or how to revise on large charts. Children may make suggestions as the teacher writes. Usually occurs during writing mini-lessons.
Small-Group Activities	Language and literacy small-group lessons	Preschool and kindergarten teachers provide direct instruction in foundational language and literacy skills
	Differentiated small-group reading lessons (guided reading)	Teachers group children with similar reading levels and needs to provide direct instruction in reading texts.
	Writing groups (revising, editing)	Teachers group children with similar problems in writing in order to provide target instruction.
Individual or Paired Activities	Centers	Preschool children work in designated spaces in the classroom such as a housekeeping dramatic play center, a blocks center, or a writing center.
	Workstations	Teachers use specific locations in which they place particular activities for children to accomplish with a partner or alone—usually used when the teacher is teaching small-group lessons.

DAILY SCHEDULE DICTATES ROOM ARRANGEMENT

AFTER TEACHERS HAVE BRAINSTORMED the types of whole group, small group, and individual activities that will occur in their classrooms, they begin to consider the time each of these activities needs. For example, in elementary school, teachers are often required to devote 90 minutes to reading instruction alone, and in preschool most programs require at least 60 minutes for center activities and 30 minutes for outdoor play.

The activities and daily schedule dictate what the actual classroom physical layout will look like. For example, both the Head Start teacher and the third-grade teacher would need a carpeted area for their whole-group activities that is large enough to comfortably seat all the children. This area would need a chair, an easel on which to place big books and chart paper, and storage bins to house teaching materials used at the easel. In the Head Start classroom, the whole-group area would need to be large enough for children and teachers to move around and not merely sit. The teacher would need access to a tape player and rhythm instruments for music and movement activities. In the third-grade classroom, the teacher will need bulletin boards or display spaces clearly visible to the whole-group area to hang summary charts of learning, or important reminders of instructional practices produced as a part of whole-group lessons.

Preschool teachers have need for areas for small-group instruction. In some preschools, the teacher and teaching assistant each take half of the children at the same time to teach a small-group lesson. If this was the plan, then the classroom would need at least two tables large enough to sit eight to ten children and the teacher during small-group time. The whole-group carpet could also be used for small-group activities, but often teachers need tables to better support children during drawing, writing, or other art activities. Other preschool teachers teach much smaller groups of children while the other children are engaged in other activities or in centers. In this case, only one small table may be needed for small-group instruction. Most elementary teachers have at least one small-group area for reading and writing small-group lessons. This space must be large enough for at least six children and the teacher and have ample storage space, display area, and an easel to hold chart paper. Some elementary teachers place at least two other small tables around the room that are not assigned seating for children. These may be part of workstations or centers and may also be used for small groups of children working together on projects.

Centers or Workstations

In addition to space for whole- and small-group lessons, language- and literacy-rich early childhood classrooms include a variety of small partitioned spaces that are used for specific purposes (Reutzel & Jones, 2010). Typically, preschools are divided into six to eight centers. Typical preschool classrooms will include a library center, a computer center, an art center, a writing center, a center for housekeeping and other dramatic play, a block center, a center for puzzles and other manipulatives, and a special center for theme-related activities (Smith, Brady, & Anastasopoulous, 2008). Other centers include a woodworking workbench and sand or water table. In order to prompt children to engage in reading and writing and extend children's opportunities for literacy learning, many centers besides the library, computer, and writing centers are stocked with materials that prompt children to engage in reading and writing (Roskos & Neuman, 2001; Vukelich, 1994). For every center, teachers supply not just materials typical of that center but also reading and writing props that are related to those typical materials, and related storybooks and information books.

For example, if children were studying light and shadow, then the science center might include a collection of flashlights that children can take apart and reassemble and use in shadow experiments. It might include objects such as stuffed animals and kitchen utensils to use in shadow experiments. This center might include a display of a labeled drawing of the parts of a flashlight created by the teacher and a poster that challenges children to identify the animal or object that created variously shaped shadows. Also displayed might be a chart giving directions on how to make two hand shadows. The teacher might provide several clipboards and booklets made of blank paper stapled together, with a typed title page saying *Scientist's Journal.* Other sheets with the title *Labeled Drawings of a Flashlight* and *Shadow Shapes I Made* might be provided in trays along with a can of pens, pencils, and markers. The center might also include books about shadows such as *Nothing Sticks Like a Shadow* (Tompert, 1988) and *What Makes a Shadow?* (Bulla, 1994).

Elementary school classrooms are typically not center-based like preschool classrooms. They may have a library and listening center, a computer center, and several literacy workstations (Diller, 2003), classroom spaces that are designated for children's individual use of materials previously used for group instruction. Materials placed in workstations are intended to promote children's meaningful practice of reading and writing strategies independent of the teacher. Typically elementary students spend time in workstations while the teacher is conducting small-group lessons. For example, a third-grade teacher planned to use the listening center as a workstation to practice comprehension work about the storybook *Blueberries for Sal* (McCloskey, 1976). The teacher placed two copies of the book and blank sheets of paper with directions for folding a sheet into four parts, drawing in one part a picture of the book's main character, writing in a second part three sentences about the character's problem, and writing in the remaining two parts an explanation of two ways that the character tried to solve the problem. The children had been carefully prepared to participate in this workstation activity during a previous whole-group lesson.

During morning whole-group time, the teacher had read *Blueberries for Sal* aloud to the whole class. She told the children the two main characters' names and asked them to be thinking about these characters' problems as they listened. While reading, she makes comments about what each main character is thinking and pauses to say, "You know, I think I just read a hint about one of the problems. Did anybody else get an idea about what the problem might be?" After discussing the problem, the teacher says, "Now that we know the problem that both Sal and the little bear had, we have to listen to find out how each of them solves that problem." After reading, the teacher has children recall several ways the characters attempted to solve the problem. Next, she demonstrates on a large sheet of chart paper hung on the easel how to divide the paper into four parts. She draws a sketch of two of the main characters in the first portion of the paper and then invites children to compose sentences telling the problem. Next, the teacher elicits from the children their recollections of at least two ways the main characters tried to solve the problem and writes these on the remaining portions of the chart. After the four-part chart is completed, the teacher announces, "Now I am going to hang this chart in the listening center to remind you what you will be doing there this week. In the listening center, you will listen to the story again; then, as workstation work, you will make your own four-part story chart." Later, the teacher might stock the listening center with an incomplete version of the same four-part chart and an unfamiliar storybook in order to see how well children can infer problems and solutions on their own and to determine who needs small-group instruction in this comprehension strategy.

In order to be effective in helping children practice what they have learned in whole- or small-group lessons, workstations should be large enough for two children to work together, and some stations may be large enough for up to four children. When there are many workstations in a classroom, and only two children in each station, teachers have found children are more on task and speak in quieter tones of voice, which is important as teachers are conducting small-group lessons (Diller, 2003). Figure 6.2 presents a list of possible literacy workstations that can be included in primary-grade classrooms. This list includes an example of one activity that might be placed in each of the centers. However, it is critical to keep in mind that all materials placed in literacy workstations are first used in small- or whole-class activities to teach children concepts or strategies that they need. Workstations provide an important opportunity for children to practice and gain fluency in reading and writing activities introduced by the teacher.

Of particular importance in language- and literacy-rich classrooms are the spaces that house the library center, writing center, computer center, and preschool/kindergarten dramatic play centers. Research has demonstrated that if these centers are well designed, they are more likely to attract children and children are more likely to stay on task for longer periods of time. That is, in addition to materials placed in these centers when they serve as literacy workstations, these centers have literacy materials for children to use during free-choice times.

Library Center

Children spend more time reading when their classrooms' libraries are well designed and stocked with an abundance and variety of reading materials than when their classroom libraries are cramped and poorly stocked (Morrow, 1997; Morrow & Weinstein, 1986; Neuman, 1999). All classrooms need a well-designed and well-stocked library. There are seven requirements of well-designed library centers and four additional, optional characteristics (adapted from Fractor, Woodruff, Martinez, & Teale, 1993; Morrow & Weinstein, 1986). Well-designed classroom libraries

- are large enough for as many as six children and the teacher.
- are partitioned off from the rest of the classroom with bookshelves or other dividers.
- have an abundance and variety of books (the number of books should be at least five times the number of children in the classroom).
- have at least one bookshelf on which book covers can be displayed facing outward.
- have additional shelving for other books.

FIGURE 6.2   Literacy Workstations and Suggested Materials

Listening

Book, audiocassette, and paper labeled *"beginning"* on the front and *"end"* on the back

Overhead

Overhead projector, transparent film with the letters *at*, transparent film with the letters *b, c, f, h, m, p, r, s, v , br, fl,* and *spl*

Writing

Red and yellow paper to cut in the shape of an apple for writing apple shape poems, collection of books about apples

Library

Books in tubs with colors indicating levels, book summary forms (which include a blank space for the title of the book, a place to circle if it is a story or information book, and a box titled *What I liked about this book*)

Retelling

Three books and three sets of props to retell each book

Word-Letter-Sound

Words written on cards for sorting into *ow* like *snow* and *ow* like *owl*

Pocket Chart

Favorite poem about snow cut up into words, a copy of the poem in an envelope for checking

Big Book

Collection of big books and a Big Book Summary Form (same as in library center)

Computer

Directions for how to get to a particular Web site for gathering information about acorns

Discovery

Directions for how to make a Halloween snack in the shape of a witch's hat, a digital camera for taking pictures of each step, including eating and enjoying the snack

- use a method of organization, such as using baskets or crates to separate books by theme or content, level of difficulty, author, or by whether the books are fiction or nonfiction.
- have soft seating.
- may include storytelling props, such as cutout pictures of characters stapled on straws or small objects related to events in a particular book.
- may include a listening center with books, audiocassettes or CDs of the books, tape players or CD players, and headphones.
- may include a special basket for the "read-aloud of the day."
- may include displays of books and related objects for children to play with as they look at those books.

Writing Center

All classrooms need a well-designed writing center. This center serves as a place for children to practice writing strategies learned during instruction and to test out personal hypotheses (Rowe, 1994). Well-designed writing centers

- are spaces devoted only to writing, not serving also as, for example, an art center.
- include a table and chairs that can accommodate comfortably up to four children and the teacher.
- have ample storage space, for example, a shelf or a rolling cart, for writing tools and other materials such as clipboards.
- include a variety of writing tools and writing surfaces and book-binding materials.
- display models of the teacher's writing, such as restaurant menus, thank-you letters, or story compositions.
- display children's writing.
- have writing reference materials, such as charts showing alphabet letters, letter-sound association charts with pictures for each letter sound, word cards related to content areas of study, and picture dictionaries.
- may include picture cards to prompt writing ideas and to give directions for writing particular genres or for completing other activities teachers assign for the writing center.

Computer Centers

All classrooms need a computer center with one or more computers, a printer, and a scanner. Digital cameras and a video camera may also be housed in this center. Even young children develop unique concepts related to the multiple ways in which literacy is used and created digitally (Labbo, 1996). The computer center also fosters children's social interactions as they learn from one another. Well-designed computer centers

- are placed in a central space to encourage movement to and from other centers.
- are large enough for at least three children to work at a single computer.
- have sufficient space around the computers so that children can bring stuffed animals or other props to use in computer play in preschool or kindergarten, and for paper for recording information in the elementary grades. For example, preschoolers might bring to the center a stuffed character related to a CD-ROM book they are viewing and fourth graders may bring a specially designed graphic organizer for gathering information from various Web sites.
- display computer-generated work by the teacher and by children—for example, checks created for pretend shopping in a housekeeping play center or menus created for a restaurant dramatic play area, or a completed graphic organizer.
- have a *Helpful Hints* poster that explains computer operations with easily interpreted icons—for example, how to use the paint brush or pencil (adapted from Labbo & Ash, 1998) and how to download digital photographs.
- use a variety of software programs, including a word-processing program, such as Word (produced by Microsoft), a graphics program such as KidPix (produced by Broderbund), CD-ROM books (e.g., *Arthur's Adventures with DW* produced by The Learning Company), and games (e.g., *Alphabet Express* produced by School Zone).

Displays in Language- and Literacy-Rich Classrooms

Classroom displays include materials placed on walls, shelves, or bulletin boards (Jeong, Gaffney, & Choi, 2010). Displays should highlight the reading and writing accomplishments of all children, whatever their writing abilities, and should include materials produced by the teacher with children (Casbergue et al., 2008). Teachers should change displays frequently in order to maintain children's motivation to write and to acknowledge continually developing writing behaviors. As teachers coordinate displays of shared writing; interactive pocket charts; and directions with changing science, social studies, art, music, and mathematics content, they keep the classroom environment fresh and interesting for their students. Notice that these examples of print displays include texts with a variety of text formats and content and use a variety of language from a few words to many words.

Another important purpose for classroom displays is to make children's thinking and learning visible (Miller, 2008). As children think aloud about a storybook the teacher is reading aloud, the teacher may record (in their words) what children are hypothesizing about the meaning of the story. As children's hypotheses change, the teacher again records the new thinking and why they have changed their hypotheses. Later, the teacher records these ideas on a chart, which serves to show children their own thinking in action. Across time, such charts allow visitors to see the learning trajectory of a group of students.

MATERIALS

MATERIALS IN A LANGUAGE- AND LITERACY-RICH CLASSROOM are abundant, varied, authentic, accessible, and located near where they are most likely to be used (Roskos & Neuman, 2001). Children need enough books and other reading materials, writing tools and surfaces, and reference materials to meet their various developmental levels, interests, and instructional needs. Because children will not all be reading and writing at the same level, teachers need a variety of materials to meet these needs. In addition to textbooks, children need **authentic materials,** which are used for instructional purposes but also serve real-world purposes outside of school (Duke & Purcell-Gates, 2003). These are books, such as reference books (dictionaries, thesauruses, encyclopedias), telephone books, catalogs, children's information books and storybooks, and such other traditional reading materials as newspapers and magazines. Environmental print items, such as maps, calendars, videotapes, and DVDs, are also authentic materials.

Children should know where to locate materials and be responsible for returning them when finished. The most efficient storage places are near where children are likely to use the materials. Preschool children are more likely to write when pencils and markers are stored in the block center near catalogs of building supplies and clipboards with lumber orders than when pencils and markers are kept only in one central location. In primary grades, children need erasable markers in the overhead-projector workstation and crayons and pencils in the listening workstation. Teachers can use the first few weeks of school to teach children routines for entering centers or workstations and for using materials found in these locations (Morrow, Reutzel, & Casey, 2005).

Children's Literature

Research confirms that the amount of experience children have with literature correlates with their language development reading achievement, and quality of writing. Children who are exposed to quality literature are more likely to learn to love literature and to include reading quality books as an important part of their lives. They are more willing to sustain their involvement with a book through writing, doing projects, and participating in discussions (Eeds & Wells, 1989). Research has also shown that children whose classrooms have a large number of books in a high-quality library center choose to read more often (Morrow & Weinstein, 1986) and have higher reading achievement (Morrow, 1992).

The process of locating a sufficient number of quality books can be daunting. Experts recommend that the number of books in a high-quality classroom collection should be eight to ten times the number of children (Fractor et al., 1993). Teachers can borrow books from local and school libraries, use bonus points from book clubs to obtain free books, and collect inexpensive books from book clubs and bookstores that offer educational discounts.

The classroom literature collection should include books from a variety of genres. Figure 6.3 presents genres of literature, their defining characteristics, and an example book for each. Figure 6.3 also includes three special kinds of picture books: wordless picture books, predictable books, and alphabet books. These books are especially enjoyable for young children from preschool through the elementary grades. They play critical roles in teaching children comprehension strategies, phonemic awareness, letter-sound knowledge, and sight words. Also included in Figure 6.3 are various reference materials.

In addition to providing books from a wide variety of genres, teachers must make sure that children have access to texts of various difficulty levels. Each page in some books will have only one or two words or a simple sentence. Other books' pages will have several lines of text and be considered easy-reading books. Finally, some books will have text that is organized in paragraphs and uses sophisticated vocabulary.

Teachers will also need sets of **leveled books.** These are calibrated and labeled by level of difficulty, from very easy, beginning-level books to middle-school-level texts. Many commercial companies sell sets of storybooks and nonfiction books at identified levels (Fountas & Pinnell, 2009). These texts are usually used in reading instruction and for reading practice during workstation activities.

DVDs and videos also present valuable information to children. Teachers can collect videos of children's stories and information books or informational television programs. Finally, language- and literacy-rich classrooms are stocked with children's magazines. Many magazines extend children's interest in science and social studies and provide examples of published writing by children.

Materials for Writing

Writing materials are located throughout the classroom, in centers and workstations, in whole-class and small-group instruction areas, and especially in the writing center. Materials are abundant, varied, accessible, and fresh (new materials are added frequently to keep children's interest high). Figure 6.4 presents a list of writing materials that might be found in language- and literacy-rich classrooms.

FIGURE 6.3　Genres of Literature Included in Literacy- and Language-Rich Classrooms

Type of Literature Definition	Example Books
Traditional Literature Tales once told by storytellers but now published in picture book or chapter book format	Zelinsky, P. (1986). *Rumpelstiltskin: From the German of the Brothers Grimm.* New York: Dutton.
Fables Traditional stories with animal characters and explicitly stated morals	Young, E. (1992). *Seven blind mice.* New York: Philomel.
Folktales Traditional stories with flat characters (good, bad, tricky) with happy endings	Pinkney, J. (2006). *The little red hen.* New York: Dial Press.
Myths and Legends Traditional stories that explain natural occurrences often including heroes or heroines with superhuman or magical abilities	Lindbergh, R. (1990). *Johnny Appleseed.* New York: Little, Brown.
Fantasy Narratives that include elements that can never occur in the real world	Long, M. (2003). *How I became a pirate.* New York: Harcourt.
Realistic Fiction Narratives about things that could plausibly happen in the real world	Booth, D. (1997). *The dust bowl.* Tonawanda, NY: Kids Can Press.
Historical Fiction Realistic fiction set in the past	Hest, A. (1997). *When Jesse came across the sea.* Cambridge, MA: Candlewick Press.
Biography and Autobiography True stories about the lives of everyday or famous people	Giovanni, N. (2005). *Rosa.* New York: Henry Holt and Company.
Information Books Nonfiction that presents realistic, accurate, and authentic information	DK Eye Wonder. (2004). *Weather.* New York: Dorling Kindersley.
Poetry Text with condensed language that may include special lining, imagery, and elements of rhythm and rhyme	Myers, W. (1993). *Brown Angels.* New York: HarperCollins.
Wordless Picture Books Books without texts in which the story is told or information conveyed only through illustrations	Wiesner, D. (1991). *Tuesday.* New York: Houghton Mifflin.
Predictable Books Text with repeated dialogue or events or patterns of occurrences and text	Ho, M. (1996). *Hush! A Thai lullaby.* New York: Orchard Books.
Alphabet Books Books using the sequence of the alphabet to present information	Pallotta, J. (1986). *The Yucky reptile alphabet book.* Watertown, MA: Ivory Tower Press.
Reference Materials Dictionaries, atlases, and encyclopedias	Scholastic. (2005). *Scholastic pocket dictionary.* New York: Scholastic.

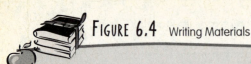

FIGURE 6.4 Writing Materials

A variety of writing tools, including

> pencils and pens with interesting shapes or fancy toppers such as feathers or objects
> markers such as highlighters, smelly markers, markers that change colors, and fat and thin markers
> alphabet stamps, tiles, cookie cutters, sponge letters, magnetic letters, felt letters
> crayons, chalk, and mechanical pencils

A variety of writing surfaces, including

> clipboards, small white boards, chalkboards, and lined and unlined paper in a variety of shapes and colors
> a variety of writing pads, including sticky notes, spiral notebooks, to-do lists
> sand tray

A variety of bookbinding materials, including

> a digital camera to take photos for "all about the author" pages
> stapled books of four to eight pages
> construction paper and other materials for making book covers

A variety of reference materials, including

> a photo book of all the children with their first and last names
> special words on index cards (such as seasonal or theme vocabulary)
> pictionaries, dictionaries, visual dictionaries
> alphabet charts and letter-sound association charts

Technology Materials

Teachers in the new millennium have especially embraced new technologies, recognizing children's sophistication in using games, Internet resources, and even personal devices such as iPods, cell phones, and other app-ready devices. Teachers are increasingly joining blogs and helping their students develop wiki pages and produce podcasts. One way that teachers are extending children's use of technology beyond using merely workbook-like exercises, or even CD-ROM books, is to carefully integrate technology with response to literature activities (Labbo, 2005). Teachers read aloud a book such as *Fly with Poetry: An ABC of Poetry* (Harley, 2000) to explore a variety of poetic techniques and enjoy powerful language, and then prepare a variety of technology-based response activities. For example, children can find poems they like at www.bbc.co.uk/cbeebies/tweenies/songs. At another site (www.favoritepoem.org/videos.html), students can listen to adults reading poems aloud. At http://home.freeuk.net/elloughton13/scramble2.htm, students can click one of

TECHNOLOGY TIE-IN

LEARNING MORE ABOUT CHILDREN'S LITERATURE

The following sites have links to author's Web pages or interviews with authors and illustrators. They have book reviews and suggested ways to build text sets of related books.

www.scholastic.com/magicschoolbus presents a Magic School Bus video along with information about all the Magic School Bus books. You can find other activities and games by moving around the site.

www.childrenslit.com presents information about authors and illustrators.

Nearly all children's authors and illustrators have their own Web pages with information about their books, and sometimes a blog, video, or games. For example Mo Willems has all of these. You will find out the real pronunciation of Knuffle Bunny's name.

http://carolhurst.com is a great reference for finding more about the literary qualities of books. Ms. Hurst has some references for building text sets of related books.

www.warriorcats.com presents information about the popular Warrior Cat series by Erin Hunter. This site presents videos of the author talking about her favorite books in the series, and an illustrator who has made Manga versions of the books. These fantasy books appeal to children 8–10 years old.

http://classroombooktalk.wikispaces.com presents VoiceThreads (audio) reviews of books by children in grades 1 through 5. Students who visit the site can select a genre of literature, then select one of the books reviewed. Ambitious teachers will be anxious to learn how to use PowerPoint or VoiceThread (http://voicethread.com) tools to help their students compose their own book reviews and post them to the site. The site also has blogs about books.

the top buttons to find a game unscrambling poems. They click and drag words on a virtual magnetic board to produce their own versions of poems. Students can select a variety of alphabet games at www.literacycenter.net. Teachers may begin a poetry pen pal project by initiating an exchange at www.teaching.com/keypals (the site has directions and suggestions for projects). This activity will require teacher supervision and reminding children not to share personal information. Children can also use *Alphabet: Play with the ABCs* (software found at Library Video Company) to build alphabet letters out of puzzles. Another software program, *Blue Clues ABC Time Activities* (Viacom & Humongous Entertainment) offers a variety of multimedia activities including answering questions and using words to make stories.

TECHNOLOGY TIE-IN

TAKE VIRTUAL TOURS OF CLASSROOMS WITH TEACHERS WHO TALK ABOUT THEIR CLASSROOM ENVIRONMENTS

To visit some of the best classrooms ever, go to www.scholastic.com and click on the Librarians tab at the top menu. Scroll down that page until you find the Author Videos button and click on that. It will immediately bring up an author interview. To the right of the video screen are icons to select other interviews. That is a great place to hear authors talk about their work. However, on the left of the video, you will see another menu list with the top one being Featured Videos. Click on that button and it will take you to a video of a kindergarten teacher and her classroom of wild children. That video is intended to teach kindergarten children appropriate classroom rules. Now on the right side of the video screen will be icons of other teachers. You can see the kindergarten teacher's library as she describes how she set it up, and then you can see another video of a tour of this entire classroom. There are tours for second-, fourth-, and sixth-grade classrooms. All have special features worth seeing.

CULTURALLY SENSITIVE AND INTEGRATED CURRICULUM

CURRICULUM IS WHAT CHILDREN LEARN related to the disciplines of language arts and literature, social studies, science, mathematics, art, music, health, and physical education. Recent research and theory regarding the literacy curriculum (language arts and literature, which includes reading, writing, and spelling) suggest that children learn better when the curriculum is integrated across the language arts and across disciplines and when it is culturally sensitive.

Culturally Sensitive Curriculum

All children belong to cultural groups that in some way shape their attitudes, beliefs, and ways of making meaning with written language. When children perceive of a writing task or a text as having content that reaffirms their cultural identities, they are more likely to become engaged in the task and to construct personal meaning (Meier, 2000). Culturally relevant topics, topics that children perceive as culturally affirming, are an important avenue to learning and literacy development (Au, 2000).

The curriculum in literacy-rich classrooms reflects sensitivity for children's cultures in both its content (what is taught and what children are expected to read and write) and its instruction (how concepts are taught). In most classrooms, one or more students have recently arrived in the United States and speak a language other than English at home. Many classrooms include children from a variety of cultural and language backgrounds. Regardless of the mixture of children in a particular classroom, all children need exposure to literature that presents nonstereotyped information about a wide variety of cultural groups.

A culturally sensitive curriculum eliminates the artificial dichotomies created when studying "other" cultures; it includes examples from many cultures as a part of all learning experiences. That is, the content that children study and the material they read naturally present many different cultures. Teachers are careful to include many examples of multicultural literature in all their literature theme units and content units. **Multicultural literature** consists of

- fiction with characters who are from cultural groups that have been underrepresented in children's books: African Americans, Asian Americans, Hispanic Americans, Native Americans, and Americans from religious minorities;
- fiction that takes us to other nations and introduces readers to the cultures of people residing outside of the United States; and
- information books, including biographies, that focus on African Americans, Asian Americans, Hispanic Americans, Native Americans, Americans from religious minorities, and people living outside the United States

The best in multicultural literature presents culturally authentic information (Bishop, 1992). **Culturally authentic literature** portrays people and the values, customs, and beliefs of a cultural group in ways recognized by members of that group as valid and authentic. Most culturally authentic literature is written or illustrated by members of the cultural group. Appendix A provides a list of multicultural literature including culturally authentic literature.

When teachers have difficulty locating children's literature representative of a child's cultural heritage, local storytellers can be invited into the classroom. For example, in one first-grade classroom were three children from Cape Verde, an island off the African coast. When the teacher failed to locate literature that included children from this cultural background, she turned to the community liaison in her school for help and learned that the neighborhood included many families from this location. The community liaison helped the teacher locate a woman who visited the class several times to share stories. After the storyteller's visits, the children retold the stories, which the teacher recorded in big book format. The children illustrated the story, and these books became class favorites.

Integrated Content Units

Curriculum integration—teaching broad topics that cover areas within the language arts and across more than one discipline—improves teaching and learning (Dewey, 1933; Vars, 1991). This kind of instruction allows children to see connections among facts and theories, provides a focus for selecting instructional activities, provides for coherence of activities, allows children to study topics in depth, and promotes positive attitudes (Lipson, Valencia, Wixson, & Peters, 1993). Integrated content units are organized around a broad theme that includes learning concepts across more than one content area, active inquiry activities, and activities incorporating all the language arts.

For example, a teacher may use the theme of "growing" as a focus for learning experiences for a group of first graders. This theme explores physical changes that occur as a part of growth in plants, animals, and humans; measurement; and the literary theme "growing up." As a part of the activities included in the theme, the teacher may read aloud folktales in which plants grow to enormous sizes (such as *The Enormous Turnip,* retold by Kathy Parkinson, 1986), stories that contrast children at different ages (such as *Stevie* [Steptoe, 1969]), poems about childhood activities at different ages (*I Want to Be* [Moss, 1993]), and information books about growing up (such as *Pueblo Boy: Growing Up in Two Worlds* [Keegan, 1991]). The teacher may guide the children in dramatizing the stories, and children may create storytelling props to use in retelling the folktales.

The teacher may also read information books about the growth of plants and animals (such as *How a Seed Grows* by Jordan, 1992; and several books from the *See How They Grow* series published by Dorling Kindersley including *See How They Grow: Butterfly* [Ling, 2007]; *See How They Grow: Frog* [Royston, 2007]; and *See How They Grow: Mouse* [Royston, 2008]).

MEASURING CLASSROOM ENVIRONMENT QUALITY

RECENTLY, SEVERAL RESEARCHERS have developed rating scales for measuring the quality of the classroom literacy environment. These rating scales take into account the physical arrangement, materials, displays, and the quality of the interactions between children and teachers. Two scales have been designed exclusively to measure the preschool language and literacy environment (ELLCO-Pre-K: Smith et al., 2008; CHELLO: Neuman, Dwyer, & Koh, 2007); and two scales have been designed for the elementary grades (CLEP: Wolfersberger et al., 2004; TEX-IN3: Hoffman, Sailors, Duffy, & Beretvas, 2004). One other scale measures the emotional and instructional quality of a classroom more generally Pre-K-3 (CLASS: Pianta, La Paro, & Hamre, 2008), but the authors make recommendations for language and literacy quality in addition to the general quality measures. All of these scales have information regarding their validity and reliability (Reutzel & Jones, 2010). In general, the **literacy and language environmental rating scales** examine the quality of

* materials and supplies.
* arrangement of the classroom spaces and materials.
* procedures and routines for using the spaces and materials.
* use of varied and effective instructional practices.
* gaining and sustaining the interest of children in literacy activities using higher-level cognitive activities.

The CLASS (Classroom Assessment Scoring System) rating system was developed following nearly ten years of research (e.g., Hamre & Pianta, 2005; Justice, Mashburn, Hamre, & Pianta, 2008; LoCasale-Crouch, Konold, Pianta, Howes, Burchinal, Bryant, et al., 2007). During this time, instructional quality was defined along five scales:

* productivity, in which teachers manage time and establish routines to maximize learning time

- instructional learning formats, in which teachers facilitate all children's active participation and focus on the lesson objective, using a variety of instructional methods
- concept development, in which teachers promote children's creative and higher-level thinking (rather than rote learning) by asking open-ended questions, and asking children to explain their ideas and problem solve
- quality of feedback, in which teachers' feedback to children focuses on developing understanding, elaborating on responses, sustaining persistence, and trying alternative strategies
- language modeling, in which teachers engage individual children in extended conversations; ask open-ended questions; use language expansion strategies of repeating, elaborating, and event casting; and use sophisticated vocabulary

The TEX-IN3 Observation System takes a unique approach by examining the quality of two different text environments: instruction with commercial texts and instruction with teacher- and student-made texts. This survey takes into account teachers' and students' use and understanding of the texts. For example, a classroom with a high-quality text environment would include a wide variety of texts that meet the diverse interests and learning needs of the classroom, are related directly to the curriculum, and reflect the diversity of the classroom members and community. Such a text environment would be the opposite of classrooms that are dominated by one set of textbooks for science, social studies, and language arts and in which all children, regardless of their current reading level, read the same books at the same time. Instead, classrooms would have some textbooks but also many tradebooks related to science and social studies topics. Student- and teacher-made texts would be highly visible throughout the classroom and would be used in support of learning. Teachers in these settings value all types of texts including teacher- and student-produced texts. The teacher demonstrates initiative, insight, and skill in weaving a variety of texts together to meet curricular needs in reading and in content and in meeting the needs of individual students. Students know how all the texts are used in the classrooms, where the texts are located, and how teacher- and student-made texts reflect and support their learning. Students know the names of classroom workstations or storage locations, are clear about the kinds and value of activities and texts used in those locations, and demonstrate with pride their own contributions to the visible productivity and learning reflected in the texts found in the classroom.

MEETING THE NEEDS OF ENGLISH LANGUAGE LEARNERS AND STRUGGLING READERS AND WRITERS

THIS BOOK DESCRIBES effective high-quality literacy and language environments that are expected to support the learning of all children. For example, high-quality classrooms have texts that reflect the diverse cultures found in the classroom and community. However, teachers may need to take extra steps to ensure that the classroom appeals to and supports the learning of ELL children and children who are struggling with reading and writing. With both ELL and struggling readers and writers, having a wide range of materials reflecting a broad diversity may not be sufficient (Vardell, Hadaway, & Young, 2006; Allington, 2008). The task of selecting books for English learners and struggling learners is more complex than merely considering their age, interest, and culture because the typical grade-level suitability may not be appropriate. It is important to take into account the actual reading level of students in the class. For example, a fourth grader reading instructionally on a first-grade level would not have sufficient reading materials if only a few texts at that level were found in the classroom library or in teachers' selection of leveled books for instruction. One estimate for the number of books needed at this level is over eighty books (Allington)!

Three suggestions may help teachers prepare their classrooms for ELL and struggling readers. First, build a school-wide lending library of leveled books that can be rotated in and out of individual classrooms. Second, have a wider range and number of picture books on sophisticated topics but which have visual accessibility (abundant illustrations) to support comprehension. Finally, have many stair-step collections of books on the same topic. *Stair-step books* address a particular topic on a variety of levels of complexity (Vardell et al., 2006). For example, there are multiple books about sharks, wolves, and insects that can be collected into stair-step sets.

DEVELOPMENTALLY APPROPRIATE INSTRUCTION AND EXPLICIT INSTRUCTION

THIS BOOK DESCRIBES the literacy environment and appropriate instructional practices for children from preschool through fourth grade, the period often called the *early childhood years*. Professional organizations concerned with education during those years have taken an active role in defining appropriate practices. In a position statement, the National Association for the Education of Young Children (NAEYC) (Copple & Bredekamp, 2009) define appropriate instruction from a developmental perspective. During the early childhood years, children experience significant development emotionally, physically, socially, cognitively, and linguistically. Developmentally appropriate practices in literacy instruction take into account interactions among those areas of development, including the ways that literacy development is influenced by linguistic, cognitive, emotional, and social development (Cunningham & Stanovich, 1997). Only recently, for example, we have begun to appreciate how critical children's emotions are to their engagement in cognitive activities and how children's literacy learning in school is influenced by the social and cultural knowledge they acquire in their homes and communities (Dyson, 2006).

Developmentally appropriate instruction is defined as setting goals for individual children that are challenging but achievable with the support of well-qualified teachers. In order to set such goals, teachers must know what to expect in children's literacy acquisition; that is, they must understand the continuum of development in language and literacy. However, the NAEYC statement about developmentally appropriate instruction also indicates that children will follow their own unique paths to reach conventional literacy. Children have individual patterns of development, grow up in different home and community environments, and have different educational experiences. Therefore, a wide range of individual variation in literacy learning is expected each year in preschool and through the elementary grades. In order to meet the needs of individual children, teachers must be able to assess each child's progress toward conventional reading and writing.

Thus, teachers have three critical roles in helping children achieve challenging goals. They must be knowledgeable about the continuum of language and literacy development; they must be able to assess individual children and determine their placement on that continuum; and they must be able to formulate goals and plan instruction that will help children reach those goals. Effective teachers carefully consider all methods of instruction in order to select those most likely to reach a particular child at a particular point in his or her literacy development.

One way to view instructional methods is in terms of directness; methods range from indirect to direct. With **indirect instruction,** teachers provide materials, but children learn from doing and from watching others. Indirect instruction occurs as teachers interact with children as they engage in activities. For example, teachers may place writing materials in a writing center, and children in kindergarten might copy, write a string of random letters to which they tell a story, attempt to use invented spellings, or merely draw a picture. As teachers sit in the writing center, they may comment and ask questions or provide help when asked. Thus, indirect methods of teaching do not mean that teachers ignore children. Rather, teachers let children take the lead (for example, teachers say, "Tell me about your writing"), but they provide children with feedback and support when invited. These interactions provide teachers with opportunities to see how children put information gained through instruction into independent action. Teachers may want to use these activities in order to collect samples of children's work and take anecdotal notes.

Other methods of instruction are more direct and more teacher-directed (Hamre & Pianta, 2005). With **direct instruction,** teachers determine goals for teaching—that is, for example, they plan to teach how to write the letters *L, T,* and *E* or how to write a lead sentence in a nonfiction description of the habitat and habits of predators. In direct instruction, teachers model how to perform tasks and talk aloud as they perform those tasks in order to provide explanations of their mental activities. Such specifying of learning outcomes, modeling of processes, thinking aloud, and explaining are also characteristics of **explicit instruction.** Teachers use terms correctly (such as rhyming words or a rime) to teach skills and make explicit the relationship between a skill and the broader purpose of reading or writing (rhyming words have the same rime, and that helps us read new words) (Justice et al., 2008).

Explicit instruction is usually part of an instructional sequence called **gradual release of responsibility** (Pearson & Gallager, 1983). Gradual release of responsibility begins with explicit teaching of a single concept or strategy, one that can be expressed in the performance of a discrete task. First, teachers provide explicit instruction about the target literacy concept or strategy. This includes a demonstration of the task that expresses knowledge of that concept or mastery of that strategy, with accompanying think-alouds and explanations. Then teachers release some responsibility for performing that task. They might repeat their demonstration of the task but with pauses for asking children to recall next steps or to participate in the demonstration. Next, teachers reduce their responsibility further, by having one child demonstrate while other children help by providing some of the thinking aloud and explaining. Now, the teacher's role is to provide feedback about the accuracy or effectiveness of the children's demonstrations, think-alouds, and explanations. After several children have demonstrated, the teacher may pair children up or assign small groups. Children in the pairs or small groups perform the task together, helping each other as the teacher circulates to give feedback. Only after all of these steps (sometimes called *I do it, We all do it,* and *You all do it*) are children asked to perform the task independently. Now the entire responsibility for knowing a concept or strategy and being able to express it in performance of a relevant task is the child's.

Direct instruction, explicit teaching, and gradual release of responsibility can meet the needs of individual children. Direct instruction is developmentally appropriate when it is based on teachers' having assessed children and determined that they have the necessary background experiences and concepts to learn a new strategy or concept. This can be the case even for whole-class groups, especially when teachers take a playful stance and provide positive feedback to children. However, providing explicit instruction to whole-class groups of children all the time without regard to individual children's levels of achievement is never developmentally appropriate. Language- and literacy-rich classrooms are the venue for all types of instruction, in a range from direct to indirect opportunities. Teachers must find the balance of direct and indirect instructional methods that will best meet the needs of their students.

In literacy-rich classrooms with many diverse learners, teachers need to consider when and how both indirect and explicit direct teaching can be culturally responsive. **Culturally responsive instruction** is instruction that is "consistent with the values of students' own cultures and aimed at improving academic learning" (Au, 1993, p. 13). That is, many children are exposed to ways of learning in their homes and communities that are different from mainstream. Learning in mainstream homes reflects the kinds of learning expected in school: adults give directions that children are expected to follow; adults ask questions to determine if children are learning and individual children are expected to answer showing their knowledge. In contrast, in many communities, children are expected to learn by observing adults without interrupting or asking questions. In other communities, children participate verbally with other children and adults rather than taking turns listening and speaking. In still other cultures, children are not expected to show individual competence but, rather, work within the group. Therefore, in order to refine instruction so that it is culturally responsive, teachers need to research how adults and children interact in their local communities by visiting community events and talking with parents or community informants. For example, in one school in Hawaii, teachers discovered that children often called out responses to questions in overlapping turns rather than individual turn taking. Teachers originally labeled children's quick responses to questions without waiting to be called upon as disruptive but later found this pattern of response was typical in the community. After discovering this practice was common, they allowed multiple children to talk and answer questions without taking turns. Children's talk about stories increased and the teachers felt children were accelerating their reading growth (Au & Kawakami, 1985).

Assessment–Based Comprehensive Literacy Instruction

IN THIS CHAPTER, we have described the elements that comprise a language- and literacy-rich environment, and the appropriate types of interactions that occur between teachers and students as students engage with the literacy materials in their classrooms. In addition to these basic components of a classroom environment, teachers must consider the results of two critical national reports on the essential components of reading instruction (e.g., *Developing Early Literacy: Report of the National Early Literacy Panel* [National Early Literacy Panel, 2008]; *Teaching Children to Read: An Evidence-Based Assessment of the Scientific Research Literature on Reading and Its Implications for Reading Instruction* [National Reading Panel, 2000]). Both of these reports suggest essential elements of instruction and provide insight into the nature of that instruction. In preschool and kindergarten, these essentials, which must be included in instruction, are knowledge of the alphabet, phonemic awareness, concepts about print, alphabetic principle, vocabulary, and listening comprehension. In kindergarten through elementary grades, the essential components of instruction include phonemic awareness, phonics, vocabulary, comprehension, and fluency. These essential components of reading also dictate assessments.

Assessment is a critical part of the instructional cycle. First, teachers assess what children know, then plan instruction based on student needs, provide instruction, and finally assess whether children have learned. Most classrooms use initial **screening assessments** at the beginning of the year. The results of these assessments help teachers plan instruction and help them group children. After instruction, teachers use **monitoring assessments** to determine children's progress in order to identify small groups of children who many need more intensive instruction. The use of initial screening assessments and monitoring assessments in the classroom is the first step in **response to intervention (RTI)**. RTI is an approach to identifying struggling students who may need extra support and intervention instruction and, later, students who may need special education (Mesmer & Mesmer, 2008). The RTI process may include up to five steps. First, good literacy practices for each age/grade level are determined and put into place in regular classroom instruction. All students are assessed for their reading level and placed in groups reading texts on that level. Then all children are screened for learning of basic literacy skills to determine if they have reached predetermined benchmark levels. Districts establish, for example, the number of alphabet letters children should recognize in one minute or the number of correct words per minute that students are expected to read at the end of the school year. Or districts may use ranges established through research (see Chapter 10 for fluency levels at the end of grades 1 though 5 that 50 percent of readers reach). Next, students not meeting benchmarks receive extra support, usually in small-group instruction. Then, after receiving intervention support, students are assessed using monitoring assessments and either return to regular instruction or are recommended for individualized interventions. Monitoring assessments used in RTI, compared to informal, teacher-made monitoring assessments a classroom teacher might routinely use, are more sensitive to small changes in performance, are given frequently, and are reliable and valid (Mesmer & Mesmer). Finally, when students still struggle with individualized and intensive interventions, they are entered into the process of determining eligibility for special education services.

The RTI approach assumes that all children are receiving highly effective and differentiated instruction in the regular classroom. It assumes that all children will have access to materials they can read with support of the teacher for guided reading and content study and materials they can read independently (Allington, 2008). Teachers may want to make a spot check in their classrooms to assess whether they have sufficient materials for guided-reading instruction and for independent reading. Select three students (one achieving above-grade-level expectations, one at grade level, and one below). Have students pull out materials they are reading in guided-reading instruction and that they are currently reading independently. Then have students find materials they have recently read in science, for example. Have students read aloud from each of those texts for three minutes (use a timer). On a sheet of paper, make a slash for each word the student read incorrectly. Then write a pencil line under the last word the student read by the three-minute timer. For each text, calculate the number of words read correctly (see Chapter 5 directions on how to take a running record to establish word reading accuracy rate). Divide by 3 and record this rate for each text. For each student, this accuracy rate should be 90 percent or higher. If it is not, teachers need to make adjustments in the materials they are asking students to read in guided reading, in helping students make more appropriate choices for independent reading (see Chapter 10), and searching for a wider range of books to use in content study.

Chapter Summary

EARLY CHILDHOOD PROFESSIONAL ORGANIZATIONS stress the importance of all aspects of children's development. Children's literacy learning should be embedded within child-centered early-childhood programs with developmentally appropriate practices. Exemplary early-childhood programs are found in language- and literacy-rich classrooms in which children are reflective, motivated readers and writers who use literacy to learn about their world.

To create language- and literacy-rich classrooms, teachers select quality classroom literature collections that include traditional literature, fantasy, realistic fiction, historical fiction, biography, information books, poetry, wordless picture books, predictable books, and alphabet books. They select reference materials, audiovisual materials, children's magazines, and writing materials.

Teachers infuse reading and writing materials throughout the room to encourage functional use of literacy. They set up a classroom library center, a writing center, and a computer center.

Teachers establish daily routines using reading and writing. Teachers read or tell stories, poems, or information books daily; they set aside time for children to read and write independently; and they plan small-group activities.

The curriculum is organized around literature content units that include talking, listening, reading, and writing activities. All units include multicultural literature.

Teachers provide instruction in a variety of settings as they demonstrate reading and writing, guide interactive discussions, and provide direct teaching through modeling. They form a variety of groups, including whole-class gatherings, small groups, and pairs, and they set aside time for children to work alone. Teachers assess children's literacy learning and use results of assessment to guide instruction including tier 1, 2, and 3 instruction in response to intervention (RTI).

USING THE INFORMATION

Use the information presented in this chapter to make a classroom environment checklist. For example, such a checklist might include the following:

LITERACY ENVIRONMENT CHECKLIST

Physical Layout of Classroom

_____ sectioned into centers

_____ carpeted whole-class area large enough for all children

_____ small-group instructional area

_____ easel for chart paper

_____ pocket chart

Library Center

_____ includes number of books equal to five times the number of children _____

Writing Center

_____

Computer Center

_____

APPLYING THE INFORMATION

Imagine that you are either the preschool or third-grade teacher who brainstormed whole- and small-group activities for their classrooms, which were discussed earlier in this chapter. Create a classroom floor plan for this teacher. Select one area of the classroom (whole-group carpet, small-group teaching table, listening center, etc.). List all the literacy materials that should be available in that area .

GOING BEYOND THE TEXT

VISIT A PRESCHOOL OR ELEMENTARY SCHOOL CLASSROOM and observe literacy instruction and activities. Look carefully at the literacy materials that are available in the room. Note how often children interact with these literacy materials. Observe the children and their teacher as they interact during literacy instruction and as the children work on literacy projects. Use the Literacy Environment Checklist you made to guide your observations. Or, obtain a copy of one of the environmental rating scales discussed in this chapter and use it to rate the quality of the classroom environment.

REFERENCES

Allington, R. (2005). *What really matters for struggling readers: Designing research-based programs* (2nd ed.). Boston: Allyn & Bacon.

Allington, R. (2008). *What really matters in response to intervention instruction: Research-based designs.* Boston: Allyn & Bacon.

Au, K. (1993). *Literacy instruction in multicultural settings.* New York: Harcourt.

Au, K. H. (2000). Multicultural factors and the effective instruction of students of diverse backgrounds. In A. E. Farstrup & S. J. Samuels (Eds.), *What research has to say about reading instruction* (3rd ed.) (pp. 392–413). Newark, DE: International Reading Association.

Au, K., & Kawakami, A. (1985). Research currents: Talk story and learning to read. *Language Arts, 62,* 406–411.

Bishop, R. (1992). Multicultural literature for children: Making informed choices. In V. Harris (Ed.), *Teaching multicultural literature in grades K–8* (pp. 37–53). Norwood, MA: Christopher-Gordon Publishers.

Bulla, C. (1994). *What makes a shadow? Let's read and find out science 1.* New York: HarperCollins.

Carle, E. (1979). *The very hungry caterpillar.* New York: Philomel Books.

Casbergue, R., McGee, L., & Bedford, A. (2008). Characteristics of classroom environments associated with accelerated literacy development. In L. Justice & C. Vukelich (Eds.), *Achieving excellence in preschool literacy instruction* (pp. 176–181). New York: Guilford Press.

Chapman, M., Filipenko, M., McTavish, M., & Shapiro, J. (2007). First graders' preferences for narrative and/or information books and perceptions of other boys' and girls' book preferences. *Canadian Journal of Education, 30,* 531–553.

Connor, C., Morrison, F., & Slominski, L. (2006). Preschool instruction and children's emergent literacy growth. *Journal of Educational Psychology, 98*(4), 665–689.

Copple, C., & Bredekamp, S. (2009). *Developmentally appropriate practice (in early childhood programs, serving children from birth through age 8).* Washington, DC: National Association for the Education of Young Children

Cunningham, A. E., & Stanovich, K. E. (1997). Early reading acquisition and its relation to reading experience and ability 10 years later. *Developmental Psychology, 33,* 934–945.

Cunningham, P. (2004). *Phonics they use: Words for reading and writing* (4th ed.). Boston: Allyn & Bacon.

Dewey, J. (1933). *How we think* (Rev. ed.). Boston: Heath.

Dickinson, D. (2001). Book reading in preschool classrooms: Is recommended practice common? In D. Dickinson & P. Tabors (Eds.), *Beginning literacy with language* (pp. 175–203). Baltimore, MD: Brookes Publishing.

Dickinson, D., & Smith, M. (1994). Long-term effects of preschool teachers' book readings on low-income children's vocabulary and story comprehension. *Reading Research Quarterly, 29,* 105–122.

Diller, D. (2003). *Literacy workstations: Making centers work.* Portland, ME: Stenhouse Publishers.

Diller, D. (2007). *Making the most of small groups: Differentiation for all.* Portland, ME: Stenhouse Publishers.

Duke, N. (2000). Print environments and experiences offered to first-grade students in very low- and very high-SES school districts. *Reading Research Quarterly, 35,* 456–457.

Duke, N., & Purcell-Gates, V. (2003). Genres at home and at school: Bridging the known to the new. *The Reading Teacher, 57,* 30–37.

Dyson, A. (2006). On saying it right (write): "Fit-its" in the foundations of learning to write. *Research in the Teaching of English, 41,* 8–42.

Eeds, M., & Wells, D. (1989). Grand conversations: An exploration of meaning construction in literature study groups. *Research in the Teaching of English, 23,* 4–29.

Fountas, I. C., & Pinnell, G. S. (1996). *Guided reading: Good first teaching for all children.* Portsmouth, NH: Heinemann.

Fountas, I., & Pinnell, G. (2009). *Leveled book list K-8+: 2010–2012 edition,* print version. Portsmouth, NH: Heinemann.

Fractor, J., Woodruff, M., Martinez, M., & Teale, W. (1993). Let's not miss opportunities to promote voluntary reading: Classroom libraries in elementary school. *The Reading Teacher, 46,* 476–484.

Guthrie, J., Wigfield, A., & Von Secker, C. (2000). Effects of integrated instruction on motivation and strategy use in reading. *Journal of Educational Psychology, 93,* 211–225.

Hamre, B., & Pianta, R. (2005). Can instructional and emotional support in the first-grade classroom make a difference for children at risk of school failure? *Child Development, 76*(5), 949–967.

Harley, A. (2000). *Fly with poetry: An ABC of poetry.* New York: Boyds Mills Press.

Hoffman, J., Sailors, M., Duffy, G., & Beretvas, S. (2004). The effective elementary classroom literacy environment: Examining the validity of TEX-IN3 observation system. *Journal of Literacy Research, 36,* 303–334.

Jeong, J., Gaffney, J., & Choi, J. (2010). Availability and use of information texts in second-, third-, and fourth-grade classrooms. *Research in the Teaching of English, 44*(4), 435–456.

Jordan, H. (1992). *How a seed grows.* New York: HarperCollins.

Justice, L., Mashburn, A., Hamre, B., & Pianta, R. (2008). Quality of language and literacy instruction in preschool classrooms serving at-risk pupils. *Early Childhood Research Quarterly, 23,* 51–68.

Keegan, M. (1991). *Pueblo boy: Growing up in two worlds.* New York: Dutton.

Labbo, L. D. (1996). A semiotic analysis of young children's symbol making in a classroom computer center. *Reading Research Quarterly, 31,* 356–382.

Labbo, L. (2005). Books and computer response activities that support literacy development. *The Reading Teacher, 59*(3), 288–292.

Labbo, L. D., & Ash, G. E. (1998). What is the role of computer-related technology in early literacy? In S. Neuman & K. Roskos (Eds.), *Children achieving: Best practices in beginning literacy* (pp. 180–197). Newark, DE: International Reading Association.

Ling, M. (2007). *See how they grow: Butterfly.* New York: Dorling Kindersley.

Lipson, M., Valencia, S., Wixson, K., & Peters, C. (1993). Integration and thematic teaching: Integration to improve teaching and learning. *Language Arts, 70,* 252–263.

LoCasale-Crouch, J., Konold, T., Pianta, R., Howes, C., Burchinal, M., Bryant, D., et al. (2007). Observed classroom quality profiles in state-funded pre-kindergarten programs and associations with teacher, program, and classroom characteristics. *Early Childhood Research Quarterly, 22,* 3–17.

McCloskey, R. (1976). *Blueberries for Sal.* New York: Puffin.

McGee, L. M. (2003). Book acting: Storytelling and drama in the early childhood classroom. In D. M. Barone & L. M. Morrow (Eds.), *Literacy and young children: Research-based practices* (pp. 157–172). New York: Guilford Press.

McGee, L. M., & Schickedanz, J. (2007). Reading books aloud in preschool and kindergarten: Accelerating language and oral comprehension. *The Reading Teacher, 60,* 742–751.

Meier, D. R. (2000). *Scribble scrabble, learning to read and write: Success with diverse teachers, children, and families.* New York: Teachers College Press.

Mesmer, E., & Mesmer, H. (2008). Response to intervention (RTI): What teachers of reading need to know. *The Reading Teacher, 62*(4), 280–290.

Miller, D. (2008). *Teaching with intention: Defining beliefs, aligning practices, taking action, K–5.* Portland, ME: Stenhouse Publishers.

Mol, S., Bus, A., & de Jong, M. (2009). Interactive book reading in early education: A tool to simulate print knowledge as well as oral language. *Review of Educational Research, 79*(2), 979–1007.

Morrow, L. (1992). The impact of a literature-based program on literacy achievement, use of literature, and attitudes of children from minority backgrounds. *Reading Research Quarterly, 27,* 250–275.

Morrow, L. (1997). *The literacy center: Contexts for reading and writing.* York, ME: Stenhouse Publishers.

Morrow, L., & Gambrell, L. B. (1998). How do we motivate children toward independent reading and writing? In S. Neuman & K. Roskos (Eds.), *Children achieving: Best practices in beginning literacy* (pp. 144–161). Newark, DE: International Reading Association.

Morrow, L. M., Reutzel, D. R., & Casey, H. (2005). Organization and management of exemplary language arts teaching: Classroom environments, grouping practices, and exemplary instruction. In C. Evertson & C. Weinstein (Eds.), *Handbook of classroom management* (pp. 559–581). Mahwah, NJ: Lawrence Erlbaum Associates.

Morrow, L. M., & Weinstein, C. S. (1986). Encouraging voluntary reading: The impact of a literature program on children's use of library centers. *Reading Research Quarterly, 21,* 330–346.

Moss, T. (1993). *I want to be.* New York: Dial Press.

National Early Literacy Panel. (2008). *Developing early literacy: Report of the National Early Literacy Panel.* Washington, DC: National Institute for Literacy.

National Reading Panel. (2000). *Teaching children to read: An evidence-based assessment of the scientific research literature on reading and its implications for reading instruction* (NIH Publications No. 00-4754). Washington, DC: U.S. Department of Health and Human Services.

Neuman, S. B. (1999). Books make a difference: A study of access to literacy. *Reading Research Quarterly, 34,* 286–311.

Neuman, S., Dwyer, J., & Koh, S. (2007). *Child/home early language and literacy observation.* Baltimore: Brookes Publishing.

Parkes, B. (2000). *Read it again! Revisiting the shared reading.* Portland, ME: Stenhouse Publishers.

Parkinson, K. (1986). *The enormous turnip.* Niles, IL: Albert Whitman & Company.

Parsons, S. (2008). Providing all students ACCESS to self-regulated literacy learning. *The Reading Teacher, 61,* 628–635.

Pearson, P. D., & Gallager, M. C. (1983). The instruction of reading comprehension. *Contemporary Educational Psychology, 8,* 317–344.

Pentimonti, J., Zucker, T., Justice, L., & Kaderavek, J. (2010). Information text use in preschool classroom read-alouds. *The Reading Teacher, 53*(8), 656–665.

Perry, N., Hutchinson, L., & Thauberger, C. (2007). Mentoring student teachers to design and implement literacy tasks that support self-regulated reading and writing. *Reading and Writing Quarterly, 23,* 27–50.

Pianta, R., La Paro, K., & Hamre, B. (2008). *Classroom assessment scoring system: Manual Pre-K.* Baltimore, MD: Brookes Publishing.

Pinnell, G., & Fountas, I. (1996). *Guided reading: Good first teaching for all children.* Portsmouth, NH: Heinemann.

Price, L., van Kleeck, A., & Huberty D. (2009). Talk during book sharing between parents and preschool children: A comparison between storybook and expository book conditions. *Reading Research Quarterly, 44,* 171–194.

Reutzel, R., & Jones, C. (2010). Assessing and creating effective preschool literacy classroom environments. In M. McKenna, S. Walpole, & K. Conradi (Eds.), *Promoting early reading: Research, resources, and best practices* (pp. 175–198). New York: Guilford Press.

Richgels, D. J. (2002). Informational texts in kindergarten. *The Reading Teacher, 55,* 586–595.

Roskos, K., & Neuman, S. B. (2001). Environment and its influences for early literacy teaching and learning. In S. B. Neuman & D. K. Dickinson (Eds.), *Handbook of early literacy research* (pp. 281–292). New York: Guilford Press.

Rowe, D. (1994). *Preschoolers as authors: Literacy learning in the social world.* Cresskill, NJ: Hampton Press.

Royston, A. (2007). *See how they grow: Frog.* New York: Dorling Kindersley.

Royston, A. (2008). *See how they grow: Mouse.* New York: Dorling Kindersley.

Schickedanz, J. A. (2003). Engaging preschoolers in code learning: Some thoughts about preschool teachers' concerns. In D. M. Barone & L. M. Morrow (Eds.), *Literacy and young children: Research-based practices.* New York: Guilford Press.

Schulman, M. B., & Payne, C. (2000). *Guided reading: Making it work.* New York: Scholastic.

Sipe, L. (2002). Talking back and taking over: Young children's expressive engagement during storybook read-alouds. *The Reading Teacher, 55,* 476–483.

Smith, M., Brady, J., & Anastasopoulous, L. (2008). *Early language and literacy classroom observation pre-K tool.* Baltimore: Brookes Publishing.

Smolkin, L., McTigue, E., & Donovan, C. (2008). Explanation and science text: Overcoming the comprehension challenges in nonfiction text for elementary students. In C. Block & S. Parris (Eds.), *Comprehension instruction: Research-based best practices* (2nd ed., pp. 183–195). New York: Guilford Press.

Steptoe, J. (1969). *Stevie.* New York: Harper & Row.

Taylor, B. M., Frye, B. J., & Maruyama, G. (1990). Time spent reading and reading growth. *American Educational Research Journal, 27,* 351–362.

Tompert, A. (1988). *Nothing sticks like a shadow.* New York: Houghton Mifflin.

Vardell, S., Hadaway, N., & Young, T. (2006). Matching books and readers: Selecting literature for English learners. *The Reading Teacher, 59*(8), 734–741.

Vars, G. (1991). Integrated curriculum in historical perspective. *Educational Leadership, 49,* 14–15.

Vukelich, C. (1994). Effects of play intervention on young children's reading of environmental print. *Early Childhood Research Quarterly, 9,* 153–170.

Wolfersberger, M., Reutzel, D., Sudweeks, R., & Fawson, P. (2004). Developing and validating the literacy profile (CLEP): A tool for examining the "print richness" of early childhood and elementary classrooms. *Journal of Literacy Research, 36,* 211–272.

Xiong, B. (1989). *Nine-in-one. Grr! Grr!* San Francisco: Children's Book Press.

Yopp, R., & Yopp, H. (2006). Informational texts as read-alouds at school and home. *Journal of Literacy Research, 38*(1), 37–51.

myeducationlab

Go to the topics English Language Learners, At Risk and Struggling Readers, and Assessment in the MyEducationLab (www.myeducationlab.com) for your course, where you can:

- Find learning outcomes for English Language Learners, At Risk and Struggling Readers, and Assessment along with the national standards that connect to these outcomes.
- Complete Assignments and Activities that can help you more deeply understand the chapter content.
- Examine challenging situations and cases presented in the IRIS Center Resources.

 **A+RISE**

Go to the Topic A+RISE in the MyEducationLab (www.myeducationlab.com) for your course. A+RISE® Standards2Strategy™ is an innovative and interactive online resource that offers new teachers in grades K–12 just-in-time, research-based instructional strategies that:

- Meet the linguistic needs of ELLs as they learn content
- Differentiate instruction for all grades and abilities
- Offer reading and writing techniques, cooperative learning, use of linguistic and nonlinguistic representations, scaffolding, teacher modeling, higher order thinking, and alternative classroom ELL assessment
- Provide support to help teachers be effective through the integration of listening, speaking, reading, and writing along with the content curriculum
- Improve student achievement
- Are aligned to Common Core Elementary Language Arts standards (for the literacy strategies) and to English language proficiency standards in WIDA, Texas, California, and Florida.

CHAPTER 7

Supporting Language and Literacy Learning in Preschools

KEY CONCEPTS

Sounding Literate
Self-Regulation
Shared Writing with
  Write On
Guided Drawing
Confusable Letters
Continuants

Tier 2 Words
Vocabulary Prop Box
Text and Toy Sets
Sit and Stay
Pattern Innovation
Sign-In Procedure
Phonemic Awareness

Phoneme Scaffolding
Utterance Length
Utterance
  Complexity
Vocabulary Variety
Language Scaffold
Portfolio

The Preschool Context

I N THIS CHAPTER, we describe exemplary preschool practices that foster high levels of language and literacy development for all children including children in day care, Head Start or Even Start, public or private preschools, and prekindergarten programs. Exemplary preschool programs foster parent involvement and attend to children's safety and aesthetic, physical, emotional, social, and cognitive development. They also provide developmentally appropriate instruction in math, language, literacy, and science.

The Critical Role of Preschool

Many preschoolers develop language and literacy concepts as a result of participating in routine activities that occur in their families and communities. Through these activities, children gain an awareness of how to use language and literacy in particular literacy events, the way that literacy operates, and how literacy use empowers family members (Gee, 2001).

In many preschools, children continue to be involved in literacy activities that are remarkably similar to those they have already experienced in their homes and communities (McGill-Franzen, Lanford, & Adams, 2002). These children have a double dose of highly effective language and literacy learning opportunities. They have supportive parents or caregivers who provide materials, opportunities, and informal teaching about how to interact with books and pretend to read, and how to draw and pretend to write. Further, they have highly skilled preschool teachers who provide additional reading and writing opportunities within a high-quality early-childhood program. As a result, they acquire high levels of literacy development.

However, some children get very few opportunities to engage in sustained language and literacy activities either in home or at preschool (Dickinson, 2001). For a variety of reasons, many parents do not read books aloud to their young children or encourage their children to pretend to write. Children growing up in poverty are more likely to attend preschools that have low-quality programs and ineffective preschool teachers (McGill-Franzen et al., 2002). Children from low-literacy preschools and homes enter kindergarten with extremely low levels of literacy development.

However, high-quality preschool experiences do make a difference in young children's lives. Effective preschool teachers can accelerate the learning of children whose parents or caregivers provide low levels of home support for literacy learning (Tabors, Snow, & Dickinson, 2001). Using the activities we describe in this chapter, preschool teachers can create opportunities that will accelerate the language and literacy learning of all children.

Most children who attend high-quality preschools can be expected to enter kindergarten with high levels of language and literacy development. At the beginning of their kindergarten year, children may be able to (McGee, 2005)

- retell a favorite story using some language of the story, past tense verbs, and other features of **sounding literate** (see Chapter 4).

- retell a familiar information book, using some information from the text, timeless present tense verbs, and other features of sounding literate.
- discuss events in a familiar text using analytic talk.
- use complex sentence structures in everyday conversation.
- use increasingly complex vocabulary learned from preschool experiences.
- demonstrate understanding of book and print organization concepts and letter and word concepts.
- recognize as many as forty of the fifty-two uppercase and lowercase alphabet letters, including most uppercase and some lowercase letters.
- write a recognizable first-name signature.
- isolate or segment the beginning sound of a spoken word or identify two rhyming words.
- learn to associate some letters with (consonant) phonemes.
- demonstrate the emergence of the alphabetic principle by beginning to invent spellings.

Learning in the Preschool Classroom

Most preschool programs are founded on common principles of learning.

1. *Three- and four-year-olds learn best when they are actively engaged in manipulating materials.* Preschoolers do not learn effectively when they must sit for long periods of time and merely listen to the teacher. Young children can participate actively in whole-class activities when teachers intersperse reading aloud with more active singing, movement activities, and recitation of finger plays. Teachers need to be mindful that small-group instruction will be more successful when each child has materials than when children must wait long periods of time to have a turn.
2. *Preschoolers learn from play.* For example, over time as children play in the block center, their block constructions and their play with the constructions become more complex. Through the explorations and trial and error that are part of playing with blocks, they discover more complex concepts about balance, size, and spatial relationships. As they play with other children, their language develops in complexity and their emotional and social development expands.
3. *Preschoolers learn from selecting their own activities.* When young children must select their own activities, they use cognitive processes that are not required when they merely are told what to do and how to do it. When children self-select, they must consciously plan, thinking ahead about what they want to do. Then, as they carry out their plan, they monitor their progress toward completing these plans. These activities of planning, carrying out the plan, and monitoring self-behavior are a critical part of self-regulation. **Self-regulation** occurs when children can inhibit behaviors that are not condoned; focus attention on others, including the teacher; willingly take on roles directed by others; and monitor their behavior in different settings. When teachers notice children roaming the room without finding an activity that attracts their attention or sustains their interest, those teachers realize they must not make play decisions for the children but instead must help the children plan and monitor their own play so that children can develop their own self-regulatory behaviors.

READING AND WRITING IN EXEMPLARY PRESCHOOL CLASSROOMS

THREE WAYS that exemplary preschool teachers can help children develop language and literacy concepts follow.

1. *By infusing literacy materials throughout the classroom in nearly every center.* Children learn as they interact with these materials in their daily play.
2. *By having extended conversations with children as they are playing and by modeling how to use literacy materials as children are playing.* Exemplary teachers play with children in such ways as to step up their play to a slightly higher language and cognitive level. They demonstrate how to use new materials and label those materials for children.
3. *By frequently and routinely providing language and instruction in whole-class and small-group activities.* In exemplary preschools, literacy activities that occur in small-group and whole-class settings form a foundation for children's later playful literacy interactions in centers. For example, after a teacher reads aloud a story and helps children dramatize the story using simple props, children enjoy dramatizing the story with a friend later in the library center. After a teacher writes a thank-you note to a classroom visitor as a shared writing activity, several children pretend to write thank-you notes in the writing center.

Much of what preschoolers can do is not conventional—many preschoolers do not yet write alphabet letters conventionally, and even their signatures are not fully developed. They ask many questions or make comments about books read aloud to them that reveal they often have confusions. Therefore, exemplary literacy programs for preschoolers take into account children's development and their unconventional approaches.

Exemplary preschool literacy programs have as their desired outcomes that children learn many conventional literacy skills that we described earlier and within this chapter. However, in exemplary literacy programs, young children are provided many playful opportunities to achieve these expected conventional literacy outcomes through discovery and experimentation. Exemplary preschool teachers find a balance between instruction geared toward helping children develop conventional literacy concepts and activities in which children are allowed and encouraged to explore literacy on their own terms. These balancing activities are systematic—they present experiences that are compatible with children's current level of literacy knowledge yet at the same time provide opportunities for children to develop more complex concepts.

Mrs. McKannon's Classroom: Preschool Literacy in an Exemplary Language- and Print-Rich Environment

We describe one morning in Mrs. McKannon's prekindergarten classroom for 20 four-year-old children. Mrs. McKannon teaches in Washington, D.C., and her children come from a nearby low-income housing project, from a homeless shelter across the street from the school, and also from middle-class parents who own condos in the building in which the school is located. Three children in Mrs. McKannon's classroom came to the school with identified special needs, and the school has a special needs teacher who serves the needs of these children. Mrs. McKannon is an exemplary teacher who arranges her classroom so that print materials are infused in authentic ways in every center, and she provides large blocks of time for children to play in the centers. As children play, she and her teaching assistant engage in many extended conversations as they join in the play. On the day we visited the classroom, Mrs. McKannon was on week 3 of a themed unit about growing things. She has read many storybooks, including *The Ugly Vegetables* (Lin, 1999), *Bigger* (Kirk, 1998), and *Make Way for Ducklings* (McCloskey, 1999). She has also shared information books, including *See How They Grow: Duck* (Royston, 2001) and a predictable book, *Just Enough* (Daniels, 2000), as a part of *Opening the World of Learning* (Schickedanz & Dickinson with Charlotte-Mecklenburg Schools, 2005), a comprehensive early-literacy program published by the Pearson Learning Group.

Children at Play.   Mrs. McKannon's classroom has many centers, including the library, writing, art, science and math, discovery, and home centers. On this morning, the sand and water table has been converted to a compost-making center, and a special dramatic play center, "The Potting Shed," has been set up as the discovery center. By midmorning, children are working and playing at nearly every center. Two children are on the rug in the library center. They are looking at several books together, commenting about the pictures and talking about the illustrations. A large, handwritten, shared writing chart hangs in the center titled "Root Vegetables" with the words *carrot, garlic, potato,* and *onion.* One child points to an illustration in a book he is viewing and asks the other child, "Is this a cabbage? Should it go on the root vegetable list?" The other child says, "I'll ask the teacher if it grows under the dirt."

Two children are at the writing center. At the center, among other writing materials, are a supply of index cards and paper with a fancy border. Earlier in the week, Mrs. McKannon had demonstrated making place cards for a soup party by folding the index cards in half and writing a friend's name on the card. She explained these would be on the table so everyone would know where to sit at the party. That day at lunch, the children were surprised to find place cards on the lunch table. They all had fun finding their own names and eating with new friends. They had earlier learned how to write invitations, and several example invitations were displayed near the writing center. This morning, one of the children at the center is drawing and writing an invitation. She announces, "I'm going to have ice cream with soup," and draws a picture of a double-dip cone. The other child comments, "I like ice cream, too. Maybe I'd better write *ice cream.*" She writes a scribble on her invitation. Next, the two girls discuss whom to invite to their party and decide to make a place card for Megan. One of the girls says, "*Megan* begins with *M*, I'll write that." Mrs. McKannon is nearby and hears this conversation. She enters the center and says, "I bet you both can write *M*. Do you need to look at *M* or do you know it?" One girl says, "It's the up, down, up, down letter"; and both write *M*'s on their paper. Mrs. McKannon says, "What can you do to write the rest of Megan's name?" Calisha replies, "Look on her cubby"; and Makalia answers, "Go ask her." Mrs. McKannon acknowledges that both are good ideas and suggests they each do it.

Two children are at the art center. It has a variety of birdseed, Popsicle sticks, and a jar of honey. Children are making bird-feeder sticks by spreading the honey on the stick and then sprinkling birdseed on the honey. Directions for making the bird-feeder sticks are posted above the center. As the children finish, they sign their names to a sign on a clipboard that says, "I made bird-feeder sticks."

Four children are at the home center. This is a typical preschool center with a small table and chairs, stove, refrigerator, shelves, and baby bed. The center houses plastic food, play cookware and tableware, several dolls and doll clothes, and dress-up clothes. The center also has three cookbooks, a box with recipe cards (with recipes), blank recipe cards, and different kinds of pens. It also has two telephones and a home-made telephone book with pictures of the children and pretend telephone numbers. Several pretend checkbooks and credit cards are in numerous wallets and purses. Today, before center time, Mrs. McKannon placed some new materials in the center and introduced these materials during whole-group time. The new materials are three blank books with the title *Vegetable Soup Recipes*. During whole-group time, Mrs. McKannon reminds children about the activity they have been working on for a few weeks, reading soup recipes and tasting different soups together. There are three shared writing charts near the home center titled *Tomato Vegetable Soup*, *Beef and Vegetable Soup*, and *Mrs. McKannon's Famous Vegetable Soup*. On three different days, Mrs. McKannon or her teaching assistant brought in a large container of soup and each child was able to try a sample. Then they read the soup recipe together, and later the recipes were put in the art center for the children to draw the ingredients. Today, Mrs. McKannon has moved the recipes to the home center for this week's new activity. Children are invited to copy their favorite recipe or write their own recipe as they play in the home center. Today, three children are in the home center. Two children decide to cook a meal for their babies, using empty food containers and plastic food in the center. One child says, "I think I'll cook some chicken. Let me look up a good recipe." She opens a cookbook on one of the shelves in the center and begins looking through the pages. Another child is sitting in a rocking chair, looking at magazines. Nearby, Mrs. McKannon steps into a telephone booth made from a large box. She looks up a number in the telephone book (class telephone book with each child's name and pretend telephone number). She says, "Ring. Ring. Is Ashanti home?" The child in the rocking chair says, "I'll get that," and answers a toy phone in the center. She says, "Ashanti is not here. Can I take a message?" "Yes," says Mrs. McKannon, "I would like to come over later and see the recipe he wrote. He told me his soup is better than mine. I'm coming over to try his recipe. Bye." Then the girl gets up, opens the soup recipe books, and writes. Mrs. McKannon enters the center and says, "Cally, are you making your own recipe for me to try?" Figure 7.1 shows Cally's recipe.

Two children are in the compost-making center. It is the sand table filled with a variety of root vegetables such as carrots with their green tops, celery, and small green onions. The children have several potato mashers and are attempting to mash the vegetables in order to make compost. The teaching assistant steps into the center and begins to mash vegetables with the children. She says, "This is hard work making compost, but I know it will make our soil in the garden richer. It will make next year's crop of vegetables grow faster and bigger." One of the boys replies, "Is this stuff going to smell nasty soon? It looks like garbage." The assistant answers, "Yes, and garbage could be gathered to use as compost, but most people don't have a garden in the city to put compost in."

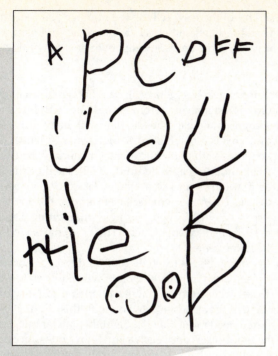

FIGURE 7.1   Cally's Recipe

The other boy pipes up, "My great-grandmother lives in Mississippi and she has a great big garden." The assistant continues, "A very large garden, umm. I bet she grows different kinds of vegetables." The conversation extends for several more minutes as the boys share their experiences with gardens, growing food, and eating vegetables.

Two children are at the easel in the art center and making prints with cut-up vegetables by dipping them in several colors of ink pads and pressing them to the paper hung on the easel. Near this center is a discreet sign for the teachers and assistant reminding them of vocabulary words they might use while they have conversations with children at this center. Words on this list include *ink pad*, *print*, *roll*, *outline*, *width*, *length*, *separate*, *shape*, *cross section*, *press*, *pattern*, and *overlap*.

One child is playing in the potting shed, and he asks the teaching assistant to come help him. In this center are yardsticks, two measuring tapes, and several taped lines on the floor, along with lots of different-size plastic flowerpots, marbles, plastic flowers, and seed envelopes. During the week, the children have been pretending to get ready to plant a garden by measuring the length of a row and then taping it down. Jacob is trying to get the measuring tape to stay out so he can measure one of the rows. The teaching assistant says, "I'll help you measure. I'll hold this end and put it down right here at the end of the row. You pull out the tape very slowly and go to the other end.

Now put it down right on that end of the row. Tell me the number you see. That will tell us how long the row is." Then the assistant helps Lyton find the clipboard with the diagram of a large garden. She says, "Now we can write down how long this row will be on our plan."

The Teacher at Work.   Mrs. McKannon teaches literacy all day. Though most of the children in Mrs. McKannon's classroom do not come from homes with rich literacy experiences, they demonstrate a willingness and eagerness to play with literacy materials in the classroom in authentic ways. This is a result of Mrs. McKannon's deliberately infusing classroom spaces and activities with authentic literacy materials she has previously used in instruction (Casbergue, McGee, & Bedford, 2008). Each of the literacy activities in her classroom was first introduced to a whole-class group or used for a small-group lesson and, finally, placed in the centers. For example, the soup recipes were created in several whole-class activities. Then, during a small-group activity, the children used the recipe charts to locate alphabet letters. Then the charts were placed in the art center and, finally, the home center.

Mrs. McKannon frequently comments, "I teach literacy all day, every day. I teach all the letters all the time. There isn't a day in which I don't invite children to write letters or words, demonstrate how to write letters, segment a phoneme, identify rhyming words, or clap out syllables. Some of my children catch on with this 'all day' teaching approach. However, some children need more. So I deliberately plan language and literacy activities each day for the whole class and teach a small-group lesson every day for all my children. We also know that we have to prepare for the center activities in order for them to be right at the cutting edge of what we want children to be doing. We introduce materials in whole and small groups, and we demonstrate how to play with the materials before we ever put them out for children."

Ms. Rodgers' Classroom: Teaching Concepts about Print, Alphabet Recognition, and Phonemic Awareness

Ms. Rodgers teaches Head Start in a rural community center. At the beginning of the school year, almost none of her children could write their names, and most children's grips on markers suggested they had had few experiences drawing, coloring, or pretending to write. Almost none of the children could recognize any alphabet letters although two children did know the first letters in their names. When assessed for concepts about print, most children knew *front, back, top,* and *bottom;* but very few realized that the left page was read before the right page or anything about directionality of print; and none could point at words one to one.

Even with these low-level skills at entry to Head Start, these children would be expected to have high levels of skills at kindergarten entry. The elementary school the children would attend is a Reading First school; that is, it receives funds through the No Child Left Behind legislation. It uses DIBELS (Dynamic Indicators of Basic Early Literacy Skills, http://dibels.uoregon.edu) to assess kindergartners' literacy progress in the early fall, winter, and spring. By the time of the winter DIBELS assessment, kindergartners are expected to identify forty alphabet letters in less than a minute and to segment beginning phonemes from spoken words. In the spring, they are expected to be able to identify some sounds in nonsense words.

In order to prepare her Head Start students for these kindergarten expectations, Ms. Rodgers and her colleagues decided to increase the intensity with which they taught concepts about print, alphabet recognition, and phonemic awareness while still meeting Head Start guidelines for balancing child-initiated activities with teacher-directed activities. They did so using shared writing with write on, guided drawing, and daily literacy lessons, at first in alphabet recognition and later in phonemic awareness.

Shared Writing with Write On. Ms. Rodgers used shared writing nearly every day to demonstrate directionality concepts and to contextualize alphabet instruction. **Shared writing with write on** is an elaboration of this. Shared writing begins with a meaningful experience and rich conversation. For example, after reading *The Three Billy Goats Gruff* (Stevens, 1995), Ms. Rodgers drew the children's attention to the picnic the goats enjoyed after getting across the bridge. She and the children talked about the tablecloth spread on the ground, the picnic basket, and the food the goats ate. Then Ms. Rodgers talked about going on a picnic in the park with her grandchildren. Finally, she showed her picnic basket in which she had packed sandwiches, apples, potato chips, juice boxes, and cookies along with paper plates and napkins. The children talked about why these were good foods for packing in a basket and which foods might not be good.

Now Ms. Rodgers introduces the writing portion of shared writing. She said, "Now we will write a list for packing a picnic basket. Let me read the title of our list. It is right up here." She points to the first word. "I'll read each word and point to it. *List, of, Picnic, Food.*" Ms. Rodgers had written the title on chart paper in preparation for this lesson. Ms. Rodgers has targeted two skills for teaching: she wants children to notice words (they have spaces around them) and to listen for the first phoneme in words. So, after reading the title, she said, "I want someone to come up here and point to the words of the title as I read it and then count the number of words." A child quickly came forward and pointed as everyone read the title again. Now Ms. Rodgers says, "I'll say the first sound of something I packed in my basket, and you see if you know what it is. I packed something that starts /s/." There are many guesses from the children, so Ms. Rodgers says, "Yes, Quadaravious, it is ssssandwich. And it starts with the letter *S*." She writes the word and then says, "Here is something else I packed, see if you can guess: /p/, /p/, /p/." She writes *potato*, then says, "*Potato chips* is two words so I have to scoot over a little bit before I start the next word, *chips.*" After writing *chips*, she says, "You can see two words, *potato chips*, see that little space between. That means another word. I'd like someone to step up and touch the SPACE between the two words *potato chips.*"

Ms. Rodgers continues saying the first sound for the words *juice* and *cookie.* After the list is complete (*sandwich, potato chips, juice, cookies*), Ms. Rodgers says, "I am going to let three people step up to the chart and find a letter they want to write. Then I am going to leave this picnic list on the easel during center time. All of you can step up and write letters or draw pictures." Three children step up, and Ms. Rodgers lets them write a letter. If they need help, she writes the letter first, reminding the class about the lines they will need to make the letter. Later that day, eight other children step up to the chart during center time and write on the chart. Ms. Rodgers invites five other children— ones she knows need more practice writing letters—to write with her and invites each one to locate the space between *potato chips.*

During this brief lesson (it lasted only fifteen minutes), Ms. Rodgers focused on concept development, vocabulary learning, concepts about print and phonemic awareness, and helping children write alphabet letters. This whole-group activity was immediately available for all children to use during center time, and Ms. Rodgers made good use of the time to target specific children for additional one-on-one guidance.

Guided Drawing.   Ms. Rodgers realized that her four-year-olds had had few experiences drawing and writing before coming to Head Start. The children's motor control was below age expectations because of their lack of opportunity to practice. She needed a way to make sure children drew every day. Unfortunately, just putting materials in a writing center and art center did not seem to promote practicing as often as the children needed. Therefore, she decided to include a teacher-directed, guided-drawing activity often as a part of morning entry activities, a small-group activity, or center activities. She decided to use guided drawing.

Guided drawing is an activity in which the teacher demonstrates how to make the basic lines and shapes used in drawing and writing (such as vertical, horizontal, diagonal, and curving lines, circles, ovals, squares, triangles, and dots). As the teacher demonstrates making the marks on a sheet of large unlined paper, she tells a story such as going on a car trip to Grandma's that would go through tall trees (as she tells this part of the story, she demonstrates writing long vertical lines, then invites the children to make tall trees), past a cow pasture (short vertical lines), crossing a bridge (long horizontal line), over some bumps (curved lines), and through mountains (diagonal lines in a V). Immediately after the teacher's demonstrations of making different kinds of lines, the children practice making them on their large, unlined paper. Ms. Rodgers took a few minutes to lead the children through one guided drawing and then invited children to draw on their own. Gradually, as most children gained better motor control, Ms. Rodgers no longer included guided-drawing activities.

Small-Group Lessons in Alphabet Recognition and Phonemic Awareness.   Ms. Rodgers presented information about alphabet letters and phonemic awareness all day, every day, in just the same way as Mrs. McKannon. However, she also took a more systematic approach during daily small-group lessons. In the fall, she focused on alphabet recognition. In the winter, she interspersed phonemic awareness activities with alphabet activities. In the spring, she added in work with sound-letter correspondences. In the fall, Ms. Rodgers taught four letters each week, two of which were confusable letters. **Confusable letters** are letters that share many of the same letter features, often causing children to confuse them. Pairs of letters such as *I* and *H*, *N* and *Z*, and *C* and *U* differ only in their orientation. So, Ms. Rodgers taught letters such as *A*, *C*, *U*, and *T* together in one week. Children sorted letter tiles, practiced writing the letters, fished for letters (letters were paper-clipped to paper fish and "fished" with a magnet pointer), fed letters to a puppet (Roberts & Neal, 2004), and played letter concentration.

When Ms. Rodgers began teaching phonemic awareness, she selected the phonemes /s/ and /m/. She chose these because of the contrasting mouth shapes involved in their pronunciation and because they are **continuants,** that is, their pronunciations can be prolonged. In contrast to /s/, which is pronounced with the lips apart, /m/ is pronounced with the lips together. Children can easily see this difference as Ms. Rodgers shows them how the two phonemes are spoken. Because /s/ and /m/ are continuants, Ms. Rodgers can stretch out their pronunciation while children listen to the sounds and observe the different mouth shapes (McGee & Dail, 2010). Later, in teaching phonemic awareness, Ms. Rodgers will demonstrate phonemes whose distinctive features are more difficult to see (such as /t/ with its distinctive tongue tap on the roof of the mouth) and whose pronunciations cannot be prolonged (such as /b/, which is "popped," that is, it can be spoken only in an instant).

In her phonemic awareness lessons, Ms. Rodgers pronounced words with stress on individual phonemes. She used scaffolding to teach children how to hear phonemes and say them in isolation by directing her students to watch her mouth as she said the sounds and words. She helped them to say phonemes in isolation; to emphasize the sounds in words; and to feel what their mouths, tongues, teeth, and vocal cords were doing (McGee & Ukrainetz, 2009). Later, the children sorted pictures with two different initial phonemes; fished for pictures and isolated the phonemes in the pictured words; and played sound concentration, matching two pictures with the same initial phoneme.

Supporting Vocabulary and Listening Comprehension

Reading and writing are ultimately about meaning—and both Mrs. McKannon and Ms. Rodgers provided many opportunities for children to explore new concepts and acquire new vocabulary. These are critical activities because readers must construct meaning out of the words as they read, and writers must convey meaning through their writing of words. Vocabulary and oral comprehension in preschool play a key role in children's later being able to comprehend highly complex books and write detailed and persuasive compositions (Wells, 1986; Senechal, LeFevre, Hudson, & Lawson, 1996). Therefore, vocabulary and concept development, experience and knowledge of books, drama and retelling, and extended conversations form a strong foundation for children's literacy success (McGinty & Justice, 2010). As a result of these activities, children are expected to retell storybooks capturing the main events, names of characters, and using past tense. They are expected to retell information books or nonfiction with most important ideas using some of the scientific vocabulary. They are expected to carry on conversations and to participate in classroom discussions with increasing use of vocabulary experienced in lessons and activities and with increasingly complex sentence structures.

Using Interactive Read-Alouds

Reading books aloud is a daily occurrence in every preschool. Teachers plan these read-alouds so that they expose children to a variety of good literature (see Chapter 6 for different genres of literature) including storybooks, nonfiction, poetry, and predictable books (Zucker & Landry, 2010). They also plan how they will read the books in order to take advantage of the rich concepts and vocabulary and to extend children's listening comprehension. Listening comprehension involves understanding what the author meant to convey and also making some inferences—stating ideas that are not in the text or the illustrations. Children also learn to reason by considering causes and effects (what caused something to happen or what will happen as a consequence of an action).

Supporting vocabulary and oral language development and listening comprehension is a matter of carefully preparing to read the book. To extend vocabulary knowledge, teachers identify vocabulary words that are considered tier 2 words (Beck, McKeown, & Kucan, 2008). **Tier 2 words** are words that are more sophisticated than everyday words. For example, the everyday word *baby* is related to the more sophisticated tier 2 word *infant.* Teachers select ten to twelve of these words in the book they will be reading and then consider how they can extend children's understanding of these words using vocabulary teaching techniques (Neuman & Dwyer, 2009):

- pointing out a word's meaning by showing it in the illustration (for example, pointing to a cradle in the illustration)
- showing pictures prior to reading
- slipping in a short definition while reading (*"Wailing* means 'crying very loudly'")
- subtly acting out a meaning during reading (demonstrating *strutting* by sitting up straight and moving from side to side with the chin up)

Teachers use the tier 2 vocabulary words in their questions and in their explanations, and they prompt children to use these words when they comment or answer questions (McGee & Schickedanz, 2007). Teachers invite children to say the words in meaningful phrases, or they have all the children repeat a vocabulary word. As teachers read books more than once, they provide even more opportunities for children to learn and use the vocabulary words. Extending opportunities to use the vocabulary during art activities, in hands-on science experiments, or in dramatic play also extends children's vocabulary learning opportunities.

Teachers can extend children's oral language by modeling the use of complex sentences as they talk about books. For example, a teacher may comment about *Henny Penny* (Galdone, 1968). "I notice that Henny Penny's legs look like she is running very fast because she is really worried about the sky falling down. I think Cocky Locky is going to know that Henny Penny is really scared." The first sentence is complex because it includes a dependent and independent clause as well as verb and noun phrases.

However, reading books aloud is more than merely focusing on vocabulary or using more complex language. It is also about enhancing listening comprehension: Teachers model thinking aloud, carefully select questions that require thinking beyond mere facts, and use good follow-up questions that prompt children to clarify and extend their responses through explanation. Composing good questions that stimulate children's thinking also requires careful planning (McGee & Schickedanz, 2007). Reading a book on the run does not allow teachers time to carefully think through how to best share the book. Good questions begin with words such as *how, why, how do we know,* or *what if.* Finally, teachers need to be prepared to clarify children's misunderstandings. As children make comments and attempt to answer questions, teachers carefully listen to acknowledge what they are trying to communicate and to provide explanations that clear up any confusion (Schickedanz, 2008).

Teachers also should select books that are related to a theme so that vocabulary extends across books and concepts are deepened. For example, the books *The Carrot Seed* (Krauss, 1945) and *Jack's Garden* (Cole, 1997) are both about gardening. To extend vocabulary, a teacher might create a **vocabulary prop box** that would contain real objects for vocabulary words that appear in the books. A vocabulary prop box for these two books might include seeds, a trowel, a small rake, a portion of a garden hose, a watering can, plastic insects, a variety of plastic flowers, and a plastic carrot (Wasik & Bond, 2001). As teachers share these props, they can invite children to "Tell me what you know about this" or "Tell me how you would use this." As they read aloud, teachers can remind children of the objects in their prop box. For example, when reading *The Carrot Seed*, a teacher paused to ask a question (p. 249):

Teacher: How did the little boy plant the seed?

Child 1: He dug a hole.

Teacher: [to same child] Tell me more [about what he did when he dug a hole].

Child 1: He dug a hole in the ground and he put the seed in.

Teacher: How did he dig the hole?

Child 2: With a shovel like this. [The child demonstrates the action of digging.]

Teacher: Kind of like the [trowel] that I showed you.

This teacher used a clarifying and extending prompt ("Tell me more") as well as repeating the children's response to encourage the children to expand their sentence (Beauchat, Blamey, & Walpole, 2009). Child 1 responded to the teacher's questions with "He dug a hole" and expanded this sentence to "He dug a hole in the ground and he put the seed in" after the prompt. Thus, after the initial question, "How did the little boy plant the seed?," the teacher prompted children to increase the sophistication of their answers and use of language as well as to use more vocabulary. Notice that the initial question began with *How* rather than *What*. Questions that begin with *What* usually require literal thinking, whereas questions that begin with *How, Why*, or *What if* usually require inferential thinking (Zucker & Landry, 2010). Literal thinking is required to talk about what is seen in illustrations or heard in the story text being read such as when children are asked to name, describe, or count objects in illustrations. In contrast, inferential thinking is required to talk about things not seen in the illustrations or heard in the book. They require the children to reason and make inferences such as when children are asked to explain why a character acted as he did. Typically, teachers should ask far fewer literal thinking questions and more inferential thinking questions.

Preschool teachers should plan to read aloud nonfiction or information books on a wide variety of topics (Pentimonti, Zucker, Justice, & Kaderavek, 2010). Information books sometimes prompt more conversation and questions than do simple stories (Smolkin & Donovan, 2002). When reading information books, teachers want to make explicit the connections among ideas. Books dealing with science concepts often include, for example, cause-and-effect relationships—how animals catch their prey or why animals hibernate in the winter. Teachers can make these connections explicit by helping children understand that a spider can catch an insect because its web is sticky. Information books can easily be incorporated into themes as they were in Mrs. McKannon's classroom.

After reading books aloud, effective teachers make sure they make those books available in the classroom book center. Children are especially interested in browsing through a book immediately after it has been read aloud. Children develop stronger literacy skills when they have access to and engage with books on their own (Neuman, 1999) and are supported in this activity by frequent teacher read-alouds.

Storytelling and Drama

Storytelling and dramatizing are favorite preschool activities. Young children's play often includes extended episodes of fantasy play in which they become their favorite characters in stories (Welsch, 2008). Text and toy sets can be used to stimulate dramatic play about particular stories (Rowe, 1998). **Text and toy sets** are realistic, small-scale toys and other props that are placed in a special box or basket in the book center along with the storybook. Props should include something the child can wear to become a specific character as well as objects that are used in a specific book. Recommended books include books with memorable characters who use repeated language and for which objects have a particular importance (Welsch). For example, *Little Red Hen (Makes a Pizza)* (Sturges, 1999) includes Little Red Hen repeatedly asking, "Cluck, cluck who will help me . . .?" The book includes specific objects, including a pizza pan, flour, mozzarella, bowl and mixing spoon, and a finished pizza. These objects can be gathered and placed in a box to prompt book-related pretend play. First, teachers read aloud the book and then introduce the props included in the text and toy set. Children are encouraged to use the materials during center time. Some children act out the story, others make up new actions for the characters, and still other children make up their own stories with the props.

Folktales and fairytales are particularly effective for whole-group drama and small-group storytelling activities. For example, teachers would read *The Three Billy Goats Gruff* (Stevens, 1995) aloud to the class on one day and on the next day would read it aloud inviting children to say each of the characters' dialogue. The following day, the teacher may give each child a drama prop: faces drawn on card stock. Several children have the face of the big billy goat, others have the face of the middle billy goat, still other children have the face of the little billy goat, and the remainder of the children have the face of the troll. The teacher acts as narrator and director, pointing to the children when it is their turn to talk and modeling the dialogue for children. Later, in small group, children may get an envelope with drama props for retelling this entire story: drawings of the faces of the four characters drawn on four sheets of paper. Teachers guide children by coaching them about which prop to hold up and what dialogue to say.

Taking Time to Talk

As surprising as it sounds, many preschoolers have few opportunities to have a one-on-one conversation with their teachers (Dickinson, 2001). Teachers are often busy with the whole class of children so that taking a few minutes each day to talk with each child seems impossible. However, when teachers **sit and stay** in centers for extended periods of time, they can capitalize on numerous opportunities for conversations with children. Effective conversations begin with children's interests and their actions. The best conversations are extended over several turns (during which each person takes a turn to talk) and in which a topic is explored in depth. Children who are learning English and children with low levels of vocabulary development need more frequent conversations to extend their language skills.

The focus of conversations with children should be on genuine communication rather than on correcting children's language errors. Young children are still acquiring proficiency in language, and attempting to be understood through rephrasing and clarifying are more effective for their language development than repeating a correct sentence. Teachers should include some sophisticated vocabulary in their conversations. One-on-one conversations provide many opportunities to explain words and to use both rare words and everyday words for the same concepts—for example, using the word *infant* as well as *baby*.

As teachers talk with children, they may engage children in conversations about past events or planning for the future. Such conversations require children to use decontextualized language that describes events, objects, and people not present in the here and now of the classroom. Teachers can prompt such conversations by talking about familiar events they have engaged in—going to the dentist, shopping at the mall, or visiting a relative.

SUPPORTING CONCEPTS ABOUT PRINT AND ALPHABET LETTER LEARNING

TO BECOME SUCCESSFUL READERS AND WRITERS, children need experiences with print. Shared reading of books with large print or reading books in which the print is salient are two ways teachers can draw children's attention to print. We have already seen how Ms. Rodgers used shared writing to teach concepts about print and letter recognition.

Shared Reading

Shared reading is a form of interactive read-aloud using big books or enlarged charts of poems or songs (Parkes, 2000). The text selected for shared reading often includes rhyming words, words with alliteration, or repeated words or phrases that make the text highly memorable. After teachers introduce the text to children, the children naturally join in saying the text—thus, it is called *shared reading* because the children share reading with the teacher. Effective books for shared reading have a limited amount of text, print that is large enough for children to see when they are seated near but not next to the book, and word spaces that are large enough so that words are easy to isolate.

For reading, teachers will need a sturdy easel large enough to support the big book or enlarged chart. As they read, teachers can pause to allow children to chime in and say parts of the text. Teachers may want to point out words that rhyme or begin with the same sound (alliteration).

Beyond enjoyment, shared reading can be used to teach children concepts about print, including book and print organization and letter and word concepts. Book and print organization concepts include knowing that left pages are read before right pages, the top and bottom of pages, print direction including the left-to-right directionality and return sweep, and one-to-one matching of words (Zucker, Ward, & Justice, 2009). To teach book and print organization concepts, teachers can merely say, "I'll read this page first (pointing to the left page). Now, I'll read this page (pointing to the right page). Now, I have to turn the page." Teachers can also use pointers to point out where to begin reading and to point to each word from left to right across the page of text.

Eventually, children can take turns pointing to the words (with a teacher's guidance) as the teacher and children chant the story or poem. As children point, teachers can make explicit pointing to the top of the page and the exact place to begin reading. They can make explicit their one-on-one matching and the return sweep each time they read (Beauchat et al., 2009).

Shared reading can be used to teach alphabet recognition (Justice & Ezell, 2002) and letter and word concepts (Zucker et al., 2009). After reading a big book or a poem written large on chart paper, teachers can ask children to step up to the book or chart paper and find particular letters. This is very effective when a letter appears frequently on a single page of text or in the text of a poem displayed on chart paper. Teachers can have children step up and find a letter that also occurs in their name or find two letters that are the same. Teachers can write a letter on a dry-erase board, have children name that letter, and then have the children step up to the displayed text and find it there. Teachers can have children find two letters that are the same, count the words on a line of text, find just one letter, then two letters, or find just one word or two words. They can find short or long words. They can count long words. They can say, "Laundromat is a long word; let's count the number of letters in that word."

Because of their familiarity with shared reading texts, children enjoy pretending to reread these books and poems on their own. Small copies of big books or poems should be included in the book center to encourage children's pretend reading.

Shared Writing

Shared writing can also be used to teach book and print organization concepts as well as letter and word concepts. First teachers produce the shared writing chart with children following a memorable activity, such as examining root vegetables and learning how they are grown. We have found that shared writing with preschoolers is easier when children dictate words or phrases to add to a list. Lists can be made quickly, because it only takes a few seconds to write a word in the list. Like Ms. Rodgers, Mrs. McKannon wrote several lists with her children related to the theme *growing things* (e.g., a list of root vegetables, soup recipes, directions for making bird-feeder sticks).

Another activity calling for shared writing is to compose a **pattern innovation.** Pattern innovations begin as the teacher reads a predictable poem or story. Once the children are familiar with the pattern created by the repeated phrases in the book, they can construct their own innovation on the pattern. For example, *A Dark, Dark Tale* (Brown, 1981) tells the story of entering a scary house, going slowly up the stairs, and looking inside a shadowy cupboard only to find a mouse. It includes the repetitive pattern, "In the dark, dark _____, there was a dark, dark _____."

A group of four-year-olds retold the story using their school as the setting:

Once there was a dark, dark school.
In the dark, dark school there was a dark, dark hall.
Down the dark, dark hall was a dark, dark classroom.
In the dark, dark classroom there was a dark, dark cubbie.
In the dark, dark cubbie there was a SPIDER!

Pattern innovations that are carefully copied on large charts become favorite reading materials for shared reading and pretend reading. Teachers can make these texts into books by typing the text on several pages and illustrating the text with magazine pictures or clip art. These books can be bound and placed in the book center; they often become children's favorites.

After producing shared writing charts, teachers can have children step up to the chart to demonstrate concepts about print. Figure 7.2 presents a list of concepts about print and activities to help children acquire those concepts.

FIGURE 7.2   Concepts about Print Instructional Activities

Directionality Concepts	Concepts about letters	Concepts about words
"Step up to the book/chart and ____"	"Step up to the book/chart and ____"	"Step up to the book/chart and ____"
Point to what I read (the print)	Point to (or circle) this letter (show magnetic letter); write this letter	Point to (or circle) this word (show a word card); Point to (or circle) an interesting word
Point to exactly where I start reading (top left word)	Point to (or circle) the letter F (teacher names a letter); point to the letter F and then write it	Point to (or circle) a short word (or the shortest word); count the number of letters
After I read this (point to first word) show me where I read next (left-to-right across line)	Point to (or circle) a letter you know; Point to a letter you know and write it	Point to (or circle) a long word (or the longest word): count the number of letters
After I read this (sweep across the first line of text) show me where I read next (return sweep)	Use your fingers and show me (or circle) just one letter; show me (or circle) two letters	Find a word that begins with F
Point to the words one-to-one as I read	Point to (or circle) two letters that are the same	Circle the first letter in this word; circle the first letter in a word
	Point to (or circle) all the A's	Circle the last letter in this word; circle the last letter in a word
		Count the number of words in the title
		Count the number of words we wrote
		Point to the first word; point to the last word

The Sign-In Procedure and Other Name Activities

Novice readers and writers who realize that written marks can communicate messages are ready for the **sign-in procedure.** In this procedure, each child writes his or her name each day on an attendance sign-in sheet (Richgels, 2003). This procedure is functional; it should actually serve as the attendance record of the classroom. With young three-year-olds, the procedure may consist of having children place a card with their name on it in a box or on a chart. Later, they may place their name card and a slip of paper (the same size as the name card) on which they have written their names in the attendance box. Eventually, children will sign in by writing their signatures on an attendance sheet. Naturally, three- and four-year-olds' signatures will not be conventional when they first begin the sign-in procedure. However, by signing in daily, children gradually refine their signatures into readable names.

Ms. Rodgers uses the sign-in procedure because many of the children who come to her classroom have had few writing experiences prior to beginning preschool. Many children do not have crayons and paper in their homes. Before she began the sign-in procedure, few children voluntarily visited the writing center. The sign-in procedure gave the children an opportunity to write each day. As they became comfortable with that very brief writing experience, they gained confidence and began visiting the writing center for more lengthy writing experiences. The children also observed that their writing was useful; Ms. Rodgers used the sign-in list to comment on children's absences. Figure 7.3 presents an example of Ms. Rodgers' sign-in sheets.

Activities to Promote Alphabet Letter Learning

Shared reading, shared writing, and the sign-in procedure provide many opportunities for teachers to talk about alphabet letters and demonstrate their conventional formation. Through "all day, all the time activities" evident in Mrs. McKannon's classroom, many children will learn to recognize many alphabet letters. They will hear about letters during shared reading and shared writing; they will locate and write letters in step-up and write-on activities. Teachers often use letter activities as transitions. For example, they may call children to line up to go to the playground by saying, "If your name begins with the letter *K*, you may line up now."

We do not recommend that preschool teachers engage children in handwriting practice or require children to copy alphabet letters merely for the purpose of learning a letter's correct formation (Schickedanz & Casbergue, 2004). However, we do recommend that teachers frequently model for children how to write letters and, as they model, that they talk about the strokes they are making (Schickedanz, 1999). This naturally occurs during shared writing as teachers spell words as they write them. However, teachers can also capitalize on other opportunities to introduce and reinforce the formation of alphabet letters. For example, one preschool teacher noticed that one child was writing a letter *S* in nearly conventional form in his sign-in signature whereas most of the other children had not yet mastered this difficult letter. During whole group, the teacher complimented the writer, "I noticed that Sakeil wrote a

Children Sign In

Date: 9/23/

Jackson	
Arick	
Cordale	
Jamyia	
Brannon	
Johnathan	

FIGURE 7.3   A Sign-In Sheet from Ms. Rodgers' Classroom

very nice *S* today at sign-in." Then she quickly demonstrated how to write the letter on a large chart and invited Sakeil to step up to the chart and also write the letter. Later, the chart was hung in the writing center and all the children were invited to practice writing *S*'s.

Another activity that directs attention to alphabet letters is teaching children to write everyone's name (Cunningham, 2000). Each day, the teacher demonstrates how to write one child's name on a large chart paper. Children practice writing the name on small wipe-off boards or on paper attached to a clipboard. As they write, the teacher and children talk about the alphabet letters they are writing. Figure 7.4 presents two

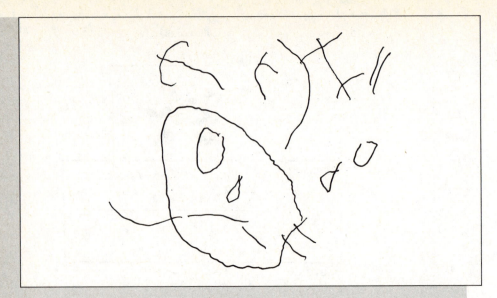

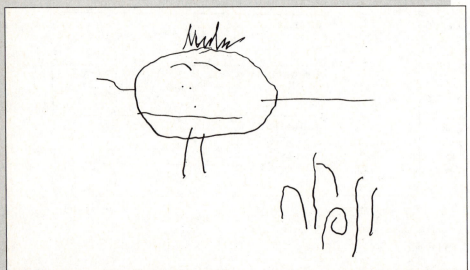

FIGURE 7.4 Writing and Drawing *Angel*

children's attempts to write Angel's name. This lesson took place early in the year in a Head Start classroom in which all the children were English language learners. Notice that one child is writing letter-like shapes that have some relationship to Angel's name and the other child has written a series of lines and circles. Both children attempted to draw *Angel* with one picture a clear tadpole (see Chapter 2) and the other with the necessary shape (circle) and lines without a clear tadpole structure.

TECHNOLOGY TIE-IN

The Internet includes many Web sites featuring alphabet letters.

www.LearningPlanet.com/act/abcorder.asp The alphabet letters are spoken aloud and children are invited to click on alphabet letters to indicate which letter comes next in a sequence. All of the alphabet letters are displayed in order so the child does not need to remember letters to play the game.

www.literacyhour.co.uk/kids/alph_char2.html. An alphabet chart is presented at this site. Children can click on the letters and a page of an alphabet book is displayed.

www.boowakwala.com/alphabet/online-alphabet-game.html Four letters are presented in both uppercase and lowercase letters. A character says a letter name and children click on that letter

http://funschool.com is more challenging. Here, children must locate alphabet letters hidden in a scary Halloween picture. The sound effects add to the pleasure of this activity. However, children need to already know the alphabet letters in order to play the game.

http://starfall.com presents several different animated alphabet letter activities.

SUPPORTING CHILDREN'S DEVELOPMENT OF PHONEMIC AWARENESS, LETTER-SOUND KNOWLEDGE, AND ACQUISITION OF THE ALPHABETIC PRINCIPLE

PHONEMIC AWARENESS, that is, conscious attention to individual sounds (phonemes) in words, is essential to learning to read and write (Adams, 1990; Goswami, 2004). Fully developed phonemic awareness, the sort of awareness that allows children to use the alphabetic principle in reading and writing, entails phoneme-by-phoneme segmentation of words. Most preschoolers do not achieve this level of awareness. However, preschoolers can develop other sorts of phonological awareness that are first steps toward this fully developed phonemic awareness (McGee & Dail, 2010). Phonological awareness occurs when children are directed to sound units larger than a single phoneme. For example, with experience, preschoolers can learn to detect syllables and recognize and produce rhyming words. They can also learn to segment or isolate the first sounds in words, the first step in phonemic awareness. This will occur as teachers read nursery rhymes and other texts with many examples of rhyme and alliteration. In the last part of this chapter, we describe many activities that allow preschoolers to develop the beginnings of phonemic awareness, including playful lessons with a systematic approach to phonemic awareness.

Attending to Syllable and Rhyme

Nursery rhymes and other rhyming jingles can be found in literature from around the world. They provide a perfect starting point for drawing children's attention to the sounds of language. In fact, three-year-olds who have had so many experiences with nursery rhymes that they have memorized some of them are far more likely to have high levels of phonemic awareness as five-year-olds than children who have not had many experiences with nursery rhymes (MacLean, Bryant, & Bradley, 1987). Children naturally learn nursery rhymes when they are repeated again and again as a part of whole-group activities in preschool. Many nursery rhymes and jump-rope jingles can be quickly recited emphasizing the rhythm created by accented syllables. Using the word syllables as children chant the rhyme raises their awareness of this unit of sound in language. Teachers can make syllables even more explicit by chanting and emphasizing the syllables in children's names.

When teachers turn to rhyme, attending to syllables should be eliminated so that children can concentrate on this new unit of sound. Teachers can draw children's attention to the rhymes included in nursery rhymes with "I can hear" talk. For example, when listening to the nursery rhyme "Hickory Dickory Dock," teachers can say, "I can hear *clock* and *dock;* they rhyme." Or, with another rhyming book, teachers can say, "I hear *mouse, house*—those two words rhyme *mmmm ouse* and *hhh ouse.*" Simply pausing to notice a few rhyming words during shared or interactive read-alouds is enough to capture some children's attention (Cunningham, 1998).

Attending to Beginning Phonemes

Teachers can continue making "I can hear" statements about beginning sounds when talking about children's names. If Miguel is chosen as helper for the day, the teacher can say, "I can hear Miguel's /mmmm/, the first sound in his name /mmmm/ *Miguel*." In a later instance of Miguel's being helper, the teacher may ask, "What sound do you hear at the beginning of *Miguel*?" Still later, the teacher may withhold display of Miguel's name card until she gets a response to "The name of today's helper starts with /mmm/. Who could it be?" Teachers can use the beginning phonemes of children's names in transition activities. For example, when calling children to line up for lunch, teachers might say, "If your name begins with /m/, you may get in our line now." *Charlie Parker Played Be Bop* (Raschka, 1992) is a picture book that can be used to heighten awareness of sounds in words. After reading the single line of text displayed across two facing pages, "Boppitty, bibbitty, bop. BANG!," a preschool teacher might say, "I can hear /b/ in those words!" and repeat all four words, emphasizing their initial *b* sound.

A more systematic approach to learning to isolate or segment beginning phonemes is to use phoneme scaffolding (McGee & Ukrainetz, 2009). In **phoneme scaffolding,** the teacher uses three levels of support: high, medium, and low in order to make sure the child learns the task of segmenting and can do so with a variety of words starting with consonant phonemes. High support in scaffolding is provided when the teacher models the task and elicits the child's participation by copying what the teacher has done. Most teachers find that when they begin teaching segmenting phonemes, children simply don't know what the teacher wants. Teachers will say, "What is the first sound in *mouse*?" Children are likely to say "mouse," simply repeating the word, or "squeak," attempting to say the sound that a mouse would make. A few children will say the letter *M*. Although this response shows lots of knowledge, it does not answer the question, "What is the first sound in *mouse*?" and children have to be able to separate the SOUND from the LETTER in order to develop phonemic awareness. Thus, to help the children complete the task, teachers use high levels of support. The teacher says, "What is the first sound in *moon*? /m/m/m/*moon*. Watch my mouth (teacher presses her fingers together close to her mouth). "*Moon* starts /m/. You say /m/." The teacher asks the question, demonstrates and gives a clue about the mouth position, provides the answer required for this task, and then elicits the answer from the child. With medium support in scaffolding, the teacher does not provide the answer but still provides plenty of help. The teacher says, "What is the first sound in *moon*? /m/m/m/*moon*, watch my lips" (and again uses the motion of pushing fingers together near the mouth). Here, the teacher does not supply the answer but waits for the child to provide it. With low support in scaffolding, the teacher only gives a single hint, "What is the first sound in *moon*? /m/*oon*." Here, she only slightly elongates the first sound and waits for the child to respond.

Modifying Instruction to Meet the Needs of Diverse Learners

TEACHERS ARE CONCERNED with supporting all children's literacy growth; with thoughtful instruction, most children do succeed in becoming reflective, motivated readers and writers. Most children develop a range of expected knowledge within a reasonable time frame when they are given adequate opportunities and instruction. For young children, this time frame and the range of expected knowledge are wide and allow for much individual variation. However, teachers also recognize that some children seem to struggle to acquire literacy, even within literacy-rich classrooms and with a wide variety of instructional experiences. These children need teachers who are especially observant and adept at modifying instructional techniques.

In preschool, the first place to meet the needs of individual learners is in interacting with children as they select and play with center materials. Teachers can engage a child in conversation and provide informal instruction while at the same time honoring and respecting the child's lead. Teachers use systematic observation and careful documentation in anecdotal notes to make decisions on when to intervene with children in a more targeted way. Within the wide range of normal language development, some specific accomplishments serve as guides. Steady preschool growth in utterance length, utterance complexity, and vocabulary variety prepare children for successful literacy learning; lack of accomplishment in those areas makes literacy success difficult (Walker, Greenwood, Hart, & Carta, 1994; Scarborough, 1991). **Utterance length** is how many morphemes a child uses on average in a turn at talking. **Utterance complexity** is how many and what kinds of phrases and clauses a child uses to make a number of different kinds of sentences. **Vocabulary variety** is the number of different words, especially rare words, that a child understands and uses (Dickinson & Sprague, 2001). Teachers can take stock of children's utterance length and complexity and vocabulary variety through observation. Typically, preschool children can speak in sentences five to seven words in length. Acquisition of verbs and prepositions is an important aspect of vocabulary development in preschool.

Targeted Classroom Interventions

Ms. Rodgers' systematic approach to targeted classroom interventions was to teach four letters each week, targeting two confusable letters and two other letters with small groups of children. All the children in her classroom received this intervention. It might be considered a tier 1 intervention from a response to intervention perspective. That is, she provided explicit instruction to all children. Each Friday, she observed her students in a small-group activity in order to assess their ability to name each of the four letters and to write them from memory. Most of her children knew far fewer than ten letters when she began this targeted approach. After the intervention, most children recognized more than half of the letters. Note that the activities used in this intervention were playful (for example, feeding alphabet letters to a puppet), and most of them included games that are engaging to young children (for example, playing concentration by matching two of the same letters). Figure 7.5 presents the four letters Ms. Rodgers selected for instruction in each of ten weeks of targeted intervention.

Despite Ms. Rodgers' targeted intervention, her careful observations showed that three children still had learned fewer than four alphabet letters. So, she prepared another intervention for these children. For ten minutes, three days a week, during center time, she pulled these children to a small-group table and taught alphabet letters, two letters per week. Because the group was so small, Ms. Rodgers was able to provide more individual support and feedback to each child. Within the response to intervention model, this instruction would be considered a tier 2 intervention because it allowed her to provide more intense instruction for the children.

Shared Reading with Planned Language Activities

One kind of planned language activity is to read aloud carefully selected books and scaffold children's attention to verbs, adjectives, and adverbs (Justice, Pence, Beckman, Skibbe, & Wiggins, 2005). For example, action verbs are a critical component of the book *Mr. Gumpy's Outing* (Burningham, 1970). The animals flap, trample, muck, and bleat. Teachers act out these animal actions as they read the story aloud (for example, by flapping their arms up and down) and then ask children to apply their new knowledge (for example, by naming other animals that can flap) (Justice et al.). Other books can be used to introduce adjectives, opposites, and time-related adverbs. For example, *The Napping House* (Wood & Wood, 1984) includes repeated adjective-noun phrases (such as *cozy bed, snoring granny,* and *dreaming child*). Teachers can ask questions such as "Who is cozy? How do you get cozy?" Then teachers can help children form their own phrases, such as *the cozy chair, the cozy couch,* and *the cozy blanket.* Again, this intervention is best provided to small groups of children who most need language support, including English language learners.

Talking about Objects Related to a Book or Theme. Another appropriate language activity for children who need more structured language support is to gather a small group of children to talk about objects related to a book that will be read later that day or the next

FIGURE 7.5   Letters for Targeted Intervention Lessons

Week	Letters
1.	A, C, U, T
2.	E, F, I, O
3.	H, L, B, I
4.	D, P, R, B
5.	G, J, L, E
6.	K, R, X, M
7.	M, W, V, S
8.	N, Q, Y, Z
9.	V, W, A, M
10.	E, F, T, L

day. For example, before reading aloud *The Little Red Hen (Makes a Pizza)* (Sturges, 1999), teachers can bring in a variety of baking dishes, including glass and aluminum baking dishes in a variety of shapes, such as round cake and pie pans and rectangular bread and muffin pans. Teachers might also bring in pizza pans and cookie sheets and different kinds of cheese. The teacher talks about and names the objects and provides some descriptive details. Teachers also use more sophisticated language with the children. For example, teachers use words such as *slanted* and *straight* (comparing the sides of a pie pan with those of a cake pan) or *shallow* and *deep* (comparing the muffin pan or pizza pan with the bread pan). Teachers can also bring in cooking utensils such as bowls, measuring cups, and spoons, so that children can pretend to use them with their baking dishes.

Meeting the Needs of Preschool ELLs

At the age of three, middle-class children's spoken language includes about 2,000 words, and they learn nearly 2,000 more each year (Roskos, Tabors, & Lenhart, 2004). Therefore, by the time they enter kindergarten, middle-class children, regardless of their home language, know about 5,000 words. Despite their acquisition of a home language, English language learners may have very little English vocabulary. Because of the critical role that vocabulary plays in learning to read and write, preschool teachers need to plan intentionally for ELLs' language and vocabulary growth. They can use language scaffolding strategies to help preschoolers to expand their English vocabularies and their sentence structure knowledge.

Language scaffolds are the teacher's intentional attempts to sustain conversation and provide children with models of new vocabulary and slightly more complex sentence structures. The following effective language strategies are adapted from Roskos and colleagues (2004, pp. 40–41):

- The teacher repeats a few of the child's words from a child's comment and inserts additional words using slightly more complex sentence structure. For example, at breakfast, a child holds his milk carton out expecting the teacher to open it for him. The teacher says, "Should I open it? Open it?" After the child nods or says "yes," the teacher says, "I will open your milk. You watch."
- As teachers perform an action, they talk about their action. For example, at the writing center when making birthday cards, the teacher says, "I will fold my paper. Now I will write *Happy Birthday*. Now you fold."
- As a child performs an action, the teacher explains what the child is doing. For example, at the home center, the teacher says, "You got a cup. A cup. Will you drink?"
- Before children are to perform an action, teachers demonstrate the action and describe in detail what they are doing. Teachers repeat the most critical vocabulary for actions and objects. For example, as children pretend to make cookies using sand for flour, the teacher says, "This is flour. We scoop up the flour. We scoop up more flour. Now it is full."
- Before children are to perform an action, teachers ask children to tell what they will do first. For example, after a child empties a cup of flour (sand), the teacher says, "Now we are scooping flour. Scooping flour. What will you do first?"

These scaffolds wrap English around the child while the child is actively participating in an activity. The actions support children's understanding even when they know very little of the vocabulary. However, the term *scaffolding* implies not just support but also that the support is removable. As children show greater competence, they need less support. As teachers provide daily language scaffolding, children gradually begin using the modeled English vocabulary and sentence structures, eventually in non-scaffolded situations (Richgels, 1995).

A COMPREHENSIVE MODEL OF ASSESSMENT AND INSTRUCTION IN ACTION

IN THE FOLLOWING SECTION, we present Ms. Clements and how she uses a comprehensive model of assessment and instruction. Ms. Clements and her preschool children are studying travel. As a part of this unit, Ms. Clements has read many stories about characters who travel away from their homes and poems about traveling (including imaginary travel of the mind). The children have learned different methods of transportation and are examining ways in which seeds travel.

A Day in Ms. Clements' Classroom

Ms. Clements teaches two half-day preschool classes in a large, urban, school district. Her schedule is divided into four time periods: whole-class gathering, center time (with small-group instruction), snack and recess or a special class, and story time. She has a systematic approach to observing her children and keeps notes about what they are learning that helps her plan instruction.

Whole-Class Gathering. After completing several whole-class activities (counting the number of girls and boys, singing a song with movement, and reading a poem from a chart), Ms. Clements introduces the day's main focus. "I have a new story today about another character who leaves home and travels to many different places. But instead of reading the story to you, I am going to tell it. The title of the story is *The Runaway Bunny*, and it was written by Margaret Wise Brown" (1942). Ms. Clements hangs a copy of the front cover of the book on a story clothesline (a clothesline strung between two chairs) as she reads the title. As she tells the story, she hangs more pictures on the clothesline. After reading, the children talk about all the things the little bunny turned into. Then children step up to the clothesline and tell what is happening in each of the story pictures. Next, Ms. Clements says, "Little Bunny sure did become a lot of things in this story. You might want to draw a picture in the art center about Little Bunny and his mother and all the different things he became. Let's write a list of all the things Little Bunny turned into, and I'll put the list in the art center to remind you what you might want to draw."

Ms. Clements uses shared writing with the children to write the list of things Little Bunny turns into. One child offers, "Little Bunny turned into a flower." Ms. Clements asks the children to tell her which letter she will need to spell the word *flower*. She says, "Flower. FFFFFlower. Everyone say out loud what letter I need to begin spelling the word *flower*." Many of the children say "*F*," some children offer other letters, and a few children are silent. Ms. Clements confirms, "Yes. *F*. FFF."

Center Time. Ms. Clements teaches a mini-lesson and observes children. The children select centers, and Ms. Clements and her assistant circulate among the children helping them find materials and making sure that everyone has settled into an activity. Then she calls five children to a table where she frequently conducts small-group lessons for a mini-lesson on phonemic awareness. She has a collection of environmental print objects and small toys that the children have brought to school in the past two weeks. The objects include toys or print objects that begin with the phonemes /t/, /r/, or /l/, including tissue, a bag of rice, a box of Tide, a toy train, a bunch of roses, and a box of lima beans. She also has lots of small pictures that begin with those same phonemes.

To begin a familiar phonemic awareness game, Ms. Clements holds up an object and emphasizes its beginning sound. She says, "Rrrrice. Now let's listen to the first sound at the beginning of *rrrice*." Several children say /r/ and Ms. Clements confirms. She shows each object and slowly articulates each word, emphasizing its beginning sound. Now she passes out a set of pictures for the children to sort. With some children, she uses high levels of scaffolding (discussed earlier in this chapter) in order for them to segment the beginning phoneme. Ms. Clements takes note that three children were able to segment the beginning phonemes of their pictures with moderate support at first but increasingly with only minimal support. The other two children needed high levels of support but before the lesson ended demonstrated segmenting at least one phoneme with moderate support.

After teaching the small-group lesson and while the children are still engaged in center activities, Ms. Clements picks up a clipboard on which she has placed six pieces of sticky notepaper with five children's names written at the top of each paper (one extra, blank piece of notepaper is included). Ms. Clements observes four or five children nearly every day. At the beginning of the year, she divided her children into two groups of four or five children. Then she assigned each group of children to a day of the week. The first group of children is observed on Monday, the second group on Tuesday, and so on. One day a week, she does not observe children but uses the day for more small-group instruction, guests, films, cooking, or other special activities.

Ms. Clements circulates among the children in the centers. Ishmail is one of her target children to observe today. She observes him as he works in the letter and word center. She watches as he dumps out the bag of *R* and *T* objects that the class has gathered and separates them into two piles. He says "ro-bot" and places the toy in the *R* bag. He says "rrr-ice," and places it in the *R* bag. He says "t-t-tums," and places it in the *T* bag. He says "tr-ain," and places it in the *T* bag. Ms. Clements writes her observations on one of the sticky notes.

In the library center, Ms. Clements observes Husalina, another focus child for today, retell *Henny Penny* using the story clothesline. Husalina includes every event in the story, recalls the characters' names correctly, and repeats the dialogue, "Wanna come? Yes. Tell king sky's falled." Ms. Clements then observes Cecelia playing in the travel dramatic-play center with Josephine and Barbara. All three girls pretend to write a letter home to their mothers. Ms. Clements observes their writing and then asks Cecelia to read her letter. Cecelia reads, "Dear Mom, I'm having fun. Cecelia."

Ms. Clements invites Rayshawn, another target child, to read a chart of a familiar song, "Wheels on the Bus," with her; she is aware that he rarely chooses to reread the classroom charts or retell stories in the library center. Rayshawn points to the text from left to right and sweeps his hand across the lines as he recites the words to the song. Ms. Clements notes that he has memorized the words to the song but is not matching the words he says with the words in the text. She gives Rayshawn a few of the word cards from the pocket chart that match with the text of the song. Rayshawn cannot match the words without Ms. Clements' support.

Ms. Clements Reflects and Plans

After the children are dismissed, Ms. Clements takes time to organize her observations and make plans for instruction. First, she takes the sticky notes off the clipboard and puts each note in her assessment notebook. As she places the sticky notes in the notebook, she reflects on what the observations show about each child's understanding

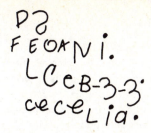

Caption: 11/2   Cecelia is using emerging letter form. Her signature is in the appropriate location for letters. She shows awareness of linearity, hyphens, and periods. Her meaning is appropriate for the situation (pretending her mother misses her) and includes language used in a letter. She uses conventional alphabet letter forms (with one reversal). She relies on contextual dependency.

Text: Dear Mom,
        I'm having fun.
        Cecelia

FIGURE 7.6   Cecelia's Letter and Caption

about reading or writing. She writes her analysis beside the sticky note in the observation notebook.

Her notes capture what she observed Ishmail and Husalina doing and saying. She indicates that Ishmail segmented the word *robot* into syllables (*ro*) and (*bot*), the word *rice* into its beginning phoneme (*r*) and rime (*ice*), and the word *train* into its onset (*tr*) and rime (*ain*) by segmenting these words in her notes. She indicated in her notes that he matched each of the words with its appropriate letter. Her analysis reflects these observations: "Ishmail segments words between syllables, onset and rimes, and beginning phonemes. He knows the sounds associated with *T* and *R*. He is making the transition from phonological to phonemic awareness."

Ms. Clements decides to put Cecelia's letter, which she collected from the travel dramatic-play center, in Cecelia's **portfolio** (a large folder in which she keeps examples of that child's work). She quickly writes a caption for Cecelia's letter and clips it to the letter. The caption includes the date and Ms. Clements' analysis of what the letter reveals about Cecelia's understanding about writing. Figure 7.6 shows Cecelia's letter and Ms. Clements' caption.

Then Ms. Clements thinks back on the day's activities and her observations. She decides that she wants to teach a small-group lesson with Rayshawn and a few other children on how to match word cards to words on charts of memorized songs and poems.

Chapter Summary

PRESCHOOLERS CAN BE EXPECTED to achieve much written language competence. They enjoy storybook read-alouds and discussions, play rhyming games, have partial alphabet knowledge and phonological awareness, and use some alphabet letters or mock letters to write meaningful words and phrases, including their names. They retell favorite storybooks and information books and write pretend messages as part of dramatic play. Although most preschoolers do not develop full phonemic awareness (segmenting every phoneme in a word), teachers help them to take first steps through enjoyable, informal phonological awareness activities, such as "I can hear" and rhyming games. In addition, they target instruction and provide scaffolding so all children make progress.

Preschoolers acquire concepts about written language when their classrooms are filled with print and when teachers model how to use that print in play, during shared writing, and shared reading. Mrs. McKannon's classroom included many games and dramatic-play opportunities in which children used print in entertaining and functional ways. Teachers also plan whole- and small-group lessons targeted on specific early literacy and language skills. Ms. Rodgers planned small-group alphabet and phonemic awareness lessons, she used guided drawing to help children learn to control the lines and shapes used in drawing and writing, and she used shared writing to teach concepts about print.

Well-planned interactive read-alouds support preschoolers' development of vocabulary, oral language, and listening comprehension. Teachers plan read-alouds to focus on specific tier 2 vocabulary words, model using complex language structures, and ask questions that call for inferential thinking. They are skillful in reading aloud nonfiction books and books grouped into themes so that vocabulary development is extended over large periods of time.

Print concepts and alphabet instruction takes place during shared reading and writing such as when teachers help children compose innovations on patterns found in predictable books. Children learn to segment beginning phonemes through scaffolded instruction. Finally, teachers differentiate instruction for children who may be at risk and struggling to acquire the literacy concepts other children are learning. Teachers provide tier 1 and tier 2 instruction for critical skills such as learning alphabet letters. They carefully use scaffolds to build vocabulary and oral language for English language learners. Teachers are systematic about observing children and use their observations to plan instruction.

Together, all the literacy activities in preschool support children's learning in five major areas of literacy development: listening comprehension, vocabulary development, concepts about print, alphabet letter recognition and writing, and phonemic awareness. For a few children, who have connected phonemes with letters, the alphabetic principle emerges.

USING AND APPLYING THE INFORMATION

Make five columns of the foundational literacy concepts developed in the preschool years: alphabet recognition, concepts about print, phonological and phonemic awareness, listening comprehension, and vocabulary development. Then, make a list of all the literacy learning instructional activities mentioned in this chapter, including (but not limited to) play, interactive reading books, shared reading and writing, writing lists, sign-in procedure, letter games, and storytelling and drama. Write each of the instructional activities under the foundational literacy concept that it is most likely to be teaching. Be prepared to justify your answers.

GOING BEYOND THE TEXT

VISIT A PRESCHOOL CLASSROOM and observe several literacy activities. Take note of the interactions among children as they participate in literacy experiences. Also note the teacher's talk with children in those experiences. Make a list of the kinds of literacy materials available in the classroom. Talk with the teacher about the kinds of literacy activities he or she plans. Compare these materials, interactions, and activities with those found in Mrs. McKannon's, Ms. Rodgers', and Ms. Clements' preschool classrooms.

REFERENCES

Adams, M. J. (1990). *Beginning to read.* Cambridge: MIT Press.

Beauchat, K. A., Blamey, K. L., & Walpole, S. (2009). Building preschool children's language and literacy one storybook at a time. *The Reading Teacher, 63,* 26–39.

Beck, I. L, McKeown, M. G., & Kucan, L. (2008). *Creating robust vocabulary: Frequently asked questions and extended examples.* New York: Guilford Press.

Brown, M. (1942). *The runaway bunny.* New York: Harper & Row.

Brown, R. (1981). *A dark, dark tale.* New York: Dial Press.

Burningham, J. (1970). *Mr. Gumpy's outing.* New York: Holt, Rinehart & Winston.

Casbergue, R., McGee, L. M., & A. Bedford. (2008). Characteristics of classroom environments associated with accelerated literacy development. In L. M. Justice & C. Vukelich (Eds.), *Achieving excellence in preschool literacy instruction* (pp. 167–181). New York: Guilford Press.

Cole, H. (1997). *Jack's garden.* New York: Mulberry Books.

Cunningham, P. (1998). Looking for patterns: Phonics activities that help children notice how words work. In C. Weaver (Ed.), *Practicing what we know: Informed reading instruction* (pp. 87–110). Urbana, IL: National Council of Teachers of English.

Cunningham, P. (2000). *Phonics they use: Words for reading and writing.* New York: Longman.

Dickinson, D. (2001). Large-group and free-play times: Conversational settings supporting language and literacy development. In D. Dickinson & P. Tabor (Eds.), *Beginning literacy with language: Young children learning at home and school* (pp. 223–255). Baltimore, MD: Brookes Publishing.

Dickinson, D. K., & Sprague, K. E. (2001). The nature and impact of early childhood care environments on the language and early literacy development of children from low-income families. In S. B. Neuman & D. K. Dickinson (Eds.), *Handbook on early literacy research* (pp. 263–280). New York: Guilford Press.

Galdone, P. (1968). *Henny Penny.* New York: Clarion Books.

Gee, J. (2001). A sociocultural perspective on early literacy development. In S. Neuman & D. Dickinson (Eds.), *Handbook of early literacy research* (pp. 30–42). New York: Guilford Press.

Goswami, U. (2004). *Linguistic factors, phonological and orthographic processing in dyslexia.* Swindon, England: Economic and Social Research Council.

Justice, L. M., & Ezell, H. K. (2002). Use of storybook reading to increase print awareness in at-risk children. *American Journal of Speech-Language Pathology, 11,* 17–29.

Justice, L. M., Pence, K. L., Beckman, A. R., Skibbe, L. E., & Wiggins, A. K. (2005). *Scaffolding with storybooks: A guide for enhancing young children's language and literacy development.* Newark, DE: The International Reading Association.

Kirk, D. (1998). *Bigger.* New York: Puffin Books.

Krauss, R. (1945). *The carrot seed.* New York: HarperTrophy.

Lin, G. (1999). *The ugly vegetables.* Watertown, MA: Charlesbridge Publishing, Inc.

MacLean, M., Bryant, P., & Bradley, L. (1987). Rhymes, nursery rhymes, and reading in early childhood. *Merrill-Palmer Quarterly, 33,* 255–281.

McCloskey, R. (1999). *Make way for the ducklings.* New York: Puffin Books.

McGee, L. M. (2005). The role of wisdom in evidence-based preschool literacy programs. In B. Maloch, J. V. Hoffman, D. L. Schallert, C. M. Fairbanks, & J. Worthy (Eds.), *54th yearbook of the National Reading Conference* (pp. 1–21). Oak Creek, WI: National Reading Conference.

McGee, L. M., & Dail, A. R. (2010). Phonemic awareness instruction in preschool: Research implications and lessons learned from Early Reading First. In M. C. McKenna, S. Walpole, & K. Conradi (Eds.), *Promoting early reading: Research, resources and best practices* (pp. 59–77). New York: Guilford Press.

McGee, L. M., & Schickedanz, J. (2007). Repeated interactive read-alouds in preschool and kindergarten. *The Reading Teacher, 60,* 742–751.

McGee, L. M., & Ukrainetz, T. A. (2009, April). Using scaffolding to teach phomenic awareness in preschool and kindergarten. *The Reading Teacher, 62*(7), 599–603. doi: 10.1598/RT.62.7.6.

McGill-Franzen, A., Lanford, C., & Adams, E. (2002). Learning to be literate: A comparison of five urban early childhood programs. *Journal of Educational Psychology, 94,* 443–464.

McGinty, A. S., & Justice, L. M. (2010). Language facilitation in the preschool classroom: Rationale, goals and strategies. In M. C. McKenna, S. Walpole, & K. Conradi (Eds.), *Promoting early reading: Research, resources and best practices* (pp. 9–36). New York: Guilford Press.

Neuman, S. (1999). Books make a difference: A study of access to literacy. *Reading Research Quarterly, 34,* 286–311.

Neuman, S., & Dwyer, J. (2009). Missing action: Vocabulary instruction in pre-K. *The Reading Teacher, 62,* 384–392.

Parkes, B. (2000). *Read it again! Revisiting shared reading.* Portland, ME: Stenhouse Publishers.

Pentimonti, J. M., Zucker, T. A., Justice, L. M., & Kaderavek, J. N. (2010, May). Informational text use in preschool classroom read-alouds. *The Reading Teacher, 63*(8), 656–665.

Raschka, C. (1992). *Charlie Parker played be bop.* New York: Orchard Books.

Richgels, D. J. (1995). A kindergarten sign-in procedure: A routine in support of written language learning. In K. A. Hinchman, D. J. Leu, & C. K. Kinzer (Eds.), *Perspectives on literacy research and practice, Forty-fourth yearbook of the National Reading Conference* (pp. 243–254). Chicago: The National Reading Conference.

Richgels, D. J. (2003). *Going to kindergarten: A year with an outstanding teacher.* Lanham, MD: Scarecrow Education Press.

Roberts, T., & Neal, H. (2004). Relationships among preschool English language learners' oral proficiency in English, instructional experience and literacy development. *Contemporary Educational Psychology, 29,* 283–311.

Roskos, K. A., Tabors, P. O., & Lenhart, L. A. (2004). *Oral language and early literacy in preschool: Talking, reading, and writing.* Newark, DE: The International Reading Association.

Rowe, D. W. (1998). The literate potentials of book-related dramatic play. *Reading Research Quarterly, 33,* 10–35.

Royston, A. (2001). *See how they grow: Ducks.* New York: Dorling Kindersley.

Scarborough, H. (1991). Early syntactic development of dyslexic children. *Annals of Dyslexia, 41,* 207–220.

Schickedanz, J. (1999). *Much more than the ABCs.* Washington, DC: National Association for the Education of Young Children.

Schickedanz, J. A. (2008). Increasing children's learning by getting to the bottom of their confusion. In L. M. Justice & C. Vukelich (Eds.), *Achieving excellence in preschool literacy instruction* (pp. 182–197). New York: Guilford Press.

Schickedanz, J. A., & Casbergue, R. M. (2004). *Writing in preschool: Learning to orchestrate meaning and marks.* Newark, DE: The International Reading Association.

Schickedanz, J., & Dickinson, D., with Charlotte-Mecklenburg Schools. (2005). *Opening the world of learning: A comprehensive early literacy program.* Parsippany, NJ: Pearson.

Senechal, M., LeFevre, J., Hudson, E., & Lawson, E. (1996). Knowledge of storybook as a predictor of young children's vocabulary. *Journal of Educational Psychology, 88,* 520–536.

Smolkin, L., & Donovan, C. (2002). "Oh, excellent, excellent question!": Developmental differences and comprehension acquisition. In C. Block & M. Pressley (Eds.), *Comprehension instruction: Research-based best practices* (pp. 140–157). New York: Guilford Press.

Stevens, J. (1995). *The three billy goats gruff.* New York: Harcourt.

Sturges, P. (1999). *The little red hen (makes a pizza).* New York: Dutton Children's Books.

Tabors, P., Snow, C., & Dickinson, D. (2001). Homes and schools together: Supporting language and literacy development. In D. Dickinson & P. Tabor (Eds.), *Beginning literacy with language: Young children learning at home and school* (pp. 313–334). Baltimore, MD: Brookes Publishing.

Walker, D., Greenwood, C., Hart, B., & Carta, J. (1994). Prediction of school outcomes based on socioeconomic status and early language production. *Child Development, 65,* 606–621.

Wasik, B., & Bond, M. (2001). Beyond the pages of a book: Interactive book reading and language development in preschool children. *Journal of Educational Psychology, 93,* 243–250.

Wells, G. (1986). *The meaning makers: Children learning language and using language to learn.* Portsmouth, NH: Heinemann.

Welsch, J. G. (2008). Playing within and beyond the story: Encouraging book-related pretend play. *The Reading Teacher, 62,* 138–148.

Wood, A., & Wood, D. (1984). *The napping house.* San Diego: Harcourt.

Zucker, T. A., & Landry, S. H. (2010). Improving the quality of preschool read-alouds: Professional development and coaching that targets bookreading practices. In M. C. McKenna, S. Walpole, & K. Conradi (Eds.), *Promoting early reading: Research, resources and best practices* (pp. 78–104). New York: Guilford Press.

Zucker, T. A., Ward, A. E., & Justice, L. M. (2009, September). Print referencing during read-alouds: A technique for increasing emergent readers' print knowledge. *The Reading Teacher, 63*(1), 62–72.

PEARSON myeducationlab

Go to the topics Oral Language Development and Phonemic Awareness and Phonics in the MyEducationLab (www.myeducationlab.com) for your course, where you can:

- Find learning outcomes for Oral Language Development and Phonemic Awareness and Phonics along with the national standards that connect to these outcomes.
- Complete Assignments and Activities that can help you more deeply understand the chapter content.
- Examine challenging situations and cases presented in the IRIS Center Resources.

A+RISE

Go to the Topic A+RISE in the MyEducationLab (www.myeducationlab.com) for your course. A+RISE® Standards2Strategy™ is an innovative and interactive online resource that offers new teachers in grades K–12 just-in-time, research-based instructional strategies that:

- Meet the linguistic needs of ELLs as they learn content
- Differentiate instruction for all grades and abilities
- Offer reading and writing techniques, cooperative learning, use of linguistic and nonlinguistic representations, scaffolding, teacher modeling, higher order thinking, and alternative classroom ELL assessment
- Provide support to help teachers be effective through the integration of listening, speaking, reading, and writing along with the content curriculum
- Improve student achievement
- Are aligned to Common Core Elementary Language Arts standards (for the literacy strategies) and to English language proficiency standards in WIDA, Texas, California, and Florida.

CHAPTER 8

Supporting Literacy Learning in Kindergarten

KEY CONCEPTS

Interactive Read-Aloud
Word Consciousness
Tier 2 Words
Finger-Point Reading
Continuants
Elkonin Boxes
Journal Writing
Kid Writing
Word Wall
"What-Can-You-Show-Us?" Activity

Writing the Room
Morning Message
Decodable Word
Guided Reading
Interactive Writing
High-Frequency Words
Alphabetic Principle
Decoding
Invented Spelling
Bookhandling Skills
Directionality Concepts

Letter-and-Word
Concepts
Sight Words
Dramatic-Play-with-Print Center
Project Approach
Environmental Print
Screening
Assessments
Monitoring Assessment
Portfolio

THE KINDERGARTEN CONTEXT: WHAT'S NEW HERE?

THE GREATEST CHANGE from preschool to kindergarten is the more explicit approach to instruction and the expectations for learning the conventions of reading and writing. At the end of kindergarten, children are expected to

- Understand concepts of print, including top, bottom, front, back, left page before right page, left-to-right and return sweep, one-to-one matching of spoken words to written words, and concepts about words compared to letters.
- Recognize and write most of the alphabet letters.
- Identify and construct rhyming words.
- Segment beginning and ending sounds in words, and segment easy, three-phoneme words.
- Know sound-letter correspondences for consonants and beginning to know vowel letter-sound correspondences.
- Use sound-letter correspondences to invent spellings with beginning and ending letters.
- Spell and read new words by using familiar rhyming word parts and consonant sound-letter correspondences.
- Use one-to-one matching of spoken and written words to finger-point read familiar stories and poems.
- Recognize twenty-five high-frequency words and spell them.
- Read little books, levels 1 through 4 or A through C.
- Write first and last names.
- Participate in read-alouds with increasingly complex comments and answers to teachers' questions, and ask questions.
- Learn and use new vocabulary from content study and read-aloud experiences.
- Retell stories and nonfiction with detail and correct sequence.

Kindergarten teachers use many of the same teaching procedures that preschool teachers use. They use daily routines in which they read aloud to children, engage children in shared reading and writing, and provide opportunities for children to practice reading and writing independently. In this chapter, we describe how these teaching strategies and other more advanced ones are adapted to fit the needs of kindergartners.

In the next sections of this chapter, we describe exemplary teachers and their approaches to kindergarten instruction. Exemplary teachers provide instruction about literacy conventions in whole-group lessons and to small groups of learners.

TEXT READING AND WRITING IN EXEMPLARY CLASSROOMS

Using Interactive Read-Alouds

Gregory and Cahill (2010) tell about an exemplary teacher they call Mrs. Hope who uses interactive read-alouds to teach children five listening strategies. **Interactive read-alouds** occur as teachers read books aloud to children, make comments that reveal their thinking, and ask questions. Children participate by answering questions and making comments. Thus, there is a great deal of interaction between the teacher, the story text, and the children. During such read-alouds, teachers have many opportunities to demonstrate active-listening strategies. The first strategy Mrs. Hope taught her kindergartners she called the *schema* (see Chapter 1) strategy. Mrs. Hope drew a picture of a person's head with many lines swirling around inside it. She told the children these swirling lines were the ideas inside someone's head. She told children that they had many ideas in their brain about lots of topics. For example, she reminded the children that when they read the book *Zach's Alligator* (Mozelle, 1995), they thought about everything they knew about alligators before she read the book. She told children that thinking about what you know is using your schema. She said, "So before you listen to a story, you click your schema on." Next, Mrs. Hope taught children to use a strategy called *make a connection.* Mrs. Hope used the picture of the brain with swirling ideas and explained that it was easier to remember ideas when they connect to something already in your brain. She told children that making connection is like Velcro. The Velcro sticks two ideas together. She taught children to say, "I can connect to that" and then tell a connection to their lives or to another book that they had made. Next, Mrs. Hope taught children to make *mind movies.* Children listened to Mrs. Hope read the first two pages of *Fireflies* (Brinckloe, 1985), then closed their eyes and tried to picture in their minds what they heard. They talked about their mind pictures and then drew them. Finally, they compared their mind pictures to the book's illustrations. Last, Mrs. Hope taught children to ask questions by saying "I wonder." One child asked about Frog and Toad, "I wonder if they will make snowballs" (Gregory & Cahill, p. 519). Mrs. Hope reminded children that as they listened to a story, they should think about their "I wonder" questions and find answers to them. She told children this was called the "using your brain" strategy. Children in Mrs. Hope's classroom used hand motions to indicate they wanted to use a strategy. As Mrs. Hope was reading, they held their hands in the shape of the letter *C* to indicate they wanted to make a connection, or held up two fingers to make a *V* indicating they wanted to describe their mind picture. A wiggling finger meant they wanted to ask a question. Mrs. Hope would stop reading and invite children to use their strategy. Before reading, they always clicked on their brains to get their schema going.

Another exemplary teacher, Mrs. Myers (Myers, 2005) taught her children to use three listening strategies—retelling, questioning, and predicting—based on reciprocal teaching (Palincsar & Brown, 1984), usually used with older readers. She used puppets to introduce her children to these strategies and used them to prompt strategy use during interactive read-alouds. Mrs. Myers used a princess puppet to teach the first strategy, retelling. Retelling is when children recount the major events in a story or nonfiction book. Mrs. Myers told the children that the princess' job is to tell a short story about a long book. To begin with, the children listened to stories, and Mrs. Myers prepared story cards. Each card had a picture of a story event. As a group, the children talked about the order of the pictures and put them in sequence. The child holding the princess puppet told the events in order using the picture cards to prompt the retelling. Next, Mrs. Myers read aloud a story but did not prepare story cards. After reading, she prompted children to tell the characters' names and something about them first, then the important events, and finally the ending of the story. All children contributed ideas, and Mrs. Myers helped them identify only the important events. Then the child with the princess puppet used those ideas and retold the story with support from Mrs. Myers.

TECHNOLOGY TIE-IN

LISTENING TO AUTHORS AND ILLUSTRATORS

www.stonesoup.com/archive/listen presents young authors who have recently published their texts in the magazine *Stone Soup.* Students can either read the pieces or listen to the authors read their own work.

www.magickeys.com/books/ presents e-stories for younger and older students, some of which include audio.

www.memfox.net/mem-reads-aloud presents Mem Fox reading her books aloud.

www.storylineonline.net. Students can click on a book and an actor or actress reads it aloud on a video. The actors and actresses also talk about why they like the book.

www.harpercollinschildrens.com/kid/gamesandcontests/features/video presents authors and illustrators being interviewed or reading from their books aloud. This site also has book trailers.

www.sillybooks.net presents e-stories that are read aloud and each word of the text is highlighted as it is read. It also has contests for children and the winners' entries are animated and posted to the site. Click on the writing contest button and you will see the animated books published by children across the country.

Next, Mrs. Myers taught children two kinds of questions: questions to clarify and questions that call for thinking. One puppet, Clara Clarifier, asked short questions that could be answered "yes" or "no" or with few words. These were clarifying questions. Quincy Questioner asked thinking questions, which were harder to answer and required a lot of talking to answer. Mrs. Myers needed to prompt children to get them to ask questions as these roles required the most critical thinking. Finally, a wizard puppet was used to predict or guess what would happen next, the last listening strategy taught. This was the easiest strategy for all the children.

After teaching the strategies, four children were selected on a rotating basis to hold each of the puppets during story time. As Mrs. Myers read the story aloud, she would prompt children to perform their role. Children holding the puppet could say "pass" if they needed ideas or help. Shy children were told to hold up the puppet and let the puppet talk. Other children were invited to help, and everyone had an opportunity to hold a puppet at least once a week. Children gradually took on more independence and needed less support from Mrs. Myers. She reported that one of her kindergartners said during a social studies lesson, "I have a clarifying question. I don't know what a condo is" (Myers, 2005, p. 322).

Lane and Allen (2010) described a final exemplary teacher whom they call Ms. Barker. Ms. Barker promoted word consciousness and vocabulary learning through her everyday routines. **Word consciousness** involves being aware of words and interested in their meanings (Anderson & Nagy, 1992; Graves & Watts-Taffe, 2002). To build word consciousness among her kindergartners, Ms. Barker brainstormed **tier 2 words** for the words she used throughout the day in her daily routines including calling on classroom helpers to do their job, walking in a line, gathering for whole-group lessons, and passing out materials, as well as words used every day such as *happy, nice, wrong, correct,* and *impolite.* Tier 2 words are sophisticated words used for everyday concepts. They carry more nuanced meanings. For example, tier 2 words for the word *happy* that Ms. Barker identified were *glad, cheerful,* and *delighted.* For *nice,* she used the tier 2 words *pleasant, thoughtful,* and *kind* (Lane & Allen, p. 367). Instead of *pass out,* she identified the word *distribute.* Tier 2 words for *wrong* included *awkward, flawed, inaccurate,* and *incorrect;* tier 2 words for describing actions of the children as they walked in line included *disorderly, halt, linger, orderly, proceed, procession,* and *rapidly.* Words for passing out classroom supplies included *accumulate, allot, amass, deplete, dispense, distribute, replenish,* and *stockpile* (p. 368).

Ms. Barker began the school year using the ordinary words used by most teachers but gradually introduced new tier 2 words for those terms. She explained that the classroom job previously called *weather watcher* would now be the *meteorologist* because a meteorologist is someone who watches the weather. She gradually shifted from saying, "Grace, can you *pass out* the papers?" to "Grace, would you *distribute* the papers?" As her language shifted, so did the children's. Further, when reading aloud, Ms. Barker would often stop and say, "Um that's an interesting word; let's listen to see if we can figure out what it means." Not long after, children would say during a lesson or an interactive read-aloud, "Um, that's an interesting word I don't know what it means."

Using Assessment to Plan Instruction

Mrs. Trimble is an exemplary kindergarten teacher who teaches in a rural school with many children who are on free and reduced lunch. Many of her kindergartners attended a very effective Head Start center in a local community center and enter kindergarten with high levels of literacy skill. Other children have very few conventions in place when they enter kindergarten. Because she knows she will have children with a wide range of knowledge about and experiences with reading and writing, Mrs. Trimble assesses her children early in the year. She begins with having children write their names; identify the uppercase alphabet letters; and point out easy concepts about print such as front, back, top, bottom, left and right page, where to begin reading, the left-to-right directionality of reading a line of text, and the return sweep movement, along with one-to-one matching. She also asks children to say the beginning sound of five words she speaks slowly for the children. For most children, these are the only assessments she gives, but for some children who know many of the concepts in the first batch of assessments she continues with a second batch of assessments: asking children to identify the lowercase letters and say the sounds of consonant letters. She also gives a dictation sentence in which children are asked to spell words the best they can as the teacher says the words, and she asks children to read words from a high-frequency list. She keeps her assessment materials in a basket with folders for each child on her small-group teaching table. These assessments take about ten minutes for each child (and she assesses four to five children each day while the other children are at their tables doing another activity).

Mrs. Trimble uses the assessment data to form instructional groups and to begin planning her whole-group instruction. Over the years, Mrs. Trimble has found several trends in her children's entry knowledge (McGill-Franzen, 2006). Children who already could identify forty or more alphabet letters could also segment the beginning sounds of words and identify most consonant letter sounds. They could also invent spellings with at least one or two letters and knew many concepts about print. Children who knew fewer than forty alphabet letters had inconsistent knowledge about letter-sound correspondences—some children could segment some beginning sounds and could identify some letter-sound correspondences. Other children knew few, if any, letter sounds and could not segment the beginning sound of words.

Therefore, Mrs. Trimble generally forms four groups of students. The first group includes children who know the least letter names and who do not yet know any letter-sound correspondences and cannot segment beginning sounds. They have few concepts about print. The target for early learning for these children is to notice letter features and learn letter names, to associate letters with sounds, and learn to write letters while gaining more concepts about print. Mrs. Trimble knows this is her *letter and sound learning group* (McGill-Franzen, 2006).

The second group includes children who know more letters and can identify a few consonant letter-sound relations or can segment some beginning sounds. These children do not yet use their knowledge to invent spellings and are not one-to-one matchers. The target for early learning for these children is to learn the remainder of the alphabet letters and all the consonant sounds and how to stretch sounds in words to spell them. Mrs. Trimble thinks of these children as her *sounds group* (McGill-Franzen, 2006) because they will be learning more letter sounds and stretching words to hear the sounds along with learning one-to-one matching.

A third group is composed of children who know nearly forty alphabet letters and many consonant letter-sound correspondences, can segment beginning sounds, and match one to one. They can spell some words with one-letter invented spellings. The early learning target for this group is to stretch sounds in words to write them, then read back their own writing and begin early **finger-point reading** in predictable books. Mrs. Trimble thinks of these children as her *finger-point readers* (McGee & Morrow, 2005), but she will also be teaching them to spell new words using familiar rhyming words.

Finally, children in the last group write sophisticated invented spellings usually with beginning and ending letters, know most letters, know most letter-sound correspondences, and have one-to-one matching. Some may know a few high-frequency words. The early target for this group is to use guided reading in predictable books to build up sight vocabulary of high-frequency words, teach them to use beginning and ending of words to monitor their reading, and to learn to read and spell new words by building new words from familiar rhyming words. Mrs. Trimble thinks of the children in this group as her *early beginning readers*.

Teaching Small Groups

Mrs. Trimble meets her letter and sound group daily and provides explicit instruction in alphabet recognition. For example, to teach the children to identify and write the letter *H*, she writes an *H* on a small whiteboard and she says, "This is an *H*. I make two down lines, and then I make a line across. Down, down, across. *H*. You say it." Then the children are given several opportunities to make, name, and describe the letter on their own small chalkboard or sand tray, repeating the teacher's letter-formation talk (McGee, 2007). Letter-formation talk occurs when teachers say words describing the letter strokes

FIGURE 8.1 Letter-Formation Talk

A	slant slant across
B	down curve curve
C	circle back stop
D	down big curve
E	down over 1 over 2 over 3
F	down over 1 over 2
G	circle back stop little line in
H	down down across
I	down little line across little line across
J	down curve up
K	down slant in slant out
L	down over
M	up slant down slant up down
N	up slant down up
O	circle back
P	down curve
Q	circle back little line out
R	down curve little slant out
S	curve curve back
T	down across
U	down curve it up
V	slant down slant up
W	slant down slant up slant down slant up
X	slant down slant over it
Y	little slant down little slant down little line down
Z	over slant down over

to make each letter. Figure 8.1 presents letter-formation talk for the uppercase letters. Mrs. Trimble uses several motivating games to practice letter naming, including fishing for letters, feeding letters to a puppet, playing concentration and other matching games, and going on letter searches in the classroom.

Mrs. Trimble usually teaches two or three letters a week to this group (a letter a week is too slow for the learning the children in this group need to make). She frequently assesses their learning and reteaches letters during the following weeks as needed. After the children have learned ten or more letters, she begins teaching children how to segment the beginning sound of a word (see Chapter 7 for Ms. Rodgers' scaffolding of this learning).

Mrs. Trimble meets with her sounds children daily as well. She is teaching them how to stretch the sounds in words and to hear more than one sound (children can already segment the beginning sound). To do this, Mrs. Trimble has selected a few words that have two phonemes, such as the words *my, we, no, shoe, lay, shy,* and *see*. She will use these words to demonstrate the task of saying words slowly. Each of these words is familiar to children and begins with a **continuant,** a consonant phoneme that can be held in the breath stream for a few seconds (McCarthy, 2008). She begins, "We are going to learn to say words slowly and stretch them out. Like this. I will say the word slowly. Watch and listen. /mmmmyyyy/ *my*. Let's do it together. Watch my mouth." On this day, she merely has children practice with the words *my, we,* and *no*. In later lessons, the children listen to and stretch out all the words. Next, Mrs. Trimble introduces Elkonin boxes (Elkonin, 1973). **Elkonin boxes** are small square boxes (about 2″×2″) for each phoneme in the word. Mrs. Trimble has prepared a sheet of card stock with two Elkonin boxes for each child. Each child has two pennies. Mrs. Trimble demonstrates using the boxes. She says, "I am going to say words slowly, and as I say each sound I'm going to push up a penny. Watch me. MMMMM (pushing up one penny) YYYYY (pushing up the other penny). Now I'll say the word and you push up the penny. Don't push up the second penny until you hear that second sound." Later, she will have children say the sound and push up the pennies (Clay, 2005; Griffith & Olson, 1992).

Mrs. Trimble meets with her finger-point reading group frequently but not daily. The children have been reading a poem with rhyming words, they have matched words in the poem with word cards, and each child has practiced finger-point reading with teacher guidance. They are now ready to learn to spell new rhyming words. The poem is presented in Figure 8.2.

Mrs. Trimble leads the group in rereading the poem and then asks children to identify rhyming words. She helps children segment each rhyming word orally into its onset and rime (e.g., the word *cold* is segmented into the onset /c/ and rime /old/). After the children orally segment the word, the teacher places a card with the written word in a pocket chart. With all the rhyming words in the chart, the teacher says, "Now we know that all these words rhyme. Our job today is to look very closely and see

FIGURE 8.2 "I Don't Like the Cold"

I Don't Like the Cold

I *told* you I don't like the *cold!*

I'm not *sold* on *cold*—

I *told* you **so!**

Take this **snow** and **go!**

I *told* you **so!**

I'll *hold* out for sun and hot—not *cold* and **snow!**

I *told* you **so!**

which ones have the same spelling pattern" (Cunningham, 1998, p. 91). Children need to understand words such as spelling pattern and vowel.

The teacher picks up a pair of rhyming word cards from the pocket chart, explains or reminds the children what *spelling pattern* and *vowel* mean, and invites children to identify the letters in the spelling pattern in the rhyming words, for example, *o-l-d* in *gold* and *told*. Then the teacher underlines the *-old* part of each word, and the teacher and children decide that *gold* and *told* have the same spelling pattern and they rhyme. "We can hear the rhyme and see the spelling pattern" (Cunningham, 1998, p. 91). Then the teacher replaces those word cards and moves on to another pair of rhyming words from the pocket chart. Finally, when the teacher and students have underlined spelling patterns in several pairs of rhyming words, they move to an application activity that involves using the word card words to read and write additional words. For the reading-new-words activity, the teacher writes words that rhyme with and have the same spelling pattern as the words of an already displayed pair (e.g., *sold* and *fold* to go with *gold* and *told*), elicits the children's telling what letters to underline in the new words, displays them in the pocket chart under the original pair of words, and helps the children to read the new words using the spelling pattern. In this part of the lesson, they are *decoding*.

For the writing-new-words activity, the teacher mentions a word the children might want to write and gives an example of a sentence in which it might be needed. For example, if one of the already displayed rhyme pairs is *dog* and *log*, the teacher might say, "What if you wanted to write *fog*, like in 'I saw *fog* on the way to school today'?" Then the teacher leads the children through a reading of all the rhyme pairs in the pocket chart, until they find the words that rhyme with *fog*: "*dog, log*" When they notice that *fog* rhymes with *dog* and *log*, the children can use the underlined spelling pattern in the two displayed words to help the teacher to spell the new word on a word card for display. Later, children can read and write words in the letter-and-word workstation.

Mrs. Trimble also teaches literacy during whole-group and other small-group activities. Journal writing is the first activity of the day. **Journal writing** is children's daily independent writing about personal topics. For kindergartners, this writing combines drawing a picture with writing a message by using what they know about letters and sounds. Mrs. Trimble uses journal writing because it is open-ended, and all learners can participate. As the children enter the classroom, they locate their journals, which are kept in color-coded plastic tubs, stamp the day's date using a date stamp, and begin drawing and writing.

Once the children are settled, Mrs. Trimble calls one of her small group of children to the small-group table to work with her on kid writing. **Kid writing** is a teacher-supported activity in which children decide on a short message, write lines to indicate each word that will be needed to write that message, listen to the sounds in each word, and write the sounds they hear (Feldgus & Cardonick, 1999). While kid writing is often described as an activity for a whole-class group, Mrs. Trimble finds that it works better in a small group. She works with a different group each day of the week so that all the children experience this supported writing activity weekly and so that her support can be targeted to the needs of her four groups of children.

To begin kid writing with the first group of children (letter and sound learners), Mrs. Trimble teaches children to draw a picture of something of personal interest. Then she teaches them to say what they will write slowly holding up a finger for each word.

While the children begin drawing their picture, Mrs. Trimble selects one student, and they compose a sentence together. They count the number of words, hold up a finger for each word, and draw a word line for each word. The teacher helps the child recall the words for each line they drew together. For children in this group, remembering what is to be written and getting the right number of lines is complex learning. For this group, Mrs. Trimble might help each child listen to only one salient word in the message, asking the child to listen for the beginning sound with increasing levels of scaffolding (see Chapter 7). She helps the child pick a letter to spell that sound and use an alphabet chart to find the letter. For example, Jamica composed the sentence, "I like playing Wii." She was able to draw four lines for her words and she wrote the word *I* when prompted by Mrs. Trimble. Mrs. Trimble pronounced the word *like* slowly, and Jamica could hear /l/ and wrote an *l*.

In other groups, Mrs. Trimble may remind children that the word they are attempting to spell is on the classroom **word wall** (a place on the classroom wall where words are posted under alphabet letters). Or, she may ask a child to say the word slowly and listen to its sounds and write the letters heard. Mrs. Trimble has found that children in her sounds learning group have difficulty saying words slowly and segmenting all the individual sounds although they have no difficulty with hearing the beginning sound. She models listening for the beginning and ending sounds. When children are consistently successful with those, she asks them to attend to middle sounds as well. The children write letters that they think go with the sounds. At the end of the lesson, the teacher asks each child what he or she wrote and quickly records each child's sentence in conventional spelling on a sticky note and places it at the bottom of the child's writing.

When each child is finished writing, the teacher makes a decision on the spot each day to highlight something one child has done that all the children might learn from. For example, someone in the early beginning reading group might have spelled the /sh/ sound with the correct digraph letters *SH* or someone might have used a familiar rhyming word to spell a word. The teacher would point out these good strategies.

At the end of journal time and kid writing, all the journals are collected and put away in their tubs for the next day's writing. At the end of each month, Mrs. Trimble reviews her students' journal writing for progress. Figure 8.3 presents Addie's kid writing in November and in January and one of her January journal entries. In November, with support Addie could spell some sounds in the word *scared* (*SCD*) when the teacher helped her; but when she wrote the words *of thunder,* she used a random string of letters. In contrast, in January, Addie heard and spelled the beginning and ending sounds of *got* and *haircut* and some middle sounds of *haircut*. Addie's January journal entry (*My favorite movie is Willy Wonka*) is equally sophisticated with spellings of many sounds in the middles of words. Her journal writing, however, without the lines on which to place words used during kid writing, sometimes lacks spaces between words.

Shared Reading

After journal time, Mrs. Trimble does shared reading activities with the whole group. She has selected shared reading for whole group because it is open-ended and introduces children to a wide range of concepts about print. Thus, it meets the needs of all her diverse learners.

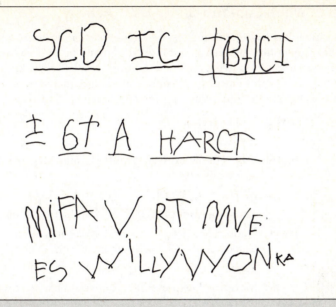

FIGURE 8.3 Addie's Kid Writing and Journal Writing

Mrs. Trimble teaches children many nursery rhymes at the beginning of kindergarten during a nursery rhyme theme unit. She teaches most nursery rhymes orally using dramatic games such as jumping over a candlestick or using finger plays. A favorite of most children is "Jack Be Nimble" because they enjoy jumping over the candlestick. They are intrigued with the new word *nimble,* which they know means being able to do something quickly without falling or spilling. When a rhyme has become familiar enough, Mrs. Trimble's class reads it aloud together from a large chart while she directs with a pointer on the chart-paper text. She knows that it is important for children to look at the print during such a choral reading. Before reading, she asks, "Where will you look to find the first word of the poem?" and makes sure that children are looking there. A child is invited to use the pointer to point to each word as the other children read. When the kindergartners are familiar with several rhymes, Mrs. Trimble introduces a rhyme written on sentence strips in the pocket chart. Children chant the rhyme while she points. Children match word cards to words on the chart, count the number of letters in words, find words that are the same, and find words that begin with a particular letter. Mrs. Trimble has found that repeatedly engaging children in simple finger-point reading and word-matching activities and in counting letters in words helps children develop strong concepts about letters and words. Each day at the end of shared reading, Mrs. Trimble invites a few children to play the **"what-can-you-show-us?" activity** (Richgels, Poremba, & McGee, 1996).

The "What-Can-You-Show-Us?" Activity

During this activity, children step up to the chart or big book, point to something in the print they notice, and talk about it. At the beginning of the year, Mrs. Trimble demonstrated stepping up to the chart and pointing to a letter she knew, a letter in someone's name, and a letter that was repeated. She even demonstrated reading a word: *Jack.* In this example, the children are stepping up to the "Jack Be Nimble" nursery rhyme.

Mrs. Trimble:	You're pointing to that *t-h-e*, Colin. Tell us about it.
Colin:	It's *the*!
Mrs. Trimble:	That's the word *the*? [Erin nods, and Mrs. Trimble points to the word and reads.] the.
Mrs. Trimble:	[to the class] Watch Eric. [His turn is next.]
Eric:	There's a *C* for *Caleb* [pointing to the first letter in Candlestick].
Mrs. Trimble:	Oooh. There's a *C* for *Caleb*. What do you mean "C for Caleb"? Does Caleb have a *C* somewhere in his name?
Eric:	Yeah.
Mrs. Trimble:	Mariposa has something she would like to show you.
Mariposa:	A *J* [pointing].
Mrs. Trimble:	A *J*! [pointing to the same *J* that Mariposa had pointed to]
Mariposa:	*j.*
Mrs. Trimble:	That's a *J*. Thank you for showing us the *J*.

The "what-can-you-show-us" activity is open-ended; it allows all children to step up to the shared reading chart and show something they know. In the beginning of the year, some of Mrs. Trimble's children merely stepped up to the chart and pointed to a letter without naming it. Then Mrs. Trimble would identify the letter and have the child name it. Other children could easily locate and name letters, and some children were beginning to notice words in their familiar rhyming context. As the year progresses, children will begin to notice more sophisticated elements of the print.

Reading the Morning Message

Mrs. Palmer teaches in an elementary school with a mixture of children from low-income families and middle-class families. Approximately 50 percent of the children qualify for free or reduced lunch. She has ninety minutes of uninterrupted time each day for reading instruction with additional time for opening activities and writing activities. She integrates reading and writing instruction in the afternoon with social studies and science topics.

As children enter Mrs. Palmer's classroom, they sign in. Mrs. Palmer's sign-in procedure is more complex than the one we discussed in Chapter 7. Each child has his or her own sign-in sheet, and children are invited to write more than their names—they can copy interesting letters or words. Each child has a clipboard and attempts to **write the room,** that is, to walk around the classroom in search of print and then to copy letters and words that interest them (Richgels, 2003).

> Dear boys and girls,
> Good morning. Today is Friday
> April 23, 2010. We will read a book
> about bugs. Do you like bug
> hunting?
>
>   Mrs. Palmer

FIGURE 8.4 Mrs. Palmer's Morning Message

Each morning after sign-in, the children read a morning message (presented in Figure 8.4). A **morning message** is a short message written by the teacher on chart paper and hung on an easel for reading (Labbo, 2005; Mariage, 2001). Teachers use morning messages to teach alphabet recognition and concepts about print early in the year and sight word recognition later. Mrs. Palmer uses the same pattern to write each day's morning message. It always begins "Good Morning" followed by the sentence "Today is _____." She always writes something that will happen that day and ends with a question about the activity.

The kindergartners look at the morning message as they come in each day; by midyear, most children can read the familiar words *Good Morning* and *Today is* on their own. They puzzle out the other words by talking among themselves. During opening activities, Mrs. Palmer reads the morning message using a pointer. Her voice is quiet as she reads familiar words and louder for new words. She knows many children know the words *We* and *will*, so she is quiet to let children take the lead. When she gets to the word *bugs*, she stops and says, "I think we can figure out this word. What sound will it start with? Does anyone see anything else to help us?" Many children talk about the letter *b* and the sound /b/, and someone recognizes the whole word *bug* in *bugs*. Then Mrs. Palmer points across the letters, slowly saying, "/b-u-g-z/. I noticed it ended with the letter *s*, so it is *bugs*." Again, Mrs. Palmer knows many children know the words *Do you like* and so she is quiet to let them read. She pauses to see which children will recognize the word *bug* in the last sentence, and many children do.

After reading the message, Mrs. Palmer leads the children in familiar work with the message. Some children come up to the chart and find a period. Some find capital letters. Others count words in the first sentence. Still others come up to use a word frame to find familiar words such as *Today, We, Do, you,* and *like*. Mrs. Palmer always leaves the morning message hanging on the easel so that during choice time, children can copy words that interest them. Sometimes she makes a small copy of the morning message cut into words to use in a special morning message workstation. Children put the words in order and then glue them to a piece of construction paper.

Teaching Small Group: Word Work That Starts with Book Reading

After opening activities (and after special classes such as library, music, physical education, or art), children are sent to workstations while a small group of children work with Mrs. Palmer. Five children sit on the carpet with Mrs. Palmer while other children consult the chart for their workstation assignments. The children in this group are finger-point readers. Mrs. Palmer gives a small whiteboard and a marker to each of the five children. She tells the children they are going to build new words. She begins by reading the book *Spring in the Kingdom of Ying* (Charlesworth, 2002), which includes many examples of words with the rime *-ing*. Then she invites children to recall a word, say it slowly, isolate the onset and spell it, then add the *-ing* rime. The children segment and spell *king, wing, sing,* and *ding* before moving to harder words with consonant cluster onsets such as *fling, swing, sting, string,* and *spring.* As the children write each word and wipe it off their boards, Mrs. Palmer writes it on a list on a chart hung on the easel. At the end of the lesson, the children read from this list the words they had spelled earlier. Mrs. Palmer ends the lessons by showing children cards printed with *ing, k, w, s, d, fl, sw, st, str,* and *spr.* Mrs. Palmer makes a word using a letter card and the *ing* card, and children read the word. Then she tells children that these word-building cards and writing paper and pencils will be in the letter and word center and that the next time they go there, they should write a list of as many words as they can make and read using those cards.

Mrs. Palmer dismisses the small group and signals that all children should go to their second workstations. Then she calls together a second small group of children who are early beginning readers. These children are reading small books using decodable words. **Decodable words** are consistent with phonics generalizations; for example, the vowel in a CVC (consonant-vowel-consonant) word is short or the first vowel in a CVCe (consonant-vowel-consonant-silent *e*) word is long. The children in this group are familiar with today's book, which has many short-*o* words.

Mrs. Palmer uses a form of guided reading to read this little book. For **guided reading** in kindergarten, the teacher introduces very-easy-to-read books and then guides children's independent reading of the books. Mrs. Palmer introduces today's book by talking with children as they look through the pictures and talk about what is happening. Mrs. Palmer sometimes says, "*Happy* is an important word in this story; what letter do you expect to see first in *happy*?" Once the children have identified the letter *H*, she has them search the text and locate the word. Then Mrs. Palmer reads aloud the first page of the book, and the children read the page quietly. Mrs. Palmer listens to one child read. The children then talk about the story before Mrs. Palmer reads the second page as a model for their later reading on their own. In this stage of early guided reading, children use the pictures, their memory of the text read by the teacher, their store of known words (many learned in the morning message), and some simple decoding skills that they have already learned (for example, to try the beginning sound and look at the ending sound).

After reading the little book, Mrs. Palmer teaches a lesson on how to decode an unfamiliar word. Decoding unfamiliar words requires more than building and reading words from a familiar rime; for example, if a word's rime is unfamiliar, the reader must look at each letter in the word in sequence from left to right and blend the sounds associated with those letters. The decodable book Mrs. Palmer and her students are reading has the words *mop* and *job*. She had put the letters *m, o,* and *p* together on the board and said, "Let's say I don't know this word and I have to figure it out. I look at the first letter and say its sound, then I look at the second letter and say its sound, and I look at the last letter and say its sound. Watch me keep my sounds going all the way through the word, *mmmooop*."

On this second day with the decodable book, Mrs. Palmer listens to each child read a page to see which children can use the decoding strategy of matching the correct sounds to the three letters of a CVC word (including the short vowel) and keeping those sounds going all the way through the word. If she finds someone who can do that, then before moving to the next page, she invites that child to demonstrate for the group. For example, she says, "Camille used our strategy of keeping the sounds going." She points to the word *job* and says, "Camille, show us how you did that on this word."

Two considerations guide such teaching of decoding strategies in kindergarten. The first is that teachers must not expect that all kindergartners will learn to decode unfamiliar words; only early beginning readers can do so. Mrs. Palmer has only a few children who are ready for the strategy of applying the CVC generalization and keeping the sounds going all the way through a word; many children will learn it as first graders. The second consideration is that not all words are amenable to such strategies. Teachers must be careful to demonstrate decoding strategies and invite children to apply them only with words that are decodable, that is, consistent with phonics generalizations. For example, pronouncing a vowel as short in a CVC word works for many CVC words (e.g., *cat, dot, pug*); it does not work for all CVC words (e.g., *car, dog, put*).

Interactive Writing in Small Group

Mrs. Palmer is going to use interactive writing with her early beginning readers. With **interactive writing,** teachers let children write some of the letters or words on a shared writing chart; thus, it is also called "sharing the pen" (Tompkins & Collom, 2004). Interactive writing proceeds in a very similar manner as kid writing. However, unlike kid writing, in which each child writes his or her own sentence, with interactive writing, a group of children decides on one sentence before writing. Then a line is written on the chart paper for each word in the sentence. The teacher helps children locate high-frequency words on the word wall and writes these words herself. **High-frequency words** are those that appear often in just about any text that is longer than a few sentences, for example, *the, is, me, am, can, is,* and *in*. These are words that teachers place on word walls (usually introducing five new words each week). For other words, the teacher demonstrates saying the word slowly and segmenting the beginning sounds. Words in interactive writing are spelled conventionally, so the teacher spells difficult middle parts of words and has children spell beginnings and endings.

Figure 8.5 presents a page of a book composed with interactive writing. Each of four days after reading a little book about go-carts during guided reading, Mrs. Palmer helped a small group of four early beginning readers and writers compose four new

FIGURE 8.5 A Page of a Book Composed with Interactive Writing

pages for their own *Go-Cart Book*. For the page shown in Figure 8.5, one child wrote *The* from memory. A second child listened to the beginning sound of *blue* and wrote the letter *b*, and the teacher completed the spelling of that word. Another child listened to *go*, said it slowly stretching out its sounds, and then spelled it. After writing *cart*, the teacher invited another child to write the period. They completed four sentences, and each of the four children selected a page, then drew and colored a picture of a go-cart. Then Mrs. Palmer assembled the papers into a book.

TEACHING CHILDREN THE CONVENTIONS

WE HAVE ALREADY SHOWN how several exemplary kindergarten teachers teach the conventions of reading and writing during their daily activities. Children's attention is drawn to alphabet letters, sound-letter associations, concepts about print, and high-frequency words. They see demonstrations of and apply phonemic awareness and decoding. They make sense of books read aloud to them by recalling information and making inferences. Kindergartners are introduced to most conventions in reading and writing during daily whole-group routines such as shared reading, journal and kid writing, and interactive read-alouds. However, teachers also provide tailored instruction during small-group lessons; and all children gain new insights into alphabet knowledge, phonemic awareness, concepts about print, the alphabetic principle, and listening comprehension. Many children learn to decode words, identify a few high-frequency words, and spell with increasingly complex spellings. Here, we discuss teaching each of these conventions.

Alphabet Instruction Including Letter-Sound Knowledge

By the end of kindergarten, children must quickly and accurately recognize most of the uppercase and lowercase letters by name, be able to write recognizable letters, and know the sounds associated with a majority of the consonant letters. Kindergarten teachers are better able to meet the needs of children when they know what children already know through systematic assessment and observation (see Chapters 3 and 4). Many kindergartners still confuse similar-looking letters and reverse letters when writing. Teachers need to confront the issue of confusable letters (such as *M* and *W* and *b*, *p*, *d*, and *q*). Teachers can select one of the confusable letters and teach children to recognize this letter using a set of letters the children already recognize. For example, if children already know *A*, *C*, *F*, and *T*, then teachers use that set of letters in games to teach an unknown but confusable letter such as *M*. Writing should accompany letter recognition. When one confusable letter is well known, teachers add another. Although teachers will not want to require perfect conformity to any handwriting system, they should demonstrate and talk through the strokes they use for making letters.

When teaching lowercase letters, teachers should begin with letters that have the same shape in both uppercase and lowercase form. These will be learned quickly. Then teachers can add lowercase letters with different shapes than their uppercase partners.

Teachers should begin teaching a letter's sound only after children can identify the letter without hesitation. If teachers are careful to teach sound-letter associations only of those letters that children can name, then sound-letter instruction need not await children's being able to identify all the letters. In addition to choosing letters that children can name, teachers begin sound-letter instruction with sounds that children have already used in phonemic awareness activities, whose manners of articulation are quite different from one another, and whose names contain that sound. For example, if children have already learned to hear /f/, /v/, and /s/ in spoken words, as demonstrated, for example, by their being able to say words beginning with those sounds and then separately say the onset and rimes of those words ("*fan*, /f/-/an/; *vine*, /v/-/In/; *soon*, /s/-/OOn/"), then they are ready to learn which letters are associated with those three consonant sounds. Some letter sounds are easier to learn than others. For example, the sound associated with the letter *V* is /v/ (see Table 1.2 in Chapter 1), and that sound can be heard as the first phoneme in the letter name "vee." It is easiest to learn. The sound associated with the letter *F* is /f/ and that sound can be heard in the last phoneme in the letter name "eff." On the other hand, the letter *G* is associated with the sound /g/, and its letter name "gee" does not contain the sound /g/. These sounds are the hardest to learn. Teachers should teach both sound-to-letter associations (listening to the sounds in spoken words and associating letters with them) and letter-to-sound associations (looking at letters in written words and identifying sounds with them).

Phonemic Awareness Instruction Including Decoding

Teaching children to segment the first sound in spoken words and, later, to segment easy three-phoneme words requires teachers to learn how to scaffold (see Chapter 6 and Mrs. Rodgers). Students are given a picture, and the teacher slowly pronounces the word. She says "mmmmmmmaaaaaaannnnnn" for *man,* for example. She tells children to watch her mouth as she says the first sound (lips are pressed together to form the /m/ phoneme); she says the word slowly, pointing to her lips. Finally, she tells the children the beginning sound, "The first sound in *mmmman* is /m/. You say it." This teaches children the task of saying just one sound—the beginning sound in the word. Later, the teacher will have children listen for the ending sound, the sound they hear last. She says, "mmmmaaaannnn. Listen to the last sound, mmmmaaannnn." She points to her mouth as she says the last sound /n/. "The last sound is /n/. Do you hear it? mmmmaaaaannnnn." After most children can segment the first and often the last sound in a word, teachers demonstrate how to hear all the phonemes in three-phoneme words using Elkonin boxes (three boxes lined up). Again, teachers would start with words with continuant consonants (and avoid any consonant clusters) such as the words *feet, jam, leaf, mom, nail, red,* and *sun* (McCarthy, 2008). After demonstrating the process of pushing up pennies or other tokens into the boxes and saying each phoneme, children are given a set of cards each with a picture of different three-phoneme words. They practice saying the words cued by the pictures, saying the words slowly, and pushing up the tokens. Later, children are given consonant letters to push into the boxes (such as pushing the *f* and *t* into the first and last boxes for the word *feet*). When children can hear the phonemes, say the word slowly, and coordinate pushing the tokens with the saying, they are developing phonemic awareness. When children can hear the phonemes, say the words slowly, and coordinate the pushing of letters with the saying, they are developing the **alphabetic principle.** The ability to use the alphabetic principle occurs during decoding and during invented spelling. **Decoding** occurs when children look at an unknown word and attempt to say it by using the sounds associated with letters. **Invented spelling** occurs when children listen to a word they need to spell and spell it by matching letters to sounds they hear.

Concepts about Print Instruction Including Learning Sight Words

Teaching children concepts about print occurs during shared reading and writing, interactive writing, and kid writing. As teachers talk about the print or about what they are writing, they share insights about how to print words. "Get your eyes up here. This is where we start reading," introduces the concept of the first word in text located at the top left line of print. "I need to scoot over a bit to start the next word. See, I've left a nice space between the words" shows children the concept of a word space. "Watch me say the words slowly and touch each word as I read" demonstrates one-to-one matching as well as left-to-right directionality. Asking "Now where do I go?" after reading the first line of text asks children to notice the return sweep. Saying, "We wrote a lot of words today; let's count the number of words we have written," then demonstrating touching each word while counting shows children what words (compared to letters) look like. Saying, "I just wrote a very long word. Let's count the number of letters in this word" contrasts for children what letters are compared to words.

From preschool experiences with books, most kindergarteners know the concepts associated with **bookhandling skills,** such as front, back, top, bottom, and left page before right page. They are beginning to learn the **directionality concepts** of left to right and return sweep and one-to-one matching across lines of text from top to bottom. They need to learn **letter-and-word concepts:** words are comprised of letters, words have first and last letters, and there are first and last words on a page. Figure 7.2 in Chapter 7 presents several activities that teachers can use to teach letter-and-word concepts during shared reading and writing.

During finger-point reading, after children can match words they say one to one with words on the page, they begin to develop sight words. **Sight words** are words that children can actually read. When their eyes see the word, they recognize the word immediately. The first sight words children learn are often high-frequency words. As noted earlier, high-frequency words are words in English that are repeated often such as the words *the, is, and, can, to, with, are,* and *a.* Other words that children learn by sight are names of their friends or brothers and sisters or words of interest such as *school* or *love.* By the end of kindergarten, children are expected to recognize approximately twenty-five high-frequency words because they have seen them so often in morning message, shared writing or reading, and in finger-point reading.

Teaching Comprehension and Vocabulary

Dramatizing books is a playful and powerful way to develop kindergartners' comprehension and vocabulary. Teachers frequently dramatize stories, but children can use drama to explore information books as well. One teacher included drama as a part of her chick-hatching unit. Mrs. Poremba's students had read many information books and posters about chick development and hatching. As the children anticipated their first chick's hatching, they applied what they had learned from their reading.

Mrs. Poremba: Let's pretend that we are a chick that's been in the egg twenty-one days. You are SO crowded, your legs and your wings and your head and your back and your beak are ALL crunched together. . . . OK, the first thing you do is you SLOOOOOWLY move your head up and you're going to poke your air sack on the top of your egg to take that breath of your first air. Poke your air sack. Okay. Take your breath. Do you like that air?

Children: Yes. Uh huh.

Mrs. Poremba: But you know what? That took a lot of work. So now you're tired again. . . . Ohhhh. Now a little bit of a rest. Now we're going to take our head and get your egg tooth up, part of the end of your beak. And we're going to make our very first pip in the shell—and that's very hard work. Find your place to pip.

Children: Pip, pip, pip. Peep, peep, peep.

Mrs. Poremba: Did you get a pip in your shell?

Children: Yeah. Yes.

Mrs. Poremba: Go back to sleep. You are so tired. This is HARD work hatching. OK, now let's look at our picture to see what we need to do next.

In this classroom, dramatic play provided a rich context for extending children's understandings of the world (Putnam, 1991). As students dramatized information from books, they showed their understandings of the meanings of words such as *air sack, pip,* and *egg tooth.*

INDEPENDENT LITERACY EXPERIENCES

CHILDREN NEED MANY OPPORTUNITIES to explore literacy on their own, for their own purposes and to practice with materials and activities introduced by their teachers. Kindergarten teachers will use a combination of centers that provide authentic real-world literacy experiences and workstations.

Real-World Literacy Experiences

One particularly effective center in kindergarten is called a **dramatic-play-with-print center.** This is a center in which children pretend around a theme that includes much real-world reading and writing. Mrs. Poremba uses several of these centers in her classroom. A popular dramatic-play-with-print center in Mrs. Poremba's room is a classroom pizza parlor. One day, Deborah was taking orders there. She had chosen this play center for at least a small part of the free-choice time several times a week. Like most of her classmates, when taking a customer's order, she always wrote a line of mock cursive for each item in the customer's order. She took a pizza order from one of the authors of this book: seven lines of mock cursive for "extra large . . . thin and crispy . . . green olives . . . sausage . . . extra cheese . . . root beer . . . large." Later, however, when delivering the order, Deborah used a different writing strategy. "Wait— you need your receipt," she said, and she used the numerals and symbols on the toy cash register to copy "¢ 25¢"and "$5" on the back of the paper she had used for writing the order.

The **project approach,** like dramatic-play-with-print centers, also emphasizes real-world literacy experiences. In dramatic-play-with-print centers, children pretend to play in real-world settings such as pizza parlors and shoe stores. They pretend to be customers, waiters and waitresses, and shoe store employees. In these roles, they pretend to read store advertisements and menus and to write receipts and order forms. The project approach involves children in constructing simulations of real-world settings for literacy activity; once established, these function like dramatic-play-with-print centers. Powell and Davidson (2005) described how their urban kindergartners decided to build a doughnut shop in their classroom. They invited bankers to their classroom to tell them how to get a loan and find potential stockholders to buy stock. They wrote to staff members in the school and a nearby college to invite them to become stockholders and wrote thank-you letters when they received money for shares. They invited building inspectors to come and describe how to get building permits. Children wrote labels for the ingredients in their doughnut store, a big book about their experience, and invitations to the grand opening of the store.

Workstations

Because kindergarten teachers work with small groups of children daily, they need to offer the other children meaningful experiences they can complete independently. Teachers may use a variety of techniques, including assigning all children a "Must do" activity such as drawing a picture of the main character of a storybook read aloud. Or, teachers may assign a small-group task to be completed after a small-group lesson, such as reading the little book used for finger-point reading to two other children. Or, teachers may assign children to workstation groups as Mrs. Palmer did. Each group is assigned to a station and they stay at the station until the teacher signals time for a change. Chapter 6 provides several ideas for workstations that can be used in kindergarten.

DIFFERENTIATED INSTRUCTION TO MEET THE NEEDS OF DIVERSE STUDENTS

SMALL-GROUP INSTRUCTION IN KINDERGARTEN should meet the needs of nearly all children by providing them with instruction appropriate to their knowledge and need profiles. Some children may need more frequent small-group instruction in even smaller groups than other children. When children are not making progress in small groups of four to seven children, then teachers should consider providing instruction in groups of two or three. Instruction needs to include what children know and build bridges to what they do not know. When children are not succeeding, teachers might consider whether instruction provided enough known items to provide success and build confidence before moving to new items. English language learners may need special attention to ensure they understand instructions, have adequate vocabulary and concepts, and can connect their background experiences with the materials to be learned.

Using Environmental Print

Environmental print is the print found in our homes and communities. It is found on packages, plastic bags, billboards, junk mail, signs, and television. It is usually the first print that children find meaningful as they learn to associate favorite toys with logos on toy packaging or favorite fast-food restaurants with logos found on signs. Environmental print is found in every home and community and is the most familiar print for all children. Kindergarten teachers can use this print to teach alphabet letters, phonemic awareness, sound-letter relationships, and decoding.

One way to find out more about the environmental print familiar to English language learners is to take a walk through neighborhoods in which they live (Orellana & Hernadez, 1999) with older children (if parents give their permission) or with someone familiar with the community. Teachers can take digital photographs of the logos and signs located in neighborhood groceries, video stores, and restaurants. Teachers can use the photographs in lessons and in classroom displays. They invite children to tell about their experiences in these locations. Children can bring in empty packages from their homes to use in show and tell and for small-group skill instruction in alphabet recognition and sound-letter associations (Xu & Rutledge, 2003). These materials can be used to make books by pasting familiar environmental print into pages stapled together. These familiar books can be displayed in the library center.

Morning Message Plus

Morning message plus is a hybrid approach to using the morning message and "What can you show us?" In this approach, the teacher plans the message she or he will write and then writes it as the children watch (in the traditional morning message, teachers write the message before children enter the classroom). Children reread along with the teacher and then predict what word will be written next. The teacher makes comments about what she or he is doing while writing. After the writing is completed, the children step up to the writing and identify letters, words, or print elements they know. Then the teacher extends each child's knowledge through a short mini-lesson (Reilly, 2007).

This activity is designed for a very small group of children with identified needs. On this day, the teacher is capitalizing on the interactive read-aloud book she read to the entire class, *Max's Dragon Shirt* (Wells, 1991), and the familiar characters Max and Ruby. She wrote, "Max went to the store to buy milk for Ruby. He paid 2$ for milk and 3$ for Red-Hot Marshmallow Squirters. How much money did Max spend?" (Reilly, 2007, p. 773). As she wrote, she elongated the /m/ sound by stretching it out for the word *Max* and asked children to say which letter spelled that sound. When she reached the word *to,* she asked children to locate it on the word wall and spell it for her to write. She continued to make comments and ask children questions as she completed the message. As she finished each sentence, she invited the children to read it back. Tyrone was invited to take a turn telling what he knew in the text. He pointed to the *M* in *Max* and named it. At this point, Tyrone only knew thirteen letters and eight letter sounds so the teacher wanted to extend this knowledge. She asked what sound the letter *M* made and took the opportunity to teach it. Now she wants Tyrone to say a word that begins with that sound. She has him go to the name board (pictures of all the children with their names written under them) and find someone's name that began with *M.* Tyrone did as instructed, and the teacher confirmed, "Good. *Mary* starts with /m/. Now you say it." (p. 775). This activity allows teachers in a brief few minutes to target instruction needed by individual children. English language learners can benefit from this instruction as the small group allows teachers to focus on their needs and to scaffold their language needs.

Using Similarities between Spanish and English

Spanish-speaking children make up nearly 80 percent of the ELL population in the United States (Harris, 2006). Understanding the similarities and differences between Spanish and English can provide teachers with a useful starting point for teaching phonemic awareness, phonics, and spelling. Figure 8.6 compares consonants and consonant digraphs in English and Spanish. Phonemic awareness and phonics lessons should begin with the sounds that are found in both languages (Helman, 2004). The sounds that are only found in English will require explicit, systematic lessons in which teachers show children how to attend to manner of articulation and compare and contrast with sounds in Spanish.

FIGURE 8.6 Phonemes in Both English and Spanish and Only in English

Both in English and Spanish	Only in English
/b/	/d/
/f/	/j/
/g/	/r/
/h/	/v/
/k/	/sh/
/l/	/th/
/m/	/zh/
/n/	
/p/	
/s/	
/t/	
/w/	
/y/	
/ch/	

Source: Adapted from Helman, 2004.

Using Finger-Point Reading

Many ELL children have experiences with printed language that do not involve left-to-right and top-to-bottom directionality (Barone, Mallete, & Xu, 2005). Some languages use a different word order, such as adjectives following verbs rather than preceding them. Thus, the activity of finger-point reading to accompany memorized text is critically important to establish directionality and letter-word concepts in English. While English-speaking children may quickly establish these concepts, English language learners may need extra practice with texts with just a few lines, very exaggerated word spaces, and few words per line. Because it is critical that all children before the end of kindergarten establish one-to-one matching and left-to-right directionality with a return sweep, teachers must be especially concerned to observe ELLs' acquisition of these concepts.

Writing and Reading in Two Languages

It is important that kindergarten teachers find a way to support children's home language learning as well as their learning English (Ortiz & Ordonez-Jasis, 2005). Traditionally, teachers have encouraged parents to support the home language by reading aloud books to their children; talking with their children as they engage in joint activities such as baking cookies or washing the car; and sharing poems, songs, and rhymes with their children (Yopp & Stapleton, 2008). Parents are also encouraged to tell their children stories. Thus, parents can support children's language learning (including awareness of rhyming and beginning sounds) in their home languages when they share books such as *¿Tu mamá es una llama?* (Guarino, 1993) or *Vamos a Cazar un Oso* (Rosen, 1993), Spanish versions of *Is Your Mama a Llama?* and *We're Going on a Bear Hunt*. In school, teachers can encourage the use of two languages during journal writing and sharing. Children can be asked to write in both English and Spanish, for example. In the early stages of learning to write, many bilingual children use letter strings (rather than letters with any sound-letter relationships in invented spellings). Many children at this stage of writing (see Chapter 1) use similar letters to write their messages but clearly indicate which letter string represents Spanish and which represents English (Rubin & Carlan, 2005). As children develop the alphabetic principle, they begin using some sound-letter correspondences but cannot match all the sounds and letters in a word. For example, Rubin and Carlan found that one child wrote *cro* and read it *carro* (in Spanish) and wrote *cro* again but read it *car* (in English). Even when teachers cannot speak Spanish (or other home languages spoken by children), they can invite their kindergartners to read to them their English writing and to read their other writing to other speakers in the classroom or the school.

PULLING ASSESSMENT TOGETHER: USING PORTFOLIOS

A PORTFOLIO IS A LARGE ENVELOPE OR FOLDER, one for each child in the classroom, into which teachers put a selection of work samples and their captions (see the work sample and caption Ms. Clements collected and wrote in Figure 7.6 in Chapter 7). They also collect anecdotal notes, results of **screening assessments,** and results of **monitoring assessments.** Thus, a **portfolio** is a collection of a variety of a child's work and assessments, which inform teachers about the child's development and accomplishments. Portfolios serve several functions in the classroom. They are used to make instructional decisions, help children reflect on what they have been learning, and share with parents information about their children's literacy growth (Hansen, 1996; Porter & Cleland, 1995). For portfolios to be useful, they must be manageable and up-to-date. Most importantly, portfolios help teachers reflect on their own practice (Bergeron, Wermuth, & Hammar, 1997; Kieffer & Faust, 1994).

Before grading periods in the elementary school, teachers pull out anecdotal notes and captions taken weekly or biweekly and gather them together in each child's portfolio. In preparation for giving grades and meeting in conferences with parents, teachers look through the anecdotal notes and work samples to determine progress and areas of needed instruction. They gather any running records and miscue analyses (see Chapter 5 for a discussion of these assessment tools). They look through all of the children's samples to make an analysis of the children's decoding and spelling strategies and their growing awareness of story and expository text structures (see Chapter 5 for a discussion of the narrative and expository text structures we expect elementary students to acquire). Finally, they consider any assessment data. Together, these data form a complete picture about the child's accomplishments, current level of understanding, and future needs.

Analyzing Children's Writing

Early-childhood classrooms for children in preschool, kindergarten, and first grade provide children with many opportunities to try their hand at telling and retelling stories and writing at the writing center. Composing activities such as these provide opportunities for teachers to gather rich assessment information about their children's literacy development. It is particularly important to gather work samples of experimenters' writing as they will display both conventional and unconventional concepts.

Analysis of Form.   Young children's writing can be examined for the following forms.

- mock cursive (indicates awareness of linearity)
- mock alphabet letters (indicates awareness of letter features)
- conventional alphabet letters (indicates knowledge of alphabet formations)
- copied words (indicates awareness of words in environment)
- spelled words such as the child's name or other learned words such as *mom, dad,* and *love* (indicates learned spellings)
- conventions (such as capitalization and punctuation)
- invented spelling

In addition, teachers note whether children's writing shows awareness of linearity, for example, writing mock letters from left to right in lines, or spacing, for example, leaving spaces between strings of conventional letters as if writing words (Feldgus & Cardonick, 1999). Young children frequently circle words, place periods between words, or separate words with dashes. These unconventional strategies indicate that children are experimenting with word boundaries.

Story Form.   Teachers take special note of children's control over story form, which includes the following elements.

- setting, which identifies time, place, and weather
- characters, who are revealed through their thoughts, actions, appearance, and dialogue
- plot, which includes a problem, episodes, climax, and resolution—episodes consist of actions toward solving the problem and outcomes
- point of view, which reveals who tells the story
- mood
- theme

Figure 8.7 presents a story composition dictated by five-year-old Kristen to her kindergarten teacher. The composition contains sixteen pages and a title page. As Kristen's kindergarten teacher analyzed the form of Kristen's story, she noted that Kristen had included three characters: a little girl, a cat, and baby cats. These characters were developed through the illustrations (which showed what the characters looked like), a

FIGURE 8.7   "The Girl with the Cat and the Babies"

Title:	The Girl with the Cat and the Babies
page 1	The little girl took her cat for a walk.
page 2	She got caught in a trap.
page 3	The little girl came.
page 4	And she pulled, and she pulled, and she pushed, and she pushed on the trap.
page 5	She opened the cage and the cat was almost out.
page 6	The little cat was out. She was happy.
page 7	The cat was purring because the little girl was rubbing her.
page 8	The little girl was taking her home.
page 9	The sun was coming down.
page 10	Tomorrow was the cat's birthday. She was happy because she was going to have a party.
page 11	It was the cat's birthday and the people were fixing it up because they were awake.
page 12	One day the cat was knocking on the little girl's door because she had four babies on her birthday.
page 13	The cat asked, "Can I go out in the woods with my babies to live?"
page 14	Far, far away they went. She waved good-bye and so did the babies.
page 15	The cat built five houses.
page 16	They were all ready to go to sleep.

few revelations of the cat's thoughts (she wanted to go home and she was happy), the girl's and cat's actions, and dialogue.

Kristen's story incorporates three plot episodes (rescuing the cat, the cat's birthday, and taking the baby cats to live in the woods). The first episode, about rescuing the cat, has a fully developed plot. It includes a problem (the cat was caught in a trap), actions toward solving the problem (the girl pulled and pulled, and pushed and pushed on the trap), a climax (the cat was almost out), and an outcome (the cat was out). The other episodes are descriptions of actions, and all the episodes are loosely connected through common characters.

Kristen relied on having the cats go to sleep to resolve the story. The story is told in the third person, with the cat's thoughts revealed. The mood of the story is pleasant except for when the cat is caught in the trap. Kristen's story shows her ability to manipulate all the literary elements of a story form except for theme.

Analysis of the Alphabetic Principle

Children are likely to begin to understand the alphabetic principle sometime during kindergarten. A few children come to school already understanding this principle as demonstrated in their invented spellings. Most children will acquire it during kindergarten; the earlier they do so, the more likely they are to be on the way to successful conventional reading and writing as they become experimenters (see Chapter 4). Children who leave kindergarten not displaying evidence of having acquired the alphabetic principle are very much at risk in first grade. Kindergarten teachers can make a quick assessment of children's understanding of the alphabetic principle either by asking children to spell words (see Chapter 4 for Zack's and Erin's spelling and for a spelling assessment); or teachers may dictate a sentence and ask children to write it word by word (Clay, 2005). An example of dictation sentences follows with the number of phonemes marked under the words. Children are expected, for the most part, to write one letter for each phoneme. For example, while the word *see* has three letters, it only has two phonemes because the *ee* together spell the phoneme. To score each word as correct, the child only needs to write a reasonable spelling (*kan* for *can* or *vere* for *very* is reasonable because *K* and *C* both spell the /k/ phoneme and both *Y* and *E* spell the /E/ phoneme). However, a child must write *th* for the words *the* and *that*. The long vowel spellings for the words *see* and *road* can be reasonably spelled with just the letters *E* and *O*. Students who score between five and twenty-six phonemes during early kindergarten and between sixteen and thirty-three phonemes at the end of kindergarten are performing on grade-level expectations. Students who fall below these scores may need more intense instruction in phonemic awareness, alphabetic knowledge, and sound-letter associations.

I can see the b i g b u s. It will g o v e r y f a s t
1 2 3 4 5 6 7 8 9 10 11 12 13 14 15 16 17 18 19 20 21 22 23 24 25 26 27 28 29
u p th a t r oa d
30 31 32 33 34 35 36 37

Chapter Summary

Kindergartners are expected to recognize and begin to write alphabet letters, match spoken and written words, know rhyming words and beginning sounds in words, know sound-letter correspondences and use them in invented spellings, understand concepts of print, write their first and last names, begin to read and write some high-frequency words, and enjoy and participate in read-alouds. Many of these expectations are in the area of meaning-form links, and their achievement depends on a related achievement—fully developed phonemic awareness. Kindergartners meet these expectations and continue to develop in all areas of written language acquisition when classrooms are filled with print, when teachers and children model reading and writing, and when children participate in functional and contextualized written language experiences.

Kindergartners' literacy learning is supported through classroom routines using print. Routines such as journal writing, "What can you show us?", and shared reading encourage children's reading and writing and provide opportunities for teachers and children to talk about written language. Shared reading is a rich context for literacy learning; teachers orient children to print, read with children, and plan response activities. Shared reading is used with poems, songs, letters, stories, and informational texts presented on charts and in big books.

Using shared writing and morning message is another context for language and literacy development in kindergarten. Teachers and students compose texts together. Students suggest ideas, teachers model writing processes, and the students participate in both the writing and the subsequent reading and rereading of the text. Finally, play is a critical component of the kindergarten curriculum. Children learn about written language in dramatic-play-with-print centers and during computer play.

APPLYING THE INFORMATION

Make a list of all the literacy-learning activities described in this chapter, including whole-group, small-group, and individual activities. For each activity, describe what children learn about written language meanings (listening comprehension), forms (letters and words and other concepts about print), meaning-form links (phonemic awareness, decoding, spelling), or functions (how print is used in real-world activities). Now write a second list. Write instructional activities that are most appropriate for letter and sound learners, for sound learners, for finger-point reading learners, and for early beginning reading learners.

GOING BEYOND THE TEXT

VISIT A KINDERGARTEN AND OBSERVE several literacy activities. Take note of the interactions among the children and between the teacher and the children as they participate in literacy experiences. Make a list of the kinds of literacy materials and describe the classroom routines in which children read and write. Talk with the teacher about the school's academic expectations for kindergarten. Find out how the teacher meets those expectations. Compare these materials, interactions, and activities with those found in this chapter.

REFERENCES

Anderson, R. C., & Nagy, W. E. (1992). The vocabulary conundrum. *American Educator: The Professional Journal of the American Federation of Teachers, 16*, 14–18.

Barone, D. M., Mallete, S. H., & Xu, M. H. (2005). *Teaching early literacy: Development, assessment, and instruction.* New York: Guilford Press.

Bergeron, B., Wermuth, S., & Hammar, R. (1997). Initiating portfolios through shared learning: Three perspectives. *The Reading Teacher, 50*, 552–561.

Brinckloe, J. (1985). *Fireflies.* New York: Aladdin Paperbacks.

Charlesworth, L. (2002). *Spring in the kingdom of Ying.* New York: Scholastic.

Clay, M. M. (2005). *Literacy lessons designed for individuals: Part two teaching procedures.* Portsmouth, NH: Heinemann.

Cunningham, P. (1998). Looking for patterns: Phonics activities that help children notice how words work. In C. Weaver (Ed.), *Practicing what we know: Informed reading instruction* (pp. 87–110). Urbana, IL: National Council of Teachers of English.

Elkonin, D. B. (1973). Reading in the U.S.S.R. In J. Downing (Ed.), *Comparative reading* (pp. 551–579). New York: Macmillan.

Feldgus, E. G., & Cardonick, I. (1999). *Kid writing: A systematic approach to phonics, journals, and writing workshop.* Bothell, WA: The Wright Group.

Graves, M. F., & Watts-Taffe, S. (2002). *The place of word consciousness in a research-based vocabulary program. What research has to say about reading instruction* (3rd ed.). Newark, DE: International Reading Association.

Gregory, A. E., & Cahill, M. A. (2010). Kindergartners can do it too! Comprehension strategies for early readers. *The Reading Teacher, 63*, 515–520.

Griffith, P. L., & Olson, M. W. (1992). *Kid writing: A systematic approach to phonics, journals, and writing workshop.* Bothell, WA: The Wright Group.

Guarino, D. (1993). *¿Tu Mamá es una llama?* (S. Kellogg, Illus.; A. E. Marcuse, Trans.). New York: Scholastic.

Hansen, J. (1996). Evaluation: The center of writing instruction. *The Reading Teacher, 50*, 188–195.

Harris, P. (2006). Teaching English language learners: NCTE guideline offers help for English teachers working with ELLs. *The Council Chronicle of the National Council of Teachers of English, 16*, 1, 5–6.

Helman, L. (2004). Building on the sound system of Spanish: Insights from the alphabetic spellings of English-language learners. *The Reading Teacher, 57*, 452–460.

Kieffer. R. D., & Faust, M. A. (1994). Portfolio process and teacher change: Elementary, middle, and secondary teachers reflect on their initial experiences with portfolio evaluation. In C. K. Kinzer & D. J. Leu (Eds.), *Multidimensional aspects of literacy research, theory, and practice* (pp. 82–88). Chicago: National Reading Conference.

Labbo, L. D. (2005). From morning message to digital morning message: Moving from the tried and true to the new. *The Reading Teacher, 58*, 782–785.

Lane, H. B., & Allen, S. (2010, February). The vocabulary-rich classroom: Modeling sophisticated word use to promote word consciousness and vocabulary growth. *The Reading Teacher, 63*(5), 362–370.

Mariage, T. V. (2001). Features of an interactive writing discourse: Conversational involvement, conventional knowledge, and internalization in "Morning Message." *Journal of Learning Disabilities, 34*, 172–196.

McCarthy, P. A. (2008). Using sound boxes systematically to develop phonemic awareness. *The Reading Teacher, 62*, 346–349.

McGee, L. M. (2007). *Transforming literacy practices in preschool: Research-based practices that give all children the opportunity to reach their potential as learners.* New York: Scholastic.

McGee, L. M., & Morrow, L. M. (2005). *Teaching literacy in kindergarten.* New York: Guilford Press.

McGill-Franzen, A. (2006). *Kindergarten literacy: Matching assessment and instruction in kindergarten.* New York: Scholastic.

Mozelle, S. (1995). *Zach's alligator.* New York: HarperCollins.

Myers, P. A. (2005). The princess storyteller, Clara Clarifier, Quincy Questioner, and the Wizard: Reciprocal teaching adapted for kindergarten students. *The Reading Teacher, 59*, 314–324.

Orellana, M. F., & Hernadez, A. (1999). Talking the walk: Children reading urban environmental print. *The Reading Teacher, 52*, 612–619.

Ortiz, R. W., & Ordonez-Jasis, R. (2005). Reading together: New directions for Latino parents' early literacy involvement. *The Reading Teacher, 59*, 110–121.

Palinscar, A. S., & Brown, A. L. (1984). Reciprocal teaching of comprehension-fostering and comprehension-monitoring activities. *Cognition and Instruction, 1*, 117–175.

Porter, C., & Cleland, J. (1995). *The portfolio as a learning strategy*. Portsmouth, NH: Heinemann.

Powell, R., & Davidson, N. (2005). The donut house: Real world literacy in an urban kindergarten classroom. *Language Arts, 82*, 248–256.

Putnam, L. (1991). Dramatizing nonfiction with emerging readers. *Language Arts, 68*, 463–469.

Reilly, M. A. (2007). Choice of action: Using data to make instructional decisions in kindergarten. *The Reading Teacher, 60*, 770–776.

Richgels, D. J. (2003). *Going to kindergarten: A year with an outstanding teacher*. Lanham, MD: Scarecrow Press.

Richgels, D. J., Poremba, K. J., & McGee, L. M. (1996). Kindergartners talk about print: Phonemic awareness in meaningful contexts. *The Reading Teacher, 49*, 632–642.

Rosen, M. (1993). *Vamos a cazar un oso* (H. Oxenbury, Illus.). Caracas, Venezuela: Ediciones Ekaré.

Rubin, R., & Carlan, V. G. (2005, May). Using writing to understand bilingual children's literacy development. *The Reading Teacher, 58*(8), 728–739.

Tompkins, G., & Collom, S. (2004). *Sharing the pen: Interactive writing with young children*. New York: Prentice Hall.

Wells, R. (1991). *Max's dragon shirt*. New York: Puffin Books.

Xu, S. H., & Rutledge, A. L. (2003). "Chicken" starts with "ch"! Kindergartners learn through environmental print. *Young Children, 58*, 44–51.

Yopp, H. K., & Stapleton, L. (2008). Conciencia fonemica en Espanol (Phonemic awareness in Spanish). *The Reading Teacher, 61*, 374–382.

PEARSON myeducationlab

Go to the topics Phonemic Awareness and Phonics, Word Study, Writing Development, Assessment, and English Language Learners in the MyEducationLab (www.myeducationlab.com) for your course, where you can:

- Find learning outcomes for Phonemic Awareness and Phonics, Word Study, Writing Development, Assessment, and English Language Learners along with the national standards that connect to these outcomes.
- Complete Assignments and Activities that can help you more deeply understand the chapter content.
- Examine challenging situations and cases presented in the IRIS Center Resources.

A+RISE

Go to the Topic A+RISE in the MyEducationLab (www.myeducationlab.com) for your course. A+RISE® Standards2Strategy™ is an innovative and interactive online resource that offers new teachers in grades K–12 just-in-time, research-based instructional strategies that:

- Meet the linguistic needs of ELLs as they learn content
- Differentiate instruction for all grades and abilities
- Offer reading and writing techniques, cooperative learning, use of linguistic and nonlinguistic representations, scaffolding, teacher modeling, higher order thinking, and alternative classroom ELL assessment
- Provide support to help teachers be effective through the integration of listening, speaking, reading, and writing along with the content curriculum
- Improve student achievement
- Are aligned to Common Core Elementary Language Arts standards (for the literacy strategies) and to English language proficiency standards in WIDA, Texas, California, and Florida.

CHAPTER

9

Supporting Literacy
Learning in First Grade

KEY CONCEPTS

Sight Words
Talk-Through Activity
Developmental Spelling
  Inventory
Mini-Lesson
Make-a-Rhyming-Word
  Activity
Word-Sort Activity
Decoding

Spelling
Phonics
Systematic Phonics
  Instruction
Explicit
  Instruction
Elkonin Boxes
Making Words
Word Wall

Automatic Sight
  Vocabulary
High-Frequency Words
Grand Conversations
Comprehensive
  Reading Program
Core Reading Programs
Language Experience
  Approach

WHAT'S NEW HERE?

THE "WHAT'S NEW?" IN FIRST GRADE is the expectation that by the end of the year all children will be reading and writing conventionally. They are expected to comprehend stories and informational texts; learn the meanings of new words; learn a few hundred sight words; and use strategies to decode unknown words, including using sound-letter relationships. They are expected to use sound-letter relationships and other strategies to spell words. They are expected to write a variety of kinds of compositions for a variety of purposes (to inform, to interact with others, to entertain). Table 9.1 summarizes the accomplishments expected in reading and writing by the end of first grade.

Many children begin first grade already reading and writing conventionally. The print-rich environment and literacy instruction provided for them in preschool and

TABLE 9.1   Reading and Writing Outcomes for First Grade

By the end of first grade, children

Read and retell familiar narrative and informational text.

Use strategies (predicting, rereading, imagining, questioning, commenting) for comprehension.

Choose to read and write for a variety of purposes.

Have an awareness of a wide variety of literary elements found in narratives, informational texts, and poetry (character, setting, problem, event, sequence, lining, rhyming, repetition).

Write personal, narrative, informational, and poetic text.

Have an interest in and strategies for learning meanings of vocabulary.

Acquire many sight words in reading and correctly spell many words in writing.

Use a variety of strategies for decoding and spelling (including strategies that build from phonemic awareness, maintain fluency, detect and correct errors, solve problems with words using multiple sources of information, and link to current knowledge, including the use of consonants, short vowels, long vowels, and high-frequency phonograms).

Use punctuation and capitalization.

Engage in independent reading and writing.

Source: Based on International Reading Association & National Association for the Education of Young Children (IRA/NAEYC), 1998; Fountas & Pinnell, 1996; and Bear, Invernizzi, Templeton, & Johnston, 2000.

kindergarten were sufficient for them to make the transition from experimenters to conventional, early beginning readers and writers. Children who begin first grade already reading and writing often make tremendous gains in reading during first grade, often ending the year reading on a third-grade level or above (Dahl, Sharer, Lawson, & Grogan, 1999).

Other children enter first grade as experimenters; they are the finger-point readers found in kindergarten classrooms (see Chapter 8). For them, beginning to read and write conventionally will be relatively easy as they participate in instructional activities such as those we describe in this chapter (Snow, Burns, & Griffin, 1998). For other children, this transition requires careful attention from a highly knowledgeable teacher (Clay, 2001). Children who begin first grade with knowledge and experiences of written language like those of novice readers and writers (the letter and sounds learners mentioned in Chapter 8) need carefully planned instruction in order to become conventional readers and writers who reach first-grade reading level by the end of first grade.

We know a great deal about what children need to learn in order to begin reading conventionally (Adams, 1990; National Early Literacy Panel, 2008). The hallmark of conventional reading is orchestrating all sources of information so attention is free to focus on meaning. Experienced conventional readers pay attention to print; they look at and read every word in a text. However, the print seems transparent; readers' attention is on the meaning. They are constructing meaning rather than focusing on the print. Attention can be focused on a text's meaning when readers automatically and fluently recognize words; know their meanings; and parse those meanings into phrases, sentences, and larger chunks. That is, readers recognize and access the meanings of words quickly (in a fraction of a second) "by sight" and chunk them together into phrases without consciously having to decode words or "sound them out." **Sight words** are words that readers recognize instantly. Learning words and hooking words together in reading and writing are critical.

As most children acquire sight words, an amazing thing happens quite unconsciously. As they read more and more text, they go beyond just learning specific words. They automatically relate letter sequences in frequently encountered words to spoken word parts. Knowing the pronunciations of word parts allows them to decode very complicated words they have never before encountered. They can do so very quickly, seemingly without stopping to "sound out." For example, for most younger readers, the word *see* becomes a sight word early in the learning-to-read process, and later they read for the first time words such as *beet* or *sneeze* without pausing to sound them out. For older readers, the letters *con, tempt,* and *ible* in the word *contemptible* automatically trigger pronunciation of /kuhn/, /tempt/, and /ibl/ even when they have never before encountered the word *contemptible* in their reading.

In this chapter, we will focus much of our attention on teaching children about reading and writing words. However, it is critical to keep in mind that reading continuous texts necessarily takes readers beyond the level of the individual word. Reading continuous texts is more than automatically identifying sight words and using word-recognition strategies with words that students cannot read automatically. In other words, readers must always attend to the ways that word meanings interact in the sentence they are reading and to the still larger, unfolding meaning of an entire text.

Reading and Writing Instruction in Exemplary First-Grade Classrooms

WE SHOW HOW EXEMPLARY TEACHERS guide reading and writing in first grade using a variety of instructional tools.

Guided-Reading Instruction in Mrs. Tran's First Grade

Mrs. Tran teaches twenty, first-grade children in a large urban district. The majority of the children in her classroom have home languages that are not English; the classroom includes six different home languages. At the beginning of the year, Mrs. Tran identified each of the children's strengths and needs in spelling, reading words in isolation, and text reading and comprehension. Then she grouped children for small-group instruction based on their text-level reading taking into consideration their other abilities (Helman, 2005).

Literacy Centers. In order to provide time for instruction of small, guided-reading groups, Mrs. Tran prepares several activities for children to work on independently, which she places in eight centers in her classroom. Mrs. Tran plans these activities carefully so they present a range of challenges to the variety of learners she has in her classroom. Mrs. Tran expects that the children will work together without teacher support in the centers, capitalizing on peer support for learning. Figure 9.1 lists the materials found in Mrs. Tran's eight literacy centers and describes activities that are typical for each center. Mrs. Tran changes the materials and activities included in the centers weekly or biweekly. During September and early October, she demonstrates how to work in the centers, showing children how to find and replace materials and sustain their activity in a center for twenty minutes.

FIGURE 9.1 Mrs. Tran's Literacy Centers

Listening Center. Tape recorder, multiple headphones, and approximately one hundred audiotapes of children's literature, including commercially available tapes as well as tape recordings of parents of present and past students, the principal and other teachers, and other guests reading books aloud. Sentences from the information book or storybook that is read aloud are placed on sentence strips. Children select a sentence after listening to the book and illustrate it. Children later write their own sentences. Children might also be directed to draw a picture of the beginning and ending of the story, of how the character changed in a story, or the sequence of events in an information book.

Big and Little Book Center. Small easel with four or five recently read big books, small children's chair, pointer, and small tubs of books for each child in the classroom, with copies of five or six books or poems read during shared or guided reading. Children take turns being the teacher and pretending to direct a shared reading experience. They also reread poems and books from their book tubs.

FIGURE 9.1   continued

Library Center. Cozy corner created by shelves with nearly 300 books, including books Mrs. Tran has recently read aloud, books included in a social studies or science unit, and books by favorite authors and illustrators. Children browse through books and use props to retell stories (during this week, the retelling props are spoon puppets for versions of *The Three Billy Goats Gruff* and transparency props for retelling *Where's Spot?* on an overhead projector, which sometimes is located in this center).

Writing Center. A large, round table with shelves stocked with a variety of writing tools and materials. This week, Mrs. Tran has included letter writing as a part of the writing center. She has posted several examples of letters children may use.

Letter and Word Center. An easel, a small table for writing, and shelves to hold letter and word games and puzzles. Mrs. Tran writes words on chart paper each day and places the paper on the easel for children to copy if they wish. This week, Mrs. Tran has written her name and invited children to write her name several times on the chart paper. This week, small clipboards are available for children to copy the names of other children in the class (located on sentences strips and clipped on a ring in the center). Children are also challenged to write ten words included on the word wall, using letter tiles. Other games include building new words from familiar rhyming words using magnetic letters and playing a rhyming word game.

Computer Center. A large table with two computers, word-processing packages, reading and other games, and Internet access. This week, children are challenged to write a grocery list. Food ads from the newspaper and alphabet books with food are located at the computer center.

Specials Center. This center is for special activities that occur in the classroom. This week, three parents have volunteered to read aloud with children. Other specials include art projects, cooking activities, and science experiments.

Respond-to-the-Book Center. This center includes activities for responding to a book that Mrs. Tran has read aloud to the entire class. Response activities include drawing and painting or using Play-Doh, making stick puppets to retell the story, or completing alphaboxes. Alphaboxes are sheets divided into twenty-four boxes (one box for the letters *A* through *W* and one box for *XYZ*). Mrs. Tran had demonstrated several times looking through the book and finding words or phrases having the target letter. For example, after reading *A House for Hermit Crab* (Carle, 1987), the children located *Anemones, big fish, coral, grown too big*, and *Hermit crab wanted to move* for the boxes *A, B, G*, and *H* (Morrison & Wlodarczyk, 2009).

Mrs. Tran assigns two to four children with mixed abilities to a center group; each center group is assigned to three centers a day. The membership of the groups changes every month so that children work with a variety of others throughout the school year. Mrs. Tran's schedule includes a large block of uninterrupted time for reading instruction, during which the children spend one hour in centers while Mrs. Tran teaches three guided-reading groups. In early November, the children are divided into four groups, and Mrs. Tran reads with each group four or five times a week. A reading specialist works in Mrs. Tran's classroom four mornings a week, and she works with another guided-reading group.

Talk–Through to Introduce Guided–Reading Texts.   The guided-reading approach uses a **talk-through activity** to prepare children to read a particular text (Clay, 2005; Fountas & Pinnell, 1996). Talk-through is intended to orient children to the text—to the overall text meaning, repetitive language patterns, particular new and important words, and unusual language structures. Teachers carefully gauge how much support to provide in a talk-through, given their awareness of the reading abilities of particular children and the level of challenge presented in a particular text. However, a general rule of thumb is that teachers begin talk-throughs with a one- or two-sentence summary of the overall story, then introduce the characters before opening the book. As children look through the pictures, the teacher repeats repetitive language patterns several times as she talks about the events in the story shown on a page of text. One or two new and important words are introduced by having children say the word and listen to its beginning sound, identify the letter they expect to see, search for the word in the text, and confirm the word by saying it slowly while running their finger under the word slowly. For English language learners or children with lower levels of language development, teachers have children rehearse repeated phrases or unusual language structures by saying them aloud. This layered approach (focusing on the overall meaning, hearing or rehearsing one or two phrase structures, and having children conduct one or two visual searches for words) helps children draw on all the sources of information they will use while reading.

In this lesson in early November, Mrs. Tran is working with six children who are making the transition from finger-point reading to early beginning reading. They are reading level 4 to level 5 texts (according to the Reading Recovery scheme), have acquired a few sight words, and can track print at the word-by-word level in pattern books by using some initial consonant sounds to monitor their reading. They know many consonant sound-letter associations, are beginning to learn vowel associations, use initial and sometimes final consonants in their invented spelling, and are developing a strong concept of written words. Mrs. Tran's goals for this group are to develop a larger store of high-frequency sight words, practice monitoring reading by using initial and final consonant cues to cross-check, and use their newly emerging understanding of short vowels to decode and spell words.

After careful consideration, Mrs. Tran decides to use the text *Where's Tim?* (Cutting, 1996). Before teaching *Where's Tim?,* Mrs. Tran reads through the book in order to make decisions about what to include in her talk-through activity. Mrs. Tran knows that the words *no, he, the, is,* and *in,* which are found in the text of *Where's Tim?,* are familiar to these children. Using these partially known sight words along with left-to-right pointing should anchor their reading. She will help children try to figure out the word *Tim* in the title by using what they already know about short vowels. Later, she will work with the short-*i* vowel in further word study.

Mrs. Tran introduces the book *Where's Tim?* using the talk-through (Figure 9.2). Notice how she establishes the repetitive pattern, focuses on locating the words *bathroom* and *fast,* has children figure out the surprise ending, and models using what the children know about vowels as they read the title.

Teaching for Strategies during Guided Reading.   Following the talk-through, the six children read the book aloud quietly, and Mrs. Tran listens to all the children as they read,

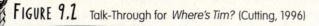

FIGURE 9.2   Talk-Through for *Where's Tim?* (Cutting, 1996)

Teacher: Today for guided reading we are going to read this book (passes out copies of book for each child), and it is a book about someone searching for someone. This man is searching. He can't find someone. I wonder who he is searching for?

(Mrs. Tran and children make guesses about who the man might be searching for.)

Teacher: How many words in the title? Let's count them together. One, two. The title is *Where's* (pauses). Um, who are they searching for? Does anybody know anything that will help me figure out the name of the person this man is searching for?

Teacher: It starts like *Tamika.*

Teacher: Yes, it starts with the sound (Mrs. Tran pauses and many children offer sounds, most of which are /t/. Mrs. Tran confirms the /t/ sound).

Teacher: Anything else that could help us? What about this vowel? Does anyone know anything that might help us? (Children offer a variety of vowel sounds, and Mrs. Tran helps the children blend /t/ /i/ /m/.)

Teacher: Now let's look through the book. Find the title page. (Mrs. Tran observes as children locate the page.) Let's look and see where the man is searching for Tim. Is he behind the door? Is he under the bed?

(Children discuss each page and where the man is looking. Mrs. Tran repeats the patterned phrase and stresses the positional words that will be read on each page, especially *under* and *behind*.)

Teacher: (page 5) Where is the man looking on this page? (Some children suggest the bathtub.) Yes, he is looking in the room where we find the bathtub. He is looking in the bathroom. Put your finger on the word *bathroom*. (Mrs. Tran makes sure everyone is on the correct word.)

Teacher: (page 8) There's Tim! Why he's fast asleep, isn't he? Who can find the word *fast*? What letter would you expect? How would you check if this word was *fast*? (Children discuss cross-checking the *f* and *t* sounds.) Ok. Now use your pointing finger and read the book softly to yourself.

noting children's tracking of print, attempts at solving problems, and monitoring what they are reading. As children are reading aloud, Mrs. Tran observes one or two children and supports them when they reach difficulty. She has a broad range of prompts that she uses to help children when they either have made an error and have not noticed or are stuck reading an unknown word. Research has shown that the most effective first-grade teachers are those who both provide explicit instruction in phonics generalizations during whole- and small-group focused lessons and teach children how to apply those generalizations during their reading and writing of continuous, authentic, and functional texts through strategy instruction (Taylor, Pearson, Clark, & Walpole, 2002). Mrs. Tran thinks of her teaching prompts as scaffolds to keep the children's attention focused on the meaning of the story (the big picture) while they attend to the small details of words. Some of her prompts for strategic reading include

- saying "Point to each word and make sure they match" (prompts the child to use one-to-one matching to coordinate what is read with the print)
- saying the beginning sound of a word softly and pointing back at the beginning of the sentence (prompts the child to reread and use the new sound information)
- prompting the child to look in a picture by asking the question, "What's happening here?" (prompts the child to monitor whether what was read fits the meaning)
- masking a part of the word, such as *ed* or *ing* (prompts the child to look at chunks of a word)
- saying, "Something didn't look right. Find the tricky word and take a look at it." (prompts the child to monitor and use more visual information)
- telling a child to make sure it makes sense and looks right (prompts the child to integrate the meaning with the visual information; adapted from Cole, 2006).
- saying, "Look in the word for something you know" (prompts the child to look closely at the visual information in a word for familiar letters, letter clusters, and word parts)
- saying, "Does this look like a word you know? Do you know a word that starts like this one? Do you know a word that has this part (showing a familiar rhyming phonogram)?" (prompts the child to notice in a word something they do know)

Mrs. Tran has already taught several reading strategies to this particular group of children using demonstrations. This group of children has some strategies firmly under control, such as moving left to right and matching word for word while reading. Mrs. Tran had earlier demonstrated "reading with her finger" and early on after her demonstration praised children for carefully reading with their fingers during guided reading. When children had difficulty matching, she prompted for this strategy by asking, "Are there enough words? Were there too many words? Try rereading it again."

Mrs. Tran demonstrated an early monitoring strategy for these children recently (Schwartz, 2005). For example, last week the children read *Can you put a shark in a sack?*, and the first page of text included the question in the title. One of the children read, "Can you fit a shark in a bag?" Mrs. Tran demonstrated what to do. "That made sense; it goes with the picture. But what you said didn't look right. Let me show you." She pointed to each word in the text as she said slowly, "Can you fit. Umm I said *fit* and it doesn't look right. See this word starts with *P*, /p/ not /fffffit/. So I need to say something that looks right AND makes sense. I'll reread. Can you put a shark in a sack? Does that make sense? Does it look right? I need to check it. Let me say it slowly and look. *pppuuuttt*. Yes, it looks right now and it makes sense." Later, when children have difficulty reading and say words that are gross visual mismatches with the words in the text, she may provide several prompts for this monitoring strategy, such as asking, "Where's the tricky word? What did you notice? What letter did you expect at the beginning? Would _____ fit there? It has to look right and make sense."

Children in this group are beginning to make more than one attempt at a word before asking for help. They are beginning to use the strategy of backing up and trying again by rereading. In this lesson, Mrs. Tran demonstrated a more complex strategy of searching for known information to figure out an unknown word using the word *Tim*. Later, she will use prompts such as, "Can you find something you know? Does it look like a word you know? Do you know a word like this? Do you know a word that starts with those letters? Do you know a word that ends with those letters? What do you know that might help?" Although Mrs. Tran has many prompts at her fingertips, she consciously uses only one or two before making a teaching point, as she did on how to notice the word *fit* did not look like the word in the text, *put*.

Other groups of children in Mrs. Tran's classroom are learning more sophisticated reading strategies, such as using decoding a new word by analogy (using a familiar phonogram to identify a new word, such as using *ham* to figure out *scram*) or decoding multisyllabic words by using several analogies (such as using *ex* and *fan* to figure out *Mexican*). Other strategies focus on expanding vocabulary knowledge, such as calling to mind related concepts for words that are only somewhat familiar. Still other strategies focus on meaning, such as inviting children to predict and confirm, pause and build a mental picture, assess whether a character's action is expected or unusual, and connect story events or characters to life experiences and acquaintances. As children read up the gradient of text difficulty, moving from text level 1 through text level 16 (the expected range of texts on the first-grade level), they learn ever more sophisticated reading strategies. Appendix A presents a list of leveled texts recommended for use in guided-reading instruction from levels 1 through 18.

Word Work and Spelling Instruction. After guiding the reading and strategy teaching, Mrs. Tran teaches her planned word-work activity: learning to use the short-*i* vowel sound in the word *Tim*. She uses a small, dry-erase board to demonstrate taking off the letter *T* on the word *Tim* and saying the rime portion of the word left behind. Then she has children use the rime phonogram *im* to build more words such as *dim, him, rim,* and *slim* by adding new consonants and even a consonant blend. Then Mrs. Tran draws the children's attention to the short-*i* sound in the *im* phonogram. Children orally segment the words into three phonemes: /t/, /i/, /m/; /d/, /i/, /m/; /r/, /i/, /m/.

Mrs. Tran also uses her guided-reading groups to teach spelling because she has found a strong relationship between their reading and spelling development in the first grade (Williams, Phillips-Birdsong, Hufnagel, Hungler, & Lundstrom, 2009). In the beginning of the year, she assessed children's spelling using a **developmental spelling inventory** (Bear, Invernizzi, Templeton, & Johnston, 2008; Ganske, 2000), which determines the level of children's spelling. At the beginning of the year, most children in her classroom were letter-name spellers (they spelled with consonants and sometimes vowels although often not the correct vowels). Only a few children had not acquired the alphabetic principle and could not even spell at the letter-name stage. Also, a few children were spelling beyond the letter-name stage and had reached the within-a-word stage of spelling (these children could spell many short vowel words but were learning to spell long vowels, *r*-controlled vowels, and other vowels). For this group of letter-name spellers, Mrs. Tran follows the scope and sequence suggested in *Word Journeys* (Ganske).

Because this group already knew something about beginning consonant sounds and a few blends, she taught very quickly all the letter-sound associations of each of the consonant letters, teaching three to four associations each week (starting with *B, M,* and *S*), and then taught the *S* blends, *L* blends, and finally the *R* blends. This systematic approach helped all the children consolidate their knowledge of consonants and consonant blends. She is now focusing on teaching the short vowels. She started with short-*a* families to introduce short *a*. Now children are ready for the short-*i* vowel, so later this week she will teach children to spell and sort words in short-*i* families (*it, in, ip,* and *ig;* see the suggested sequence for teaching of short vowels in Ganske, 2000, p. 122).

Mrs. Tran will guide children to read the words and sort them into groups, to spell new words by deleting and adding new consonants and blends, and to search for words with these spelling patterns in texts. In later lessons, Mrs. Tran will use interactive writing to consolidate children's knowledge of the *it, in, ip,* and *ig* phonograms they have studied. For this activity, Mrs. Tran uses folders with the tops cut in the shape of a roof. On the first folder, Mrs. Tran has written "*in* family." On this folder, the children will share the pen to write a list of all the words they know in the *in* family. These folders are displayed around the room and become an important resource during independent writing. Figure 9.3 presents Mrs. Tran's systematic approach to teaching decoding and spelling. She will expect her children to be able to use this information during both reading and writing.

Interactive Writing. For another of her guided-reading groups, Mrs. Tran has decided to use an interactive writing activity using the pattern found in *Where's Spot?* (Hill, 1980). Mrs. Tran is particularly concerned about these children because of their need to develop many foundational concepts. These children do not have a firm grasp of

FIGURE 9.3   Mrs. Tran's Systematic Study of Words for Decoding and Spelling

Beginning and ending consonants	*b, m, s, r, t, n, p, g, d, h, l, c, f, w, j, k, y, v, z, qu*
Digraphs	*sh, ch, th, wh*
S blends	*st, sp, sk, sn, sc, sm, sl, sw*
L blends	*sl, fl, pl, bl, cl, fl, gl*
R blends	*cr, fr, gr, pr, dr, tr, dr, br, gr*
Short-*a* word families	*at, an, ad, ag, ap*
Short-*i* word families	*it, in, ip, ig*
Short-*o* word families	*ob, op, ot*
Short-*e* word families	*ed, en, et*
Short-*u* word families	*ub, ug, un, ut*
Mixed short vowel families	variety of families
Final consonant blends and digraphs	*ch, th, sh, ack, ick, eck, ock, uck, ang, ing, ong, ung, ank, ink, unk, all, ell, ill*

identifying and writing all alphabet letters and are just beginning to control the left-to-right, one-to-one matching of spoken and written words. They have only recently demonstrated a use of the alphabetic principle in their invented spelling attempts. They need more instruction in matching sounds and letters and are still in the finger-point reading stage with only a few sight words.

This group has already heard Mrs. Tran read *Where's Spot?* (Hill, 1980) several times. Mrs. Tran has made a pocket chart of the text from this book for finger-point reading experiences. The children have practiced using a pointer to reread the story from the pocket chart, pointing to the words from left to right. They have participated in many pocket-chart extensions, such as matching words on word cards to words on the pocket chart.

Now Mrs. Tran has decided they will use interactive writing to compose pattern writing. The children decide to compose a pattern story called "Where's Mrs. Tran?" For this lesson, the children will only write the title of the story together during the interactive lesson. Mrs. Tran guides the children by having them repeat the title ("Where's Mrs. Tran?") and count the number of words. She writes three lines on chart paper from left to right, emphasizing that they will write the three words in the title across the paper on these lines.

Mrs. Tran reminds the children of the first word in the title that they will write. Now she will teach a specific spelling strategy she expects children to be able to use in their own independent writing. These strategies are actions children can take to figure out a spelling for themselves. She tells the children they will use the strategy of finding the word somewhere in the room and copying its spelling. She asks the children, "Where could we look for the word *Where's*? Where do we know to find this word?" Mrs. Tran recognizes that an important reading and spelling strategy for children at this stage is to draw on resources such as familiar stories, poems, and charts to read and write words (Sipe, 1998). The children find the word *Where's* both on the book *Where's Spot?* and on their pocket chart. Then the children spell the word, saying its letters left to right. Mrs. Tran briefly discusses the apostrophe. She invites first one child and then another to come to the chart and write the first four letters in the word *Where's*. Mrs. Tran quickly writes the remaining letters on the chart as the children tell her the letters.

Next, Mrs. Tran has children remember the second word in their title—*Mrs.* Mrs. Tran will teach a second spelling strategy she will expect these children to attempt in their independent journal writing—saying the word slowly and listening for sounds and letters they know. Mrs. Tran has children say the word *Mrs.* slowly and identify its beginning sound. She teaches a **mini-lesson** on the /m/ sound's association with the letter *M*. One child is selected to write the letter *M*. Then Mrs. Tran again has children think of where they could find the remainder of the word's spelling. They locate five different places in the classroom where Mrs. Tran's name is written and confirm that *Mrs.* begins with the letter *M*. Again, they name the letters in the word, and children are selected to write them on the chart. Figure 9.4 presents the interactive writing result of "Where's Mrs. Tran?" After this short interactive writing lesson, Mrs. Tran teaches a word-work lesson for this group. She presents a group of pictures in a pocket chart, some beginning with the sound /m/ and some beginning with the sound /t/ taught in a previous lesson. The children sort the pictures and then do a guided-writing activity in which Mrs. Tran shows each picture and the children independently spell its first letter (*M* or *T*), then Mrs. Tran supports the children in segmenting the last sound in the word and writing a letter for that sound. After spelling each word, Mrs. Tran has

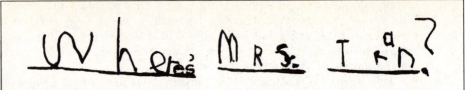

FIGURE 9.4   Interactive Writing of *Where's Mrs. Tran?*

children run their fingers under the word while they say it slowly to check that the letters match what they hear.

Mrs. Tran uses interactive writing with all the groups in her classroom. Depending on what the children know, she adjusts what she expects children to write, the amount of support she provides, and how much text will be written in one lesson. In some groups, children write sight words quickly and spend more time discussing how to write words with complex vowel spelling patterns or adding suffixes, such as consistent spelling of *ed* and *s*. In other groups, children focus on writing the beginning, middle, and final sounds in words.

As she engages the children in interactive writing, Mrs. Tran will also teach children strategies for spelling words when they are writing independently. She has taught children the strategy of saying the word slowly and listening for the sounds they hear and to look on the word wall. Soon she will capitalize on all the phonogram words she has taught to show children the strategy of thinking of a rhyming word they know and using that to help them spell (Williams et al., 2009). The spelling strategies she will teach include (Williams & Lundstrom, 2007, p. 207) the following instructions.

- Look for a word on the word wall.
- Find a word on the word wall that will help you (*could* for *would*).
- Look for the word in print around the classroom.
- Say the word slowly and listen for the sounds you hear.
- Think about different spelling patterns that can spell the sound you hear (*out* versus *down*).
- Say the word slowly and listen for any parts you know how to spell (*and* in *candy*).
- Think about the word in your head. Can you "see" the word?
- Think of a word you already know how to spell that will help you spell this word.
- Think of a word you know that rhymes with the word you're trying to spell.

Whole-Class Word Study.   During the second half of the year, all students engage in whole-class word study using **make-a-rhyming-word activities.** Mrs. Tran selected two familiar word families that she knows are frequently found in words that first graders encounter, such as *ack, ail, ain, ame, eat, est, ice, ide, ick, ock, oke, op, uck, ug,* and *ump.* Figure 9.5 presents thirty-seven phonograms that are most frequently found in English spellings (Adams, 1990, pp. 321–322). Each child is given a card with the phonogram written on it, several cards with individual consonants, and a folder that has been stapled to hold the cards. Mrs. Tran says, "I have the word *eat*; now what do

FIGURE 9.5   Thirty-Seven Phonograms That Are Most Frequently Found in English Spellings

ack	ail	ain	ake	ale	ame	an
ank	ap	ash	at	ate	aw	ay
eat	ell	est	ice	ick	ide	ight
ill	in	ine	ing	ink	ip	ir
ock	oke	op	ore	or	uck	ug
ump	unk					

Source: Adams, 1990, pp. 321–322.

we need to make the word *beat*? Who can show me?" She emphasizes the sound of the letter *b* by repeating it. The children use their letter and phonogram cards to spell words while Mrs. Tran or the other children pronounce them.

Mrs. Tran places making-a-rhyming-word activities in her letter and word center. She writes several words on a sheet of writing paper and challenges children to write additional words when they are in the center. Figure 9.6 presents a word-building activity that Sindy completed in the letter and word center. She composed the words *bat*, *mat*, *rat*, *sat*, and *vat* using the pattern Mrs. Tran provided in her word *cat*. Then Sindy went on to build words from another pattern, one that Mrs. Tran did not suggest. She wrote *Mom* and *Tom*.

Later in the year, Mrs. Tran will also introduce a **word-sort activity** (Bear et al., 2008). Children will collect and sort words according to particular spelling patterns. For example, over several days, children may collect words that have the long-*a* sound. All the words will be collected and placed on cards. Then children can sort the words to discover all the patterns used to spell long *a,* such as in the words *fade, rage, fail, raise, pale, paste,* and *straight.*

Writing in Mr. Schultheis' First Grade

Mr. Schultheis is a first-grade teacher who has been identified as an exemplary teacher, one whose students' literacy development far exceeds that of average teachers' students (Pressley, Allington, Wharton-McDonald, Block, & Morrow, 2001; Wharton-McDonald, 2001a, 2001b). Children in his classroom sit in clusters of desks. They begin the day with independent reading of books selected from tubs placed at each cluster of desks. Independent reading is followed by whole-class read-aloud. Next, during the reading block, Mr. Schultheis meets with guided-reading groups. Some children read copies of children's books at their level; other children may read decodable books in which the text is primarily composed of words following expected phonics patterns. Other children may read a class book composed by the

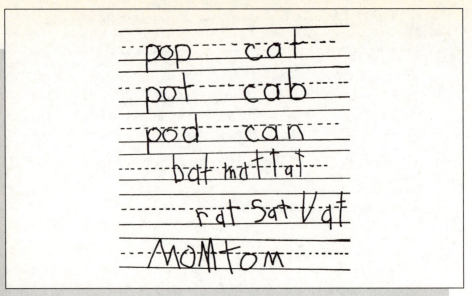

FIGURE 9.6 Sindy's Word-Building Activity

children during writing block. Other children may be reading big books used in shared reading.

The writing block begins with a mini-lesson. The teacher gives a short whole-class lesson on some aspect of writing. This may include reading a short excerpt, such as the beginning sentence or paragraph from a text shown to the class on an overhead projector. They discuss the writing, and the teacher models writing a similar beginning. Mini-lesson topics may be about characteristics of texts:

- beginnings that grab readers' attention; middles that keep that attention and provide much of the information; and endings that resolve conflicts, summarize, or present conclusions
- a paragraph as a set of sentences related to one another because they develop a single idea
- indenting at the beginning of a paragraph
- the parts of a story (characters, an initiating event that sets up a problem, attempts at solving the problem, obstacles, and solutions)
- the parts of a how-to description
- the parts of a compare-and-contrast informational text
- the elements of imagery in poetry

Alternatively, mini-lessons may be about processes writers use, including the following:

- selecting a topic
- reworking a draft, with attention both to conventions, such as grammar, spelling, punctuation, and capitalization, and to features of story grammar or expository

text structure, with the goal of making the text comprehendible to a reader who is not the author (The author has to assume the role of a reader.)

• editing, including the use of grammar, spelling, punctuation, and capitalization to make a text that is "finished," that is, one that meets the class's standards for publication (which depend on what students have been taught and have mastered about those conventions)

Then children begin the second part of the writing approach, an extended writing period during which they are asked to write for as long as thirty minutes (but shorter in the beginning of the year). Children are expected to use the strategies and skills just taught, and the teacher circulates to work with them individually, to observe their successes, and to determine their needs. Children select topics from a list of topics in their writing journal, or they write on a topic the teacher has suggested. During extended writing, some children attend small-group writing conferences where they receive instruction focused on their demonstrated needs, which they have in common with other members of the small group.

Mr. Schultheis carefully reads his students' writing frequently in order to note common needs and group students for targeted instruction in writing conferences. Some children may need to provide more details in their writing; others may need to reread and rework drafts to vary sentence structure; others may need to be more careful about capitalization and punctuation.

Children's writing in Mr. Schultheis' classroom at the end of the year is far different from children's writing in typical teachers' classrooms. In Mr. Schultheis' classroom, children write from four to eight sentences and from forty to over eighty words. Across the year, they have written many genres including personal journal entries and personal narratives; science, math, and response journals; letters; informational texts; and stories about fictional characters. Their plotting includes beginnings, middles, and ends; their characters are consistent; and their structures conform to story grammar. Coherence is demonstrated not just in stories but in all genres. Finally, they use capitals and periods consistently and accurately, and they frequently use question marks and exclamation marks (Wharton-McDonald, 2001b).

Informational Writing in Mrs. Duthie's First Grade

Mrs. Duthie is a first-grade teacher who has written about her experiences helping students read and write informational texts (Duthie, 1996). She knows that informational reading and writing are inspirational to all children but especially to those children who naturally select this kind of text for their independent reading and writing (Caswell & Duke, 1998). Mrs. Duthie's classroom library has a special section for information books, and she makes a special effort to read information books as part of whole-class read-alouds, as well as stories and poems. The class learns about as many information book authors and illustrators as authors and illustrators of stories and poems. Children draw on this wealth of information during their study of science and social studies topics.

Mrs. Duthie also uses mini-lessons to teach about informational writing. First, she shares one or more information books that have a special feature. Children talk about these special features and sometimes construct a group drawing or composition that

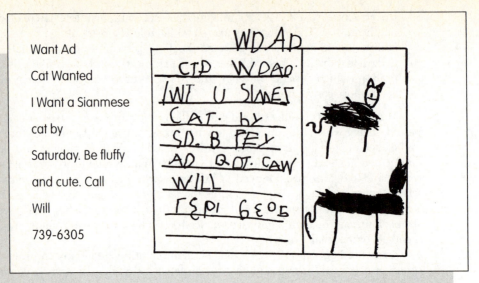

Want Ad

Cat Wanted

I Want a Sianmese

cat by

Saturday. Be fluffy

and cute. Call

Will

739-6305

FIGURE 9.7 A First Grader's Want Ad

includes the feature. For example, Mrs. Duthie showed *Oil Spill!* (Berger, 1994) to illustrate labeled drawings, *Jack's Garden* (Cole, 1995) to illustrate cutaway drawings, and *Water* (Asch, 1995) to illustrate cross-sectioned drawings. As children study topics in science and social studies, they find information using these special features of information books and use these features in their own report writing.

As a part of mini-lessons about informational writing, children can learn how to put information into sets or groups, write about one part at a time, or lead with a question. They may discover and use captions, headings, tables of contents, and indexes. They may experiment with many different kinds of informational writing beyond that found in information books. For example, Figure 9.7 presents a first grader's want ad composed after several mini-lessons about the kinds of information found in newspapers.

WORD STUDY: DECODING PRINT AND SPELLING WORDS

EFFECTIVE READERS AND WRITERS have many flexible strategies that allow them to be successful decoders and spellers. **Decoding** is the ability to look at an unknown word—that is, a word that is not a sight word, that the reader cannot identify automatically on sight—and to produce a pronunciation that is accurate—that is, a pronunciation that identifies the word as one that the reader knows from his or her spoken vocabulary. Later, children will decode an increasing number of words that are not in their speaking vocabulary. Here, children will need to hear their teacher pronounce the word to incorporate both the new meaning, new visual form, and its new spoken pronunciation.

Spelling is a system for associating word parts (individual sounds or larger chunks of spoken words) with individual letters or combinations of letters. First attempts at spelling unknown words often are not perfect. When writing a word whose spelling they are not sure of, children may use a sounding-out strategy by applying knowledge of letter-sound associations to produce a close approximation. Then they can compare that approximation with what authorities (books, more knowledgeable classmates, a teacher) tell them about correct spelling. In first grade, teachers help children learn a variety of strategies (review the list earlier in this chapter of spelling strategies that Mrs. Tran teaches).

Early Decoding Strategies and Building Sight Words

Early decoding involves using what children know about letter-sound relationships to figure out a word's pronunciation. Once children have successfully decoded an unknown word, that word gradually should become a sight word—one that children no longer have to decode or spend time thinking about.

Phonics. **Phonics** is the more-or-less regular linking of letters and combinations of letters with sounds and combinations of sounds that children draw upon to decode unknown words. We say "more-or-less regular" because a letter or combination of letters can have a very high frequency of association with a sound or combination of sounds but not always be so associated. For example, the letter combination *st* is very frequently linked to the consonant blend /st/ (as in *step, faster,* and *list*) but not always (consider, for example, *fasten* and *listen*).

In first grade, many children have already learned many consonant sound-letter correspondences. We teach these relationships first (in kindergarten and early first grade) because they are fairly regular. Children can learn to expect a particular consonant letter to represent a particular consonant sound, even though the full range of phonics generalizations is more complex than that. For example, children may come fairly quickly to associate the letter *f* with the sound /f/. Such an understanding helps to consolidate the alphabetic principle in the mind of the young reader and writer. With more experience and instruction, however, that reader and writer will learn about the greater range and complexity of phonics generalizations, for example, that sometimes other letters and combinations of letters represent the sound /f/ (as with *ph* in *phone* and *graph, ff* in *cuff,* and *gh* in *laugh*).

Phonics Generalizations. In first grade, children must begin to grapple with such complexity. Not only can a sound have more than one spelling, as in our /f/–*f-ph-ff-gh* examples, but a letter can represent more than one sound. Consider, for example, the letter *s,* which represents both /s/ (as in *sit*) and /z/ (as in *his*); or the letter *g,* which represents both /g/ (as in *go*) and /j/ (as in *gem*). Most importantly, first graders learn about vowels, which are the most variable of all letters. For example, the letter *o* can represent the sound /O/ as in *go* or the sound /o/ as in *got*. During first-grade phonics instruction, all children will learn about initial consonants, final consonants, initial and final consonant blends, consonant digraphs, and short vowels (see Figure 9.3 for Mrs. Tran's systematic approach to teaching these concepts).

More advanced children may be taught more complex phonics:

- long vowels
- *R*-controlled vowels—vowels whose distinctiveness is diminished by their being combined with /r/: /ar/, /er/, /or/
- other vowels—the remaining American English vowels: /aw/ as in *fawn*, /oi/ as in *boy*, /oo/ as in *book*, /OO/ as in *boot*, and /ow/ as in *town*
- silent letters, for example, *w* and *e* in *write* and *h* in *ghost*
- the influence of the patterning of consonants and vowels on the sounds of vowels (for example, the vowel in CVC, CCVC, and CVCC words is usually short—as in *bed*, *bled*, and *bes*—and the first vowel in CVCe words is usually long and the final *e* silent—as in *cake*, *pine*, and *tone*)
- the association of some patterns of letters with two or more different sounds (for example, *ea* with /e/ in *bread* and /E/ in *bead*; and *ow* with /O/ in *snow* and /ow/ in *cow*

Systematic, Explicit Instruction in Phonics.

Children will have multiple opportunities to learn phonics generalizations and apply them in their reading and writing. To make sure that all children have the strong decoding skills of good readers and writers, teachers provide **systematic phonics instruction;** that is, they teach with a sequence of phonics skills in mind (see the sequence Mrs. Tran uses in Figure 9.3).

Not all reading programs use the same sequence of instruction, but all programs use a systematic approach to phonics instruction; and effective programs provide teachers with information about how to provide explicit instruction. With **explicit instruction,** teachers deliberately and clearly put into words what students are to learn from a particular lesson. Teachers explicitly state the target sound-letter correspondences or other phonics generalizations around which the lesson is planned. For example, when teachers present a list of words to illustrate a sound-letter correspondence (such as *bed, boat, bike, bell, bear, bake,* and *bee* for the /b/–*b* correspondence) they tell the students what they are to learn ("We are going to learn that the sound of the letter *B* is /b/"). If teachers demonstrate a decoding skill (for example, recognizing a CVC pattern and using that information to determine that the vowel will have a short vowel sound such as in the word *bed*), they talk through what they are doing. For example, they may say, "I see that this word has a consonant, then a vowel, then a consonant. That means the vowel will probably be short *e* /e/, not long *e* /E/. Let's see if I'm right—I'll try the short *e*. 'Goldilocks lay in the bed'— that makes sense."

Teachers may use letter boxes in explicit instruction These are extensions of the **Elkonin boxes** usually introduced in kindergarten. Children say a word, slowly segmenting its phonemes. They push up a token into a box for each phoneme in a word. In kindergarten, children usually practice listening and pushing up tokens for two phoneme words and for three phoneme words that have beginning consonant continuants. In first grade, teachers begin using letter boxes in which children will listen to

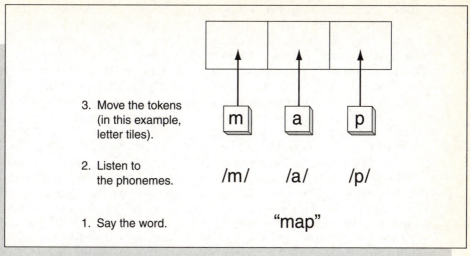

3. Move the tokens
   (in this example,
   letter tiles).

2. Listen to
   the phonemes. /m/   /a/   /p/

1. Say the word. "map"

FIGURE 9.8 Letter Boxes

the phonemes, but their focus will be on identifying letters associated with those phonemes (McCarthy, 2008). For example, using letter boxes shown in Figure 9.8, one box for each phoneme in a target word, a teacher may say, "Today we are going to listen to the short-*a* /a/ vowel sound. Listen for the /a/ sound in this word as I say it slowly: *mmmaaap*. That is the word *map* and it has the /a/ sound right in the middle. Let me show you on our letter boxes." The teacher points one by one, left to right to the empty letter boxes as she pronounces the three phonemes in *map*. She says, "I'll push up the letters as I say the sounds." The teacher says the word slowly again and pushes up the letters *m, a,* and *p* (on alphabet tiles) as she says each of the sounds /m/, /a/, and /p/. Now the children attempt to say the sounds and move their letters into their letter boxes. Then the teacher introduces several more words with /a/ (*pan, fat, gas*), demonstrating how to say the words slowly in order to isolate their component phonemes and showing children how to construct the words with letter tiles pushed into letter boxes.

Whole-Class Word Study. Word study is careful examination of how words are put together and how sound-letter associations work in reading and writing words. Because children begin first grade with different levels of phonemic awareness, alphabet knowledge, and knowledge of sound-letter associations, their teachers must plan whole-class word study that allows children with little word knowledge to participate while also challenging children who have considerable word knowledge (Bear et al., 2008). Making Words (Cunningham & Hall, 1994) and Word Walls (Cunningham, 2005; Wagstaff, 1997–1998) offer structures within which to provide such flexibility.

Making Words (Cunningham, 2005) is an activity in which children change or add just one letter at a time within words to construct new words. For example, children are given a set of six to ten letters such as *a, b, c, f, g, h, n, r, s,* and *t*. Teachers might help children form the word *can* and then challenge children to change just one letter to make the word *tan*. Then children would be challenged again to change just one letter to make the word *tag*. Children can continue, making *bag, bat, fat, fan, ran, rat,* and *hat*. Later, teachers add more letters so that children can make words with digraphs and blends such as *bath, black, stamp,* and *crash* (Combs, 2006). Teachers help children develop skill with vowels by including sorts, in which children change both consonant and vowel sounds. For example, teachers can give children the letters *a, b, e, h, i, l, m, p, s,* and *t* and they can make *bat, bit, hit, hat, sat, sit, set, met, mat, map, math, mash, lash, slash,* and *splash*. The final step is to use all the letters to construct a single word.

The first steps in implementing Making Words are to prepare materials and to demonstrate with large letters and a pocket chart. Each child has a notebook with plastic sleeves (like those in a baseball card collection notebook) in which to store his or her set of alphabet letters. The letters are printed on cards and placed in the notebooks in alphabetic order. The teacher has a similar set of much larger letters. The teacher tells children which letters will be needed for a lesson and assists them in removing those letters from their notebooks. The teacher forms the first word placing his larger, easy-to-see letter cards in a pocket chart. The teacher names the word ("We will begin with the word *bat*"), uses it in a sentence ("A baseball player uses a *bat* to hit the baseball"), and divides it into its phonemes while pointing from left to right across the word ("I hear three sounds in bat, /b/-/a/-/t/"). Next, the teacher announces the new word to be made, giving a meaning clue—"It's what Snow White did to the poison apple: She bit the apple." Then the teacher gives a hint about the new sound—"Change only one letter and make *bat* into *bit*. It's a vowel letter." The teacher guides children's discovery of how the word in the pocket chart differs from the word to be spelled—"Now let's listen while I slowly say the old word and the new word: *baaaat, biiiit*. What is the different vowel in *biiiit*? Can you hear the /i/ sound in *bit*?"—and helps children find the correct letter to make the new word. A child is selected to come to the pocket chart to demonstrate the correct new spelling.

A **word wall** is a wall in the classroom on which teachers place word cards grouped by initial letter. Figure 9.9 presents a portion of a first-grade word wall. It contains important words such as the children's names and high-frequency words children are learning to read and spell. These words are in the texts children are reading during instruction and are words that children frequently use in their daily writing. Many teachers add five or six new words each week to their word walls.

During the week, the children practice reading and writing the words. Teachers use the word wall daily for a variety of activities as part of their phonics and spelling instruction. For example, the children might use the words on the word wall to find words with short-*a* and short-*i* sounds. Other times, teachers might add words to the wall when an occasion arises, such as when several children need the same high-frequency words (e.g., *they, where,* or *this*) in their writing. They may add words from social studies and science units; later in the year, they may add words with suffixes such as *s, es,* and *ing*.

Teachers frequently lead children in activities using the words on the word wall. For example, they may give children a "spelling test." Teachers call out five or six words on the wall, have children quickly locate the words with their eyes and then write the words. After the "test," teachers and children check the spellings. Later, teachers can urge children to see the words in their minds and then check the spelling by

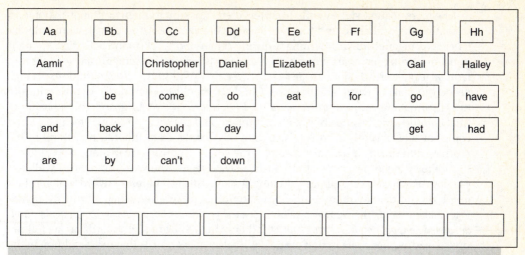

Aa	Bb	Cc	Dd	Ee	Ff	Gg	Hh
Aamir		Christopher	Daniel	Elizabeth		Gail	Hailey
a	be	come	do	eat	for	go	have
and	back	could	day			get	had
are	by	can't	down				

FIGURE 9.9   Portion of a First-Grade Word Wall

looking at the word wall. These short "spelling tests" and checks provide many opportunities to discuss first letter and sound, last letter and sound, vowels, and unusual spellings. Effective teachers make this activity playful and help all children locate the correct words. Practice using the word wall during whole-class activities like these increases the likelihood that children will use it successfully during their independent writing and reading. For example, children who have practiced using the search strategy of first identifying a word's initial letter will not make the mistake while writing in their journals of looking on the word wall for *was* but instead copying *saw*.

Building Automatic Sight Vocabularies

Automatic sight vocabularies are all the words that can be read immediately, on sight, without having to use decoding strategies; a reader looks at a sight word and recognizes it in less than one-tenth of a second. It is fortunate for children beginning the conventional phase of reading that on a list of a few hundred **high-frequency words,** they can find over 70 percent of the words in almost any continuous text. An example of such a list is *Fry's Instant Words* (Fry & Kress, 2006). Many high-frequency words are not decodable words; their pronunciations cannot be derived from phonics generalizations. For example, the CVCe generalization does not produce the correct pronunciation of the word *come*; although that generalization calls for a long vowel sound, *come* is pronounced /kum/, not /kOm/. Children must learn to read undecodable words "by sight." With words like *come*, phonics generalizations will not help them and, in fact, will mislead them. When an undecodable word is also a high-frequency word, readers cannot afford to be bogged down by frequently and pointlessly sounding it out.

Readers acquire sight words from repeated exposure to them both in isolation and in continuous, authentic, and functional texts. For example, assembling a word letter by letter on a magnetic board, writing it during center and workstation activities, seeing it in poems written on chart paper and in directions written for centers, and reading it in familiar, easy-to-read books are just a few of the ways children get the multiple exposures needed to make a word a sight word. Children should have multiple opportunities to reread familiar texts from finger-point reading, interactive writing, and guided reading. Mr. Schultheis made sure children had a tub of books at their desks in which he placed copies of their recently read text. Children read books from this tub first thing in the morning and during a special rereading time when all children read aloud to partners.

Other ways of learning sight words include seeing the word on a word wall and playing search games (such as "spelling tests") with it. Therefore, word walls in first grade should display many of the words found in a high-frequency word list, such as *Fry's Instant Words* (Fry & Kress, 2006)—see the words *a, and, are, be, by, come, could, can't, do, day, down, go, get, have,* and *had.* Still other ways to learn sight words are as follow-ups to reading. Teachers in first grade daily select a few words that most children in the small-group lesson did not know automatically, and the teachers systematically teach that word. The children locate the word in text, cover up the word, and attempt to write it on a whiteboard. They check the spelling and correct it as necessary. They erase the word and attempt to write it again, and again. Teachers prepare the word on a small word card, and it is added to a small stack of other words this group of children is learning. These word cards are shown to children daily to practice reading, and when a word is not automatically read, then children practice writing it again.

Teaching for Comprehension

The guided-reading approach uses leveled texts, and many first graders begin reading books with very predictable text or with easy-to-understand stories. These books, of course, have meaning, but their meanings are obvious from the illustrations. Not much interpretation—going beyond the literal words of the text—is needed to enjoy and understand these texts. Although children are having a heavy dose of these kinds of texts during guided-reading instruction, they should also be engaged in comprehension activities from teacher read-alouds. Children should be encouraged to ask questions, make predictions, insert comments, and draw conclusions during teacher read-alouds. Teachers should extend the listening strategies children have learned in kindergarten—asking clarifying questions, asking "I wonder" questions, summarizing the story, and making connections to the story.

Children may be part of small or large groups that have grand conversations about a book their teacher has read aloud (McGee, 1996). **Grand conversations** are directed by children's comments and questions rather than by a teacher's asking of questions. Teachers begin the conversation by asking, "What did you think?" or "Who has something to say about the book?" Children take turns talking and teachers limit their talk to a few comments and helping children gain the floor to talk. Improved understandings result from the comprehension work that emerges from the talk during a grand conversation. Figure 9.10 presents a grand conversation among first graders and their teacher about the book *Hey, Al* (Yorinks, 1986). In this story, Al is dissatisfied with his life as a janitor. When a fantastic bird one day invites him to an island in the sky, he escapes his old life to what he thinks is paradise. However, he begins to turn into a bird

FIGURE 9.10   Grand Conversation about *Hey, Al* (Yorinks, 1986)

Teacher:	What did you think about the story?
Child:	I like the part when the bird stuck his head in.
Child:	It was funny when he was in his underwear in the bathroom.
Child:	He started to look like a bird, and then he got back and painted his room.
Teacher:	Why did you like that part?
Child:	It looked like he was happy and his shirt was like the island.
Child:	The dog was sad. I didn't think he was going to make it.
Child:	Al really was happy to see the dog and he gave him a big ol hug.
Teacher:	Are there any happy and sad parts in the story?
Child:	Dog was sad at the beginning but I don't think Al was so sad.
Child:	I wouldn't be happy as a janitor washing the floor.
Child:	I wouldn't want to turn into a bird.
Teacher:	Why wouldn't you want to turn into a bird?
Child:	I couldn't play baseball, but I could fly.
Teacher:	Let's look at this page here. Did you see this (teacher points to the wing of one of the birds in which it ends in a human hand)?
Child:	Look, look, it's a hand. They are people. Those birds might have been people.
Child:	Al is going to turn into a bird like those other birds.
Child:	They were all people? Those birds, they were all people?
Child:	Yes, look at that hand. Al would have stayed up there as a bird.
Teacher:	I think he is happy to be back to his old home, and he is going to fix it up like a paradise, but a safe one.

and decides to return home with his dog. On the way home, the dog plunges into the ocean, but he later makes his way safely to Al.

During this grand conversation, children talked about events they remembered, clarified details, made inferences, and extended their own understanding of the story. Grand conversations such as these are not dominated by teacher questions; instead, they are exchanges among children. Grand conversations can be initiated by having children identify topics or "seeds" that they would like to talk about (Villaume, Wordon, Williams, Hopkins, & Rosenblatt, 1994), or teachers can generate a list of possible discussion questions from which children select a few (Vogt, 1996).

However, some first graders cannot productively participate in grand conversations. English language learners may find it difficult to get the floor to talk, struggle to be able to phrase what they want to say, or even have difficulty in adequately understanding the story. Many students need more structured experiences such as continued learning about the components of a story (main character, setting, problem, attempts to solve the problem, and the solution to the problem) and how to retell a story with each of the components. Research has shown that at-risk kindergartners and first graders only recall about two events from a story after listening to their teacher read aloud (Stevens, Van Meter, & Warcholak, 2010). Thus, an explicit approach to teaching each of the components of stories and having students recall the information related to those components could be an effective instructional strategy. First, teachers would assess whether many children in their classrooms need such instruction. They can have children retell stories in small groups. When children fail to tell more than a few ideas about a story, they will need explicit instruction. To do so, teachers can define a story component: "The main character is the character that does the most in a story. Listen as I read this story and see if you can figure out the main character, and be able to tell me why." Teachers would then read aloud a book about a strong central character using interactive techniques and enhancing techniques such as asking questions, making comments, providing examples, providing a

---

TECHNOLOGY TIE-IN

CREATING A PODCAST

Free software allows you to make podcasts using any computer with a microphone built in.

1. Go to http://audacity.sourceforge.net and click on the download tab.
2. Click on the version appropriate for your computer.
3. Open audacity and press on the Record button to record your message.
4. When you are finished with your message, click on the yellow Stop button.
5. Pull down the file menu and hit Save. You will give your recording a project name and save it to a location on your computer.
6. Now go back to http://audacity.sourceforge.net and click on the Help tab. This will provide a link to LAME and give directions for downloading this program. At this site, click on Audacity on Windows and click on the program recommended. It will be a zipped program that you must save to your computer in the same location as you saved the Audacity program.
7. Go back to the Audacity file menu again and pull down the Export to MP3 button. Save in the same location as LAME with its own file name. The file should appear on your computer with the blue note indicating it is a music file.
8. You can play and listen to the podcast on your computer by opening the file. You can also send the file as an attachment through e-mail or post it to a blog. You can even use the files in Moviemaker or iMovies as the audiofile.

definition or a synonym for vocabulary, and clarifying students' comments or asking for extending comments (Kindle, 2009). After reading, they would ask several children to identify the main character and to tell why this is the main character. Teachers would then teach another component (such as setting) and ask children to listen for the setting and the main character.

Once teachers have taught all the components of a story, children should practice retelling many different stories. One way to make storytelling more exciting is to have children create podcasts of their story recounts. The Technology Tie-In presents information on making easy podcasts that teachers can post to their Web sites for parents and children to listen to.

MODIFYING INSTRUCTION TO MEET THE NEEDS OF DIVERSE LEARNERS

WE HAVE DESCRIBED EXEMPLARY TEACHERS' INSTRUCTION using guided reading of leveled books and other kinds of texts, a writing approach that includes interactive writing, and word study in focused, explicit lessons and in embedded lessons during reading and writing. These teachers were not required to use a commercial basal reading program. Their instruction was guided by district guidelines and standards for students' reading and writing achievement rather than by a commercial program. Nonetheless, increasingly, teachers are required to teach from commercial programs. Teachers working with required commercial reading programs will need a systematic approach to modifying the activities in that program to meet the needs of their diverse learners.

Modifying Commercial Reading Programs

Many schools, as part of their comprehensive reading programs, require teachers to use a core reading program. A **comprehensive reading program** is an approach to teaching all children in an elementary school. It includes a scope and sequence of skills that will be taught at each grade level, materials that are to be read at each grade level, assessments for determining what children need to learn and for checking whether they have learned what they have been taught, and materials for reteaching when children demonstrate a need for it. A comprehensive reading program also includes provisions for reading intervention. That is, when children are identified as struggling and not making grade-level progress, the school must develop a plan to intervene with extra, targeted instruction. Intervention programs are designed to bring children up to grade-level expectations.

Core reading programs are commercial products promoted as having all that teachers and students need for the students to achieve grade-level expectations through daily instruction and practice in phonics and phonemic awareness, vocabulary, comprehension, and fluency. Some core reading programs are scripted, telling teachers what to say as they teach, what to expect students to say, and how to respond to students. These programs also are sequenced; teachers are expected to teach all parts of all lessons and to teach them in the order given in the teachers' manuals.

In order to modify instruction to meet the needs of individual children, teachers need to consider where in the sequence of instruction to begin a small group of children. Because first graders are so different in their beginning competency in reading, teachers cannot expect all children to begin with lesson 1 and move lesson by lesson through the rest, sometimes as many as 160 lessons. Basal reading programs that are not scripted and strictly sequenced are more easily modified. They provide a wide variety of activities in each lesson, allowing for teachers to select those few that fit the needs of individual children with whom they are working.

As teachers know more about their students, they are better able to skip activities provided for teaching skills and strategies that their children already know. Effective instruction is based on the kind of assessments described in Chapters 2 through 5. It is focused only on what students need to know, not on what they already know. This saves time, facilitates students' progress, and spares them frustration.

Modifying Instruction for English Language Learners

Shared reading of big books is enjoyable and beneficial for all children, but especially for ELL children. Teachers should select big books that have comprehensible language such as simple sentence structures, direct matches between the text and illustrations, repetitive sentence and event patterns that support prediction, and words used in everyday conversations. The words should be large enough to see in a small-group lesson, and word spaces should be large and prominent. Before reading aloud a big book in shared reading with English language learners, teachers can use a talk-through approach, pointing to important parts of the illustrations, speaking slowly, and focusing on simple explanations of a few words. Teachers invite children to talk about what they know. During a talk-through, the teacher can begin to use some of the language patterns that are used in the book. Then teachers read the book slowly, carefully articulating the words (Barone, Mallette, & Xu, 2005).

If teachers cannot find big books with text that is supportive of their English language learners, they can find little books at levels 1 and 2 (according to Reading Recovery leveling). We recommend books called *PM Magenta* (found at Rigby publishers) or from Pioneer Valley Books (this publisher allows you to preview some of its books before purchasing).

After reading, teachers select a few of the words to highlight in oral vocabulary instruction and a few words to teach as sight words. When strengthening oral vocabulary, teachers select rich-content words illustrated clearly in the book. For example, in the book *Mom* (Randell, Giles, & Smith, 1996), one page shows Mom digging. The word *digging* would make an excellent word for oral vocabulary learning as children talk aloud using various forms of the word *dig* (*is digging, dug, will dig, has dug, who might dig,* and *why someone might be digging*). When teaching sight vocabulary, teachers select one or two high-frequency words used in a repeated sentence pattern (in this book, the word *is* is repeated on every page). To teach sight words, teachers write the word on a chalkboard for children to trace. Then children practice writing the word on a whiteboard or making the word using magnetic letters or writing the word in a sand tray.

Teachers can use the linguistic structure of the big or little books to compose story innovations (Griffin & Ruan, 2007). Story innovations use the sentence structures found in stories (e.g., *Mom is sleeping, Mom is running, Mom is digging*) but insert new subjects (names of children or use the words *I* or *we*) and new verbs (*is jumping, is hiding*) to create a new story. Easy sentence patterns to use in story innovations include the following:

- I can _____.
- Look at me _____.
- I see a _____.
- Here comes a _____.
- I am at the _____.
- We are going to the _____.
- I have a _____.
- I can put a _____ in my bag.
- There is a _____.
- Where is the _____?
- Look at the _____.
- I see a _____ looking at me.

Each child contributes by writing a page of text and illustrating the text. Teachers can create digital stories by scanning in the child's illustrations onto a PowerPoint and then using the narration feature to record each child reading his or her own page of text.

Modifying Instruction for Struggling Readers

We have shown how Mrs. Tran organizes her instruction for children who are most at risk for reading failure. She identifies their needs early in the year, groups the children for instruction, and plans instruction that uses their strengths to teach what they need to learn next. We have shown that she uses finger-point reading of texts placed on the pocket chart (familiar nursery rhymes or short poems or songs) and engages children in short interactive writing experiences. Another instructional activity she uses is the **language experience approach** (Landis, Umolu, & Mancha, 2010). With this approach, teachers engage children in a discussion of an activity they have participated in (an art activity or cooking) or talking about a special community event. Individual children dictate or tell a sentence and the teacher writes it down. Teachers may modify children's sentences slightly but are careful not to completely change a child's words. This activity works best with only two or three children.

ASSESSING STUDENT PROGRESS IN FIRST GRADE

AN INITIAL AND ONGOING ASSESSMENT is critical for teaching first graders. Teachers need to make sure that they are providing instruction that puts children at the cutting edge of what they can do, that ensures that children are continuing to make adequate progress, and that helps teachers determine when to initiate a response to intervention plan for those few children not making gains. The critical assessments for first grade include

- recognition and production of the uppercase and lowercase alphabet letters
- one-to-one tracking of print and locating a word using finger-point reading
- high-frequency sight words
- segmenting two- and three-phoneme words
- spelling
- decoding simple short vowel words
- reading leveled text with above 90 percent accuracy and with adequate comprehension

It is critical that first graders identify uppercase and lowercase letters quickly and accurately. Appendix B presents lists of letters that can be used to assess letter recognition. First graders should also produce readable alphabet letters. Teachers can use the list of uppercase letters to ask children to write the letters in random order. Assessing writing of both uppercase and lowercase letters is needed; children should be able to accomplish this assessment as a whole group. First graders should know nearly all the letters and be able to write most letters early in the year. When individual children show difficulty with these tasks, a response to intervention plan should be considered.

Being able to track print and match each spoken word with each written word is a watershed accomplishment in learning to read. Appendix C presents a finger-point reading task with two activities: matching words one to one and locating words. This is not an assessment of actual reading, and children who are reading text level 4 or above do not need this assessment. Children reading text levels below 4 should be able to accomplish this task nearly perfectly.

Children's ability to read sight words can be assessed using the *Fry's 300 Instant Sight Words* list. This list can be found at www.usu.edu/teachall/text/reading/frylist .pdf. First graders should know a few words at the beginning of the year and gain words rapidly throughout the year. The first one hundred words on this list are expected to be learned in first grade.

The Yopp Singer Test of Phonemic Segmentation (see Chapter 4) can be used to assess segmentation of two- and three-phoneme words. At first-grade entry, children should be able to segment a few words. By the end of first grade, children should be nearly perfect on this assessment and show steady improvement through the year. Spelling can be assessed using the spelling list in Appendix C or in a developmental spelling inventory. First graders are expected to move through the stage of letter-name spelling.

Appendix C presents a decoding and writing familiar rhyming assessment that children in first grade should be able to do easily by midyear. Teachers can prepare a list of decodable CVC short vowel words to check on decoding using words such as *tap, bet, fin, rug, mat, top, fed, rig, rob*, and *bud*. These words should be unknown to the child as sight words (teachers should test this first), and children's strategies for decoding them should be noted.

Appendix A presents a list of leveled tests that teachers can use to determine the level of children's actual reading. Reading texts at levels 1 and 2 means that children are really finger-point readers relying on the simple patterns of text and one-to-one matching. Reading texts at levels 4 through 9 means that children can read preprimer texts and that they are early beginning readers. Reading texts at levels 9 through 12 means that children can read primer texts and that they are beginning readers. Reading texts at levels 14 through 16 means that children have reached first-grade reading level, and reading at level 18 or above indicates second-grade reading. Teachers can take running records of texts and ask children questions to determine if they are making progress reading up the gradient of text difficulty during first grade.

Chapter Summary

FIRST GRADE MARKS AN IMPORTANT TIME in children's schooling. They are expected to begin "really" reading and writing; at the end of first grade, society expects children to have made great strides toward conventional reading and writing. We have shown that there are many ways in which this journey is taken.

We described Mrs. Tran's guided-reading methods, including her use of talk-through before guided reading, guided-reading lessons, teaching for strategies, systematic approach to teaching phonics and spelling, and use of interactive writing. Mr. Schultheis' literacy instruction used flexible groups for revising and editing writing and varied materials used in mini-lessons. Mrs. Duthie used mini-lessons to teach reading and writing of informational texts.

Children in first grade receive instruction that strengthens their phonemic awareness, phonics, vocabulary, and comprehension, along with their knowledge of spelling and writing. Successful children in first grade gain 200 to 300 automatic sight words, especially high-frequency words, that they can both read and write; they are able to decode and spell single-syllable words that follow regular spelling patterns; and they read increasingly complex texts, moving from level 1 through level 16 according to Reading Recovery levels, or A through I according to Fountas and Pinnell (2009) (or preprimer, primer, and first-grade level texts according to basal reader levels). They write increasingly complex texts in several genres and can apply several strategies for understanding complex picture stories and informational books that are read aloud to them. They are able to independently read and write using several strategies for solving problems at points of difficulty.

Teachers modify their instruction as needed to meet the needs of struggling readers and English language learners. They may need to modify the instructional suggestions in commercial reading materials to fit the needs of their learners. Teachers also use assessment to make sure students are making adequate progress learning to read and write.

APPLYING THE INFORMATION

Make a list of all the strategies for reading, spelling, and listening that children are taught in first grade. With a partner, practice showing how children use these strategies using some of the prompts suggested in this chapter. Next, make a list of the instructional activities introduced in this chapter. For each activity, describe what children learn about written language meanings (listening comprehension), forms (sight words, spelling patterns, punctuation), meaning-form links (phonemic awareness, decoding, spelling), or functions (how print is used in real-world activities).

GOING BEYOND THE TEXT

VISIT A FIRST-GRADE CLASSROOM and observe several literacy activities. Make a list of all the print and literacy materials in the classroom. Take note of the interactions among the children and between the children and the teacher during literacy activities. Talk with the teacher about his or her philosophy of beginning reading and writing. Compare these materials, activities, and philosophies with those of Mr. Schultheis, Mrs. Duthie, and Mrs. Tran.

REFERENCES

Adams, M. (1990). *Beginning to read: Thinking and learning about print.* Cambridge, MA: MIT Press.

Asch, F. (1995). *Water.* New York: Harcourt Brace.

Barone, D., Mallette, M., & Xu, S. (2005). *Teaching early literacy: Development, assessment and instruction.* New York: Guilford Press.

Bear, D. R., Invernizzi, M., Templeton, S., & Johnston, F. (2000). *Words their way: Word study for phonics, vocabulary, and spelling instruction.* Upper Saddle River, NJ: Merrill.

Bear, D. R., Invernizzi, M., Templeton, S., & Johnston, F. (2008). *Words their way: Word study for phonics, vocabulary, and spelling instruction* (2nd ed.). Upper Saddle River, NJ: Merrill.

Berger, M. (1994). *Oil spill!* New York: HarperCollins.

Carle, E. (1987). *A house for Hermit Crab.* New York: Simon & Schuster.

Caswell, L., & Duke, N. (1998). Non-narrative as a catalyst for literacy development. *Language Arts, 75,* 108–117.

Clay, M. (2001). *Change over time: In children's literacy development.* Portsmouth, NH: Heinemann.

Clay, M. (2005). *Literacy lessons: Designed for individuals, part two: Teaching procedures.* Portsmouth, NH: Heinemann.

Cole, A. (2006). Scaffolding beginning readers: Micro and macro cues teachers use during student oral reading. *The Reading Teacher, 59,* 450–459.

Cole, H. (1995). *Jack's garden.* New York: Greenwillow Books.

Combs, M. (2006). *Readers and writers in primary grades: A balanced and integrated approach K-4.* Upper Saddle River, NJ: Pearson.

Cunningham, P. M. (2005). *Phonics they use: Words for reading and writing* (4th ed.). Boston: Allyn & Bacon.

Cunningham, P., & Hall, D. (1994). *Making words: Multilevel, hands-on, developmentally appropriate spelling and phonics activities.* New York: Good Apple/Frank Schaffer.

Cutting, J. (1996). *Where's Tim?* (Illus., J. van der Voo). Bothell, WA: Wright Group.

Dahl, K. L., Sharer, P. L., Lawson, L. L., & Grogan, P. R. (1999). Phonics instruction and student achievement in whole language first-grade classrooms. *Reading Research Quarterly, 34,* 312–341.

Duthie, C. (1996). *True stories: Nonfiction literacy in the primary classroom.* York, ME: Stenhouse Publishers.

Fountas, I., & Pinnell, G. (1996). *Guided reading: Good first teaching for all children.* Portsmouth, NH: Heinemann.

Fountas, I., & Pinnell, G. (2009). *The Fountas and Pinnell leveled book list K-8, 2006–2008 edition.* Portsmouth, NH: Heinemann.

Fry, E. B., & Kress, J. E. (2006). *The reading teacher's book of lists* (5th ed.). San Francisco: Jossey-Bass.

Ganske, K. (2000). *Word journeys: Assessment-guided phonics, spelling, and vocabulary instruction.* New York: Guilford Press.

Griffin, P., & Ruan, J. (2007). Story innovation: An instructional strategy for developing vocabulary and fluency. *The Reading Teacher, 61,* 334–338.

Helman, L. (2005). Using literacy assessment results to improve teaching for English-language learners. *The Reading Teacher, 58,* 668–677.

Hill, E. (1980). *Where's Spot?* New York: Putnam.

International Reading Association & National Association for the Education of Young Children (IRA/NAEYC). (1998). Newark, DE: International Reading Association.

Kindle, K. (2009). Vocabulary development during read-alouds: Primary practices. *The Reading Teacher, 63,* 202–211.

Landis, D., Umolu, J., & Mancha, S. (2010). The power of language experience for cross-cultural reading and writing. *The Reading Teacher, 63,* 566–579.

McCarthy, P. (2008). Using sound boxes systematically to develop phonic awareness. *The Reading Teacher, 62,* 346–349.

McGee, L. (1996). Response-centered talk: Windows on children's thinking. In L. Gambrell & J. Almasi (Eds.), *Lively discussions: Fostering engaged reading* (pp. 194–207). Newark, DE: International Reading Association.

Morrison, V., & Wlodarczyk, L. (2009). Revisiting read-aloud: Instructional strategies that encourage students' engagement with texts. *The Reading Teacher, 63*(2), 110–118.

National Early Literacy Panel. (2008). *Developing early literacy: Report of the National Early Literacy Panel.* Washington, DC: National Institute for Literacy.

Pressley, M., Allington, R. L., Wharton-McDonald, R., Block, C. C., & Morrow, L. M. (2001). *Learning to read: Lessons from exemplary first-grade classrooms.* New York: Guilford Press.

Randell, B., Giles, J., & Smith, A. (1996). *Mom.* Austin, TX: Harcourt Achieve.

Schwartz, R. (2005). Decisions, decisions: Responding to primary students during guided reading. *The Reading Teacher, 58,* 436–443.

Sipe, L. (1998). Transitions to the conventional: An examination of a first grader's composing process. *Journal of Literacy Research, 30,* 357–388.

Snow, C., Burns, S., & Griffin, P. (1998). *Preventing reading difficulties in young children.* Washington, DC: National Academies Press.

Stevens, R., Van Meter, P., & Warcholak, N. (2010). The effects of explicitly teaching story structure to primary grade children. *Journal of Literacy Research, 42,* 159–198.

Taylor, B. M., Pearson, P. D., Clark, K., & Walpole, S. (2002). Effective schools and accomplished teachers: Lessons about primary-grade reading instruction in low-income schools. In B. M. Taylor & P. D. Pearson (Eds.), *Teaching reading: Effective schools, accomplished teachers* (pp. 3–72). Mahwah, NJ: Lawrence Erlbaum Associates.

Villaume, S., Wordon, T., Williams, S., Hopkins, L., & Rosenblatt, C. (1994). Five teachers in search of a discussion. *The Reading Teacher, 47*, 480–487.

Vogt, M. (1996). Creating a response-centered curriculum with literature discussion groups. In L. Grambell & J. Almasi (Eds.), *Lively discussions! Fostering engaged reading* (pp. 181–193). Newark, DE: International Reading Association.

Wagstaff, J. (1997–1998). Building practical knowledge of sound-letter correspondences: A beginner's Word Wall and beyond. *The Reading Teacher, 51*, 298–304.

Wharton-McDonald, R. (2001a). Andy Schultheis. In M. Pressley, R. L. Allington, R. Wharton-McDonald, C. C. Block, & L. M. Morrow (Eds.), *Learning to read: Lessons from exemplary first-grade classrooms* (pp. 115–137). New York: Guilford Press.

Wharton-McDonald, R. (2001b). Teaching writing in first grade: Instruction, scaffolds, and expectations. In M. Pressley, R. L. Allington, R. Wharton-McDonald, C. C. Block, & L. M. Morrow (Eds.), *Learning to read: Lessons from exemplary first-grade classrooms* (pp. 70–91). New York: Guilford Press.

Williams, C., & Lundstrom, R. P. (2007, November). Strategy instruction during word study and interactive writing activities. *The Reading Teacher, 61*(3), 204–212.

Williams, C., Phillips-Birdsong, C., Hufnagel, K., Hungler, D., & Lundstrom, R. (2009, April). Word study instruction in the K–2 classroom. *The Reading Teacher, 62*(7), 570–578.

Yorinks, A. (1986). *Hey, Al!* New York: Farrar, Straus & Giroux.

PEARSON myeducationlab

Go to the topics Phonemic Awareness and Phonics, Word Study, Comprehension, Writing Development, Assessment, English Language Learners, and At Risk and Struggling Readers in the MyEducationLab (www.myeducationlab.com) for your course, where you can:

- Find learning outcomes for Phonemic Awareness and Phonics, Word Study, Comprehension, Writing Development, Assessment, English Language Learners, and At Risk and Struggling Readers along with the national standards that connect to these outcomes.
- Complete Assignments and Activities that can help you more deeply understand the chapter content.
- Examine challenging situations and cases presented in the IRIS Center Resources.

A+RISE

Go to the Topic A+RISE in the MyEducationLab (www.myeducationlab.com) for your course. A+RISE® Standards2Strategy™ is an innovative and interactive online resource that offers new teachers in grades K–12 just-in-time, research-based instructional strategies that:

- Meet the linguistic needs of ELLs as they learn content
- Differentiate instruction for all grades and abilities
- Offer reading and writing techniques, cooperative learning, use of linguistic and nonlinguistic representations, scaffolding, teacher modeling, higher order thinking, and alternative classroom ELL assessment
- Provide support to help teachers be effective through the integration of listening, speaking, reading, and writing along with the content curriculum
- Improve student achievement
- Are aligned to Common Core Elementary Language Arts standards (for the literacy strategies) and to English language proficiency standards in WIDA, Texas, California, and Florida.

CHAPTER 10

Supporting Literacy Learning in Second through Fourth Grades

KEY CONCEPTS

Lexile Book Measure
Individualized Reading
  Inventory
Prosody
Literature Text Set
Motif
Multiple-Character
  Perspective Approach
Modern Folktale Variants
Perspective
Grand Conversation
Instructional Reading
  Level
Character Cluster
Word Wall
List, Group, and Label
  Activity

Content-Specific
  Vocabulary
Fluent Reading
Readers' Theater
Mini-Lesson
Guided Spelling
Homophones
Homographs
Word-Sort Activity
Word Hunt
Making Big Words
Morpheme
Free Morpheme
Bound Morpheme
Affix
Prefix
Suffix

Independent Reading
  Level
Book Talk
Response Journal
Book Club
Process Approach
  to Writing
Writing Workshop
Prewriting
Drafting
Revising
Editing
Publishing
Inquiry Unit
Internet Workshop
K-W-L Chart
Rubric

WHAT'S NEW HERE?

THIS CHAPTER DESCRIBES INSTRUCTION that moves children into and beyond conventional transitional reading and writing described in Chapter 5. While many of the same kinds of instructional activities we described in Chapter 9 continue to be important during this phase of reading and writing, teachers can expand reading and writing activities to capitalize on children's new competencies.

In the second through fourth grades, there are increasing expectations for students to display traditional skills and new competencies. Perhaps the largest challenge in the second grade and beyond is meeting the very diverse needs of the children found in these grade levels. When some children begin second grade, they are reading and writing far above grade-level expectations. They are already transitional readers capable of reading more complex picture storybooks, information books, and chapter books independently. Their instructional level in reading is often far above their grade level and continues to accelerate. Other children begin second grade not yet reading on second-grade level and not yet exhibiting the strategies and skills expected of transitional readers. However, these children will have in place many literacy skills and strategies expected of end-of-the-year, first-grade-level readers. They are on their way but need continued teacher support and extended practice to move into and beyond the transitional text levels. These children tend to stay around grade-level reading levels or slightly above. Unfortunately, some children come to second grade who have not yet accomplished very much of what we expect in first grade. They may be reading only at the very beginning stage of reading at the preprimer or primer level. They need considerable teacher support and extensive amounts of practice in texts at their instructional level to enhance their early literacy skills and strategies. Without powerful teaching, these children are likely to fall further behind and the gap between their reading and their peers' reading levels will only widen. Therefore, it is clear that teachers must continue to provide a common core of experiences for all children but increasingly provide differentiated instruction to meet the needs of these diverse learners.

In a simple sense, teachers in grade 2 and beyond are expected to teach the five scientific components of the reading process: phonemic awareness, phonics, vocabulary, comprehension, and fluency (Cassidy, Valadez, & Garrett, 2010). But what children must learn is far more complex. First, they are expected to read and understand increasingly complex texts from second-grade through fourth-, fifth- or sixth-grade levels. One way to examine the complexity of books that children are expected to be able to read is to examine the recommended ranges of Lexile book measures at grades 2 through 5. A **Lexile book measure** is a metric that takes into account the difficulty of a passage using measures of word frequency and sentence length. Words that are more unusual are considered more difficult, and longer sentences usually have more complex syntax. Thus, books with higher Lexile book measures are considered more difficult, although it is important to consider that these measures do not take into account the content of the book or the quality of writing.

Consider the range of Lexile book measures for the following popular books and when they are typically read.

- *Frog and Toad Are Friends* (Lobel, 1999), 400L—typically read in second grade
- *Sarah, Plain and Tall* (MacLachlan, 2004), 560L—typically read in the third or fourth grade
- *Owl Moon* (Yolan, 1987), 630L—typically read aloud in kindergarten and first grade
- *The Chocolate Touch* (Catling, 1952), 770L—typically read in third grade
- *Harry Potter and the Sorcerer's Stone* (Rowling, 2008), 880L—typically read in third grade and up
- *Bud, Not Buddy* (Curtis, 2004), 950L—typically read in fifth or sixth grade

In order to read books at these challenging levels, transitional readers will need to acquire a very large store of sight words that they recognize accurately and automatically (without attention to the words' printed details as are needed when decoding a word). Transitional readers usually have already acquired many high-frequency sight words. For example, they can quickly read (and write) the 300 high-frequency words included on *The New Instant Word List* (Fry, 1980). Now students are learning content words found in their daily guided-reading texts, independent reading books, or content study. **Individualized reading inventories** (assessments used to determine a student's instructional and independent reading levels) include a list of graded words that children are expected to able to read that teachers can use to assess students' sight word knowledge.

In addition to a large store of sight vocabulary words, students will need sophisticated strategies for solving unknown words in reading and spelling new words in writing. They will need strategies for determining vocabulary word meanings and ways to use increasingly more nuanced vocabulary in their writing. They will need more sophisticated strategies for comprehending the highly complex text they are now encountering and an increasing array of revision techniques to craft compositions in a variety of new genres. Students will be expected to read with appropriate fluency including a rapid rate, appropriate **prosody** (expression achieved by use of pace, pitch, and stress), and phrasing. Increasingly, students will be expected to read information books in order to learn and remember new information, and to share their new knowledge through presentations using a variety of media.

In this book, we argue that teachers can best teach students the variety of skills and strategies they will need to learn through a balanced literacy program. A balanced literacy program provides a balance of explicit teaching of strategies and skills with guided and independent practice in reading quality books and other literature. We recommend using seven instructional activities:

- literature study, vocabulary instruction and comprehension instruction in daily, whole-class, interactive read-alouds and response activities
- guided-reading and spelling activities in small groups
- independent reading by individual children and in small, flexible book club groups
- advanced word work in whole-class word study activities
- guided and independent writing in daily writing workshop
- content study in Internet workshops and inquiry units, which include instruction in reading and writing to gain and share information
- frequent culminating activities involving extended, self-directed projects

LITERATURE STUDY THROUGH INTERACTIVE READ–ALOUDS

CHILDREN NEED TO EXPERIENCE BY LISTENING TO TEACHERS READ TO THEM challenging literature that they cannot read, even with teacher guidance. Teachers provide this challenge by systematically planning a read-aloud program in which they read to children literature from **literature text sets**—that is, selections of books with a common theme (e.g., that friends are often found in unusual places), author or illustrator (e.g., books illustrated by Jerry Pinkney), literary element (e.g., tricksters or dynamic characters), or genre (e.g., poetry or animal fantasy). As children listen to read-alouds for the enjoyment and vicarious experiences, it also stretches their vocabularies and increases their comprehension and appreciation of very complex texts. Good books read aloud by sensitive and thoughtful teachers offer children opportunities to experience good writing, gripping plots, admirable and despicable characters, and moral dilemmas. With appropriate guidance, children experience emotions, reflect on life, and engage in critical thinking.

Reading aloud to children also offers them the opportunity to engage with the very best of children's literature. Not all literature children encounter in school is of sufficient quality to provoke strong reactions and complex thinking. But more importantly, children rarely study literature for itself; often, the primary purpose for reading most books is to improve their reading ability—not extend their appreciation of literature (Sipe, 2008). Therefore, it is critical that teachers expand their notion of the purpose of read-alouds at these grade levels. Now, children are ready to learn more about the characteristics of specific kinds of genre, such as mysteries or graphic novels, or the fantastic elements included in fantasy, such as time slips (places where characters move from one setting in time to another). Another reason to study literature is that according to high-stakes tests (National Assessment of Educational Progress [NAEP], 2003), very few children in the United States can take a stand about a character or event and present evidence from the story to support their stand. Interactive read-alouds of high-quality literature, supported by teaching children literary reading strategies and following up reading with activities designed to extend children's comprehension in open-ended response activities, can close this gap.

Selecting a Text Set and a Literary Focus for Discussion

Teachers will select five to ten books related in some way. Figure 10.1 presents a list of suggested literary elements that may be studied in the elementary grades. This list suggests studying characters, types of conflict, or special genres of literature.

One exemplary third-grade teacher, Ms. Meddors, decided to study folk and fairy tales with her third-grade children. She wanted them to learn about motifs, locate motifs in stories she read aloud, and use the motifs to write their own versions of a folk or fairy tale. A **motif** is a kind of character, event, or other story element recurring across many folk or fairy tales. Motifs include the following elements:

- Events or characters occur in threes.
- The weakest or smallest character usually saves the day.

FIGURE 10.1   Literary Elements to Include in Text Sets for Interactive Read-Alouds

Character Studies to Identify

Character traits (enduring qualities of a character such as brave, secretive, kind-hearted, stubborn, happy-go-lucky, thoughtful)

Well-rounded characters (characters with several different kinds of character traits)

Dynamic characters (characters who change during the story)

Conflict Studies

Conflict between two characters is the central problem

Conflict between a character and himself or herself is the central problem

Conflict between a character and nature is the central problem

Conflict between a character and society is the central problem

Study of Special Genres

Fantasy
    Animal fantasy
    Toy fantasy
    Little ones
    Time slip
    High fantasy

Realistic Fiction
    Friendships
    Growing up
    Family
    Facing danger
    Making a difference

Traditional Literature
    Myths and legends
    Noodlehead stories
    Trickster tales
    Talking animal tales
    Modern variants of folk and fairytales

Post Modern Picture Books

Wordless Picture Books

Nonfiction
    How-to books
    Graphic Illustrations in nonfiction
    Gripping writing in nonfiction

Poetry
    Shape and line in poetry
    Language in poetry
    Humor in poetry

Design Elements in Illustrations
    Color, shape, line
    Perspective
    Type of Media

- Some characters are all good or all bad.
- Some characters are tricky, whereas other characters are tricked.
- Some items are magical.
- Some characters must perform tasks, whereas other characters are helpers.
- Some characters are magical.
- Some characters are clever, whereas other characters are silly or stupid.
- There are many opposites (clever/stupid, good/bad, rich/poor).

Ms. Meddors read aloud a different book from her text set of high-quality folk and fairy tales each day, and each day she had a different focus for reading. During the first read-aloud of the text set, she introduced the idea of motifs by listing three motifs on the chalkboard and defining them. As she read, she challenged the children to raise their hands when they thought they had recognized a motif. Ms. Meddors read aloud *Borreguita and the Coyote* (Aardema, 1998); and the children identified the trickster, the character who was tricked, the clever character, and the stupid character.

The next day, she introduced three additional motifs, then she read aloud *Rumpelstiltskin* (Zelinsky, 1986). After reading, Ms. Meddors introduced the concept of opposites (Temple, 1991). She defined *opposites* and asked the children which opposites could be found in the book. The children noticed that the miller and his daughter were poor but the king was rich; also, the miller's daughter became rich when she was queen. They thought Rumpelstiltskin, the miller, and the king were greedy, but they thought the miller's daughter was generous and giving. They noted that the miller's daughter and the king were tall and beautiful and handsome; Rumpelstiltskin was small and ugly. They noted that, at night, the miller's daughter was with Rumpelstiltskin, and during the day, she was with the king.

After listing such opposites in *Rumpelstiltskin,* Ms. Meddors initiated a question-making activity (Commeyras & Sumner, 1995). In this activity, children construct questions that will lead to long discussions about literature. The teacher models asking questions that could be easily answered and would not generate much talk versus questions that could generate many different ideas and opinions. Good questions are those that have no single correct answer, generate many different ideas, and take a long time to discuss. This class called these kinds of questions "long questions."

Ms. Meddors invited children to suggest long questions to use for talking about *Rumpelstiltskin.* They posed the following questions with the teacher's guidance:

If the miller was poor, why did he give a daughter to the king?

What kind of father was the miller to lie to the king in a way that might harm his daughter?

Why would the daughter fall in love with a king who demanded she spin gold or be killed?

Why are the king and Rumpelstiltskin so alike in character but not in looks? Did the miller's daughter think about this?

Another approach to help children perceive multiple perspectives in a story is the **multiple-character-perspective approach** (Shanahan & Shanahan, 1997). This approach calls for children to understand the story from different characters' points of view and to compare and contrast those different perspectives. For this approach, Ms. Meddors read aloud *Mufaro's Beautiful Daughters: An African Tale* (Steptoe, 1987), which includes two characters, Nyasha and Manyara, who are in conflict. First, she asked the children to discuss the story from Nyasha's perspective, and then from Manyara's perspective, focusing especially on the characters' conflicting character traits, goals, motivations, and actions.

As a culminating project, Ms. Meddors had students read several versions of **modern folktale variants**. These are folktales authored by real people who create different settings for the story or transform people characters into animals. For example, her students read several versions of the "Little Red Riding Hood" tale, including *Ruby* (Emberley,1990), and *Little Red Riding Hood: A Newfangled Prairie Tale* (Ernst, 1995); and several versions of the "Cinderella" tale including *Bigfoot Cinderrrrrella* (Johnston, 1998), *Dinorella* (Edwards, 1997), and *Cinderhazel* (Lattimore, 1997); among many others. Then students wrote their own variant folk tales in small groups, practiced reading them with fluency and interpretive style, and created podcasts, which were posted on Ms. Meddors' Web site. The stories they posted were *Little Red Riding Pants, Little Red Low Rider in the Hood, Cinderfootballer,* and *Cinderpretzel.*

Other teachers who want their students to learn more about the literary elements found in all narratives can use the Web site www.learner.org/interactives/story/index.html. Here, students can listen to a version of *Cinderella.* Then the Web site teaches students the literary elements found in good stories. This site presents fairly sophisticated information for each literary element, and students are presented with an interactive activity to complete related to the literary element. The final activity is a quiz of knowledge about all the literary elements. If teachers have an interactive whiteboard (Smart Board), this would make an excellent group activity to examine the literary elements in narratives (Dymock, 2007). Teachers would pull up the Web site and study one literary element such as point of view, then present children with several books with different points of view for them to read and discuss how each point of view positions the reader differently inside the heads of the characters.

Read-alouds can also be used to systematically introduce children to the elements of design in illustration and how these affect the meaning readers construct. For example, children can examine illustrators' use of color, line, shape, and different media. Figure 10.2 presents a text set selected by a fourth-grade teacher to teach children the use and effect of perspective in illustrations. **Perspective** is achieved by the illustrator by positioning the reader to view the illustrations from a particular viewpoint. Most perspectives are straight on, viewed as if the reader and the world of the illustrations were on the same level. Other perspectives put the reader below the horizon line of the illustrations. Here, buildings seem very tall and the reader feels uneasy (see the illustrations in *The Garden of Abdul Gasazi* [Van Allsburg, 1979]). Other perspectives, like a bird's eye view, put the reader looking down at the world in the illustrations (see *Owl Moon* [Yolan, 1987]). Here, readers feel powerful. Another use of perspective is one in which the illustrators take us very close in to characters or objects (see *Foolish Rabbit's Big Mistake* [Martin, 1985]). Close-ups make us look at certain characteristics of, for example, an animal or emotions of a character. This teacher introduced children to perspective, and they enjoyed finding illustrations using perspective as well as talking about what the illustrations added to their understanding of the book.

Selecting and Teaching Literary Reading Strategies

One set of literary reading strategies that teachers may teach during read-alouds is consideration of the relationships between characters and the events in a story (Taberski, 2000). For example, character traits, that is, the enduring qualities of a character that determine how he or she acts, often account for problems in a story. When children identify character traits and consider how these are related to a story's problem and its eventual solution, they are moving from what happened in the story (literal comprehension) to why (inferential comprehension).

FIGURE 10.2   Text Set on Perspective

Browne, A. (1992). *Zoo*. New York: Alfred Knopf.

Dorros, A. (1995). *Isla*. New York: Dutton Children's Books.

Johnson, S. (1998). *City by numbers*. New York: Viking.

Martin, R. & Young, E. (1988). *Foolish rabbit's big mistake*. New York: G.P. Putnam's Sons.

Perrault, C. (1990). *Puss in boots*. New York: Farrar, Straus and Giroux.

Pinkney, J. (2009). *The lion and the mouse*. New York: Little, Brown & Company.

Raschka, C. (1992). *Charlie Parker played be bop*. New York: Orchard Books.

Van Allsburg, C. (1979). *The garden of Abdul Gasazi*. Houghton Mifflin.

Van Allsburg, C. (1981). *Jumanji*. New York: Scholastic Inc.

Van Allsburg, C. (1991). *The wretched stone*. Boston: Houghton Mifflin.

Van Allsburg, C. (1992). *The widow's broom*. Boston: Houghton Mifflin.

Weisner, D. (2001). *The three pigs*. New York: Clarion Books.

Wisniewski, D. (1996). *Golem*. New York: Clarion Books.

Wood, A. (1984). *The napping house*. New York: Harcourt Brace & Company.

Yolan, J. (1987). *Owl moon*. New York: Philomel.

Young, E. (1989). *Lon Po Po: A red riding hood story from China*. New York: Philomel Books.

Another literary reading strategy is to create mental images while reading. Good readers visualize characters in action. They use images to anticipate future actions and to fill in detail. When they stop and ask themselves why characters might have acted as they did, good readers often make images and predict what might happen next. Good readers use additional strategies when reading information books. They use special text features such as flowcharts, graphs, and labeled drawings. They make note of information and make decisions about which information is most important to remember. Figure 10.3 summarizes literary reading strategies that teachers should model during read-alouds.

One way to teach literary reading strategies during read-alouds is for teachers to stop reading and to think aloud about what they are doing as they use a strategy. Then they explain why it is important to use that strategy. For example, Miller (2002) starts strategy instruction by telling what the strategy is that she will be demonstrating and why it is important: "Thinking about what you already know is called using your schema, or using your background knowledge. Schema is all the stuff that's already in your head, like places you've been, things you've done, books you've read—all the experiences you've had. . . . When you use schema, it helps you use what you know to better understand [what you read]" (p. 57). She identifies and explains the strategy she wants children to learn, "Today we are going to talk about one way [you use schema]: using schema to make connections from our reading, or the text, to ourselves. We'll call these text-to-self connections" (p. 57).

FIGURE 10.3 Literary Reading Strategies

Using schema

Text-to-self connections
  stopping to think about big ideas in a story and making connections to my life
Text-to-text connections
  comparing characters in different or the same texts
Text-to-world connections
  stopping to think about big ideas in a story and connecting to events in life
Schema for story elements
  considering characters and their enduring qualities
  determining the relationship between character traits and problems, plot, and theme
  moving from what happens, to how, and why it happens
Activating, building, and revising schema related to story events and activities

Creating mental images

Creating images of the character-in-action from readers' schema and words in the text
Changing images to incorporate new information

Inferring

Inferring the meaning of words
Predicting
  making more than one prediction and using text as support
  confirming predictions along the way
Stopping to think what happened and why it happened (from what to why)
Stopping to think why the character acted as he/she did (from what to why)
Inferring answers to questions (when the answers are not in the text)

Asking questions

Asking "I wonder why"
Asking questions before, during, and after reading
Determining whether questions can be answered in text, in schema, or from outside source

Using special strategies for informational text

Noticing and remembering when we learn something new
Using informational text features and structure
Distinguishing important from unimportant information

Synthesizing

Summarizing what's important and makes sense, but not telling too much
Moving from literal level to inferential level
  I'm thinking that, now I'm thinking, I used to think—but now I'm thinking

---

Source: Adapted from Miller, D. (2002). *Reading with meaning: Teaching comprehension in the primary grades.* Portland, ME: Stenhouse; Taberski, S. (2000). *On solid ground: Strategies for teaching reading K–3.* Portsmouth, NH: Heinemann.

Next, Miller (2002) demonstrates using the strategy, "Let me show you what I mean. I'm going to read a story to you; its title is *The Relatives Came* by Cynthia Rylant. I'll read for a while, then I'll stop and think out loud to show you how I use my schema, or what I already know, to make connections from my life to the story" (pp. 57–58). She reads the book, then stops at a page and puts the book down in her lap signaling she will be talking about the book rather than reading. She says, "[T]his page made me laugh. You see right here, where I read to you 'It was different going to sleep with all that new breathing in the house'? I understood exactly what Cynthia Rylant meant. That's because at the same time I was reading I was making a connection to when I was a little girl, remembering how my family and all my cousins and aunts and uncles would visit my grandparents in their farmhouse on old Route 92 near Oskaloosa, Iowa. Sometimes it was so hot and sticky at night that we'd all pile down to the living room—just like this picture. We'd sleep together on the black carpet with the pink and red roses" (p. 58). Next, Miller makes explicit that she has modeled using the strategy, "Do you see how using my schema helped me understand just how the people in the book feel?" (p. 58).

Strategy instruction helps children reflect on how and why strategies help to make them better readers. One student reflected that "If we connect to a word, like *mailman* or *cat* or *soccer ball*, that doesn't really help us, but if we connect to a bigger idea, like if it's on almost all the pages and it's what the book is really about, like a big idea or something, then it can help you" (Miller, 2002, p. 61). Miller makes a chart that summarizes children's reflections about using strategies. She wrote: "We think about big ideas in the story and then we think about those big ideas in our experiences."

After-Reading Response Activities

After reading aloud, teachers will want children to discuss and write about the text in ways that deepen their understanding and build literary knowledge. One activity that extends children's comprehension is a **grand conversation** (McGee, 1995), that is, a book discussion prompted by a teacher's open-ended question, such as "What did you think?" and guided by children's comments and questions rather than by the teacher's continued questioning (see Chapter 9 for an example of a grand conversation).

Another after-reading response activity (when students have copies of the texts read aloud), is to write in double-entry journals. That is, teachers might want to make sure all students have a copy of a chapter book that is read aloud. Then each student would be given a double-entry journal (booklets of paper with a vertical line dividing each paper into half). After a chapter is read aloud, students would reread the chapter in order to locate three or four quotes, which they record on one side of their double-entry journal. Then they write their responses on the other side—why they selected this quote, what this quote made them think about, or connections they made while reading the quote (Tompkins, 2006).

An open-mind portrait is another response activity designed to help students make inferences about what characters are thinking or feeling. On one side of a paper, students draw the head of the character. These are cut out; then on the back, students write their inferences. Or students might make a Venn diagram comparing and contrasting two characters. One other way to have students consider character traits is for them to make missing-person posters (Johnson & Louis, 1987). Figure 10.4 presents a third grader's missing-person poster for Amos from *Amos and Boris* (Steig, 1971).

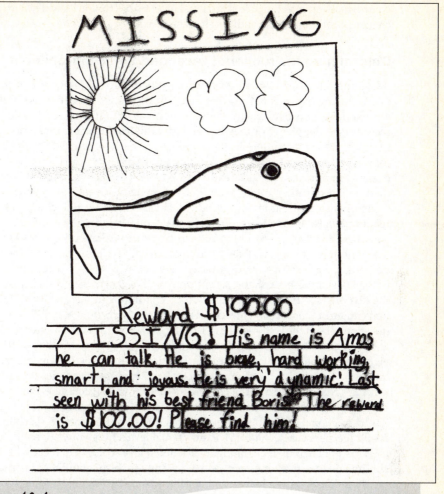

FIGURE 10.4 Missing-Person Poster for *Amos and Boris* (Steig, 1971)

GUIDED READING AND SPELLING

GUIDED READING OCCURS when groups of children, reading on similar levels, are taught reading strategies and practice reading texts under the guidance of the teacher (Fawson & Reutzel, 2000). Teachers select books at each group's instructional level. **Instructional reading level** text is of moderate difficulty. Children can read the words with 90 to 95 percent accuracy and can answer correctly 70 to 90 percent of comprehension questions. Instructional level texts provide children with just the right challenge for them to learn through teacher guidance.

Determining Instructional Level and Selecting Children

Assigning students to small groups for guided reading requires that teachers know every child's instructional reading level. To determine this, they ask children to read aloud books whose levels are known (Brabham & Villaume, 2002) and take running records (see Chapter 5) or they use an individualized reading inventory, a commercial assessment that determines instructional level. Teachers can identify the difficulty level for books they already own by consulting published lists (e.g., Fountas & Pinnell, 2010), or they can purchase books already leveled. Basal or core reading publishers level their own books, and they often provide assessments, with leveled reading passages and comprehension questions that teachers can use to determine children's instructional reading levels. To assess children's instructional reading levels, teachers need short passages (approximately 100 to 200 words in length) taken from books on a range of different difficulty levels. They have children begin reading from the easiest passage—perhaps at the first- or second-grade level (level 16, 18; or I, J). Teachers can make copies of the texts of these passages. As children read, teachers record miscues on the copy of the text, then count the number of words children read incorrectly and determine the percentage of words read correctly. Then the teacher would ask children to answer five questions about the tests—some at the literal level, some at the inferential level, and one about a vocabulary meaning. For example, a child who reads a 100-word passage with eight errors demonstrates word-identification accuracy of 92 percent. A child who answers four out of five questions correctly has a comprehension level of 80 percent. This indicates that the passage the child read was at the instructional level.

Once each child's instructional level is determined, teachers select children with similar instructional levels to form guided-reading groups of four to six children (Taberski, 2000). Teachers check children's instructional levels frequently so that they can regroup children to match their changing instructional levels. Teachers meet with each group of children three to five times per week for twenty to thirty minutes of instruction.

In guided-reading instruction, teachers begin by having children reread a familiar book to gain fluency. They then provide an introduction to a new book, and children read a few pages of this book silently (children reading at the second-grade level are expected to make the transition to silent reading). Then teachers guide discussion about that portion of the text. The children continue reading through the text with the teacher demonstrating strategies as needed. Lastly, teachers will teach predetermined skill lessons such as demonstrating a new decoding or comprehension strategy, helping children clarify and extend new vocabulary words, discussing and clarifying difficult bits of text, or helping children infer character traits or locate words with a particular suffix.

Explicit Teaching of Orthographic Decoding and Vocabulary Using Shared Reading in Guided-Reading Instruction

Shared reading is especially useful in helping children learn strategies for decoding words and learning to make inferences about a word's meaning; during shared reading, the children and teacher see the same text together in enlarged format. For example, a third-grade teacher used *Golem* (Wisniewski, 1996) in a shared reading experience to demonstrate how to decode difficult words and to infer their meanings in one of her guided-reading groups. She scanned the first page of the book and projected it on the class Smart Board. The children in the group took turns reading the text. As they came to the difficult words, the teacher demonstrated how to break each word apart and to find chunks they knew. Then they discussed what they already knew about the word's meaning. The children decoded and discussed the meanings of *Protestant, ignorant, matzoh, incited,* and *vicious.* Each time the students encountered a new and difficult word, the teacher modeled how to stop and look all the way through the word; break the word into parts; and use familiar word parts, such as *tes, tant, ig, ant, mat, in,* and *ous,* to decode the word. She modeled rereading the entire sentence saying the new word. She also modeled how to read the surrounding text to look for clues that would help her infer the word's meaning. Later, she supported the children as they began practicing using the strategy.

At the end of the shared reading lesson, she guided the children in summarizing the steps in the decoding and word meaning strategy and wrote them on an anchor chart. Over the next several days, the teacher used the anchor chart in guided-reading lessons to remind children how to use this strategy upon need.

Explicit Teaching of Comprehension Strategies and Vocabulary Meanings in Guided-Reading Instruction

Transitional readers in second grade and beyond need to learn how to transfer the comprehension strategies they are learning in read-alouds to their own reading (see Figure 10.3). For example, they need to be able to infer character traits and see how a story's problems, its plot, and possible themes are related to these traits (Taberski, 2000). *Fox and his Friends* (Marshall, 1982) is a perfect text for helping second-grade readers learn how to use this strategy. First, the teacher reminds children about this strategy (usually strategies are introduced first in whole-class, interactive read-alouds). She has already taught the meaning of character traits (enduring qualities), how they can be inferred (by what the character does, says, and thinks and by what others say about the character), and demonstrated thinking aloud to find a trait. Now she wants children to do this while reading in guided reading.

To prepare for reading, the teacher usually decides how much text the children will read. She also plans a focus for the discussion after reading, depending on their purpose for reading. Transitional readers in second grade and beyond can read several pages of text, but in this case the teacher wants the children to decide where to stop reading when they think they have discovered information about Fox's character traits. Now the children read, stop when they find information about Fox, and turn to a neighbor to tell what character trait they have inferred and what evidence they have. When all the children have shared with a partner, the teacher leads a discussion about the traits children have discovered. As they talk, the teacher has children reread portions of the text aloud to support their ideas.

Next, the teacher asks the children to use what they have discovered about Fox to predict a problem that will occur in the story. As the children leave guided reading, the teacher asks them to finish reading the book on their own and to fill in a character cluster for Fox. A **character cluster** is a circle with the character's name written in it, with rays out to other circles in which children write the character's traits and the supporting evidence.

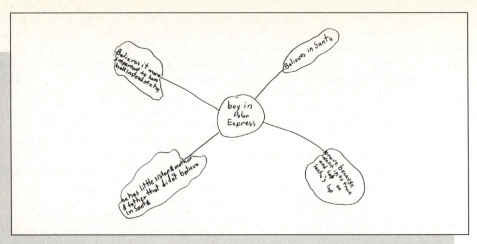

FIGURE 10.5   Character Cluster for *The Polar Express* (Van Allsburg, 1985)

For example, Figure 10.5 presents a character cluster written by a third grader for the main character—the boy—in *The Polar Express* (Van Allsburg, 1985). This child noticed the boy's altruism (although she did not have the sophisticated vocabulary to label this concept) when she said, "[I]t was more important to have the bell instead of a toy." She also clearly identified the boy as a believer and as brave, two character traits strongly implied in the text. She was able to find two details from the text as support for one character trait (the boy was brave "because he went on the train" and "he sat on Santa's lap").

Children also need to attend to the rich vocabulary found in the texts they read during guided reading. One way to stimulate children's active thinking about words and their meanings is to construct **word walls** for specific books. As children in a guided-reading group read a book together, they can select interesting and important story words to place on a special word wall. After gathering the words on the wall, teachers can help children extend their understandings of these words using a **list, group, and label activity** (Tompkins & McGee, 1993). A group of third graders constructed a *Keep the Lights Burning, Abbie* word wall (Roop & Roop, 1985). The word wall included the words *Puffin, medicine, lighthouse, trimmed, wicks, towers, pecked, scraped, waded, henhouse, dangerous, weather, whitecaps, steered, ruffled, Hope, Patience,* and *Charity.* Next, pairs of children used the words in a list, group, and label activity. They selected three to five words from the word wall list to form a group. Then they described how the words were alike (the label portion of the activity). They wrote the words on a transparency along with the label for their group of words. Then, using the overhead projector, they shared their group of words and title with the guided-reading group. One pair of children grouped the words *scraped, waded, trimmed, pecked,* and *steered* with the title "things you can do"; another pair of children grouped *pecked, ruffled,* and *henhouse* with the title "words related to hens"; and a third pair of children gathered *weather, whitecaps,* and *dangerous* with the title "words related to a storm."

Sometimes teachers can alert students to vocabulary they will encounter before reading and then engage children in discussions about words after reading. For example, before reading *The Watsons Go to Birmingham—1963* (Curtis, 1995), the teacher prepared a chart with the categories of "setting," "character," "action/problem," and "describing word." Then students predicted in which category the words *hostile place, vital, incapable, emulate,* and *intimidate* would be used in the story and after reading found evidence to indicate the actual categories (Baumann, Ware, & Edwards, 2007, p. 110). Another strategy is called "ten important words plus" (Yopp & Yopp, 2007). After reading a selection, students are instructed to find ten words they believe are the most important words to convey the meaning of the text. They write each of their words on a sticky note. Then teachers help students place the sticky notes across a whiteboard in a graph format. First, one student lays out his or her words across the bottom of the board. Then the next student adds his or her words, putting words that are the same right above the first student's words. This continues until all students have laid out their words. Most teachers find that some words are gathered by several students, some words are gathered by a few students, and some words are unique to particular students. They help students discuss the "most critical words," those that the most children selected in common, and then talk about the unique words and why they were selected. Next, students do the plus activities (adapted from p. 159):

- Use a thesaurus to locate synonyms of a word.
- Use a thesaurus to locate antonyms of a word.
- Generate sentences using the word.
- Write the word in different forms (verb, noun, adjective, adverb).
- Draw two pictures to depict the meaning of the word.
- Dramatize the meaning of the word.

Reading Information Books in Guided Reading

Guided reading should include instruction in special techniques for reading information books. For example, informational texts have much **content-specific vocabulary,** words that have specific scientific meanings and that do not appear in everyday conversation (Leu & Kinzer, 1999). Information books intentionally introduce scientific terms that are used to explain phenomena. For example, *Bald Eagle* (Morrison, 1998) provides definitions and illustrations of *nestling, prenatal down, natal down, egg tooth, eye shield, fledgling, thermal soaring, kettle, eyrie,* and *embryo*. Most information books provide more than one source of information about content-specific vocabulary. Definitions are embedded in text, provided in glossaries, and illustrated in diagrams and drawings.

Using Guided Reading and Readers' Theater to Foster Fluency

Fluent reading involves quick and accurate word recognition and appropriate prosody (voicing and phrasing) (Kuhn, 2003). It includes a component of comprehension because readers cannot read with appropriate phrasing if they do not understand what they are reading (Deeney, 2010). Fluency can be built through repeated reading of familiar text, with each reading bringing a reader to quicker, better-phrased reading. In most guided-reading groups, teachers begin the lesson by having students spend five to eight minutes rereading familiar texts. These texts can be read silently to build silent reading fluency or pairs of children can read a text aloud to build oral reading fluency.

Teachers sometimes need to address fluency problems more directly with students who read word by word and with slow plodding rate and intonation. English language learners may be learning how to use punctuation to determine phrasing, and teachers may need to demonstrate how to locate commas or divide long stretches of sentences into phrases. Students need to make their eyes move to the next phrase and read the phrase as a whole rather than try to read individual words more quickly. Echo reading, in which the teacher reads a sentence first followed by the students echo reading, is one method to teach phrasing and intonation. In general, teachers would want all students to reach the average fluency rate for end-of-the-year targets (adapted from Hasbrouck & Tindal, 2006):

- First grade: 55 words correct per minute
- Second grade: 90 words correct per minute
- Third grade: 110 words correct per minute
- Fourth grade: 125 words correct per minute
- Fifth grade: 140 words correct per minutes

In order to find the words correct per minute, teachers use a timer set at one minute and have students read a familiar text aloud. The teacher, on a copy of the text, writes the miscues and then counts the numbers of words read correctly. When students do not reach the target rate for their grade, they can listen to it read again by the teacher or listen to it read on audio tape or podcast and then reread it again. For example, a fifth-grade student reading on the third-grade level read ninety-five words with five miscues or errors in one minute. His reading rate is

$$95 - 5 = 90 \text{ correct words per minute}$$

He has not achieved the rate that third-grade-level readers are expected to reach (110 correct words per minute) and is far below the expected rate at fifth grade (140 correct words per minute). His teacher would begin more intensive instruction in fluency and work to reach at least third-grade-level rate (because that is his instructional level).

Readers' theater is an effective activity for increasing reading fluency and comprehension. Readers' theater is a simple form of dramatization in which players read their lines rather than memorize them (Trousdale & Harris, 1993; Wolf, 1993). Players usually sit on stools but may stand in groups. There are no props or costumes. To begin readers' theater, teachers write or select a script. The teacher and children read the script together, and then children break into groups to practice reading the script on their own.

An exemplary second-grade teacher, Mr. Young used a systematic approach to readers' theater to provide an authentic context for children to practice reading the same text repeatedly using appropriate prosody and expression (Young & Rasinski, 2009). Mr. Young's approach to reading instruction was to first teach a **mini-lesson** in reading to the entire class as the first part of his ninety-minute reading block. Following the mini-lesson, all children read books independently (books at their independent reading level or books previously read in guided reading). During this time, Mr. Young taught two guided-reading groups. Then all the children were assigned in pairs to workstations (using a pocket chart to show the workstation rotation for each week). Also during this time, Mr. Young taught two additional reading groups. His highest reading group participated in literature circle rather than guided reading (see the discussion on literature circles later in this chapter) and met a few times a week to have literature discussion with and without Mr. Young.

On Mondays, Mr. Young introduced the readers' theater scripts that would be read that week. He would read the title and have students predict; as he read through the script (demonstrating reading with phrasing and appropriate interpretation), he would pause and ask questions or have students revise their predictions. After reading, he would clarify vocabulary and discuss the overall meaning of the script. Then children were assigned to a script based on their guided-reading group. Children reread the script at home that night. On Tuesday, ten minutes of the mini-lesson time was devoted to small groups of children who read the same script to decide on parts (again, a problem-solving method was used to resolve conflicts). Then, during independent reading that day, everyone highlighted their parts and practiced reading them. On Wednesday and Thursday, during ten minutes of mini-lesson, each group practiced reading the script aloud. Mr. Young taught students to be supportive of each other and offer alternative interpretations for reading. He stressed that reading together the entire script as a whole group was one way to prepare for a presentation. He circulated around to the different groups supporting a group as students read parts and was especially mindful of being available to help struggling readers. Everyone used part of their independent reading time to rehearse their parts again—and many children used arrival time to gain another minute or two for practice. All scripts were performed each Friday to as many authentic audiences as possible. Readers' theater works just as well using poetry or nonfiction books (Young & Vardell, 1993).

Explicit Teaching of Spelling

Guided spelling also occurs in small groups of children with similar abilities. Here, instruction is about spelling patterns the members of a group are just beginning to recognize and use. For example, some children may be working on particular vowel spellings, others on suffixes or prefixes, and still others on dropping a final *e* or doubling a final consonant before adding *ing*.

Children in second grade and beyond are likely to be beyond the stage of letter-name spelling discussed in Chapter 9. They will be within-a-word or syllable juncture spellers (Bear, Invernizzi, Templeton, & Johnston, 2008). Within-a-word spellers learn about vowels: long, *r*-controlled, and others, as well as complex consonant clusters and contractions. Syllable juncture spellers learn about open and closed syllables (syllables that have long and short vowels), how to add suffixes to words, and about the spelling and meaning of a variety of prefixes and suffixes. For example, children learn that words having a CVC pattern require doubling the final consonant before adding the suffix, as with *hop* and *hopping*. Also important is learning to differentiate the appropriate spellings of homophones and homographs. **Homophones** are words that sound alike but are not spelled alike, as in *bear* and *bare*. **Homographs** are words that are spelled alike but do not sound alike, such as the words *bow* (weapon used to shoot arrows) and *bow* (to bend from the waist). Again, **word-sort activities** and word-locating activities are appropriate. For example, children can sort words that take *s* or *es* or *ies* as their plural spellings (Fresch & Wheaton, 1997). Other activities include **word hunts,** in which children search for words with specific patterns in books, magazines, and newspapers. Children work with a spelling each week using open and closed sorts, word hunts, and writing sorts (Bear et al., 2008). As children learn about new spelling patterns, they locate the patterns in words they can already read and practice learning to spell these words. Then children practice using these patterns in new and unknown words in order to decode the words. Spelling instruction in second grade and above always includes a spelling portion of the lesson and then an application part of the lesson in which children use the patterns to read new words.

Advanced Word Study

Whole-class word study in second grade and beyond increasingly focuses on multisyllable words, such as *elephant, writing,* and *rewrite.* The texts that children read both for reading instruction and for content study increasingly have sophisticated vocabulary with more than one syllable, with specific scientific meanings, or with multiple meanings beyond children's everyday experiences. Therefore, studying words and their structures is critical for all children, but especially for children who are English language learners. In order to focus on multisyllable words, children must increasingly use word "chunks" in their decoding and spelling. Their word identification relies less on applying phonics generalizations that merely match one or two letters with a single phoneme (e.g., the letter *m* and the sound /m/ or the letters *oa* and the sound /O/) and more on recognizing combinations or "chunks" of sounds and letters that function predictably and reliably in many words (e.g., *at* in *fat, flat,* and *flattered*). Many English words are constructed from such chunks. For example, among the chunks in *complete, balloon, emotion, presuppose, imaginary,* and *supplement* are *com, oon, tion, pre, up, pose, ary,* and *ment,* which are also found in *compare, spoon, election, predict, cup, impose, fragmentary,* and *complement.* Some of these chunks are merely common sound combinations; and others are meaningful root words, prefixes, or suffixes. Being able to quickly see these chunks of letters that are common across many different words allows speeded and nearly automatic word recognition of words children have never seen before; thus, it is critical that teachers help them see these letter combinations.

Learning about Sound Chunks in Making Big Words

One way to help children develop an intuitive sense of syllables and how to break words apart into familiar chucks is to use the making-big-words approach (Cunningham & Hall, 1994). **Making big words** begins with a big word's letters, for example, the letters in *pickpockets* (p. 83). Teachers help children make one-syllable words that highlight a variety of familiar word parts such as the words *pet, sit, tick,* and *sock.* Then children build multisyllable words, again focusing on the use of multiple familiar word parts in these words, including *picket, pocket,* and *cockpit.* Finally, they build *pickpockets.* Throughout the activity, the teacher and children discuss the words' meanings. Teachers can keep a list of familiar word parts (such as *ick, ock, et,* and *it*) that can be used to decode and spell big words on a spelling word-part word wall.

Learning about Morphemes, Base Words, and Affixes

Increasingly, word study will introduce children to morphemes. **Morphemes** are units of meaning. A word may be a single unit of meaning, as in *flow,* which means to move along in a stream, and as in *flower,* which means the blossom of a plant. Or a word may have more than one morpheme. For example, *flowed* has the meaning of *flow* plus the meaning of "already happened" or past tense; and *flowers* has the meaning of *flower* plus the meaning of "more than one" or plural. As we discussed in Chapter 1, **free morphemes** may stand alone; like *flow* and *flower,* they need not be attached to another morpheme. **Bound morphemes,** like *-ed* and *-s* in *flowed* and *flowers,* must be attached to another morpheme. Much depends on context; *-ed, -s,* and *-er* are not always morphemes. We have seen that *-ed* and *-s* are morphemes in *flowed* and *flowers,* but they are not in *red* and *is.* And *-er* is not a morpheme in *flower,* but it is in *flatter,* in which it means "more" (if something is flatter, it is more flat than that to which it is being compared), and in *farmer,* in which it means "one who" (a farmer is one who farms).

Affixes are bound morphemes, either at the beginning of a base word, where we call them **prefixes,** or at the end, where we call them **suffixes.** Suffixes are either inflectional suffixes (e.g., *-s, -es, -ed, -ing, -'s, -s', -er,* and *-est*), which signal such meanings as number (*dog/dogs, box/boxes*), tense (*walk/walked/walking*), possession (*boy/boy's/boys'*), and degree of comparison (*flat, flatter, flattest*) or derivational suffixes (e.g., *-less, -ment, -ly, -ful, -able, -ish, -ize, -ify,* and *-ion*), which change a word's part of speech, as when *-ful* changes the verb *help* to the adjective *helpful.*

When teaching about suffixes, teachers may show children the base word and then carefully add suffixes. Inflectional suffixes are easier to learn than derivational suffixes because inflectional suffixes usually do not change the part of speech of base words. Teachers demonstrate putting on and removing suffixes, compare words' meanings with and without suffixes, and help children construct sentences using various forms: *help, helps, helped, helping, helper, helpless, helpful, unhelpful, helpfully, helplessly.*

A prefix alters the meaning of a base word in a predictable way. For example, the prefix *re-* usually means "again" as in *rewrite,* while the prefix *un-* usually means "not" as in *unhappy.* To teach prefixes, best practice suggests teaching them in "families," in which all the prefixes in the family have similar meanings (Baumann et al., 2007) and focus on the most frequently used examples in the families (Kieffer & Lesaux, 2007). Figure 10.6 presents a list of prefixes in meaning-related families that are of high and medium frequency that teachers can use to plan instruction.

FIGURE 10.6 Prefixes in Meaning-Based Families of High and Moderate Frequency

Meaning-Based Family		Prefix	Sample words
Again		re*	Restart, reboot
Not, opposite of		un*	Uneven, unstoppable
		in*	Incorrect, inconvenient
		im*	Impossible, impertinent
		ir*	Irreverent, irregular
		il*	Illformed, illequipped
		dis*	Disconnect, disarray
		non*	Nonfunctioning, nondisclosure
Against		anti*	Antisocial, antigovernment
Position:	before	pre	Preview, preorder
	between	inter	Intersperse, intermittent
	middle	mid	Midpoint, midline
	across	trans	Transcontinental, transaction
Value:	too little	under*	Undervalued, underdog
	too much	over	Overvalued, overboard
	under	sub	Subfloor, subbasement
	over, more	super	Supercooled, superconductor,
	half	semi	Semiprecious, semiannual
Add to		en*	Entitle, enlarge
		em	Empower, emancipate
Wrongly		mis	Misrepresent, mismatch

Source: Adapted from Baumann, Ware, & Edwards, 2007, p. 115, and Kieffer & Lesaux, 2007, p. 141.

INDEPENDENT READING PRACTICE

CHILDREN NEED TO READ many more texts than the few they read during guided-reading instruction. They need to read easy books thirty minutes or more each day in school with the same amount of time again at home (Allington, 2008). This volume of reading is necessary to build stamina or endurance, consolidate sight word knowledge, and encourage independent practice of skills and strategies taught in whole-class and small-group instruction. Therefore, most classrooms have children engage in silent, independent reading for up to thirty minutes, shorter at the beginning of the year (while other children might be engaged in guided-reading groups). To manage independent reading and make it productive for all children, teachers need to (Reutzel, Jones, Fawson, & Smith, 2008)

- plan how to help children select books,
- arrange books so that children can easily browse and make decisions on book selections,
- foster students' motivation to read
- hold them accountable for reading, and
- monitor how well independent reading is going with individual children.

Selecting and Arranging Books for Independent Reading

In the beginning of the year, and for younger or struggling readers, the teacher carefully helps each child select ten to fifteen picture books at his or her **independent reading level** as a part of guided-reading instruction (Taberski, 2000). These would be books recently read or books the teacher is very confident the child can read with ease. From these books, each child is expected to have available two to four books for a particular day's independent reading. Many teachers have children keep these books in bags that hang on their chairs. For older readers, and later in the year, teachers expect students to be able to select on their own chapter books at their independent level. An easy rule is to begin reading a text and make a mark for each difficult word that is encountered. If more than five difficult words are located on a page of text, it is likely too difficult. A "just right" book will have only one to three challenging words per page. Students are expected to have a "just right" book in their desk before school starts and may use only five minutes of reading time to select a new "just right" book.

A more challenging approach to helping students find the "just right" book that they will enjoy, understand, and complete is to use the BOOKMATCH approach (Wutz & Wedwick, 2005). Students consider nine questions. Teachers who use this approach put the questions on a bookmark, which the students use during book-browsing time (adapted from Wutz & Wedwick, 2005, p. 17):

- Is the **B**ook length OK for me, not too long and not too short?
- Does the book have **O**rdinary language that I can understand?
- Do I feel comfortable with the book's **O**rganization, the size of print, and number of words per page?
- When I read the title and back cover, do I **K**now something related to the book?
- Will this be **M**anageable for me? After reading a bit, do I think I will be able to finish it?
- Does this genre **A**ppeal to me?
- Do I know something about the book's **T**opic?
- When I read the title and summary, do I **C**onnect to the story already?
- Overall, do I think I will have **H**igh interest in the characters, plot, genre, and topic?

To organize books for browsing, most teachers place baskets of books in various locations around the classroom to avoid a jam of students in any one location such as the book center. Teachers label baskets with the genre and then put stickers on each book indicating difficulty level (Reutzel et al., 2008). Teachers may have a map of where all the baskets are located so children can easily find the graphic novels, for example. In general, students know the range of difficulty that usually produces "just right" books for them. They start browsing at a favorite genre basket, then look for difficulty levels or interesting titles. Teachers can help children select books by giving book talks frequently. **Book talks** are short explanations of a little bit about books. Teachers show the book and then tell a little about its characters and plot. Amazon .com and other bookstores online frequently have book trailers that students can watch. Teachers also have a book review bulletin board in which classmates review books using a rating scale similar to the one movie critics use.

Fostering Motivation and Accountability

Many teachers have children complete a reading log or **response journal** several times a week that lists the books and number of pages they have read. Teachers demonstrate writing in their journal by recording the date, title, author, genre of the book, and the current page number they are on. Then they respond by answering prompts such as (Kelley & Clausen-Grace, 2006, p. 153)

- *I'm wondering*
- *I remember*
- *I'm thinking that*
- *I feel sorry for*
- *Can you believe*
- *When I read _____, I was reminded of*
- *WOW!*

Often, teachers respond to children's response journals by writing a reply to each student about once a week. Other teachers have children locate three or more new and interesting words from their independent reading and record these in their reading logs.

Monitoring an Individual Student's Reading

Although most children quickly find books for independent reading, sustain their reading, and often produce insightful responses, this is not true for all children. Therefore, teachers need a way to monitor how much students are reading, how well they are reading, and how broadly they are reading across genres. We recommend that the first five to eight minutes of independent reading time should be spent in a modified "status of the class" (Kelley & Clausen-Grace, 2006) and conferences (Reutzel et al., 2008). Each day of the week five or six students can be targeted for short conferences in which teachers first record the status of reading for each of the students in a notebook by having these students tell the title of the book and page they are reading. Then teachers meet with individual students and ask them to read a paragraph of a book they are currently reading and to talk about it. This is a quick check on whether the book is "just right" and students are comprehending appropriately. The teacher may check on the volume of reading across the week (whether an appropriate number of pages have been read) and encourage students who seem to be in a genre rut to try a new genre.

Using Book Club as an Alternative to Independent Reading

An alternative to self-selected independent reading is sometimes to form **book clubs** (Raphael & McMahon, 1994) to read and discuss the same book and occasionally do book-related response activities together as a group. The following are activities of a book club:

- Children or teachers select a book.
- Teachers model how to talk during book discussions.
- Children read the book without teacher guidance alone or in pairs.
- Children participate in literature discussions without the teacher.
- Children sometimes participate in response activities.

The heart of the book club approach is the actual book discussions (Goatley, Brock, & Raphael, 1995). To start a book club, the teacher provides multiple copies of several books, previews them for the class, and then signs up a club of children who are interested in each of the different books. The book club meets and sets the number of chapters to be read and a date to have the first book club discussion. Children read the book without teacher guidance and then have a discussion. Children can have very productive literature discussions without the involvement of the teacher (Almasi, 1995); however, children are sometimes given particular roles to play in the discussion. One child might be responsible for locating three or four new and interesting words and defining them and putting them in a sentence. Another student might be responsible for coming up with three ideas to talk about. Another student might be responsible for asking a "long question," one that requires considerable talk. Another student might be responsible for giving a summary of the main events. Another student might be the leader who asks an open-ended question to get the discussion going: "Who has a question they want to ask first. Now, let's have the new words. Now let's have the ideas." After the three ideas are talked about, the leader would call upon the long questioner to pose the question. Finally, the summarizer would give the summary.

Book clubs focusing on poetry can be exciting additions to children's independent reading practice. Poetry is an important literary genre that all too often is neglected in elementary school. However, teachers have discovered that poetry "not only [is] accessible to primary children, [but] can be the genre that excites children and motivates them to read and write" (Duthie & Zimet, 1992, p. 14).

Using Literature Circles or Strategy Groups instead of Guided Reading

We recommend guided-reading groups for most readers and especially for struggling readers and English language learners reading below grade-level expectations. However, teachers have found that opening reading instruction to groups of children who read the same selection of literature in literature circles or grouping and regrouping children into strategy groups are alternatives to guided-reading instruction. With literature circles, teachers use mini-lessons with whole groups to teach strategies and skills; then they monitor small groups of children who are in a literature circle as they more independently discuss literature selections (great for advanced readers and self-regulated learners). Teachers sometimes meet with literature circles to extend discussions and to teach new and important strategies. Teachers often confer with individual children about their reading to teach individualized and very short strategy lessons. Literature circles can be considered book clubs, but they form the heart of a reading program rather than being used sometimes as an alternative to individual independent reading practice.

Other teachers use strategy groups as an alternative to guided reading (Boushey & Moser, 2009). Here, students are reading different books on different levels, but they need to learn the same strategy such as chunking words or checking for understanding (who did what?). Teachers pull this group of students together to teach the strategy, then call the group again a day or so later to see if students are now using the strategy in their own independent reading. Again, conferring with individual children is a critical part of this approach as it is used to identify which children need to be included in a particular strategy group lesson.

WRITING

CHILDREN IN THE SECOND GRADE AND BEYOND know from their experiences in kindergarten and first grade the beginnings of a **process approach to writing:** they have prepared to write, written first drafts, and then revised and edited their drafts with support from the teacher. Children learn more independently how to use these processes to craft sophisticated tests in a variety of genres and publish them in diverse media in second grade and beyond during writing workshop. **Writing workshop** usually consists of a mini-lesson taught by the teacher, extended periods for student writing (in which small groups of students might meet to revise or edit together), and sharing.

Components of Writing Workshop: Explicitly Teaching the Writing Processes

Generally, there are five writing processes: prewriting, drafting, revising, editing, and publishing. **Prewriting** includes a writer's search for a topic, identification of audience and purpose, and collection of ideas about which to write. Many young children plan for writing during prewriting by talking to a friend or to their teacher, by writing a list of ideas, by role-playing an experience, by creating a cluster or semantic web, by listening to or reading literature, or by simply thinking. The purpose of rehearsing and planning during prewriting is to generate ideas and formulate plans for writing.

Mrs. Giovanni is an exemplary third-grade teacher who uses the writing workshop to teach children how to capitalize on the writing processes to craft highly complex texts. Based on an experience she had one morning with one of her students, Mack, she planned a series of mini-lessons to take her third graders through the writing process as they wrote about memorable experiences. Mack had gone camping with his family and friend for his birthday and had come to school bubbling with information about his great trip. Mrs. Giovanni and Mack talked for six or seven minutes before school on the playground about all the activities Mack did on his trip. Later, Mrs. Giovanni decided to have students write about their memorable experiences. She gathered several touchstone texts (Ray, 1999) (texts that model a specific writing style, genre, or technique) to use to teach this lesson including *The Relatives Came* (Rylant, 1985), *Too Many Tamales* (Soto, 1993), and *Knuffle Bunny* (Willems, 2004). Her students were very familiar with these stories and had heard her read them aloud several times. Each one told of a memorable event in a child's life. During the first lesson, she taught the concept of a "memorable experience" as one in which the writer experiences an event that causes strong emotions. Writers of memorable experiences share details of what they thought, felt, heard, saw, tasted, and smelled in order to show what they were feeling and why. She used the touchstone texts to read portions of their descriptions of a memorable moment. The students brainstormed their memorable moments with partners as part of prewriting. Next, they were asked to describe the setting of these experiences in as much detail as possible with their partner and several children shared with the whole group, again as a scaffold for prewriting. Finally, they wrote their first draft of their memorable moment.

Drafting is the writing process in which children first write their ideas. First drafts of inexperienced and struggling writers can be short, sometimes consisting of only a few words or sentences even when prewriting activities have been robust. More accomplished writers write longer first drafts and more consciously consider the necessity of writing details—but all writers struggle to get their ideas written down in a first draft. Mrs. Giovanni was not surprised at Mack's first draft. It had six sentences and lacked emotion or detail (Figure 10.7). There were many reluctant writers in her classroom, and like Mack, their first drafts would need extensive revision activities in order to produce a gripping account of an experience that evoked strong emotion.

Revising is the writing process in which children rethink what they have written. In revising, children reread their drafts and add, move, or delete words, phrases, sentences, and even paragraphs. The first revision mini-lesson that Mrs. Giovanni planned was to teach the illustrating-images strategy (Heard, 2002). In this revision strategy, students look at a piece of writing and underline an activity or event that they wrote about and then draw a picture illustrating that activity. Mack was highly motivated to select the art medium for this activity: colored pencils. He underlined the word *tubeing* [sic] and drew a picture of himself tubing in the river. Then Mrs. Giovanni challenged the students to think of another event that took place during their memorable experience—one they wrote about or didn't include in their first draft—and to draw an illustration for that event. Mack drew a picture of riding down a very tall and twisty hill on his bike, the pop-up tent

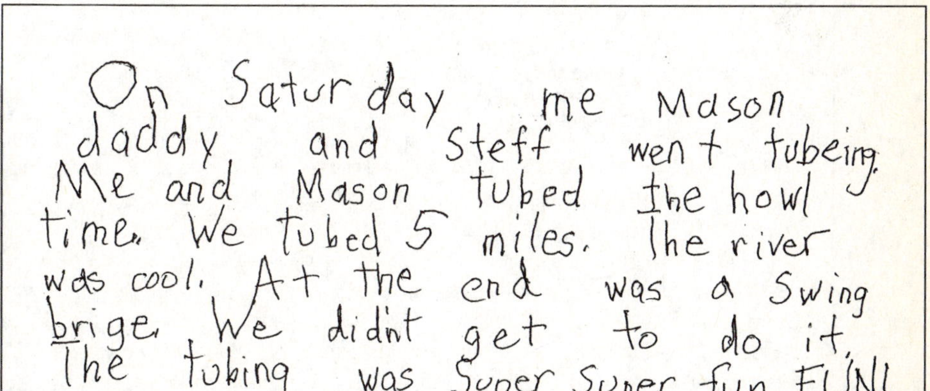

> On Saturday me Mason daddy and Steff went tubeing. Me and Mason tubed the howl time. We tubed 5 miles. The river was cool. At the end was a Swing brige. We didnt get to do it. The tubing was Super Super fun FUN!

FIGURE 10.7 Mack's First Draft of "My Birthday Weekend"

they slept in, and his parents kayaking. None of these ideas were included in his first draft. The lesson ended as several children, including Mack, told about their illustrations.

During a second mini-lesson, Mrs. Giovanni taught the slow motion revising strategy. She talked with the students about "slowing down time and playing it in slow motion" so they could recall what they were thinking, feeling, hearing, seeing, tasting, and smelling (Heard, 2002). She read an example from one of the touchstone texts (*The Relatives Came*) showing how Cynthia Rylant (1993) shared one night of sleeping with all the relatives on the living room floor. She told the students that the more vivid the details are that a writer adds, the more the reader is right there in the moment with the writer. Then she had each student select one of the pictures they drew and quickwrite without thinking of spelling what they saw, heard, felt, smelled, and tasted. Mack's quickwrite about his tubing illustration included *the cool river, the brown muddy river, screaming, rope, swim, canoes, rafts, tubes, trees, grass, hot, sunny, bright, tipping,* and *splashing.*

Now Mrs. Giovanni thought students were ready to write a second draft, but before they did she wanted to help them organize all the new information that they had gathered by drawing images and slowing down time to add details. Each student was challenged to look over all their materials and web their ideas to find the major parts of their story. Mrs. Giovanni demonstrated how one of the touchstone texts, *Knuffle Bunny* (Willems, 2004), had five parts (walking to the Laundromat, at the Laundromat, walking home and discovering Knuffle Bunny was missing, the rushing trip back, and the search for the missing bunny). She demonstrated webbing the ideas using Kidspiration software projected on the whiteboard. During conference time, Mrs. Giovanni helped five children web their memorable experiences. Figure 10.8 presents Mack's web indicating he had four parts to his story: putting up the camper, riding his bike, tubing, and the river itself.

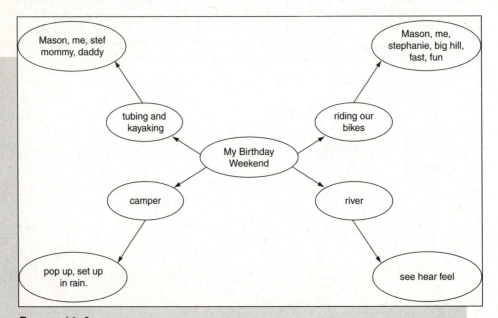

FIGURE 10.8   Kidspiration Web of "My Birthday Weekend"

Then Mack wrote a three-page second draft across two days of the writing workshop using his illustrations, the brainstorm of details, and his web organization. He read the second draft during a conference meeting, and several students asked questions. Later, Mack added in several clarifying words and phrases to his draft. During the conference, Mrs. Giovanni slipped in a lesson on the cracking-open-ordinary-words strategy (Heard, 2002) and challenged Mack to think of other words for *went* (*down the hill*). Mack came up with the words *raced* and *zoomed*.

Now Mrs. Giovanni considered **editing,** the writing process in which children focus on misspellings and errors in capitalization, punctuation, and usage; and **publishing,** which consists of sharing writing with an audience. She decided that because the students had focused so much on revising, she would support the editing process. In addition, the stories were now so good that Mrs. Giovanni wanted to publish them. So she helped her students scan their images into PowerPoint slides and use the program's narration function to record students reading to make digital stories. One of the pages of Mack's digital story is presented in Figure 10.9.

Poetic Elements

Writing workshop is an excellent place to begin a poetry unit or to prepare for a poetry festival in which children present to their parents or other classrooms of children their

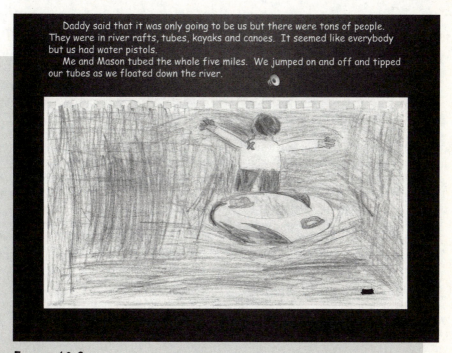

FIGURE 10.9   A Page from Mack's Digital Story: "My Birthday Weekend"

TECHNOLOGY TIE-IN

DIGITAL STORYMAKING

There are two ways to make digital stories using Web-based tools. The easiest way is to use the PowerPoint program available on most computers (and most children and teachers are comfortable with this application). Open the PowerPoint program. Students can type in titles and text, import clip art, download digital photographs and import them from a file, or import scanned pictures or movies. To insert any of these, go to the insert tab and click on the picture; clip art; or, on the far right, the movie icon. Once the PowerPoint is loaded with text and illustrations, students can narrate the show by clicking on the sound icon under the insert tab. Use the pull-down menu under sound icon and click on record sound. The computer must have a built-in microphone and the sound should be adjusted as needed. Different students can narrate each slide of the PowerPoint presentation, and as the slides are advanced each narration will play.

The second way to make digital stories is to use the iMovie (Apple) or Movie Maker (Microsoft Windows) software program. This allows users to capture audio and video materials. A tutorial can be found at www.microsoft.com/windowsxp/using/moviemaker/getstarted.

favorite poems and poems they have written (Durham, 1997). During mini-lessons in a poetry-writing workshop, children learn that not all poems have rhyme, but many do. They learn effective sound elements, such as repetition, alliteration (repeating beginning sounds), rhyme, and assonance (repeating vowel sounds). They learn about using invented words, focusing on a single image, and saying common things in uncommon ways. Finally, children learn about lining, shape, and special uses of punctuation, capitalization, and spaces (Duthie & Zimet, 1992). Together, the teacher and children discuss the impact of using poetic elements in a poem. For example, children noticed that indentations in the poem's lines make the shape of stair steps in the poem "Descent" (Merriam, 1989, p. 36) and different-length lines and special indenting created the shape of a wiggly snake in "The Serpent's Hiss" (Merriam, p. 48). A third grader composed the poem "Tree House," making use of line length and indenting to create a tree-shaped poem appropriate to the topic of his poem.

Tree house
Just you and me house
Kick up your feet house
Tree house
Free
House

Writing Informational Texts

Information books are often neglected both in reading instruction and in writing instruction. However, many children find these texts especially engaging (Duke, 1998; Duthie, 1996). Ray (2004) recommends that teachers use mini-lessons in the writing workshop to introduce children to "Wow! Nonfiction." All information books provide facts, but Wow! Nonfiction books do so in a fashion that especially interests readers in their topics. In writing workshop, the teacher reads aloud portions of a Wow! Nonfiction book, and the children analyze what the writer did to capture their interest. For example, children observed the following (adapted from Ray, 2004, p. 104).

- *I Call It Sky* (Howell, 1999) has facts placed at the end, related to the story.
- *Atlantic* (Karas, 2002) uses first-person narrative so the writer is speaking directly to the reader.
- *Tiger Trail* (Winters, 2000) uses created spellings.
- *Bat Loves the Night* (Davies, 2001) is written in present tense and makes readers believe the activities are happening right this minute.
- *Red-Eyed Tree Frog* (Cowley, 1999) follows the action of one animal.
- *Gentle Giant Octopus* (Wallace, 1998) uses very short sentences with dramatic verbs.

The children recorded their observations on a large poster that remained in the classroom. The teacher in conferences encouraged children to think of which of these techniques would be useful in writing their own informational pieces. Children were expected to use some of the techniques and to be able to explain why they used particular ones to write their own Wow! Nonfiction.

Inquiry Units during Content Study

A balanced literacy program for children in second grade and beyond includes instruction in reading and writing within the context of content study (Williams, Stafford, Lauer, Hall, & Pollini, 2009). Study of content (social studies, science, math, or a combination) takes place in inquiry units and during Internet workshops. **Inquiry units** involve the study of particular topics in social studies and science, using hands-on experiences, a variety of informational texts, and reading and writing activities. The purpose of inquiry units is to increase children's reading and writing abilities as well as their understanding of science and social studies concepts (Reutzel, Smith, & Fawson, 2005). **Internet workshops** are much like writing workshops but with a focus on children's learning to use the Internet to gather information for inquiry units.

Integrating Reading and Writing Nonfiction with Content Exploration

READING AND WRITING INFORMATIONAL TEXTS are important parts of content-area learning. Children need a variety of reading strategies including how to search for specific information, evaluate whether information is relevant for their topic or question, and integrate and summarize information across several texts (Connor, Kaya, Luck, Toste, Canto, Rice, et al., 2010). They need strategies for writing nonfiction texts that communicate their new understandings of content such as writing notes during observation and how to write texts that compare and contrast, provide descriptions of processes, and explain phenomena. They need to learn the connections between everyday words and scientific words, and how to analyze information observed, and pose questions. We recommend that teachers use five steps during inquiry units: engage, explore, explain, extend, and evaluate.

Inquiry Units

Engage.   During the engage step, teachers create interest and generate curiosity in the topic of study; they raise questions to explore students' prior knowledge. To engage children's interest in a particular topic, teachers might show illustrations from nonfiction books or read a selection of children's literature aloud. Viewing video clips or photographs from the Internet are other possibilities. In order to determine what children already know about a topic, teachers can introduce a **K-W-L chart** (in which the teacher lists what students *know,* what student *want* to learn, and, later, what they *learned*) before or after reading or viewing. For example, one group of second graders brainstormed what they knew about earthworms and how they helped the soil (Connor et al., 2010) as an engage activity in their inquiry unit about soil habitats. Another group of children who were studying garden flowers participated in an initial discussion about flowers. As the children shared information, the teacher wrote headings related to the different kinds of information that children shared on one chart and questions they had about flowers on another chart. For example, the teacher wrote the following headings: *height* (as children compared and contrasted different flowers and how tall they grew), *color, foliage,* and *fragrance* and the questions *What happens to flowers in the winter?* and *Why do we have to plant some flowers every year and other flowers grow by themselves?* Teachers use these discussions as opportunities to introduce scientific vocabulary that will be used throughout the unit.

Explore.   During the explore step, children observe objects and events from the natural world. For example, in a unit on birds, children can observe a variety of birds in zoos or museums. They can examine different kinds of bird nests, feathers, and bird bones. They can observe and record behavior of birds at a bird feeder. This is the opportunity for students to form hypotheses, record observations and ideas, and suspend judgment. Simple lab worksheets can support children as they observe. For example, second graders who were engaging in a study of soil habitats were given a lab worksheet prior to an observation experience. On one-half of the sheet was written: "Why do you think earthworms help soil? Write your hypothesis or prediction." On the other side of the lab worksheet was written: "What have you observed or learned about your earthworms?" Before beginning the actual observations, the teacher taught a short lesson on how to take notes while doing observations. Then she gave groups of students a clear plastic container with soil and worms to observe. Later, the teacher facilitated a group discussion about the observation, and posed questions: "Why are spaces appearing in the soil? What is the worm doing? What would happen if we put water in the soil? Any hypotheses? What have you observed after a rainfall on the sidewalk or road?" The teacher helped the whole group summarize after its explorations. She prepared charts with several of her prompting questions and supported students in making hypotheses and then connecting these to what they observed.

Explain.   In the explain step, students use nonfiction books to learn more about the topic of study. Previous observations are extended by carefully reading selected portions of information books that provide facts and present drawings related to the observations. This careful searching and gathering of information is different from the open-ended browsing that occurs during the engage phase of the unit. For example, second graders studying soil habitats were taught to use headings and the table of contents to find more information about earthworms. They were encouraged to explain the information they located in their own words. They were taught to use both scientific terms and everyday words and to compare and contrast how scientists would make explanations compared to other people. The teacher again used her scientific question charts she made for the explore phase of the unit to help children begin to consolidate their growing knowledge. Teachers may help children gather information from several sources and keep track of the information using a data recording grid. The teacher and children would gather a variety of resource books, including children's information books, adult information books, and pamphlets about flowers, for example. The teacher would prepare a data recording grid using headings such as *height, spread, color, foliage,* and *fragrance* across the top and the names of three flowers down the side. Over several days, each child would fill in the recording grid with information about a flower of his or her choice. To begin the work, the class would brainstorm a list of flowers, which the teacher would record on a chart.

Elaborate.   In the elaborate step, students apply concepts and skills in new (but similar) situations and use new scientific terms. Students learn to craft explanations using evidence. The second graders built an earthworm habitat terrarium. They talked about what materials (e.g., sand, pebbles, soil, and leaves) to include and in what order. One student argued that the bottom layer of materials should be pebbles or sand to "'keep the soil from getting too moist, because earthworms will not be able to breathe if the soil is too wet'" (Connor et al., 2010, p. 478).

Evaluate.   Finally, during the evaluate step, children locate information to answer questions they generate for themselves. For example, third graders generated the questions, What are the body parts of your bird? and How do these body parts help this bird to survive? (Guthrie, Van Meter, McCann, Wigfield, Bennett, Poundstone, et al., 1996, p. 326). Children selected birds of choice, located information about body parts, and wrote explanations for how the body parts allowed the bird to adapt to its environment through breeding, feeding, and protecting itself. Here, children needed to read carefully in order to detect critical information relevant to the question, integrate information across different texts, and find meanings of specialized vocabulary they were encountering. Children capitalized on knowing how to read graphs, diagrams, and other illustrations. They learned how to break up the question into parts, gather information, and then put the parts back together. In the final phase, children communicated their information in reports, group-authored books, charts, and informational stories. The teacher presented several strategy lessons on how to write scientific comparisons, process descriptions, and explanation texts. Teachers evaluated students' independent use of all the strategies previously used in group lessons.

Internet Workshop

Internet workshop (Leu, 2002) consists of children's searching, reading, and using information from the Internet around a topic of inquiry. The purpose of the Internet workshop is simultaneously to help children learn more about how to use the Internet and develop the special reading strategies needed for this kind of text as well as to help them learn to evaluate and integrate Internet information with other sources of information. Unfortunately, the Internet is now so well used—and abused—by students, that teachers are frustrated with students' copying information from sites that may or may not even be relevant to their topic of study. Therefore, teachers must teach children to effectively search for information, evaluate the information on the sites they select for research, synthesize information, and cite sources (Henry, 2006). Good Web sites will be readable for individual students, will have trustworthy information, and will have useful information for the specific research project. Further, after students have located sites that are readable, trustworthy, and useful, they learn to synthesize the information into their own words without copying and pasting and to use appropriate citations.

To begin, students need to identify a focused purpose for searching the Internet and employ effective search strategies. For example, the more explicit the search string (words typed into the search engine), the more likely the resources identified by the search engine will be actually useful. For example, two students were researching naval battles in the Pacific Ocean during World War II in which the United States Navy participated. To begin their search, their search string was "World War II" and that brought up over six million possible Web sites (Henry, 2006, p. 614). In contrast, the search string "World War II Pacific Naval battles and American involvement" located approximately 174,000 sites—still a large number but an easier beginning than the first search string (p. 623). Students should also learn to read the description of each Web site and examine its URL address for clues about whether they need to click on that site (rather than automatically clicking to the site before doing any preliminary investigation). URL addresses will reveal such information as whether it is a library ("lib" will be in the address), university, museum, or government site.

To teach whether sites are readable, teachers can provide sample pages from three sites (one that is very easy to read with lots of supportive graphics; one that is on grade level with some challenging words but with some supportive graphics; and one above grade level, with very small print, very challenging vocabulary, and difficult-to-understand graphics). Students can discuss whether they would be able to get information from the site and why or why not. Students should conclude that they need to read the site to determine if the words are too hard, if they can understand the information mostly on their own, and whether the graphics are helpful (Baildon & Baildon, 2008).

To help students consider whether a site is trustworthy, teachers may help them locate the author of the site and determine the author's credibility, or search several sites to confirm information is located in more than one site. The date of the site also might influence trustworthiness. Finally, to determine if the information on a particular Web site is useful, teachers should have students brainstorm exact questions they will be researching. For example, if students are studying what plants and animals live in the layers of a rain forest, sites that tell about destruction of the rain forest or use of rain forest to discover new drugs would not be useful.

Once students have found readable, usable, and trustworthy sites, they need to begin to take notes, synthesize information, and keep track of their sources. Taking notes requires students to locate relevant information and to write the source of that information on a note card or a page in a research journal. After notes have been taken on one page, students should read a second site and begin to analyze what information is repeated and what is new information. Gradually, students should begin to see a pattern of organization and be able to write their notes into categories (early battles, battle tactics, etc.). Using a webbing program such as Kidspiration can be helpful in laying out organization.

CULMINATING ACTIVITIES

ONE OF THE MOST IMPORTANT ASPECTS of reading and writing instruction is to create experiences that allow children to develop self-motivation and self-regulation (Perry, Hutchinson, & Thauberger, 2007). Six characteristics of activities that promote self-regulated learning are those that (based on Parsons, 2008, p. 633)

- engage students in tasks that closely resemble tasks that people use in their daily and work lives;
- call upon collaboration among students;
- are challenging, but achievable;
- have a culminating product;
- allow students input into the selection and creation of the end product; and
- require sustained work over several days.

In this book, we have described several culminating projects. For example, we shared how Ms. Meddor's students wrote and published podcasts of their modern folktale variants and Mrs. Giovanni's students published digital stories about memorable events. Other culminating projects mentioned in this chapter include writing reports in a science inquiry unit on how particular parts of birds help them survive and on World War II Naval battles. These are examples of how students used what their teachers had taught them about using reading and writing strategies to accomplish a more independent project on their own or within a small group of peers. These projects called upon using real-world skills such as revising first draft writing or synthesizing information from more than once source. Students were challenged to create an end product worthy of publication using a variety of media. Finally, these activities required sustained engagement over several days. Teachers would not want to use culminating activities with every teaching cycle, every book, or every unit they teach. But they would want to include enough of these challenging activities in order to support self-regulated and self-motivated learners.

Differentiating Instruction for Diverse Learners

THE BALANCED READING AND WRITING APPROACH described in this chapter supports learners who are reading and writing at many different levels. Children are taught in small, guided-reading groups in which they read text matched to their levels of reading ability. They practice spelling words matched to their level of spelling development. They read books independently that their teacher has helped them to select to meet their individual needs as readers. In their writing workshop, the teacher intentionally selects a small group of children for a writers' conference to focus on the strategies those children are working on.

Supporting Struggling Readers with Attention to Fluency

Despite differentiated instruction offered to all children, struggling readers need considerable support in order to make accelerated progress that will catch them up with the average of their peers. The most at-risk struggling readers in grade 2 and above are those children who have not yet made it beyond the first-grade reading level. That is, they have not been able to read texts beyond level 16 or I and are still struggling to read texts at the preprimer or primer level. As students reach third grade or higher and still have instructional reading levels within the first-grade range, they are increasingly likely to have experienced one or two tiers of RTI (response to intervention) and are perhaps on their way to being identified as needing special education. Though many children will need the long-term support of specialists to continue to make progress in reading and writing, other children can make progress in reaching second-grade reading instructional levels and above.

Why is it so critical that children get beyond first-grade reading levels? First, the materials written at those text levels are usually little books that are geared for young six- and seven-year-olds. They have short texts with few words (exactly what young children need to begin reading). But faced with these books again in second grade and then third grade, children rebel at being given "baby books." There are several companies that produce longer books, with contemporary topics of interest to older readers. However, nearly all of these companies produce books with the lowest readability at grade 2 (see Orca Book Publishers). In fact, one of the ways that average and good readers make acceleration is when they begin to read short chapter books in series (e.g., Junie B. Jones books, Magic Tree House books) often written at the second-grade readability level. These books have similar plot structures and the same characters. The vocabulary remains relatively similar across books. Children increase their volume of reading as they begin reading silently and can sustain reading for over an hour. Thus, reaching even second-grade reading level opens up the world of texts for students and provides them with many, many exciting and interesting books they can read and are not ashamed to carry home.

One technique that can be used with struggling readers still reading on the first-grade level in order to get them to the second-grade reading level is to select a text at a slightly higher level than their current instructional level (primer if children are at the preprimer level, or first grade if children are at the primer level). Then the teacher provides high levels of support for reading this text. They provide direct instruction in decoding three or four one-syllable words (words that will be read in the upcoming text), teach a few new sight words (again that will be read in the upcoming text), introduce the text using a talk-through, and then use echo reading to familiarize children with the content of the text. In very small groups, the teacher reads a sentence or two (or a short paragraph or page of text, depending on the amount of support needed), then the student reads. After echo reading, the student rereads the text and the teacher supports the reading by prompting for strategies (see the list of strategies Mrs. Tran uses with her first graders in Chapter 9). On following days, teachers introduce a new text but also students reread the familiar passage and teachers time the rate (correct words per minute) and graph it. Echo reading and repeated readings of the same text are designed to increase accuracy and automaticity of reading (Deeney, 2010). The goal of this kind of fluency-oriented instruction is to increase the level of text until students can reach second-grade reading level. Now teachers will have a wider range of texts that students can read at home, at school for greater practice, and in instructional activities.

Explicit Attention to Vocabulary for Strugglers and English Language Learners

Children in second grade and beyond make a transition from using language to communicate about immediate and everyday concerns to using language to demonstrate understanding of academic topics. The vocabulary demands of this transition are especially great for English language learners (Cummins, 2003). Typically, they have smaller vocabularies for communicating about content-area topics than do their native English-speaking peers. However, struggling readers often have similar problems with the specialized vocabulary found in content materials. Teachers must provide introductions to vocabulary before ELLs and strugglers read content materials, and more extensive practice with vocabulary after reading.

One way of introducing vocabulary before reading is to capitalize on books with labeled drawings (Barone, Mallette, & Xu, 2005). Visual dictionaries such as *The Scholastic Visual Dictionary* (Corbeil & Archambault, 2000) define over 5,000 words using labeled drawings. Many nonfiction books include at least one or two labeled drawings. For example, *Apples* (Gibbons, 2000) has labeled drawings of the parts of an apple and an apple blossom that provide good introductions to the words *stem, seed chambers, skin, core, pollen, stamen,* and *stigma.*

Explicit Attention to Narrative and Expository Text Forms for Strugglers and English Language Learners

In Chapter 5, we described elements typically found in narrative and expository texts. Elementary students demonstrate in their writing that they know some information about narrative and expository text structures. Nonetheless, during the elementary years, teachers will provide direct instruction about how to notice these elements during reading and how to incorporate them in writing. English language learners and struggling readers and writers need this explicit instruction more frequently before reading and writing. For example, narratives generally

- have specific characters who are named
- have a setting, which identifies the location, time, and climate
- have a plot structure based around a problem and conflict, that has a climax and solution
- include sophisticated tier 2 words
- are told from a particular point of view (which may be first or third person)
- are told in the past tense except for dialogue, which is in the present tense
- have a text supported and extended by illustrations of events and settings

In contrast, expository texts may also have text features, such as headings, sidebars, and endnotes or footnotes, and specialized illustrations such as graphs, charts, and illustrated drawings. Expository texts generally

- have generic animals or people
- include a topic introduction
- include a description of attributes
- present characteristic events in a sequence
- may use a compare/contrast, cause/effect, problem/solution, sequence, or descriptive structure
- include sophisticated tier 3, or content-specific words
- have text supported by a variety of illustrations (graphs, diagrams, figures, maps, labeled drawings, cut-away illustrations, lists)

Teachers make sure ELLs know about these features and how to read them by teaching about them prior to reading text with these features (Barone et al., 2005).

Assessing Student Performance for Differentiated Instruction

SECOND, THIRD, AND FOURTH GRADES are times of rapid growth in reading and writing, so teachers need a plan for systematic assessment. Assessment in cycles every eight or nine weeks (or perhaps every twelve weeks) helps teachers pinpoint each student's growth so that more flexible grouping patterns can be used to plan differentiated instruction.

Individualized Reading Inventory

Figure 10.10 presents one systematic plan for assessment. According to this plan, every nine weeks the teacher will administer an Individualized Reading Inventory to each student. An Individualized Reading Inventory is a commercial assessment that includes grade-level word lists that students read in isolation, narrative and expository

FIGURE 10.10   Assessment Plan – Required Every Nine Weeks

Word Study	Comprehension	Fluency	Writing
Weekly spelling assessments of patterns taught	Informal reading inventory—IRI (alternate narrative and expository passages or select one most in need)	Use IRI instructional passages to rate fluency and calculate rate	Rubric scores for writing projects across genres required
End of nine weeks spelling assessment of patterns taught during nine weeks	Assess questions answered on IRI (vocabulary, factual, inferential), retelling as needed		
Cumulative spelling assessment across all nine week periods	Think aloud on alternative version of IRI at the instructional level with silent reading		
Developmental spelling inventory pre and post	Oral or written summary, optional	Fluency assessment on current instructional text in guided reading, optional	
Decoding assessment, as needed	Transcription of grand conversation, optional		

passages at each grade level, and accompanying questions to assess comprehension. Most have alternative passages so that they can be given up to three times a year, but alternating among the narrative and expository passages provides enough for assessing children up to four times a year. These assessments allow teachers to determine if sight word reading is at grade level, the independent and instructional reading level, and level of fluency.

When assessing fluency (which is a combination of phrasing, appropriate use of punctuation, expression, and rate), most IRIs have checklists for phrasing (two-, three-, or four-word phrases), use of punctuation, and expression. Rate must be calculated by counting the number of words in the passage and then timing the reading. The total number of words read correctly is determined by subtracting the errors from the total number of words in the passage. For example, if the passage had 256 words and the student made 16 errors, then the number of correct words read would be 256 – 16 = 240 correct words read. Then the time is calculated into seconds (if the reading took 2 minutes 35 seconds, that would be 155 seconds). The following steps are taken to find the number of correct words read per minute.

1. number of words in the passage = 256
2. number of errors = 16
3. number of words read correctly (subtract: #1 − #2): 256 − 16 = 240
4. multiply number of words read correctly (#3) by 60: 240 × 60 = 14,400
5. calculate number of seconds to read the passage = 155 (2 minutes and 35 seconds)
6. number of words read correctly by minute (divide: #4/#5): 14,400 ÷ 155 = 92 correct words read per minute

For every other assessment cycle, the teacher should have students read the narrative then the expository passage because most students read these slightly differently. When the reading comprehension, fluency, or accuracy rate of one kind of passage is very different from the other, teachers should keep track of the type of passage that is most difficult. Across time, students' fluency should improve and the text levels that are independent and instructional should increase.

Once the instructional reading level is determined, then teachers should use an alternative form (either narrative or expository) and have students read it silently or orally one or two sentences at a time, and after reading do a think-aloud. Students say what they just read in their own words and what this makes them think about. Teachers demonstrate thinking aloud and expanding on what the text says by making inferences, connections, or evaluations. Students are expected to produce most of the following information in their think-alouds:

- literal recall of the sentence gist
- inferred information that expands on the gist of the information
- connections to other texts or students' experiences that expand the information
- connections to previous portions of the texts to the current text being read
- visualizations (or references to what they were picturing in their minds) that expand the gist
- summarizing statements that tie the information so far read together
- critiques of the text in which students evaluate the information from their perspective
- questions that students have about meaning or vocabulary
- appropriate use of vocabulary, especially specialized vocabulary (tier 2 or tier 3 words) in any of the preceding

When students' think-alouds do not include many of these mental actions, teachers will teach each one during a strategy lesson. Across time, students' think-alouds should become richer with the use of most of these activities.

Assessing Writing Using Rubrics

Rubrics are assessment tools that show how well children have learned to use particular features of a genre taught during the writing workshop. Rubrics identify key areas or elements that should be included in a high-quality work sample. Rubrics are even

FIGURE 10.11   Shape Poem Scoring Rubric

Excellent Shape Poem	Good/Adequate Shape Poem	Poor Shape Poem
best handwriting	good handwriting	sloppy handwriting
all words spelled correctly	most words spelled correctly	many words misspelled
good title	has a title	no title
appeals to two or more senses	appeals to one sense	does not appeal to senses
words written in obvious shape of poem's topic	words written in a shape but not clearly related to topic	words written in lines and no shape is obvious
very interesting ideas	some interesting ideas	no interesting ideas

more effective when children and teachers develop the rubric together. Figure 10.11 presents a scoring rubric developed by second graders and their teacher as a part of a poetry writing unit. In the unit, the children learned to use words that appeal to the five senses, lining and shape, alliteration and rhyme, and other poetic elements. They wrote shape poems and developed the rubric to evaluate their poems. The children determined that excellent shape poems would have good ideas, use correct spelling and effectively use punctuation, and be written in good handwriting. Then the teacher guided the children to also think about some of the poetic elements that she had been teaching: the poem's title, the shape of the poem, and appeals to the five senses. Finally, children thought about what an adequate poem and a poor poem might be like compared to the excellent poem.

Figure 10.12 presents Lane's shape poem. His poem was judged to be an excellent shape poem because it had a good title, the shape was related to the poem's topic, it appealed to two senses: taste and sight, he used good handwriting, and he spelled words correctly.

CHAPTER SUMMARY

SECOND, THIRD, AND FOURTH GRADES are an exciting time for children and their teachers. The great strides that students make as they enter and move beyond transitional reading present teachers with great challenges, opportunities, and satisfactions.

During read-aloud of literature, teachers select text sets focused on particular literary elements they wish to teach. They demonstrate literary reading strategies

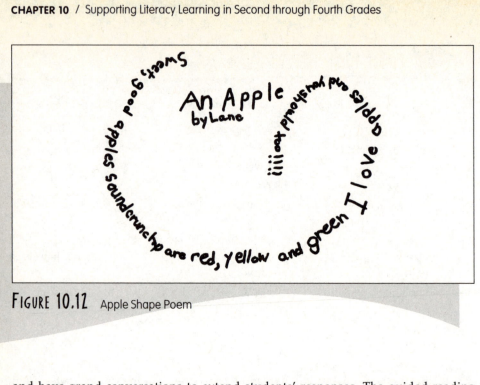

FIGURE 10.12   Apple Shape Poem

and have grand conversations to extend students' responses. The guided-reading approach involves small groups of children reading and discussing a book together at their instructional level. Teachers extend children's understanding of these texts and teach strategies for comprehending, decoding, and discovering vocabulary meanings. They extend children's vocabulary knowledge with activities such as list, group, and label. Children read self-selected easy books daily.

In writing workshop, children use five writing processes: prewriting, drafting, revising, editing, and sharing. Teachers model a variety of writing strategies for each of these processes in mini-lessons and provide guided practice in conference groups. Teachers extend children's understanding of poems and nonfiction in writing workshop by calling attention to poetic elements and having them write Wow! Nonfiction. Word study continues in second grade and beyond, extending children's abilities to spell and decode multisyllabic words. Teachers show children how prefixes and suffixes are useful tools for reading new words and learning about their meanings. A program for learning the spellings of words is also critical.

Readers' theater and repeated reading allow children to enjoy poetry, nonfiction, and stories and provide opportunities for fluency development.

Children read and write informational texts in inquiry units in science and social studies. Children learn to locate, retrieve, and comprehend informational text as they learn new content information. They pay particular attention to the content-specific vocabulary they encounter in information books and learn strategies for independent vocabulary learning. Children also learn more strategic uses of the Internet and to determine whether Web sites are trustworthy, usable, and readable. Finally, they sometimes demonstrate their growing independence and self-regulated learning in culminating activities.

Applying the Information

We suggest two activities for applying the information. Use Figure 10.1 to identify one literary unit you would like to teach. Use the Internet to search more information about this literary element, then put together a text set you would use to teach this unit. Second, visit the Lexile Web site. Select twenty books you would use in guided-reading instruction and use its book-finder function to locate each book's Lexile level. Or, locate a list of the last twenty years of Caldecott winners. Predict which book is most difficult and which one is easiest. Use the Lexile site to identify the books' Lexile levels to check your predictions. Discuss the strengths and weaknesses of using Lexile levels to determine the difficulty of a book.

Going Beyond the Text

Visit a second-, third-, or fourth-grade classroom and observe several literacy activities. Write a list of the elements of the daily routine and note all the opportunities each student has to read and write. Note the print and literacy materials used by the children in the classroom. Take note of the classroom layout and the interactions among the children and between the children and the teacher during literacy activities. Talk with the teacher about his or her philosophy of literacy instruction. Compare these materials, activities, and philosophies with those presented in this chapter.

References

Aardema, V. (1998). *Borreguita and the coyote.* New York: Alfred A. Knopf.

Allington, R. (2008). *What really matters in response to intervention: Research-based designs.* Boston: Allyn & Bacon.

Almasi, J. (1995). The nature of fourth graders' so-ciocognitive conflicts in peer-led and teacher-led discussions of literature. *Reading Research Quarterly, 30,* 314–351.

Baildon, R., & Baildon, M. (2008). Guiding independence: Developing a research tool to support student decision making selecting online information sources. *The Reading Teacher, 61,* 636–647.

Barone, D., Mallette, M., & Xu, S. (2005). *Teaching early literacy development: Development, assessment, and instruction.* New York: Guilford Press.

Baumann, J., Ware, D., & Edwards, E. (2007). "Bumping into spicy, tasty words that catch your tongue": A formative experiment on vocabulary instruction. *The Reading Teacher, 61,* 108–122.

Bear, D., Invernizzi, M., Templeton, S., & Johnston, F. (2008). *Words their way: Word study for phonics, vocabulary, and spelling instruction* (3rd ed.). Upper Saddle River, NJ: Prentice Hall.

Boushey, G., & Moser, J. (2009). *The CAFÉ book: Engaging all students in daily literacy assessment and instruction.* Portland, MD: Stenhouse Publishers.

Brabham, E., & Villaume, S. (2002). Leveled texts: The good and the bad news. *The Reading Teacher, 55,* 438–441.

Cassidy, J., Valadez, C., & Garrett, S. (2010). Literacy trends and issues: A look at the five pillars and the cement that supports them. *The Reading Teacher, 63,* 644–655.

Catling, P. (1952). *The chocolate touch.* New York: William Morrow.

Commeyras, M., & Sumner, G. (1995). *Questions children want to discuss about literature: What teachers and students learned in a second-grade classroom* (NRRC Reading Research Rep. No. 47). Athens, GA: University of Georgia and University of Maryland, National Reading Research Center.

Connor, C., Kaya, S., Luck, M., Toste, J., Canto, A., Rice, D., et al. (2010). Content area literacy: Individualizing student instruction in second-grade science. *The Reading Teacher, 63,* 474–485.

Corbeil, J., & Archambault, A. (2000). *Scholastic visual dictionary.* New York: Scholastic.

Cowley, J. (1999). *Red-eyed tree frog.* New York: Scholastic.

Cummins, J. (2003). Reading and the bilingual student: Fact and friction. In G. Garcia (Ed.), *English learners reaching the highest level of English literacy* (pp. 2–33). Newark, DE: International Reading Association.

Cunningham, P., & Hall, D. (1994). *Making big words.* Torrance, CA: Good Apple.

Curtis, C. (1995). *The Watsons go to Birmingham—1963.* New York: Delacorte Press.

Curtis, C. (2004). *Bud, not buddy.* New York: Laurel-Leaf Books.

Davies, N. (2001). *Bat loves the night.* New York: Scholastic.

Deeney, T. (2010). One-minute fluency measure: Mixed messages in assessment and instruction. *The Reading Teacher, 63,* 440–450.

Duke, N. (1998, December). *3.6 minutes per day: The scarcity of informational texts in first grade.* Paper presented at the annual meeting of the National Reading Conference, Austin, TX.

Durham, J. (1997). On time and poetry. *The Reading Teacher, 51,* 76–79.

Duthie, C. (1996). *True stories: Nonfiction literacy in the primary classroom.* York, ME: Stenhouse Publishers.

Duthie, C., & Zimet, E. (1992). Poetry is like directions for your imagination! *The Reading Teacher, 46,* 14–24.

Dymock, S. (2007). Comprehension strategy instruction: Teaching narrative text structure awareness. *The Reading Teacher, 61,* 161–167.

Edwards, P. (1997). *Dinorella: A prehistoric fairy tale.* New York: Scholastic.

Emberley, M. (1990). *Ruby.* Boston: Little, Brown.

Ernst, L. (1995). *Little Red Riding Hood: A newfangled prairie tale.* New York: Scholastic.

Fawson, P., & Reutzel, D. (2000). But I only have a basal: Implementing guided reading in the early grades. *The Reading Teacher, 54,* 84–97.

Fountas, I. C., & Pinnell, G. S. (2010). *Teaching for comprehending and fluency: Thinking, talking, and writing about reading, K–8.* Portsmouth, NH: Heinemann.

Fresch, M., & Wheaton, A. (1997). Sort, search, and discover: Spelling in the child-centered classroom. *The Reading Teacher, 51,* 20–31.

Fry, E. (1980). The new instant word list. *The Reading Teacher, 34,* 284–289.

Gibbons, G. (2000). *Apples.* New York: Scholastic.

Goatley, V. J., Brock, C. H., & Raphael, T. E. (1995). Diverse learners participating in regular education "Book clubs." *Reading Research Quarterly, 30,* 352–380.

Guthrie, J., Van Meter, P., McCann, A., Wigfield, A., Bennett, L., Poundstone, C., et al. (1996). Growth of literacy engagement: Changes in motivations and strategies during concept oriented reading instruction. *Reading Research Quarterly, 31,* 306–332.

Hasbrouck, J., & Tindal, G. (2006). Oral reading fluency norms: A valuable assessment tool for reading teachers. *The Reading Teacher, 59,* 636–644.

Heard, G. (2002). *The revision toolbox: Teaching techniques that work.* Portsmouth, NH: Heinemann.

Henry, L. (2006). SEARCHing for an answer: The critical role of new literacies while reading on the Internet. *The Reading Teacher, 59,* 614–627.

Howell, W. (1999). *I call it sky.* New York: Walker.

Johnson, T., & Louis, D. (1987). *Literacy through literature.* Portsmouth, NH: Heinemann.

Johnston, T. (1998). *Bigfoot Cinderrrrella.* New York: Scholastic.

Karas, G. B. (2002). *Atlantic.* New York: Putnam.

Kelley, M., & Clausen-Grace, N. (2006). R5: The sustained silent reading makeover that transformed readers. *The Reading Teacher, 60,* 148–156.

Kieffer, M., & Lesaux, N. (2007). Breaking down words to build meaning: Morphology, vocabulary, and reading comprehension in the urban classroom. *The Reading Teacher, 61,* 134–144.

Kuhn, M. (2003). How can I help them pull it all together? A guide to fluent reading instruction. In D. Barone & M. Morrow (Eds.), *Literacy and young children: Research-based practices* (pp. 210–225). New York: Guilford Press.

Lattimore, D. (1997). *CinderHazel: The Cinderella of Halloween.* New York: Scholastic.

Leu, D. (2002). Internet workshop: Making time for literacy. *The Reading Teacher, 55,* 466–472.

Leu, D., & Kinzer, C. (1999). *Effective literacy instruction* (4th ed.). Columbus, OH: Merrill.

Lobel, A. (1999). *Frog and toad are friends.* New York: HarperFestival.

MacLachlan, P. (2004). *Sarah, plain and tall.* New York: HarperCollins.

Marshall, E. (1982). *Fox and his friends.* New York: Scholastic.

Martin, R. (1985). *Foolish Rabbit's big mistake.* New York: Putnam.

McGee, L. (1995). Talking about books with young children. In N. Roser & M. Martinez (Eds.), *Book talk and beyond* (pp. 105–115). Newark, DE: International Reading Association.

Merriam, E. (1989). *Chortles.* New York: Morrow.

Miller, D. (2002). *Reading with meaning: Teaching comprehension in the primary grades.* Portland, ME: Stenhouse Publishers.

Morrison, G. (1998). *Bald eagle.* Boston: Houghton Mifflin.

National Assessment of Educational Progress (NAEP). (2003). Washington, DC: Office of Educational Research and Improvement.

Parsons, S. (2008). Providing all students ACCESS to self-regulated literacy learning. *The Reading Teacher, 61,* 628–635.

Perry, N., Hutchinson, L., & Thauberger, C. (2007). Mentoring student teachers to design and implement literacy tasks that support self-regulated reading and writing. *Reading & Writing Quarterly, 23,* 27–50.

Raphael, T., & McMahon, S. (1994). Book club: An alternative framework for reading instruction. *The Reading Teacher, 48,* 102–116.

Ray, K. (1999). *Wondrous words: Writers and writing in the elementary classroom.* Urbana, IL: National Council of Teachers of English.

Ray, K. (2004). Why Cauley writes well: A close look at what a difference good teaching can make. *Language Arts, 82,* 100–109.

Reutzel, D., Jones, C., Fawson, P., & Smith, J. (2008). Scaffolded silent reading: A complement to guided repeated oral reading that works! *The Reading Teacher, 62,* 194–207.

Reutzel, D., Smith, J., & Fawson, P. (2005). An evaluation of two approaches for teaching reading comprehension strategies in the primary years using science information texts. *Early Childhood Research Quarterly, 20,* 276–305.

Roop, P., & Roop, C. (1985). *Keep the lights burning, Abbie.* Minneapolis: Carolrhoda Books.

Rowling, J. (2008). *Harry Potter and the sorcerer's stone.* New York: Scholastic.

Rylant, C. (1985). *The relatives came.* New York: Simon & Schuster.

Shanahan, T., & Shanahan, S. (1997). Character perspective charting: Helping children to develop a more complete conception of a story. *The Reading Teacher, 50,* 668–677.

Sipe, L. (2008). *Storytime: Young children's literary understanding in the classroom.* New York: Teachers College Press.

Soto, G. (1993). *Too many tamales.* New York: Putnam.

Steig, W. (1971). *Amos and Boris.* New York: Farrar, Straus & Giroux.

Steptoe, J. (1987). *Mufaro's beautiful daughters.* Boston: Houghton Mifflin.

Taberski, S. (2000). *On solid ground: Strategies for teaching reading K–3.* Portsmouth, NH: Heinemann.

Temple, C. (1991). Seven readings of a folktale: Literary theory in the classroom. *The New Advocate, 4,* 25–35.

Tompkins, G. (2006). *Language arts essentials.* Upper Saddle River, NJ: Pearson.

Tompkins, G., & McGee, L. (1993). *Teaching reading with literature: From case studies to action plans.* Columbus, OH: Merrill.

Trousdale, A., & Harris, V. (1993). Missing links in literary response: Group interpretation of literature. *Children's Literature in Education, 24,* 195–207.

Van Allsburg, C. (1979). *The garden of Abdul Gasazi.* Boston: Houghton Mifflin.

Van Allsburg, C. (1985). *The polar express.* Boston: Houghton Mifflin.

Wallace, K. (1998). *Gentle giant octopus.* Cambridge, MA: Candlewick Press.

Willems, M. (2004). *Knuffle Bunny: A cautionary tale.* New York: Hyperion Books.

Williams, J., Stafford, K., Lauer, K., Hall, K., & Pollini, S. (2009). Embedding reading comprehension training in content-area instruction. *Journal of Educational Psychology, 101,* 1–20.

Winters, K. (2000). *Tiger trail.* New York: Simon & Schuster.

Wisniewski, D. (1996). *Golem.* New York: Clarion Books.

Wolf, S. A. (1993). What's in a name? Labels and literacy in readers' theatre. *The Reading Teacher, 46,* 540–545.

Wutz, J., & Wedwick, L. (2005). Bookmatch: Scaffolding book selection for independent reading. *The Reading Teacher, 59,* 16–32.

Yolan, J. (1987). *Owl moon.* New York: Philomel Books.

Yopp, R., & Yopp, H. (2007). Ten important words plus: A strategy for building word knowledge. *The Reading Teacher, 61,* 157–160.

Young, C., & Rasinski, T. (2009). Implementing readers theatre as an approach to classroom fluency instruction. *The Reading Teacher, 63,* 4–13.

Young, T., & Vardell, S. (1993). Weaving readers theatre and nonfiction into the curriculum. *The Reading Teacher, 46,* 396–406.

Zelinsky, P. O. (1986). *Rumpelstiltskin.* New York: Dutton Children's Books.

PEARSON myeducationlab

Go to the topics Phonemic Awareness and Phonics, Word Study, Writing Development, Assessment, and English Language Learners in the MyEducationLab (www .myeducationlab.com) for your course, where you can:

- Find learning outcomes for Phonemic Awareness and Phonics, Word Study, Writing Development, Assessment, and English Language Learners along with the national standards that connect to these outcomes.
- Complete Assignments and Activities that can help you more deeply understand the chapter content.
- Examine challenging situations and cases presented in the IRIS Center Resources.

 **A+RISE**

Go to the Topic A+RISE in the MyEducationLab (www.myeducationlab.com) for your course. A+RISE® Standards2Strategy™ is an innovative and interactive online resource that offers new teachers in grades K–12 just-in-time, research-based instructional strategies that:

- Meet the linguistic needs of ELLs as they learn content
- Differentiate instruction for all grades and abilities
- Offer reading and writing techniques, cooperative learning, use of linguistic and nonlinguistic representations, scaffolding, teacher modeling, higher order thinking, and alternative classroom ELL assessment
- Provide support to help teachers be effective through the integration of listening, speaking, reading, and writing along with the content curriculum
- Improve student achievement
- Are aligned to Common Core Elementary Language Arts standards (for the literacy strategies) and to English language proficiency standards in WIDA, Texas, California, and Florida.

CHAPTER
11

Meeting the Needs
of English Language Learners

KEY CONCEPTS

English Language
  Learner (ELL)
Preproduction
Total Physical
  Response (TPR)
Early Production
Speech Emergence
Intermediate Fluency
Sheltered Instructional
  Observation
  Protocol (SIOP)

Scaffolding
Concepts about Print
  (CAP)
Phoneme Repertoires
ELL Interactive Read-
  Aloud Procedure
Additive Approaches
Subtractive Approaches
Shared Language
Story Grammar
Multiliteracy

Alphabetic Principle
Orthography
Developmental
  Spelling Inventory
Cognates
Homophones
Homographs
Simple Sentence
Compound
  Sentence
Complex Sentence

English Language Learners as a Special Case of At-Risk Learners

E NGLISH LANGUAGE LEARNERS NEED SPECIAL SUPPORT in school in order to make a transition into academic learning in English. The support provided for ELLs in gaining English and learning content when they come to school differs from school system to school system, and different states have different requirements about the use of English in instruction and testing. Some school systems provide bilingual programs in which children learn both English and home languages. In some school systems, specially trained teachers provide English-as-a-second-language (ESL) instruction. In ESL programs, children are taught English at school; teachers expect that children will continue to develop their home language through experiences at home and in the community. However, in many school systems, the regular classroom teacher provides the only instruction that ELLs receive (Au, 2000). In all cases, the classroom teacher must be aware of the special needs of ELLs in developing their English language, reading, and writing.

Second Language Acquisition

Coming to school can be challenging for all young children. However, **English language learners (ELLs)** face unique challenges. Many live in communities where only their home language is spoken; the language used in business transactions, conversations, television, and radio is not English. Going to school may be the first encounter these children have with a language different from their familiar home language. Even adults are overwhelmed when faced with such an environment in which the language to which they are accustomed is never spoken and where even street signs and other environmental print are unfamiliar.

ELLs face another challenge, called the "double bind," when they are in school situations in which they are expected to learn to speak English (Tabors, 1997, p. 35). They can only gain competence as English speakers by communicating with other English speakers (Barone, Mallette, & Xu, 2005). However, in order to play with other children, they need to be able to communicate with those other children. They are faced with needing to make friendships without the English to do so and with needing to develop English without having friends with whom to speak it. Teachers will need to support ELLs' interactions with other children so that they do have the opportunities both to learn English and to form friendships.

Theories.   Theories of second language acquisition have emphasized the role of input (VanPatten, 2003). Input is the quality and amount of language children hear and understand. This hypothesis arose from Krashen's (1985) concept of "comprehensible input" as a necessary and sufficient condition for second language learning. Krashen suggested that if children received language they could understand, they would learn the language.

More recent conceptions of second language acquisition have also considered output. Output is the language that children themselves speak. In a traditional sense, output was viewed as the product of what children had learned. If a child used a new vocabulary word in an appropriate context, the implication was that this child had learned this vocabulary word's meaning. More recent conceptions of output suggest that children's output may have a learning component. That is, children may use their speech as a first draft of what they might be attempting to say, using an adult's or another child's feedback to construct a better, second draft of the speech attempt (Anthony, 2008). In fact, when learning to use correct word order and word forms (morphology), speakers require feedback on their output attempts (Swain, 2005). Later, we will show two exemplary teachers of English language learners that will highlight effective use of input and output.

Stages of Language Development.   As we described in Chapters 2 and 5, children go through four phases of oral language development as they acquire a second language. Figure 11.1 presents an overview of these phases, which are similar to the stages of first

FIGURE 11.1   Stages of Second Language Acquisition

Speech	Instruction	Books
	Preproductive Stage	
Silent in English	TPR survival words	Label books
Listen actively	Dramatic play	Letter books
Learn intonation, speed, pause, pitch, loudness		
Understand simple commands		
	Early Production Stage	
Imitate peers and teacher	TPR with verbal response	Alphabet and concept books on survival topics
Use formulaic phrases	Classroom conversations in shared experiences	
Compose telegraphic sentences		
Understand more complex commands		Predictable books with short, simple sentences
	Speech Emergence Stage	
Use wider range of sentence structures	Comprehensible input	Predictable and cumulative books
Overgeneralize syntactic rules	ELL interactive read-aloud	Simple stories and information books
Basic communicative language		
	Intermediate Fluency Stage	
Academic language	Modifications for vocabulary, sentence structure, and text structure	Complex stories and informational texts

language acquisition (Hadaway, Vardell, & Young, 2002). Knowing which phase of second language acquisition children are in helps teachers plan instruction.

Preproduction.   During **preproduction,** the first phase of second language acquisition, children speak very little English, and teachers perceive them as being silent during the school day. Though they do not speak, English language learners are actively listening to the sounds of the English spoken around them and trying to connect the actions they see with the sounds they hear. They intuitively acquire information about English intonation, pacing, pausing, loudness, and pitch. Children in this phase comprehend and respond to short commands, such as "Get out your math book" or "Come sit in the circle," after teachers physically demonstrate the actions while slowly speaking the commands.

For young children, dramatic play using realistic props is an excellent activity to build early language comprehension and use (Genishi & Dyson, 1984). The structure provided by familiar objects and activities supports children's language learning. To be effective, the objects must be real and the children must use them in real activities. Just as many toddlers first learn familiar phrases or words associated with repeated activities (called "routines"), so do English language learners first learn familiar phrases and words in English (Urzua, 1980). Many children learn to say "Night night," "go to sleep," and "read books" because these routine phrases are repeated daily as they participate in the activity of getting ready for bed. Preschool and kindergarten English language learners can learn the same phrases as they interact with their teacher and other children in their play with dolls, blankets, beds, and books in the housekeeping center. Many dramatic-play activities, such as grocery shopping, visiting the dentist, and taking a trip to McDonald's, provide rich language-learning experiences. Teachers can join in play and provide models of language. At first, many English language learners will be silent in their play as they internalize the sounds of English and discover the actions of routines. They may switch between using English and using their home language; this practice should not be forbidden (Lara, 1989).

Even in elementary school, props and dramatic play can be used as a bridge to English. All children enjoy a pretend trip to McDonald's that includes such props as bags, hamburger containers, drink cups, and hats for the employees. As part of the McDonald's play, children learn the English words *hamburgers, french fries, Coke, milk, ketchup, salt,* and *money.* They might learn routine phrases such as "Welcome to McDonald's," "May I take your order, please?" "I'd like a hamburger," or "Give me a Coke." Pictures of familiar activities can also be used to increase English language learners' oral language proficiency (Moustafa & Penrose, 1985). These experiences can be used to write a language experience story jointly dictated by students and the teacher. This story, when written, can be illustrated and read many times.

During this first phase of production, teachers should plan to build children's listening comprehension of familiar words and phrases used in school. English language learners should learn to comprehend and speak such words as *scissors, marker, glue, paper, chair, table, rug, calendar, book center, blocks, book, reading, coloring, painting,* and *building,* as well as the names of the colors, days of the week, shapes, body parts, food, clothing, family concepts, parts of houses or items in the home, and animals. Teachers may teach children this vocabulary using **total physical response (TPR)** (Asher, 1982; Hadaway et al., 2002). Teachers hold up an object or a picture of an object and say its name. Children respond physically rather than verbally to indicate their understanding. For example, if the teacher says the correct name for the pictured object, children would stand up. This is especially fun when teachers often say the wrong name for the object. Alternatives to standing are for children to tap their feet, clap their hands, or touch their noses. Gradually, teachers can ask children to repeat the name of the object in English. To collect pictures for vocabulary instruction, teachers can borrow sets of photographs from speech/language specialists, take digital photographs of objects around the classroom, or copy pictures from clip art. Figure 11.2 presents one hundred words that can be learned through TPR.

Like all children, English language learners even in the preproductive stage should be familiar with classroom routines. However, teachers must explicitly teach the words

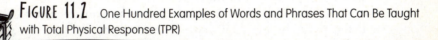

FIGURE 11.2   One Hundred Examples of Words and Phrases That Can Be Taught with Total Physical Response (TPR)

Found in the Kitchen

Cup, plate, bowl, knife, fork, spoon, napkin, dish, table, chair, pan, oven, stove, sink, faucet, counter, cupboard, refrigerator

Found in the House

Door, key, doorknob, open the door, close the door, ring the doorbell, knock on the door, bed, chair, sofa, rug, carpet, coffee table, end table, lamp, pillow, window, curtain, light switch, electrical plug, telephone, television, closet, mirror, toilet, towel, toothbrush, toothpaste, chest, sink, bathtub, bathroom, living room, kitchen, bedroom, garage

Food

Flour, sugar, bread, coffee, rice, nuts, yogurt, candy, hamburger, hot dog, chicken, corn, green beans, broccoli, lettuce, apple, banana, orange, plum, grapes, fig, raisins, lemon, watermelon, tomato, zucchini, onion, carrot, potato, lettuce, celery

Drinks

Water, milk, juice, soda, coffee, tea, smoothie

Related to Cars

Car, car door, front seat, back seat, driver's seat, steering wheel, seat belt, speedometer, hood, headlight, fender, license plate, trunk, tire, put on your seatbelt, drive, stop, lock the door used in each routine and demonstrate the action the children should take. We recommend that teachers display a printed list of events in the daily schedule along with a photograph of children engaging in each event and a picture of a clock indicating the beginning time of the event (Barone et al., 2005). For example, to call children's attention to the transition from whole-class interactive read-aloud to guided-reading groups, teachers point to the picture of the classroom in which a small group of children is sitting with the teacher and say, "It is time for guided reading" [holding up the word card for *guided reading*]. "It is 10:00" [pointing to the picture of the clock]. "We will go to guided reading. Come with me" [gesturing].

Early Production.   During **early production,** the second phase of second language acquisition (Hadaway et al., 2002), children attempt to speak, but they use very limited language, drawing on the words and gestures learned during vocabulary games or other interactions during the silent period. They frequently imitate formulaic phrases spoken by the teacher or their peers (e.g., "Hi, Wanna come?" "Let's go"). Children also point and use other gestures and facial expressions to communicate along with their small store of English words. Children at this stage can comprehend more complicated commands than in the first stage, including ones children frequently use during play, such as "Gimme that block," "You be the mama," or "It's time to clean up."

During the early production phase of language acquisition, children begin to generate speech rather than merely imitate what they have heard or use formulaic language. Early "sentences" are telegraphic, using only one or two words to convey the meaning of an entire sentence such as saying "Chips" when meaning "I want some chips." Children at this stage of second language learning focus on words related to *who, what,* and *where* rather than *how* and *why* (Hadaway et al., 2002). Teachers are helpful at this stage when they expand what children have said. For example, the teacher could ask the child who said "Chips," "Do you want some chips?" while handing the child a bag of chips.

Children in the early production stage benefit from classroom instruction that is more like conversation (Martinez-Roldan & Lopez-Robertson, 1999/2000). With such instruction, teachers demonstrate and teach, but within the back-and-forth structure of a conversation. Teachers are responsive to students' contributions; they validate and expand students' comments. They do not give up on students when their utterances seem limited. In a shared writing activity with four kindergartners, one teacher stayed with Carlos until he revealed the full meaning of a one-word comment about what the teacher had written so far (Williams, 2001, p. 753).

Carlos: (pointing to a word at the end of a line) Spot.

Teacher: What do you mean, Carlos?

Carlos: Spot. (points again to the last word in a line)

Teacher: Tell me more. What do you mean?

Carlos: No room. (pointing to the end of the first line)

Teacher: (recognizing Carlos's point that there was no more room on the line to write another word) Oh, I see, Carlos. There is no more room for words on this line, so I will continue writing on the next line.

Highly predictable pattern books are also excellent read-alouds for the phase of early production. These books have short, repeated, and very predictable phrases and strong picture clues to meaning. From these predictable books, children learn to use very simple English sentences such as

> *I am _____.*
> *I like _____.*
> *I can _____.*
> *I have _____.*

Commercial materials intended for beginning readers are excellent for ELLs' first read-alouds. For example, *Well Done, Worm!* (Caple, 2000) includes four little books using the simple sentences:

> *Worm paints a _____.*
> *Worm sees a _____.*
> *Worm is a _____.*
> *Worm gets a _____.*

Appendix A provides a list of predictable and language play books that teachers can use with English language learners as read-aloud books and for children's writing of pattern innovations.

Speech Emergence and Intermediate Fluency.

Speech emergence (Hadaway et al., 2002) is the third stage of language acquisition. By the end of this stage, children develop conversational competence in English and during social interactions can appear to be fluent. They have acquired everyday, tier 1 vocabulary and use simple and compound sentences. However, they may not always use syntactic rules perfectly, and so their use of incorrect sentences should be expanded by teachers during conversations rather than highlighted and corrected. They will be learning to understand, construct, and read complex sentences just as their peers who are native language speakers.

Shared activities in which a small group of children complete a project together provide many opportunities for conversations. Activities such as composing a shared writing chart in a small group or retelling a pattern story in which several children take turns hanging pictures on a story clothesline facilitate conversations among children who have different home languages. During these conversations, teachers use *comprehensible input* (Krashen, 1985); that is, they reduce the number of words they use, slow down their rate of talking, and limit their words to those that are very familiar. Teachers support their simplified language by pointing and using other gestures, repetition, pictures, and dramatic movements.

The last stage of second language acquisition is **intermediate fluency.** This is the stage of language proficiency in which students begin to develop more academic language and use the scientific and specific uses of words in content studies. They are able to control most syntactic patterns used in spoken conversations; like native English speakers, they are learning more sophisticated language patterns found in complex narratives and expositions they are reading. Thus, at this stage of language development, English language learners perform similarly to native English speakers. Unfortunately, for most children, it takes up to six years to acquire this competency from the time children are first exposed to and expected to learn English.

In the following sections, we provide examples of exemplary teachers of English language learners. They provide their learners with input that is comprehensible. They use conversation to teach so that students have extended output opportunities to talk and receive feedback.

Exemplary Teachers of English Language Learners

Researchers have recently identified the most effective instructional practices for producing superior academic achievement for diverse learners (e.g., Echevarria, Vogt, & Short, 2004) called **Sheltered Instructional Observation Protocol (SIOP)**. This model of instruction includes five characteristics (adapted from McIntyre, Kyle, Chen, Kraemer, & Parr, 2009, p 15):

* Joint productive activity, in which teachers and students work together on joint products
* Focused language learning instruction, in which teachers help students learn key literacy strategies and develop language competencies both in content study and during reading and writing instruction
* Instruction that occurs in conversations, in which teachers use small groups to engage students in conversation as a tool for learning
* Contextualization of instruction, in which teachers connect instruction to students' experiences
* Instruction that forms a rigorous curriculum, in which teachers provide experiences across several lessons designed for students to reach complex levels of understanding and use higher-level thinking

Each of these characteristics of effective instruction for English language learners includes scaffolding. **Scaffolding** is anything a teacher does to support a student in accomplishing a task that could not be done independently or at a higher level than would be expected without support. Scaffolding can take many forms, including asking probing or clarifying questions, making suggestions, providing sentence starters, or modeling a process. Teachers repeat key vocabulary; provide explicit instruction; clearly enunciate; and use gestures, body language, visual aids, and eye contact. Clearly, to deliver lessons that embody the five characteristics of effective instruction for English language learners with sufficient scaffolding, teachers must carefully prepare not only the content to be learned but also the language and literacy goals and objectives.

The most effective way to learn to read and write English is to transfer what is already known about reading and writing in the home language. This implies that instruction should first be in the child's home language before attempting to teach reading and writing in English and that the most effective teachers are teachers who are native language speakers. However, this is not the reality in most schools. Increasingly, monolingual teachers who speak only English are expected to provide instruction for a diverse group of learners, including children who have just begun to speak English.

TECHNOLOGY TIE IN

WEB SITES THAT SUPPORT ENGLISH LANGUAGE LEARNERS

http://babelfish.yahoo.com allows users to type in a message in English and have it translated into several languages including Chinese, Dutch, French, German, Greek, Italian, Japanese, Korean, Portuguese, Russian, and Spanish. Teachers can use the site to translate messages for parents or to translate greetings to use in the classroom.

www.enchantedlearning.com/Dictionary.html provides students with illustrated vocabulary words in several languages including Dutch, French, German, Italian, Japanese, Portuguese, Spanish, and Swedish. Teachers and students can use the site to locate cognates in English and other languages.

http://readingrockets.org/webcasts/2001 presents a Web cast on teaching English language learners featuring Diane August, Margarita Calderon, and Fred Genesee. The site also has some downloadable materials for teachers and a multilingual reading tip pamphlet for parents that is available in twelve languages.

http://brainpopjr.com/readingandwriting/word/nouns shows an animated movie explaining the different kinds of nouns. The site also has an interactive quiz students can take to show their understanding of this grammatical concept. This site does require a subscription, but some activities are free, such as the noun movie. Online reviews of this site praise its graphics and downloadable materials that go beyond the typical coloring sheet. The educators who designed the site also aligned it with standards in the various subject areas included: math, science, reading and writing, the arts.

Iddings, Risko, and Rampulla (2009) present a case study of an exemplary teacher they call Seth. Seth, who spoke only English, taught many Hispanic children including children who had recently arrived from Mexico and spoke no English at home. His teaching not only demonstrates the five characteristics of effective instruction for English language learners with strong scaffolding but also shows how he

- provides time during instruction to build students' collective understanding by restating and expanding children's utterances,
- allows and encourages children to use both English and their native language to take on the "role of teacher" in supporting other children's understandings,
- selects texts that are comprehensible through illustrations and makes activities comprehensible by repeating actions so that core concepts are examined repeatedly, and
- relates writing activities to reading activities so that vocabulary and concepts taught in reading can be used in writing.

In the first lesson, Seth prepared to read aloud *Curious George* (Rey, 1969). He selected this book because there are several books about Curious George, and he knows that reading multiple books about a single character with similar plots and conflicts naturally extends children's comprehension. In addition, these picture books provide strong support for understanding the story line through illustrations. He has also been teaching children to use a story grammar chart in which they keep track of the setting, character, problem, events, solution to problems, and feelings of characters. The story grammar chart is part of his explicit instruction in comprehension and is now a predictable teaching routine for these children. Before reading this book aloud, Seth engaged the children in a talk-through. This discussion took place at the point in the story in which the man with the yellow hat is introduced (Iddings et al., 2009, p. 55).

Seth: What else could happen? Did you think about anything that could happen?

Pedro: They do . . . about where he lives and then, he see that monkey, and then . . .

Seth: They? Who is the other person?

Pedro: Ah . . . the large yellow hat?

Seth: The man with the yellow hat, right?

Pedro: And the Curious George he like, he is so curious he went to . . .

Alicia: La ciudad (the city).

Seth: So, what do all of those, what do all of those events have in common?

Alicia: A problem.

Seth: They're all problems. But why does he always have problems?

Pedro: Because he is just curious.

Seth: Right. George is curious.

In this interaction, Seth not only taught the students about components in stories (characters and their problems) but also reaffirmed and expanded for students their language (he expanded "large yellow hat" to "the man with the yellow hat"). He also used a questioning, open stance in his replies (". . . right?") in order to extend the conversation. Alicia's extension of Pedro's sentence in Spanish was a natural part of the conversation as she seemed to step into the teacher's role of expanding a sentence.

Later, as Seth was reading the book aloud, he paused to ask a question to ensure that students were making critical inferences necessary for understanding a story event. In the part of the story in which the man in the yellow hat was delivering George, tied up in a bag, to a ship, Seth stopped and asked, "How do you think George feels right now?" (Iddings et al., 2009, p. 56). When one of the children answered this question, "Happy," Seth asked the child to tell why he thought George was happy. The student made a reasonable inference, "Because he is going to a ship." Seth confirmed, "So maybe he might be excited to be on a big ship," but then probed further. "How do you think George would feel about being tied up inside a bag, though?" (p. 56). Again, Alicia stepped in to play the role of the teacher when she said, "Como te sentiras si alguien te amarrara y te llevara en una bolsa y te llevara a un . . . a . . ." [How would you feel if someone tied you up and took you away in a bag on a . . .] At this point, she turned to another student and asked, "Como se dice 'ship'?" [How do you say 'ship'?] Now Pedro understood. Seth said, "Maybe [Curious George is] a little scared?" Pedro nodded "yeah" (p. 56).

The next day, the students composed a story about Curious George and they decided to title it "Curious George Goes to Mexico." In the story, George met up with a girl monkey that he was curious about. He got in trouble by stealing a banana for his new girlfriend, Marisol. After the police released him, George took Marisol to a taco shop where El mesaro [the waiter] asked them for their order [the best banana split]. They got married and everyone danced "La Cucaracha" at the wedding.

These two lessons demonstrate the five characteristics of effective teaching of English language learners. First, the children and teacher were engaged in a joint activity— creating background knowledge for and understanding the Curious George book and writing the Curious George story. Seth had focused goals for teaching; he taught the students components of story grammar and helped students use these to better understand the story. The two lessons were contextualized to the students' experiences by allowing them to draw upon their home language and cultural knowledge. Seth called for higher-level thinking in making inferences about character emotions. Finally, reading and writing were surrounded with rich conversations in which all partners worked at creating common understandings using their current level of English language use but receiving feedback with language at just one level more complex.

Ms. Page is another exemplary teacher who uses the resources of her children's languages to construct comprehensible sentences for writing in English (Manyak, 2008). Each morning, two children dictate Daily News sentences with the help of other children. Ms. Page writes the Daily News and collects each day's news stories into a book at the end of the month. These books are added to the class library. Today's news is dictated by Ana who shares in Spanish that she was going to the movies. Notice how the children work together in a collaborative dialogue to solve the problem of translating Ana's Spanish into English (Anthony, 2008) and how Ms. Page expands their words into an acceptable written sentence (Manyak, p. 454):

Ms. Page: Let's try to do that in English. Ana, can you help me out and think how to say that in English?

Ana: [shakes her head "no"]

Ms. Page: Are you sure? Sandra?

Sandra: Ana went to a movie.

Karen: Is going to a movie.

Student 1: A movie.

Student 2: The movies.

Ms. Page: The movies. Which day is she going to the movies?

Students: El sabado.

Ms. Page: On Saturday. Ana is going to the movies on Saturday. OK, all eyes up here on the board. Ana, help me out with the words.

In this teaching event, Ms. Page and her students jointly constructed a sentence for the Daily News—a natural way to contextualize learning for students as they bring in their experiences outside of school. The sentence was originally told in Spanish but became jointly owned in English as the children conversed together to construct an acceptable sentence that would be written in a published book.

Considerations for Teachers

ELLs face many obstacles in learning to read and write in English that are the result of cultural incongruities. Cultural incongruities arise when teachers are unfamiliar with the cultures or languages of their English language learners or when books present concepts that are different from children's cultural expectations.

Teachers who have little or no experience with minority cultures in the United States or other cultures abroad and do not speak another language must seek ways to become more knowledgeable. They must find out more about their students' home languages and experiences and about languages in general in order to bridge the gap between school cultures and children's home cultures. One resource for learning more about different languages is to read children's books that present familiar phrases in different languages such as *Hello World!* (Stojic, 2002), which presents greetings in forty-two languages.

Learning about the Community and Family.   Perhaps one of the most critical ways that teachers can become more familiar with the languages and cultures of their students is to conduct family interviews. Schools in which there are many ELLs have interpreters for teachers to use when conducting family interviews. Or teachers may use school or district parent liaisons as translators during parent interviews. During the interview, teachers seek out the parents' pronunciation of their children's names in the home language and gather information about the home language. Teachers should have parents write their child's name in the home language. This label can be displayed along with the child's picture and name written in English on the child's cubbie or in classroom displays (Schwarzer, Haywood, & Lorenzen, 2003). Teachers ask parents to characterize their children's home language development and to relate experiences the children have had reading everyday print items such as newspapers, magazines, catalogs, or children's books.

Teachers can gain a wealth of information about the language and culture of English language learners by taking a tour of the school's intake neighborhood (Orellana & Hernandez, 1999) with children (if parents give their permission) or with an adult who is familiar with the community. During the tour, they can take digital photographs of the environmental print and signs they see in busy markets, video stores, and restaurants frequented by the residents of the neighborhoods. They can use the photographs as writing prompts in shared writing or in writing workshop. Children may bring print from their homes that can be used for small-group instruction in alphabet recognition and sound-letter associations (Xu & Rutledge, 2003). Children can also make environmental print books to be housed in the classroom's book center.

Considering Differences in Print and Language.   **Concepts about print (CAP)** vary across languages. Some languages are not written from left to right and top to bottom. Therefore, these critical directional concepts in English may be more difficult for some children to develop than for others. Letter and word concepts may also cause confusion. For example, all Chinese characters are the same size and have the same blocklike shape, whereas English words can vary from long (many letters) to short (few letters). Even when words are the same length, the different shapes of the letters from which the words are composed can result in very different word profiles (compare *slipped* and *sooner*) (Barone et al., 2005).

Languages also differ in their **phoneme repertoires.** Some languages have phonemes not found in English (e.g., the trilled *r* sound in Spanish that is absent in English), and English has phonemes not found in other languages (e.g., the /ng/ sound in English that is absent in Spanish). Not surprisingly, an English-language-learning child experiences difficulty detecting and producing English phonemes absent in his or her native language.

Finally, languages use different sentence structures, or syntax. The syntax of some languages depends more on word order than does the syntax of other languages. English uses subject-verb-object word order. For example, in the sentence *The goat kicked the boy*, English speakers and readers know *the boy* is the direct object of the transitive verb *kicked* because of its position after *kicked*. Not all languages treat transitive verbs in this way. For example, Korean sentences typically end with a verb. This means that both the subjects and the direct objects of transitive verbs appear before the verbs. It does not matter in which order one says or writes those nouns so long as neither of them takes the final position in the sentence (that is reserved for the verb). To let listeners and readers know which of the nouns appearing before that final verb is the direct object, Korean speakers and writers label it with an extra syllable. Children whose home language is Korean will be used to looking for that extra syllable and not accustomed to paying attention to word order. When confronted with the written sentences *The goat kicked the boy* and *The boy kicked the goat*, what they may notice is that *boy* looks the same in both sentences. They may wonder, "Where is the direct object label?" What they have to learn is that word order matters, that *boy* is the direct object (receiver of the kicking) in the first sentence and the subject (doer of the kicking) in the second sentence by virtue of its positions in those sentences.

Selecting Books for English Language Learners and Adjusting Read-Aloud Techniques

Figure 11.1 presented suggestions for books to read aloud to English language learners at each of the first three levels of English acquisition. Books to be read aloud during the preproduction stage of language acquisition are very simple, with one or two words on a page and clear illustrations. Letter books, each page of which presents photographs of four objects whose names begin with the same sound, are quite useful at this stage (for example, the *Cambridge Alphabet Books*, published by Cambridge University Press). Similarly, teachers can make books for children by scanning photographs and pictures used in TPR activities to create personalized concept books. During this early language learning stage, teachers will read books with a clear match between text and illustrations. Teachers accompany their reading with gestures, pointing to illustrations, and dramatic movements.

Slightly more complex alphabet and concept books make excellent read-aloud materials for English language learners at the stage of early production. These and other concept books can focus on basic survival topics and extend the vocabulary children learned earlier from simple pictures and TPR activities. As teachers read aloud, they should slow down their rate of reading so that children can pick out critical vocabulary words from the rapid flow of language (Echevarria, Vogt, & Short, 2000). Teachers should also point to the salient parts of illustrations and repeat words slowly. Teachers plan vocabulary activities for after reading reinforcing critical vocabulary introduced in the book using TPR activities. In addition, easy predictable books with simple language patterns are excellent choices. The text and illustrations should continue to be related, and there should be only a few words of text on each page. For example, as they read *Mouse Paint* (Walsh, 1995), teachers can have children stand up and say the color words when they hear them in the story. Finally, teachers should also read aloud very simple, short stories and information books. Figure 11.3 presents a list of basic survival topics and some suggested books to expand those topics. Teachers can either read these books when the text is simple, or tell information when the texts are too complex for children in early production phase of language learning.

In the stage of speech emergence, teachers should continue to read aloud predictable and cumulative books but also search for books, such as *The Napping House* (Wood, 1996), that include more complex sentences. Books such as *Where Is My Baby?* (Ziefert, 1996) or *Where's Spot?* (Hill, 1980) that ask and then answer questions are particularly useful in providing models of language use. Children at this stage of language production can begin to listen to slightly more complex stories and information books; however, they still need introduction to unfamiliar vocabulary, concepts, and sentence structures. Appendix A provides a list of easy storybooks appropriate for very young children that can be used with English language learners in early speech emergence. Appropriate choices of books should include the use of varied sentence structures and an increasing number of words on each page. Wordless picture books provide excellent visual support for English language learners at this stage of language acquisition as they attempt to tell the story themselves. Illustrations in these books provide direct information about actions, characters' thoughts and emotions, and the relationship between actions and characters' feelings. Children can be invited to tell stories in their home language using a parent or community volunteer when the teacher does not speak the home language (Hadaway et al., 2002).

ELL Interactive Read-Aloud Procedure

The **ELL interactive read-aloud procedure** (Hickman, Pollard-Durodola, & Vaughn, 2004) is a technique that teaches vocabulary and comprehension using longer, more complex picture books, both narrative and informational. These are books that teachers would normally read aloud to native English-speaking kindergarten and first-grade children. However, without modification, English language learners would not be able to understand them. The ELL interactive read-aloud procedure is designed to make these books easier for ELLs to understand and to teach them vocabulary used in the books.

The ELL interactive read-aloud procedure is similar to that used in interactive read-aloud, which we described in Chapter 6. First, teachers divide the book into three or four segments, and each of these segments are read on successive days. Thus, ELLs hear a segment of text each day; thus, teachers need to carefully select books

FIGURE 11.3 Books on Survival Topics

Colors

Cabrera, J. (2000). *Cat's colors*. New York: Puffin.

Baker, A., (1995). *White Rabbit's color book*. New York: Kingfisher.

Lionni, L. (1994). *Little blue, and little yellow*. New York: Morrow.

Lionni, L. (1997). *A color of his own*. New York: Bantam Doubleday Dell.

Walsh, E. (1995). *Mouse paint*. New York: Sandpiper.

Food

Anderson, A. (2008). *Vegetables*. Sarah Anderson's Children's Books.

Ehlert, L. (1989). *Eating the alphabet: Fruits and vegetables from A to Z*. San Diego: Harcourt Brace.

Ehlert, L. (1991). *Growing vegetable soup*. New York: Sandpiper.

Rosa-Mendoza, G. (2002). *Fruits and vegetables*/frutas y vegetales. Me + mi Publishing.

Westcott, N. (1987). *Peanut butter and jelly: A play rhyme*. New York: Dutton.

Families

Crews, D. (1998). *Bigmama's*. New York: Greenwillow.

Rosa-Mendoza, G. (2001). *My family and I/Mi familia y yo*. Me +mi Publishing.

Ryder, J. (1994). *My father's hands*. New York: Harper Collins.

D. Shannon. (1998). *No! David*. New York: Blue Sky Press.

Williams, V. (1982). *A chair for my mother*. New York: Scholastic.

Seasons

Borden, L. (1991). *Caps, hats, socks and mittens: A book about four seasons*. New York: Scholastic.

Fleming, D. (1997). *Time to sleep*. New York Holt.

Fleming, D. (2000). *Autumn leaves are falling*. New York: Scholastic.

Carle, E. (1998). *The snowy day*. New York: Viking Press.

Maass, R. (1996). *When autumn comes*. New York: Scholastic.

Robbins, K. (1998). *Autumn leaves*. New York: Scholastic.

Weather

Branley, F. (1999). *Flash, crash, rumble, and roll*. New York: Collins.

Gibbons, G. (1990). *Weather words and what they mean*. New York: Holiday House.

Rockwell, A. (2008). *Clouds*. New York: Collins.

Wallace, K. 1999). *Whatever the weather*. Dorling-Kindersley.

Going to School

Davis, K. (2008). *Kindergarten rocks*. New York: Sandpiper.

Penn, A. (2006). *The kissing hand*. New York: Tanglewood.

Shannon, D. (1999). *David goes to school*. New York: Blue Sky Press.

Wells, R. (1981). *Timothy goes to school*. New York: Dial.

Wells, R. (1998). *Yoko*. New York: Hyperion.

that have natural breaks in the story. For each segment, teachers select three or four vocabulary words in the text to teach, giving ELLs more opportunity to repeat and use these few words as they talk about the story. The words selected for focus in ELL interactive read-alouds should not be in children's current vocabularies but should be likely to be encountered again in other books or in real life. Each day, teachers introduce a few new vocabulary words, but they also continue to review previously introduced words.

Each day, a segment of the book is read and reread, and on the final day, the entire story is reread and retold. Thus, each day, ELL children review previously read text and vocabulary, and they add a new segment of text and some new vocabulary. As teachers read each day, they ask *who* and *what* questions that require recall of information from the text. They do not ask *why* questions because children's language at this level of acquisition makes these questions very difficult to answer. The steps each day of the ELL interactive read-aloud procedure include the following elements:

- Introduce three new vocabulary words in a book introduction by pointing to illustrations in the book, displaying objects, or providing dramatizations.
- Read the segment of the text, highlighting the three vocabulary words by providing short definitions, pointing to illustrations, or using dramatic gestures or facial expressions.
- After reading the text segment, ask three questions requiring children to use the ideas and the vocabulary from the story.
- Help children recall story events in the text segment and have children talk about their experiences related to the story or to the three vocabulary words.
- On the second and third days, have children recall the events of the story previously read before reading the new segment of the book.

Figure 11.4 presents an example of a book appropriate for the ELL interactive read-alouds, *Knuffle Bunny: A Cautionary Tale by Mo Willems* (2004) and three or four vocabulary words for each of the three segments of the book. On the first day of the ELL interactive read-aloud, the teacher introduces the vocabulary words, reads the first segment of the book, rereads it, and has students recall the events and discuss the segment of the story using the focus vocabulary. The second day of ELL interactive read-alouds is very similar. First, the teacher and children summarize the first segment, then the teacher introduces the vocabulary, and next reads the second segment followed by having children recall and discuss the story events in this segment. The same routine is followed the third day. On this final day, after reading and recalling the final segment, the teacher rereads the entire story. Students retell the entire story using all of the focus vocabulary.

Teachers need to preview books carefully to select segments of text that occur at natural breaks in the stories and to select vocabulary words. Vocabulary words can be introduced before reading by referring to illustrations in the book; then, as each word is read, the teacher slips in its definition. For example, before reading the first segment of *Knuffle Bunny*, a teacher may say during the book introduction, "In this story, a daddy and his little girl have to go on an errand. An *errand* is when you leave home to do a job. You say *errand*. The errand they are doing is going to the Laundromat to wash clothes. Wow, what an interesting word. You say *Laundromat*. A *Laundromat* is a store

FIGURE 11.4 Using the ELL Interactive Read-Aloud Technique with *Knuffle Bunny* (Willems, 2004)

Segment 1: The Walk to the Laundromat and Putting the Clothes into the Washer

Vocabulary:

Errand:	Go out to get something or do a job
Block:	On a sidewalk, from one street to the next street
Laundromat:	A place where you can wash your clothes
Machine:	The washing machine that cleans your clothes in water

Segment 2: The Walk Home and Realization that Knuffle Bunny is Missing, Mother Asks Where is Knuffle Bunny?

Vocabulary:

Realized:	When you first know something
Replied:	Answered
Bawled:	Cry very, very loudly
Boneless:	Like you have no bones

Segment 3: The Rush Back to the Laundromat, Searching and Finding Knuffle Bunny.

Vocabulary:

Block:	On a sidewalk, from one street to the next street
Zoomed:	Ran very fast
Nowhere to be found:	Lost and couldn't be found

with lots of washing machines. Let me show you the Laundromat in the book. See the washing machines. There is one more word I want you to think about. In this story, they walk down the block to get to the Laundromat. But this word *block* is different than what you probably think of when you hear the word *block,* like a block you build with. In the story, they walk down the block, that is, they walk on the sidewalk by all the houses until they reach another street. The sidewalk from one street allllll the way to the next street is called a block. Let me show you how they are walking down the block in the book."

Using Oral Language to Support Reading and Writing

Additive approaches build on children's home language and culture (Cummins, 1986) and are in contrast with **subtractive approaches**, which replace children's home language and culture with English and mainstream values. We have shown how exemplary teachers take an additive approach to their literacy instruction when they allow students to use their home language in some reading and writing activities.

A third-grade teacher who had several Spanish-speaking children in her class introduced the characters and events in *Mirandy and Brother Wind* (McKissack, 1988) by using simple props to act out important parts of the story. As part of her introduction, the teacher used descriptive phrases from the story and illustrated the meaning of these phrases through her dramatic portrayal of the characters in action. Then the children formed pairs to read the story. Next, the children gathered to have a grand conversation about the story. As part of the conversation, the teacher shared many responses in which she used several of the vocabulary words from the story. These portions of the lesson were all conducted in English. Finally, the class broke into small groups to act out portions of the story; and several children planned their dramatic reenactments in Spanish. Although most groups presented their dramas to the class using English, one group used Spanish in its enactment.

Effective teachers of English language learners realize that students can be easily overwhelmed by too many changing instructional techniques. These children need repeated use of familiar instructional routines and activities using shared language. **Shared language** refers to vocabulary that is used repetitively when talking about a reading or writing task (Gersten & Jiménez, 1994). For instance, one teacher who taught many children with limited knowledge of English repeatedly used a few familiar words when talking about literature. She taught her children the components of a **story grammar** (see Chapter 2 for a description of a story grammar and its components), and her students understood the English words *character, setting, problem, obstacle, outcome*, and *character's emotions*. The students knew how to look for character clues because the teacher frequently asked questions such as, "What kind of character is he? What are the clues?" (Gersten & Jiménez) and modeled answer-finding techniques.

Another teacher taught students the vocabulary needed to conduct writers' conferences with partners. Using whole-class mini-lessons, the teacher taught children to talk about "'favorite part,' 'part you didn't understand,' 'part you'd like to know more about,' and 'part you might like to work on'" (Blake, 1992, p. 606). Through modeling, the teacher showed children the kinds of language that he expected them to use and the kinds of information that he expected them to talk about in a writers' conference.

These teachers focused on teaching their children how to participate in highly successful activities. They did not use many different strategies but instead used only a few strategies routinely. As children gained confidence using these strategies, these teachers gradually added other instructional strategies.

Teaching Reading and Writing Using a Multiliteracy Approach

In this chapter, we have provided information for teaching reading and writing in English and have assumed that the teacher is English-speaking. However, we want to make clear our recognition that children's experiences reading and writing in their first language support their learning to read and write in English (Freeman & Freeman, 2001). Increasingly, educators have sought ways of teaching that promote children's spoken and written language development in their first language in order to prevent first-language loss and to make available those abilities as resources for second-language learning

(Peyton, Ranard, & McGinnis, 2001). Educators have sought methods, usable by all teachers, even those who speak only English, that preserve **multiliteracy** (in which both the home language and English are honored and used).

As a first start, we recommend that teachers learn how to write all children's names in their home language. Parent volunteers or community liaisons can be helpful in guiding a teacher's practice. Teachers should also learn to say simple phrases in the children's home language such as *Good morning* or *How are you today?* (Schwarzer et al., 2003). Teachers can also obtain posters of the alphabet in each of the children's home languages and purchase a few books in each language.

One kindergarten teacher used all five of the home languages in her classroom to conduct a special theme study of insects and spiders. Volunteers wrote the words *insects* and *spiders* in each of the five languages, and parent volunteers taught children the words to the song "Itsy Bitsy Spider" in each language. All the children attempted to sing the song and write the words in all five languages (Schwarzer et al., 2003).

In another school, teachers at all primary grades decided to purchase dual-language picture books and to launch a dual-language writing project. Teachers purchased books that were available in two or more languages. Where possible, they purchased books with two languages in the same book. Later, children used writing project time to draw illustrations and to write texts in English. They took their books home, and their parents helped them to write the same text in their home language (Cummins, Chow, & Schecter, 2006).

Teaching Decoding and Spelling to English Language Learners

Because many English language learners lag behind native speakers, it is especially critical that teachers assess their knowledge of the **alphabetic principle** and **orthography.** Because decoding and spelling are so linked, giving English language learners a **developmental spelling inventory** (Bear, Invernizzi, Templeton, & Johnston, 2008) would provide insight into specific features that children control, confuse, and do not yet know (Helman, 2005). Chapter 5 presented more information about developmental spelling inventories, and Chapters 4 and 5 presented a discussion of different levels of spelling. Chapter 9 presented Mrs. Tran's systematic approach to teaching decoding and teaching spelling to small, guided-reading groups. Mrs. Tran's students included many students who were English language learners; and her explicit, systematic approach is recommended.

Teaching Vocabulary to English Language Learners

English language learners need extra attention to both learning the meanings of new vocabulary words and acquiring sight words. Earlier chapters have presented many instructional strategies for teaching new meanings for words and for helping children acquire automatic sight word recognition. One consideration for teaching English language learners sight words is their level of English competence (Helman & Burns, 2008). Researchers have found that students' scores on the Language Assessment Scales-Oral (LAS-O; De Avila & Duncan, 1994) predict the number of sight words that they can learn during a lesson. Children with very limited oral English proficiency can learn about three sight words in a lesson; children with limited English proficiency can learn about five sight words; and children with fluent English proficiency can learn about seven sight words and new meanings associated with these words. At all levels of reading, it is critical that teachers help children acquire new sight words and, later, when the words are more sophisticated, new meanings associated with those words.

In Chapter 10, we presented several after-reading vocabulary learning activities including creating a word wall of words from a book, using the list-group-label activity with word wall words or using the ten-important-words-plus activity. We mentioned introducing words to students prior to reading, then revisiting their meanings after reading. It is these before- *and* after-vocabulary learning activities that English language learners need. As in the ELL interactive read-aloud technique, English language learners need to see and hear words spoken before reading and then revisit those same words after reading. They need to hear and see new and important vocabulary words and connect the words' meanings to their experiences before reading, then consider how the new words were used in the book to expand their meanings beyond their current understandings.

Using vocabulary charts during content study or a genre study in guided reading is an effective approach for examining words prior to reading, accumulating vocabulary through extended reading experiences across several texts, and revisiting vocabulary often after reading. Teachers can use the vocabulary chart activity with read-alouds or with guided reading. This approach requires that teachers select a text set, a set of books in the same genre or on the same topic (Blachowicz & Obrochta, 2005). For example, teachers could gather a text set, six to ten books on various difficulty levels, about weather and climate, rain forests, the human body, or soil habitats; or they might gather many different versions of "The Three Billy Goats Gruff" or "Little Red Hen" stories. Teachers preview the books and select a set of core vocabulary words that are used across more than one text and critical for understanding the books in the text set. For example, core vocabulary for a text set exploring soil habitats might include the words *soil, living, nonliving, nutrients, roots, decomposition, organisms, earthworms, survive, adaptations, habitat, basic needs*, and *moisture*.

Next, teachers prepare a vocabulary chart. On a large chart, teachers place two or three pictures related to the topic of the text set. For example, the vocabulary chart for the soil habitat would have those words written at the top with a close-up picture of a forest floor (scanned from one of the books in the textbook), and a picture of an earthworm emerging from dirt (scanned from another book). The pictures leave plenty of room for adding vocabulary words to the chart during study of the text set. Before talking about the topic or introducing any vocabulary words, teachers would prepare a sheet for a first write (Blachowicz & Obrochta, 2005). This is a sheet for the child to draw a picture, then write as many words as he or she knows about the topic. The child draws a circle around these words because this same sheet will be used for a final write (explanation follows). Figure 11.5 presents a first-write sheet for a third grader who will be reading the text set on soil habitats.

The first-write sheet in Figure 11.5 shows that this child knows three words related to the topic: *dirt, worm* (*werm*), and leaves (*leefs*). After writing these words, the student circled the words to indicate this was his "first write." Undoubtedly, these words were generated by looking at the soil habitat vocabulary poster and its pictures. Now the teacher engages the children in a group conversation about the pictures. Here, children

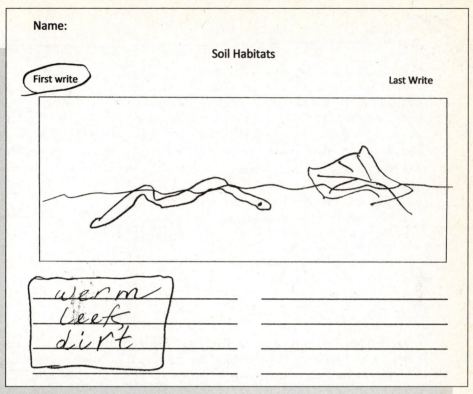

Name:

Soil Habitats

First write

Last Write

werm
leef
dirt

FIGURE 11.5   First Write for Study of a Text Set on Soil Habitats

contribute more words: *leaves, dirt, earthworm, digging,* and *soil.* The teacher writes these words on sticky notes and attaches them to the vocabulary chart. As she writes the words, she asks for clarifications and personal experiences: "Where have you seen earthworms? What were they doing?" Next is the reading phase. Either teachers read a text aloud, followed by further discussion of the words on the vocabulary chart and adding still more, or students read. If students read, teachers will want to make sure that important new vocabulary words not dictated by students are shown to students and their meanings are discussed. After reading, students add additional words to the vocabulary chart. Students then do an activity with the words on the vocabulary chart. They might select words that go together such as selecting words about living things and nonliving things; or they may act out their meanings, write different forms of the words, or draw pictures (much like the plus activities in the ten-important-words-plus activity presented in Chapter 10).

Before each text is read in the text set, teachers and students revisit the vocabulary chart. After each new book is read, more words are added to the chart. At the end of the

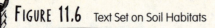

FIGURE 11.6 Text Set on Soil Habitats

Beal, R. (2000). *A handful of dirt*. Walker Books.

Himmelman, J. (2001). *An earthworm's life.* Children's Press.

Llewellyn, C. (2002). *Earthworms.* Children's Press.

Pfeffer, W. (2003). *Wiggling worms at work.* Collins.

Silverstein, A., & Silverstein, V. (2000). *Life in a bucket of soil.* Dover Publications.

Books from the Seeds of Science/Roots of Literacy Curriculum; http://scienceandliteracy.org

   K. Beals. *Earthworms underground*

   K. Beals. *My nature notebook*

   K. Beals & G. Cervetti. *Walk in the woods*

   L. Bergman & P. Pearson. *Into the soil*

   M. Bravo & K. Hosoume. *Handbook of forest floor animals*

study, students do a final write. Here they write all the words they now know (after the vocabulary chart has been removed). Students who constantly discuss words and their meanings not only learn new vocabulary but also achieve *word consciousness*, the conscious attention to the words used in conversations and in texts. Figure 11.6 presents the texts that were read about the topic *soil habitats*. Some of these books were read aloud by the teacher, and some of the texts were read by students (several books in the text set are part of the *Seeds of Science/Roots of Literacy* curriculum developed at the University of California Berkeley and can be purchased at Delta Education).

Using cognates is another strategy for increasing vocabulary knowledge. **Cognates** are words in different languages that have similar spellings, pronunciations, and meanings. Examples of cognates in English and Spanish include *dentist/dentista, map/mapa*, and *necessary/necesario*. Using cognates allows English language learners to draw upon their home language as a resource for understanding text. To teach the strategy, select a text and identify some words in English that have Spanish cognates, for example. A Spanish-English dictionary can be helpful in identifying cognates. Before reading the text, introduce students to cognates by writing two cognates on the board and asking students what they notice about the two words. Students use the words in sentences and discuss their meanings. Now present the students with the cognates in Spanish for words they will be reading in English. Have students read the text and locate the English cognates. After reading, students can select four cognates to write, draw a picture of, and put in a sentence (Ogle & Correa-Kovtun, 2010). Figure 11.7 presents one student's vocabulary cognate activity after reading *The News about Dinosaurs* (Lauber, 1989).

Vocabulary Cognates			Name_____
English	Spanish	Picture	Sentence
dinosaur	dinosauria		This dinosaur is a plant-eater
Scientist	cientifico		Some scientists study dinosaurs.
meteorite	meteorito		Scientists believe dinosaurs became extinct when a meteorite hit the earth.
Volcano	volvan		Volcanos may have caused dinosaurs to become extinct.

FIGURE 11.7 Vocabulary Cognate Activity after Reading *The News about Dinosaurs* (Lauber, 1989)

Teaching Fluency and Comprehension to English Language Learners

Chapters 8, 9, and 10 presented many strategies that teachers taught children to use for listening and reading comprehension. English language learners need these same strategies and learn through the same explicit modeling and practice lessons. Exemplary teachers use shared reading (enlarged copies of a text) projected by an overhead projector, a document camera, or on a Smart Board to teach these strategies (Fisher, Frey, & Lapp, 2008).

However, English language learners require more careful analysis of the text before presenting it to students in either shared reading or guided reading. This analysis is needed to detect problems that would create confusion for English language learners. For example, figurative language and idioms are possible areas in which ELLs may have difficulty comprehending (Avalos, Plasencia, Chavez, & Rascon, 2007). Consider the phrase "he flew the coop." This idiom would require explanation that the person was not really flying, nor was he flying away from a chicken coop. Rather, the person looked like a scared chicken who was running very quickly. Homophones and homographs are another source of confusion. **Homophones** are words that sound the same but have different meanings (*bear* versus *bare*). **Homographs** are words that have different meanings but are spelled the same (*bat*). English language learners are more likely to select the wrong meaning when reading these tricky words. When possible confusions are located, teachers consider how to introduce students to these text elements before reading to debug the book. For example, when reading *Knuffle Bunny* (Willems, 2004) aloud, teachers would note the use of the word *block* as meaning a city block that stretches from one street to the next rather than the block that is used to build in play.

English language learners also need explicit instruction about expository text structures and the language used in texts to signal these structures (Dreher & Gray, 2009). To teach the compare-and-contrast structure, teachers select a book with that structure and prepare the text for shared reading. Prior to reading, the teacher explains the structure. Some parts of texts compare two things. They tell us "how things are alike, the same." Some parts of texts contrast two things. They tell us "how things are not alike, are different." Teachers might use a Venn diagram as a visual aid to teach the lesson. As teachers read the text aloud, they would demonstrate how they think: "This tells me how crocodiles and alligators are alike so I write this under the word *both* because both crocodiles and alligators have sharp teeth and short legs." Later, they say, "This tells me how an alligator is different from a crocodile. Alligators have fatter, round snouts, and crocodiles have longer, pointed snouts. I write *fatter, round snouts* under Alligators, and I'll write *longer, pointed snouts* under Crocodiles" (adapted from Dreher & Gray, pp. 135–136).

Explicit Attention to the Sentence Structures of Written Text for English Language Learners

Teachers need to pay special attention to helping English language learners read complex sentences and obtain critical information from those sentences. The more advanced the level of a text, in general, the more complex are its sentence structures. Teachers can point out different kinds of sentences and help children collect examples of each sentence structure (Tompkins, 2006).

A **simple sentence** is composed of a subject and its predicate (e.g., "Patrick bought groceries," in which *Patrick* is the subject and *bought groceries* is the predicate). A **compound sentence** has two or more independent clauses, each with its own subject and predicate and joined by a conjunction (e.g., "Patrick went to town, and he bought groceries"). A **complex sentence** has at least one dependent clause and one independent clause (e.g., "Patrick bought groceries when he went to town," in which *when he went to town* is the dependent clause because although it has a subject and predicate, it could not stand alone as a sentence). A group of third-grade English language learners collected the following sentences from *Apples* (Gibbons, 2000).

- *An apple is a fruit.*
- *Some apples are grown at home, but most are grown commercially.*
- *As the colonists moved westward, they brought apple seeds and seedlings with them.*

Another way to scaffold English language learners' understanding of sentence structure is to make a special outline that organizes the material presented in a paragraph of a text students will read (Echevarria, Vogt, & Short, 2004). First, the teacher reads the passage that the students will read. Then, the teacher composes a short simplified paragraph that includes the major concepts from the passage that the children will be reading. Sentences are modified slightly, but most of the specialized vocabulary is included. Figure 10.8 presents a simplified paragraph and outline a third-grade teacher prepared for the book *Apples* (Gibbons, 2000). The sentences in the paragraph are not directly from the book, but each of the sentences contains phrases from sentences in the book. The sentence structure is simplified, and the concepts are defined more directly than in the book's sentences. This provides ELLs with opportunities to gain prior knowledge and learn a book's important concepts in simpler sentence structure. Children read the simplified paragraph with the teacher's support, discuss the information using the vocabulary introduced in the text, and then together fill in the outline using words from the paragraph. Children cannot copy from the sentences, but they must read carefully to select which information to use. Finally, children read the actual text.

Teaching Grammar to English Language Learners

Teaching grammar is controversial. Most experts recommend against direct teaching of grammar and instead argue that students will learn through reading and writing the various ways in which sentences work. We have seen that English language learners in classrooms with exemplary teachers often do not use English with completely well-formed sentence structures, and these utterances are expected. Teachers model for

FIGURE 11.8   Modified Paragraph and Outline for *Apples* (Gibbons, 2000)

In the springtime, apple blossoms begin to bloom on the apple trees. They are the apple flowers. Each blossom has a stamen with tiny grains of pollen on it. Bees visit the blossoms and they catch pollen on their feet. When they land on another apple blossom, they put the pollen on that flower. When pollen moves from one apple blossom to another, it is pollinated. Now the blossom can get ready to turn into an apple.

Pollination:

First, _____ from the apple tree begin to bloom in _____.

Tiny grains of pollen are found in each blossom on its _____.

Bees catch _____.

When bees visit another blossom, they _____.

Pollination is when the pollen from one blossom _____, _____.

students more correct usage by repeating and expanding what children have said. Teachers do focus more on grammar during the editing process in writing. In this stage of writing, teachers show children how to identify grammatical errors such as incorrect use of past tense forms, lack of subject-verb agreement, or incorrect use of *I* and *me*. Teachers can examine students' writing and identify the kinds of errors many students are making and then teach a mini-lesson about those errors.

Further, English language learners in the upper grades need to know grammar terms and their meanings. Figure 11.9 presents the seven parts of speech and a simple definition for each with examples. Students learn how these various kinds of words work in a sentence by examining sentences. One way to teach parts of speech is to introduce a part of speech and present a page of a book on the overhead projector or

FIGURE 11.9   Definitions and Examples of English Parts of Speech

Part of Speech	Definitions	Examples
Verb	Words that show action or states of being. Verbs can be singular or plural; present, past or future tense; or helping verbs that create tenses	*jump, jumps* *jump, jumped* *will jump, has jumped*
Adverb	Words that modify a verb, an adjective, or another adverb; Shows how, how often, how much, when, where, why	*happily, weekly, short* *tomorrow, inside*
Noun	Words used to name a person, place, thing, or idea; can be proper to name a particular person, place, or thing; otherwise nouns are common	*Mother Teresa, mother* *White House, house* *Tupperware, container* *honesty*
Pronoun	Words used in place of a noun	*I, we, you, he, she, me*
Adjective	Words used to describe a noun or pronoun; proper adjectives refer to the particular; otherwise adjectives are common	*Presidential (debate),* *high school (debate)* *best, prettiest, glowing*
Preposition	Words or group of words that indicate how ideas are related	*between, within, to, in*
Conjunction	Words that connect words	*and, although, because*

Smart Board. Then teachers demonstrate how to find, for example, all the verbs that show action. Next, students use their own book to find other verbs that show action. Third graders found these verbs on page 3 of *Stone Fox* (Gardiner, 1980): *lay, stared, looked, thought, lived, felt, dressed, took, laughed,* and *cried.*

Students also need to become familiar with different grammatical features of words. For example, three ways that plurals are made include adding *s, es,* or *a* (*run-runs, match-matches, curriculum-curricula*). Many verbs have two-form or three-form irregular tenses (*sweep-swept* and *drink-drank-drunk*). Adjectives become comparative when *er* is added and superlative when *est* is added (*big, bigger, biggest*). Students can also learn about the related noun/verb forms of words (*collection-collect; publication-publish, baby-babied*), noun/adjective forms of words (*happiness-happy, magic-magical*), and verb/adjective forms of words (*happiness-happily, magic-magically*).

Mr. Martinez is an exemplary fourth-grade teacher who takes a direct approach to teaching grammar (Tompkins, 2006). His students study verbs for four weeks. He teaches his students that there are four kinds of verbs: those that do not change form in present to past tense, regular verbs in which *ed* is added to the present tense to make the past tense, irregular verbs with two forms (present and past), and irregular verbs with three forms (present, past, and past participle). To teach verbs with three forms, he placed a large chart on which he had written Irregular Verbs: "present," "past," and "past participle." The chart had one example of each of the irregular verb tenses: *see, saw,* and *seen.* After reviewing the chart, he gave small groups of students a small copy of the chart and a set of words to sort in the irregular tenses. Students sorted the words by writing them onto the chart under the correct verb form. Figure 11.10 presents the word sort of irregular verb tenses one group of students completed.

FIGURE 11.10   Word Sort of Irregular Verbs

Present	Past	Past Participle
see	saw	seen
shake	shook	shaken
hide	hid	hidden
give	gave	given
begin	began	begun
fall	fell	fallen
shrink	shrank	shrunk
choose	chose	chosen
drink	drank	drunk
drive	drove	driven
know	knew	known

A final way to make students more aware of grammar is to unscramble sentences, imitate sentences, and combine sentences. For sentence unscrambling, teachers present the phrases of a sentence in scrambled order for students to reorder. For example, the following is a scrambled sentence from *Stone Fox* (Gardiner, 1980, p. 5):

which was over ten years ago

she was an old dog

actually born on the same day as little Willy

Unscrambled, this sentence is "She was an old dog—actually born on the same day as little Willy, which was over ten years ago." After unscrambling the sentence, the teacher presents it as written in the text and discusses with students the use of punctuation. In this sentence, the punctuation marks a phrase. The dash in the sentence could have been another comma, but teachers show how this dash brings importance to the next phrase in the sentence.

In sentence imitating, students are given a sentence from a book being read in the classroom and are challenged to write the sentence with the same structure but with different words. Teachers start with easy sentences and then move to ones more complex. Here are examples from *Stone Fox* (Gardiner, 1980, p. 21) and sentences composed by third graders.

Book: Little Willy held up two handfuls of money.

Students: Big Sally pulled out two fistfuls of hair.

Book: Little Willy inspected the potatoes, threw out the bad ones, and put the rest into sacks.

Students: Big Sally looked at the apples, took out the rotten ones, and put the rest into baskets.

In sentence combining, students put more than one sentence into a long, more complex sentence. Here are seven phrases that can be combined into one complex sentence:

Mr. Leeks was a tall man

Mr. Leeks had a thin face

Mr. Leeks was riding a horse

The horse was tall

The horse had a thin face

Mr. Leeks came out to the farm

Mr. Leeks bought the potatoes

The combined sentence is: "Mr. Leeks, a tall man with a thin face, riding a horse that was also tall and had a thin face, came out to the farm and bought the potatoes" (Gardiner, 1980, p. 21). Teachers start with sentences with three phrases to combine, and work up to more complex sentences. After combining sentences, teachers discuss the use of punctuation.

Assessment for English Language Learners

ALL CHILDREN BENEFIT FROM FREQUENT ASSESSMENT of their learning. Assessments given early in a school year should be carefully selected to help teachers quickly determine which students should be grouped together, and provide targets for instruction. Assessments provided in Chapters 3, 4, 7, and 8 are appropriate for preschoolers and kindergartners. The assessments discussed in Chapters 5 and 10 are very appropriate for English language learners who are in grades 1 and higher. As an alternative, the PALS 1-3 (Phonological Awareness Literacy Screening, 2007), a multilayered assessment that provides critical information for children in grades 1 through 3, has proven helpful in identifying specific needs of English language learners (Helman, 2005). In this assessment, all students are expected to take three subtests: word recognition in isolation, developmental spelling, and oral reading in context. For students who do not reach benchmark ranges on these assessments, they are also assessed on the foundational concepts of letter knowledge, phonemic awareness, and concept of word. Word recognition in isolation assesses children's ability to identify grade-level words automatically. Children are asked to spell words in the developmental spelling inventory, and the words spelled have different spelling features. Children at different grade levels are given more challenging words with more complex spelling features. In the oral reading in context assessment, children read a graded passage (on different difficulty levels). Word accuracy, fluency, and comprehension are measured.

Though Spanish-speaking children score lower on these assessments than their English-only peers, the results of the assessments provide teachers with valuable information (Helman, 2005). For example, at the end of first grade, most English-only students are reading at the first-grade level whereas most Spanish-speaking children are reading at the primer level. However, individual children's profiles on these assessments provide more specific targets for instruction. For example, one Hispanic first grader read a primer-level text and answered six out of six questions. However, he only identified nine of twenty words in isolation. Another Hispanic first grader read a first-grade level text with accuracy but only answered three out of six questions. She read fifteen of twenty words in isolation correctly (pp. 672–673). The results of this one assessment suggest that the first student is in need of intense instruction in sight words and the second student demonstrates an urgent need for more explicit instruction in comprehension.

Another assessment that we recommend for English language learners is the Word Writing CAFÉ. This is an assessment of a student's fluency in writing words, accuracy in writing words, and growing word complexity (Leal, 2005/2006). It is similar to Clay's (2005) Writing Vocabulary assessment in which children are given ten minutes to write all the words they know, and the correct spellings are counted and compared to national norms. This assessment can be given to large groups of students and is easy to interpret. For first graders, we recommend that teachers use Clay's procedures and the norms presented in her assessment book (p. 180). For second graders and above, teachers can use the Word Writing CAFÉ. Here, students are presented with several sheets of paper, each divided into thirty boxes. Students are told they will be writing for ten minutes and writing as many different words as they know. They are to write one word in each box, without repeating words or writing names (such as the names of their friends or family members). Before writing, students are asked to think of things they can hear, taste, smell, feel, or see; things that tell about their home or the classroom; or, things they like to do. Students are reminded to spell all the little words they know such as *the* and *we*. Finally, they are told to write every word they know how to write. Teachers give students exactly ten minutes, then all students stop writing. Of course, this assessment needs to be given after teachers have covered much of the words in the classroom, or it might be given in the school library where less print is available.

Teachers count the total number of different words each child spelled correctly and the number of words spelled correctly with one syllable, two syllables, three syllables, and more than three syllables. In second grade, the students in one school wrote a mean of seventy-eight correct words including sixty-five one-syllable words, twelve two-syllable words, and one three-syllable words. Third graders wrote a mean of seventy-nine words but more two-syllable words and fewer one-syllable words. Across the grades, the number of two-syllable words written correctly was the biggest indication of increase in word writing fluency (Leal, 2005/2006, p. 344). Teachers can use this group assessment to make sure students are learning to spell a variety of words— eighty would be a good goal—and that students are increasingly able to spell words with more than one syllable. This assessment is a quick check and would easily identify students who need more intensive spelling and sight word instruction.

CHAPTER SUMMARY

ENGLISH LANGUAGE LEARNERS who learn to listen and speak in English and to read and write in English require the same kind of exemplary teaching as all children. However, there are special considerations that need to be taken into account when planning instruction for these children. Teachers need to become familiar with the cultural opportunities in the neighborhoods where children live, interview families about the language spoken in the home, and find out more about the written properties of the home language versus English. Teachers also need to know what stage of English language learning each student has reached: preproduction, early production, speech emergence, or intermediate fluency. This level of language influences the kinds of books read aloud and the language learning experiences that are most effective. It also determines the number of sight words children can learn.

Five characteristics of highly effective instruction for English language learners are joint activity, focused literacy and language instruction, rigorous curriculum calling for higher-level thinking, use of conversation in small groups, and contextualization. The use of home language is accepted, and teachers draw upon the language resources of all students to support English language learning. Teachers plan for ways to bring the home language into instructional activities using parent or other volunteer support for special projects.

English language learners need direct instruction in decoding and spelling using a systematic approach. They learn vocabulary by seeing and hearing new words both before reading and after reading. Using vocabulary charts with text sets is an effective vocabulary learning technique. Comprehension is expanded through a special ELL interactive reading technique, when children's language and comprehension indicate this need. English language learners need to learn more about the parts of speech and forms of English verbs. Sentence unscrambling, imitating, and combining are appropriate techniques for helping students understand sentence structures, the role words play within sentences, and how punctuation serves as a guide to comprehension and phrasing in fluent reading.

Applying the Information

Julia Felix is a first-year teacher in a large urban school that serves children from a variety of cultural and language backgrounds. This year, she will be teaching third grade [or you may assume that she will be teaching kindergarten]. She opens her class list and reads the following names (X = ELL student) (Faltis, 1993, p. 5).

1. Leon	13. Kyung X
2. Kimberly	14. Gina
3. Xiancoung X	15. Frank
4. Daniel	16. Chatty
5. Lisa	17. Guadalupe X
6. Maria Eugenia X	18. Kathy
7. Jeffrey	19. Do Thi X
8. Aucencio X	20. Jimmy X
9. Concepcion X	21. Amy
10. Jessica	22. Leonard
11. Tyrone	23. Antonin
12. Sean	

Julia thinks to herself, "I especially want the ELL students to fully join in my class" (Faltis, 1993, p. 6). How will Julia accomplish this task? What suggestions can you make about her room arrangement, the materials she will need, and the modifications she can be expected to make in instruction? Suppose that Julia decides to teach a unit about wild animals. Make suggestions for materials that she can include in the unit, and plan at least one lesson that will meet the needs of the English language learners in her class.

GOING BEYOND THE TEXT

VISIT A PRESCHOOL OR ELEMENTARY SCHOOL that has many English language learners. Observe the children in their classroom as they interact with the other children and during literacy activities. Take note of ways in which the English language learners are similar to and different from the other children. If possible, talk to a teacher about supporting the literacy learning of English language learners. Take at least one reading and one writing activity that you can share with an English language learner. For example, take a children's book and literature props for the child to retell the story; plan a hands-on experience, such as popping corn, that will stimulate writing; or prepare a special book that you can give to the child for his or her own journal. Carefully observe the child's language and behaviors during these literacy activities. Be ready to discuss what this child knows about literacy.

REFERENCES

Anthony, A. (2008). Output strategies for English-language learners: Theory to practice. *The Reading Teacher, 61*, 472–482.

Asher, J. (1982). *Learning another language through actions: The complete teachers' guidebook*. Los Gatos, CA: Sky Oaks Productions.

Au, K. H. (2000). Multicultural factors and the effective instruction of students of diverse backgrounds. In A. E. Farstrup & S. J. Samuels (Eds.), *What research has to say about reading instruction* (3rd ed.) (pp. 392–413). Newark, DE: International Reading Association.

Avalos, M., Plasencia, A., Chavez, C., & Rascon, J. (2007). Modified guided reading: Gateway to English as a second language and literacy learning. *The Reading Teacher, 61*, 318–329.

Barone, D. M., Mallette, M. H., & Xu, S. H. (2005). *Teaching early literacy: Development, assessment, and instruction*. New York: Guilford Press.

Bear, D., Invernizzi, M., Templeton, S., & Johnston, F. (2008). *Words their way: Word study for phonics, vocabulary, and spelling instruction* (3rd ed.). Upper Saddle River, NJ: Prentice Hall.

Blachowicz, C., & Obrochta, C. (2005). Vocabulary visits: Virtual field trips for content vocabulary development. *The Reading Teacher, 59*, 262–268.

Blake, B. (1992). Talk in non-native and native English speakers' peer writing conferences: What's the difference? *Language Arts, 69*, 604–610.

Caple, K. (2000). *Well done, Worm!* Cambridge, MA: Candlewick Press.

Clay, M. (2005). *An observation survey of early literacy achievement*. Portsmouth, NH: Heinemann.

Cummins, J. (1986). Empowering minority students: A framework for intervention. *Harvard Educational Review, 56*, 18–36.

Cummins, J., Chow, P., & Schecter, S. (2006). Community as curriculum. *Language Arts, 83*, 297–307.

De Avila, E., & Duncan, S. (1994). *Language assessment scales*. Monteray, CA: CTB Macmillan/McGraw-Hill.

Dreher, M., & Gray, J. (2009). Compare, contrast, comprehend: Using compare-contrast test structures with ELLs in K-3 classrooms. *The Reading Teacher, 63*, 132–141.

Echevarria, J., Vogt, M., & Short, D. (2000). *Making content comprehensible for English language learners: The SIOP model*. Boston: Allyn & Bacon.

Echevarria, J., Vogt, M., & Short, D. (2004). *Making content comprehensible for English language leaners: The SIOP model* (2nd ed.). Boston: Allyn & Bacon.

Faltis, C. (1993). *Joinfostering: Adapting teaching strategies for the multilingual classroom.* New York: Merrill/Macmillan.

Fisher, D., Frey, N., & Lapp, D. (2008). Shared readings, modeling comprehension, vocabulary, text structures, and text features for older readers. *The Reading Teacher, 61,* 548–556.

Freeman, D., & Freeman, E. (2001). *Between worlds: Access to second language acquisition.* Portsmouth, NH: Heinemann.

Gardiner, J. (1980). *Stone fox.* New York: Harper-Collins.

Genishi, C., & Dyson, A. H. (1984). *Language assessment in the early years.* Norwood, NJ: Ablex Publishing.

Gersten, R., & Jiménez, R. (1994). A delicate balance: Enhancing literature instruction for students of English as a second language. *The Reading Teacher, 47,* 438–449.

Gibbons, G. (2000). *Apples.* New York: Scholastic.

Hadaway, N. L., Vardell, S. M., & Young, T. A. (2002). *Literature-based instruction with English language learners, K–12.* Boston: Allyn & Bacon.

Helman, L. (2005). Using literacy assessment results to improve teaching for English-language learners. *The Reading Teacher, 58,* 668–677.

Helman, L. A., & Burns, M. K. (2008, September). What does oral language have to do with it? Helping young English-language learners acquire a sight word vocabulary. *The Reading Teacher, 62*(1), 14–19. doi: 10.1598/RT.62.1.2.

Hickman, P., Pollard-Durodola, S., & Vaughn, S. (2004). Storybook reading: Improving vocabulary and comprehension for English-language learners. *The Reading Teacher, 57*(8), 720–730.

Hill, E. (1980). *Where's Spot?* New York: Putnam.

Iddings, A., Risko, V., & Rampulla, M. (2009). When you don't speak their language: Guiding English-language learners through conversations about text. *The Reading Teacher, 63,* 52–61.

Krashen, S. (1985). *Inquiries and insights: Second language teaching: Immersion and bilingual education, literacy.* Hayward, CA: Alemany Press.

Lara, S. G. M. (1989). Reading placement for code switchers. *The Reading Teacher, 42,* 278–282.

Lauber, P. (1989). *The news about dinosaurs.* New York: Bradbury Press.

Leal, D. (2005/2006). The Word Writing CAFÉ: Assessing student writing for complexity, accuracy, and fluency. *The Reading Teacher, 59,* 340–350.

Manyak, P. (2008). What's your news? Portraits of a rich literacy activity for English language-learners. *The Reading Teacher, 61,* 450–458.

Martinez-Roldan, C. M., & Lopez-Robertson, J. M. (1999/2000). Initiating literature circles in a first-grade bilingual classroom. *The Reading Teacher, 53,* 270–281.

McIntyre, E., Kyle, D., Chen, C.-T., Kraemer, J., & Parr, J. (2009). *6 principles for teaching English language learners in all classrooms.* Thousand Oaks: Corwin Press.

McKissack, P. (1988). *Mirandy and Brother Wind.* New York: Alfred A. Knopf.

Moustafa, M., & Penrose, J. (1985). Comprehensible input PLUS, the language experience approach: Reading instruction for limited English speaking students. *The Reading Teacher, 38,* 640–647.

Ogle, D., & Correa-Kovtun, A. (2010). Supporting English language-learners and struggling readers in content literacy with the "partner reading and content, too" routine. *The Reading Teacher, 63,* 532–542.

Orellana, M. E., & Hernandez, A. (1999). Talking with the walk: Children reading urban environmental print. *The Reading Teacher, 51,* 612–619.

Peyton, J., Ranard, D., & McGinnis, S. (Eds.). (2001). *Heritage languages in America: Preserving a national resource.* McHenry, IL: Delta Systems.

Phonological Awareness Literacy Screening. (2007). Retrieved August 7, 2010. http://pals.virginia.edu/tools-1-3.html.

Rey, H. (1969). *Curious George.* Boston: Houghton Mifflin.

Schwarzer, D., Haywood, A., & Lorenzen, C. (2003). Fostering multiliteracy in a linguistically diverse classroom. *Language Arts, 80,* 453–460.

Stojic, M. (2002). *Hello World!: Greetings in 42 languages around the globe.* New York: Scholastic.

Swain, M. (2005). The output hypothesis: Theory and research. In E. Hinkel (Ed.), *Handbook of research in second language teaching and learning* (pp. 471–483). Mahwah, NJ: Lawrence Erlbaum Associates.

Tabors, P. O. (1997). *One child, two languages.* Baltimore, MD: Brookes Publishing.

Tompkins, G. (2006). *Language arts essentials.* Upper Saddle River, NJ: Pearson.

Urzua, C. (1980). A language-learning environment for all children. *Language Arts, 57,* 38–44.

VanPatten, B. (2003). *From input to output: A teacher's guide to second language acquisition.* Boston: McGraw-Hill.

Walsh, E. (1995). *Mouse paint.* New York: Red Wagon Books.

Willems, M. (2004). *Knuffle Bunny: A cautionary tale by Mo Willems.* New York: Hyperion Books.

Williams, J. A. (2001). Classroom conversations: Opportunities to learn for ESL students in mainstream classrooms. *The Reading Teacher, 54,* 750–757.

Wood, A. (1996). *The napping house.* New York: Harcourt.

Xu, S. H., & Rutledge, A. L. (2003). "Chicken" starts with "ch"! Kindergarteners learn through environmental print. *Young Children, 58,* 44–51.

Ziefert, H. (1996). *Where is my baby?* Brooklyn, NY: Handprint Books.

myeducationlab

Go to the topic English Language Learners in the MyEducationLab (www.myeducationlab.com) for your course, where you can:

- Find learning outcomes for English Language Learners along with the national standards that connect to these outcomes.
- Complete Assignments and Activities that can help you more deeply understand the chapter content.
- Examine challenging situations and cases presented in the IRIS Center Resources.

A+RISE

Go to the Topic A+RISE in the MyEducationLab (www.myeducationlab.com) for your course. A+RISE® Standards2Strategy™ is an innovative and interactive online resource that offers new teachers in grades K–12 just-in-time, research-based instructional strategies that:

- Meet the linguistic needs of ELLs as they learn content
- Differentiate instruction for all grades and abilities
- Offer reading and writing techniques, cooperative learning, use of linguistic and nonlinguistic representations, scaffolding, teacher modeling, higher order thinking, and alternative classroom ELL assessment
- Provide support to help teachers be effective through the integration of listening, speaking, reading, and writing along with the content curriculum
- Improve student achievement
- Are aligned to Common Core Elementary Language Arts standards (for the literacy strategies) and to English language proficiency standards in WIDA, Texas, California, and Florida.

Children's Literature

Alphabet Books

Archambault, J., & Martin, B. (1989). *Chicka chicka boom boom*. New York: Scholastic.

Carle, E. (2007). *Eric Carle's ABC (The world of Eric Carle)*. New York: Grosset & Dunlap.

Castella, K. (2006). *Discovering nature's alphabet*. Berkeley: Heyday Books.

Ehlert, L. (1989). *Eating the alphabet*. New York: Harcourt.

Elting, M., & Folsom, M. (1980). *Q is for duck*. New York: Clarion Books.

Isadora, R. (1983). *City seen from A to Z*. New York: Greenwillow Books.

Johnson, S. T. (1995). *Alphabet city*. New York: Penguin.

Lobel, A. (1981). *On Market Street*. New York: Greenwillow Books.

McMillan, B. (1986). *Counting wildflowers*. New York: Lothrop, Lee & Shepard Books.

Moon, J. (2006). *Making letters: A very first writing book*. Columbus, OH: Brighter Minds Media.

Schnur, S. (1997). *Autumn: An alphabet acrostic*. New York: Houghton Mifflin.

Seeger, L. (2010). *The hidden alphabet*. New York: Roaring Brook Press.

Seuss, Dr. (Theodore Geisel). (1963). *Dr. Seuss's ABC*. New York: Random House.

Shannon, G. (1996). *Tomorrow's alphabet*. New York: Greenwillow Books.

Books to Read Aloud to Young Children

Baker, K. (1994). *Big fat hen*. New York: Harcourt.

Berenstain, J., & Berenstain, S. (1971). *Bears in the night*. New York: Random House.

Brown, M. (1942). *The runaway bunny*. New York: Harper & Row.

Brown, M. (1947). *Goodnight moon*. New York: Harper & Row.

Burningham, J. (1971). *Mr. Grumpy's outing*. New York: Henry Holt & Company.

Chorao, K. (1977). *The baby's lap book*. New York: Dutton Children's Books.

Clifton, L. (1977). *Amifika*. New York: E. P. Dutton Children's Books.

Crews, D. (1978). *Freight train*. New York: Greenwillow Books.

Eastman, P. D. (1960). *Are you my mother?* New York: Random House.

Freeman, D. (1968). *Corduroy*. New York: Viking Press.

Galdone, P. (1973a). *The little red hen*. New York: Scholastic.

Galdone, P. (1973b). *The three bears*. New York: Scholastic.

Galdone, P. (1986). *Three little kittens*. New York: Clarion.

Havill, J. (1986). *Jamaica's find*. Boston: Houghton Mifflin.

Hort, L. (2000). *The seals on the bus*. New York: Henry Holt & Company.

Hughes, S. (1985). *Bathwater's hot*. New York: Lothrop, Lee & Shepard Books.

Hutchins, P. (1971). *Rosie's walk*. New York: Macmillan.

Lewis, K. (1996). *One summer day*. Cambridge, MA: Candlewick Press.

Lewis, K. (1997). *Friends*. Cambridge, MA: Candlewick Press.

*Ormerod, J. (1981). *Sunshine*. New York: Puffin Books.

*Oxenbury, H. (1982). *Good night, good morning*. New York: Dial Press.

Pinkney, J. (2009). *The lion and the mouse*. New York: Little, Brown.

Rice, E. (1981). *Benny bakes a cake*. New York: Greenwillow Books.

Shannon, D. (1998). *No, David!* New York: Scholastic.

Slobodkina, E. (1947). *Caps for sale*. New York: Addison-Wesley.

Steen, S., & Steen, S. (2001). *Car wash*. New York: Putnam.

Wells, R. (1973). *Noisy Nora*. New York: Dial Press.

Willems, M. (2004). *Knuffle bunny: A cautionary tale*. New York: Hyperion Books.

Willems, M. (2007). *Knuffle bunny too: A case of mistaken identity*. New York: Hyperion Books.

Tolstoy, A. (1968). *The great big enormous turnip*. Danbury, CT: Franklin Watts

Predictable and Language Play Books

Brown, M. (1994). *Four fur feet*. New York: Hyperion Books.

Burningham, J. (1978). *Would you rather . . . ?* New York: Crowell.

Carle, E. (1977). *The grouchy ladybug*. New York: Crowell.

Edwards, P. M. (1996). *Some smug slug*. New York: HarperCollins.

Fleming, D. (1993). *In the small, small pond*. New York: Scholastic.

Fox, M. (1987). *Hattie and the fox*. New York: Bradbury Press.

Ho, M. (1996). *Hush! A Thai lullaby*. New York: Orchard Books.

Kavalski, M. (1987). *The wheels on the bus*. Boston: Little, Brown.

Martin, B., Jr. (1983). *Brown bear, brown bear*. New York: Henry Holt & Company.

Most, B. (1996). *Cock a doodle moo*. New York: Harcourt.

Plourde, L. (1997). *Pigs in the mud in the middle of the rud*. New York: Blue Sky Press.

Root, P. (1998). *One duck stuck*. Cambridge, MA: Candlewick Press.

Schneider, R. M. (1995). *Add it, dip it, fix it*. Boston: Houghton Mifflin.

Sendak, M. (1962). *Chicken soup with rice*. New York: Harper & Row.

Smith, M., & Ziefert, H. (1989). *In a scary old house*. New York: Penguin.

Sweet, M. (1992). *Fiddle-i-fee*. Boston: Little, Brown.

Tabak, S. (1997). *There was an old lady who swallowed a fly*. New York: Scholastic.

Westcott, N. B. (1987). *Peanut butter and jelly*. New York: Trumpet Club.

Wilson, K. (2006). *Moose tracks*. New York: McElderry Books.

Wilson, K. (2007). *A frog in the bog*. New York: McElderry Books.

Wood, A. (1982). *Quick as a cricket*. Singapore: Child's Play (International).

Ziefert, H. (2002). *Who said moo?* New York: Handprint Books.

*Wordless books.

Multicultural Books

Barnwell, Y. (1998). *No mirrors in my nana's house.* New York: Harcourt.

Bruchac, J., & Longdon, J. (1992). *Thirteen moons on turtle's back: A Native American year of moons.* New York: Philomel Books.

Bryan, A. (1986). *Lion and the ostrich chick and other African folk tales.* New York: Atheneum Books.

Caines, J. (1982). *Just us women.* New York: Harper & Row.

Choi, S. (1993). *Hal Moni and the picnic.* Boston: Houghton Mifflin.

Clifton, L. (1970). *Some of the days of Everett Anderson.* New York: Henry Holt & Company.

Coutant, H., & Vo-Dinh. (1974). *First snow.* New York: Alfred A. Knopf.

Crews, D. (1991). *Big Mama's.* New York: Greenwillow Books.

Cruz Martinez, A. (1991). *The woman who out-shone the sun/La mujer que brillaba aun mas que el sol.* San Francisco: Children's Book Press.

Delacre, L. (1989). *Arroz con leche: Popular songs and rhymes from Latin America.* New York: Scholastic.

Delacre, L. (1990). *Las Navidades: Popular Christmas songs from Latin America.* New York: Scholastic.

Dorros, A. (1991). *Abuela.* New York: Dutton Children's Books.

Garza, C. (1990). *Family pictures.* San Francisco: Children's Book Press.

Giovanni, N. (1985). *Spin a soft black song.* New York: HarperCollins.

Goble, P. (1989). *Iktomi and the berries.* New York: Orchard Books.

Goble, P. (1992). *Crow chief: A Plains Indian story.* New York: Orchard Books.

Greene, B. (1974). *Philip Hall likes me. I reckon maybe.* New York: Dial Press.

Greenfield, E. (1988a). *Grandpa's face.* New York: Philomel Books.

Greenfield, E. (1988b). *Nathaniel talking.* New York: Black Butterfly Children's Books.

Hamilton, V. (1985). *The people could fly.* New York: Alfred A. Knopf.

Havill, J. (1989). *Jamaica tag-along.* Boston: Houghton Mifflin.

Howard, E. (1991). *Aunt Flossie's hats (and crab cakes later).* Boston: Houghton Mifflin.

Johnson, A. (1989). *Tell me a story, Mama.* New York: Orchard Books.

Levine, E. (2007). *Henry's freedom box.* New York: Scholastic.

Lin, G. (2009). *Where the mountain meets the moon.* New York: Little, Brown.

Martin, F. (2000). *Clever tortoise: A traditional African tale.* Cambridge, MA: Candlewick Press.

Martinez, E., & Soto, G. (1993). *Too many tamales.* New York: Putnam.

Mathis, S. (1975). *The hundred penny box.* New York: Viking Press.

McKissack, P. (1986). *Flossie and the fox.* New York: Dial Press.

Mollel, T. (1993). *The king and the tortoise.* New York: Houghton Mifflin.

Park, L. (2008). *Bee-bim bop!* Boston: Sandpiper Books.

Park, L. (2009). *The firekeeper's son.* Boston: Sandpiper Books.

Pena, S. (1987). *Kikiriki: Stories and poems in English and Spanish for children.* Houston: Arte Público Press.

Price, L. (1990). *Aida.* New York: Harcourt.

Say, A. (1990). *El Chino.* Boston: Houghton Mifflin.

Say, A. (1993). *Grandfather's journey.* Boston: Houghton Mifflin.

Sneeve, V. (1989). *Dancing teepees: Poems of American Indian youth.* New York: Holiday House Publishing.

Soto, G. (1993). *Too many tamales.* New York: Putnam.

Steptoe, J. (1969). *Stevie.* New York: Harper & Row.

Steptoe, J. (1987). *Mufaro's beautiful daughters.* New York: Lothrop, Lee & Shepard Books.

Strete, C. (1990). *Big thunder magic.* New York: Greenwillow Books.

Tafolla, C. (1987). *Patchwork colcha: A children's collection.* Flagstaff, AZ: Creative Educational Enterprises.

Takeshita, F. (1988). *The park bench.* New York: Kane/Miller.

Xiong, B. (1989). *Nine-in-one grr! grr! A folktale from the Hmong people of Laos.* San Francisco: Children's Book Press.

Young, E. (1989). *Lon po po.* New York: Putnam.

Recommended Books for Guided-Reading Instruction in First Grade

Title	Basal Level	Publisher
	Levels 1–2	
	Readiness/Kindergarten	
Dad		PM Starters (Rigby)
Ghost		Wright
Mom		PM Starters
Pets		PM Starters
The Birthday Cake		Wright
Gabby Visits Buster		Pioneer Valley
Packing My Bag		PM Starters
The Go-Karts		PM Starters
The Pencil		PM Starters
The Way I Go to School		PM Starters
	Levels 3–4	
	Preprimer 1	
Fun with Mo and Toots		Pacific Learning
The Little Red Hen		Pioneer Valley
Tiger, Tiger		New PM
Wake Up, Dad		New PM
The Big Kick		New PM
Copycat		Wright
Let's Have a Swim		Wright
Little Chimp and Big Chimp		PM Plus
Little Pig		Wright
Shark in a Sack		Wright
	Levels 5–6	
	Preprimer 2	
Bella's Birthday		Pioneer Valley
Ben's Treasure Hunt		New PM
Father Bear Goes Fishing		New PM
Gabby Is Hungry		Pioneer Valley
Kitty Cat and Fat Cat		PM Plus
Look for Me		Wright
Tom Is Brave		New PM
Baby Hippo		PM Extension
Blackberries		PM Plus
Bread		Wright
The Hungry Kitten		New PM
Jolly Roger the Pirate		PM Extension
Little Chimp Runs Away		PM Plus
Where Are You Going, Aja Rose?		Wright Group
Where Is Miss Pool?		Pacific Learning

Levels 7–8
Preprimer 3

Baby Bear Goes Fishing	New PM
Bella and Rosie Play Hide and Seek	Pioneer Valley
Ben's Dad	New PM
Jolly Roger and the Treasure	PM Plus
Nick's Glasses	Pacific Learning
Pat's New Puppy	Pearson/Reading Unlimited
The Red Rose	Wright
Bella and Rosie Trick or Treat	Pioneer Valley
Kitty Cat Plays Inside	PM Plus
Little Chimp and Baby Chimp	PM Plus
A Lucky Day for Little Dinosaur	PM Extensions
Seagull Is Clever	New PM

Levels 9–11
Primer

Baby Bear's Present	New PM
The Biggest Cake in the World	Pacific Learning
Kitty Cat and the Paint	PM Plus
The Lion's Tale	Pearson/Reading Unlimited
Magpie's Baking Day	New PM
The Three Billy Goats Gruff	Pioneer Valley
The Best Cake	New PM
Jane's Car	New PM
The Lion and the Rabbit	New PM
Gabby and the Christmas Tree	Pioneer Valley
Gabby Runs Away	Pioneer Valley
Greedy Cat	Pacific Learning
The Hungry Giant	Wright
Little Chimp and the Termites	PM Plus
Ten Little Bears	Pearson/Reading Unlimited
The Three Bears	Pioneer Valley

Levels 12–14
Primer–Early First Grade

Bella Is a Bad Dog	Pioneer Valley
Brave Triceratops	New PM
Candlelight	New PM
The Clever Penguins	New PM
House Hunting	New PM
The Hungry Giant's Soup	Wright
Red Socks and Yellow Socks	Wright
Terrible Tiger	Wright
Father Bear's Surprise	PM Extensions
The Fox Who Foxed	New PM

The Little Red Bus	New PM
Mrs. Spider's Beautiful Web	New PM
Ratty-Tatty	Wright
The Three Pigs	Pearson/Reading Unlimited
The Missing Necklace	Pearson/Reading Unlimited

Levels 15–18
First Grade–Early Second Grade

Poor Sore Hungry Giant	Hameray
The Hungry Giant's Shoe	Hameray
Mrs. Wishy Washy and the Big Farm Fair	Hameray
Mrs. Wishy-Washy and the Big Wash	Hameray
Mrs. Wishy-Washy and the Big Tub	Hameray
The Hungry Giant's Baby	Hameray
Are You My Mother?	P. D. Eastman
Goodnight Owl	Pat Hutchins
Just Me and My Dad	Mercer Mayer
Kiss for Little Bear	E. H. Minarik
Noisy Nora	Rosemary Wells
There's a Nightmare in My Closet	Mercer Mayer
Mouse Soup	Arnold Lobel
Mouse Tales	Arnold Lobel
More Tales of Amanda Pig	Jan Van Leeuwen

APPENDIX

B

Preschool and Kindergarten Monitoring Assessments

Uppercase Alphabet Recognition
Child Administration Sheet

(Copy letters as presented on one sheet of paper for older children or copy each line of letters on separate index cards for younger children.)

O	B	S	A	T	M
Q	K	D	U	R	Z
C	F	N	W	Y	G
L	E	H	P	I	X
V	J				

Lowercase Alphabet Recognition
Child Administration Sheet

(Copy letters as presented on one sheet of paper for older children or copy each line of letters on separate index cards for younger children.)

o	a	c	e	g	m
b	s	r	u	t	z
f	n	w	y	d	l
h	p	i	x	v	j
q	k				

Preschool and Kindergarten Monitoring Score Sheet

Name of Child _____   Date of Administration _____

Uppercase Alphabet Recognition Task

(Use child administration sheet provided. Have child identify each letter. Circle letters correctly identified on score sheet.)

O	B	S	A	T	M
Q	K	D	U	R	Z
C	F	N	W	Y	G
L	E	H	P	I	X
V	J				

Lowercase Alphabet Recognition Task

(Use child administration sheet provided. Have child identify each letter. Circle letters correctly identified on score sheet.)

o	a	c	e	g	m
b	s	r	u	t	z
f	n	w	y	d	l
h	p	i	x	v	j
q	k				

Name Writing Task

(Give child a sheet of paper and have child write his/her name.) Score the signature:

Level 0:   Uncontrolled scribble
Level 1:   Controlled scribble such as mock cursive
Level 2:   Separate marks that do not resemble letters
Level 3:   One or two recognizable letters (may have orientation difficulties)
Level 4:   Mostly recognizable letters (may have orientation difficulties)
Level 5:   Recognizable and correct signature with few orientation difficulties
Level 6:   First and last name using mostly correct formation

Writing Alphabet Task

(If child can write a signature at level 3 or higher, ask child to write letters in order presented on uppercase alphabet recognition task. Score correct letters that are recognizable even if they have orientation difficulties.)

Concepts about Print Task

(Use a picture book with two pages that have just two to three lines of text.)

Bookhandling
(Hand the book to the child and ask child to)
1. Show front.   2. Show back.

(Open book and point to right-hand page, ask child to)
3. Point to top.   4. Point to bottom.

Directionality
(Gesture down right-hand page, and ask child, "Where do I read next?")
5. Child must turn to next page.

(Ask child on double spread, "Which page do I read first?")
6. Child must point to left page.

(Gesture down left-hand page, and ask child, "Where do I read after I read this page?")
7. Child must point to right page.

(Gesture down left page, and ask child, "Where exactly would I begin to read this page?")
8. Child must point to first word in first line of text.

(Point to first word in first line of text, and ask child, "After I read this word, where do I read next?")
9. Child must point to next word or sweep left to right across first line of text.

(Sweep finger across first line of text, and ask child, "After I read this line, where do I read next?")
10. Child must point to first word in second line of text.

Letter and Word Concepts
(Gesture down right page, ask child to)
11. Show one letter.   12. Show one word.

(Ask child to)
13. Point to short word. (Child must point to word with three or fewer letters.)
14. Point to long word. (Child must point to word with five or more letters.)

(Sweep finger across the first line of text, and ask the child to)
15. Count words in line of text. (Child must count words accurately.)

Phonological Awareness Task: Generating Rhyming Words

1. "Let's see how many rhyming words you can name for *bat*. I know one. *Hat.* Now you tell me words that rhyme with *BAT.*" Count number of rhyming words generated for *BAT* (may count nonsense words).

2. "Now you tell me words that rhyme with *LAKE.*" Count number of rhyming words generated for *LAKE* (may count nonsense words).

Phonemic Awareness Task: Isolating Beginning Sounds

("Today we are going to listen to sounds in the beginning of words. My word is *boat. Boat* begins with /b/; you say /b/. Let's try another one. My word is *feet. Feet* begins with /f/; you say /f/. Remember; say the beginning sound of the word." If child gives the letter name, say, "That is the letter name. Say the sound." Only score the beginning sound correct, not the letter or portion of word.)

1. /r/ *rain*	2. /b/ *bed*	3. /k/ *kite*	4. /h/ *horse*
5. /b/ *bunny*	6. /w/ *wig*	7. /h/ *house*	8. /d/ *duck*
9. /t/ *tire*	10. /s/ *sun*		

Oral Comprehension and Vocabulary Task: Retelling Checklist for *Owl Moon* (Yolen, 1987)

"Here is the book we have been reading (show only front cover of book). Now you tell me everything you remember that happened in this story." Put a check beside each statement child makes in retelling (use gist of child's statement). Circle bolded words that best describe the child's retelling. If child makes statements not included in checklist, write statements on the checklist.

_____ late one winter night past my bedtime

_____ Pa and I went owling

_____ As Pa and I walked toward the woods

_____ Pa did not call out

_____ you have to be quiet if you go owling

_____ Pa stopped at the pine trees

_____ he called who-who-whoooo

_____ the sound of a great horned owl

_____ he was silent and we listened

_____ there was no answer

_____ we walked on and I felt cold

_____ you have to make your own heat if you go owling

_____ we went into the woods

_____ the woods were dark, black

_____ you have to be brave if you go owling

_____ we came to a clearing

_____ Pa called who-who-whoooo

_____ An echo came through the tree who-who-whoooo

_____ Pa called back who-who-whooooo

_____ Just as if he and the owl were talking

_____ The owl's shadow flew over us

_____ Pa turned on his flashlight

_____ just as the owl was landing on a branch

_____ we stared at one another

_____ then the owl flew back into the forest

_____ Pa and I walked back

_____ When you go owling you need hope

_____ like hope that flies on wings under an owl moon

Ideas _____/28

Past tense: consistent   inconsistent   none

Sequence: correct   incorrect   random

Characters: all by name   some   no names

Main events: most   some   few   none

Setting: place   time

Overall summary statement: yes   no

Class Profile Preschool and Kindergarten Monitoring Assessments

Name	ABC	abc	name	Write abc	CAP	rhyme	Begin pho	Retell ideas	Retell vocab

APPENDIX

C

Preschool and Kindergarten Monitoring Assessments

Advanced Assessments

Letter-Sound Association Child Administration Sheet

(Copy letters as presented on one sheet of paper.)

B	S	T	M		
K	D	R	Z		
C	F	N	W	Y	G
L	H	P			
V	J				

Finger-Point Reading Child Administration Sheet

(Make a booklet with four pages. Put the title on the first page.) Pages:

2.   I'm a little teapot,
short and stout

3.   Here is my handle.
Here is my spout.

4.   When I get all steamed up,
then I shout.

5.   Tip me over,
and pour me out.

"I'm a Little Teapot"

I'm a little teapot,

short and stout.

Here is my handle.

Here is my spout.

When I get all steamed up,

Then I shout.

Tip me over,

and pour me out.

Preschool and Kindergarten Monitoring Score Sheet:
For Advanced Assessment

Name of Child _____   Date of Administration _____

Letter-Sound Association Task

(Use child administration sheet provided. Have child identify the sound of each letter. Circle on this score sheet letters for which child correctly identified sounds.)

B	S	T	M		
K	D	R	Z		
C	F	N	W	Y	G
L	H	P			
V	J				

Invented Spelling:

(Give the child a piece of paper. Say, "We're going to listen to sounds in words and then spell them. Like the word *tea*. I like hot tea in the winter and iced tea in the summer. I'm going to listen to the sounds in the word *tea*. /t/ I know that sound is spelled *T*. Let me listen again /t/ /E/ I hear *E*." **Write *Te* on the child's paper**. "Now it's your turn. I'll say some words and you spell them by listening to the sounds."

1. man
2. bug
3. fit
4. trade

Scoring:

1. one sound represented with logical letter
2. beginning consonants represented with correct letter
3. beginning and ending consonants are represented
4. blends, long vowels and short vowels are represented but some may not be spelled conventionally
5. conventional spelling of blends, long vowels, and short vowels

Finger-Point Reading

Prepare "I'm a Little Teapot" booklet with large font and extra large word spaces. Sing the nursery rhyme until child can say it verbatim from memory. Say, "Here is a book with the teapot rhyme in it. Watch as I say it and point to each word." Say the rhyme and point to each word. Invite the child to read along. Say, "This time I'll point to the words and you say the rhyme." Prompt children so that they successfully say each word as you point to that word. Say, "Now you can point to the words and we'll say the rhyme together." Correct child's pointing as needed. Say, "Now you point at the words and say the rhyme." Teachers score one point for each line of text in which the child correctly points to each word while saying that exact word. No score is given if any word is incorrectly matched.

_____ I'm a little teapot

_____ short and stout.

_____ Here is my handle.

_____ Here is my spout.

_____ When I get all steamed up

_____ Then I shout.

_____ Tip me over

_____ and pour me out.

Locate Words in Finger-Point Reading Text

Say, "This poem has the word _teapot._ Let me show you." Reread the first line of text. Point to the word _teapot_ and say, "Here is the word _teapot._ Now you show me the word _short._" Continue with all words. Score one point for each word correctly located.

1. short
2. here
3. spout
4. I
5. up
6. shout
7. tip
8. me

Reading Familiar Rhyming Words

Write the word *bat* on a small whiteboard. Say, "This is the word *bat*. Now I am going to wipe off the letter *b* and make another word. I'll put on an *f*. Now the word is *fat*. Now let me wipe off the letter *f* and make another word. I'll put on an *r*. Now the word is *rat*. Now it's your turn. I'll put on some new letters and you read the words." Add the letters and have children read the word. Score one point for each word read correctly.

1. h   hat
2. m   mat
3. s   sat
4. v   vat
5. c   cat

Writing Familiar Rhyming Words

Write the word *big* on the whiteboard. Say, "I wrote the word *big*. Now I am going to change it to the word *pig*. That word starts with /p/; I need a *p*." Erase the *b* and put on a *p*. "Now you are going to write some words. Write the word:" Score one point for each word correctly spelled.

1. fig
2. jig
3. mig
4. wig
5. zig

Class Profile Preschool and Kindergarten Monitoring Assessments: Advanced Assessments

Name	Letter-sound	Invented spelling	Finger-point reading	Locating words	Reading rhyming words	Writing rhyming words

Glossary

Additive Approaches Instructional methods that build on students' home languages and cultures. These contrast with subtractive approaches that attempt to replace children's home languages and cultures with English and mainstream culture. See *Subtractive Approaches*.

Affix A bound morpheme attached either at the beginning of a base word, in which case it is a prefix, or at the end of a base word, in which case it is a suffix. See *Bound Morpheme, Prefix*, and *Suffix*.

Alphabetic Principle A guiding rule for reading and writing whereby both processes depend on the systematic use of sound-letter correspondences.

Analytic Talk Discussion that goes beyond the literal meaning presented in a text or in illustrations; children infer character traits and motivations, infer problems, connect events across parts of a book, infer cause-and-effect relationships, and construct explanations for why characters act as they do. For example, a child is engaged in analytic talk when he or she says, "I think Goldilocks should have known that that chair would break. It looks pretty flimsy to me." In contrast, a child who says, "Goldilocks sat on Baby Bear's chair, and it broke" is not engaged in analytic talk.

Approximations The not fully realized products of children's incomplete literacy knowledge and ability. For example, their invented spellings are approximations of conventional spellings, their finger-point readings are approximations of correct word identification, and their mock letters are approximations of accurate alphabet writing.

Authentic Materials Materials that, although used for instructional purposes in school, also serve real-world purposes outside of school, for example, telephone books, catalogs, newspapers, magazines, maps, calendars, videotapes, and DVDs.

Automatic Sight Vocabulary All the words that one can read immediately, on sight, without having to use decoding strategies. A reader looks at a sight word and recognizes it in less than one-tenth of a second. Efficient reading depends on readers' having most high-frequency words, especially those that are undecodable, in their automatic sight vocabularies. See *High-Frequency Words* and *Decodable Word*.

Basic Interpersonal Communication Skills (BICS) Language competence needed to interact with and communicate with friends and others in social and play situations. Basic Interpersonal Communication Skills include use of context and concrete vocabulary. This is one way that they differ from Cognitive Academic Language Proficiency (CALP), which uses more abstract vocabulary. See *Cognitive Academic Language Proficiency (CALP)*.

Beginners Children in the first of the four broad phases of literacy development described in this book (see Chapter 2). Beginners are dependent on others for their reading and writing experiences. See *Novices, Experimenters*, and *Conventional Readers and Writers*.

Being Precise A child's taking care about how he or she matches saying particular words with seeing particular parts of text. Being precise, although not an act of word identification, does involve reading a text the same way across multiple readings because of using the exact words of the author and correctly matching the saying of those words with given parts of text. For example, a child cannot say "House" whenever shown a word card with the written word *house*. However, suppose his or her favorite storybook tells the story of the three little pigs and that one page's text is *The big, bad wolf huffed and puffed and blew their house down. The three little pigs ran into the forest*. A child who always says, "Huffed and puffed and blew their house down" when coming to that page is being precise. A more advanced form of being precise—but that still is not accurate word identification—is finger-point reading. See *Finger-Point Reading*.

Book Club A small group of children who decide to read a particular book or set of books together. They read the books independently or with partners but discuss the books and engage in response activities as a group.

Book Orientation Concepts Understandings of *top* and *bottom* with regard to a book's cover and its pages and of *one-by-one* and *front-to-back* page turning. Book orientation concepts are a subcategory of concepts about print. See *Concepts about Print*.

Book Talk A short presentation of a book, showing the physical book and telling a little about its characters and plot.

Bookhandling Skills Ways of looking at, holding, turning pages in, and otherwise manipulating books in order for their texts and illustrations to be accessible for accurate meaning making. See *Concepts about Print*.

Booksharing Routines Familiar, expected actions and language that accompany book reading.

Bound Morpheme A morpheme that must be attached to another morpheme; cannot stand alone. See *Morpheme* and *Free Morpheme*.

Character Cluster A diagram describing a story character. A central circle contains the character's name; peripheral circles, connected by spokes to the central circle, contain the character's traits and supporting evidence.

Cognates Words in different languages that have similar spellings, pronunciations, and meanings, for example, in English and Spanish, *dentist/dentista*, *map/mapa*, and *necessary/necesario*.

Cognitive Academic Language Proficiency (CALP) Language competence needed to learn science,

social studies, mathematics, and other school subjects. Cognitive Academic Language Proficiency includes abstract vocabulary. This is one way that it differs from Basic Interpersonal Communication Skills (BICS), which uses more concrete vocabulary. See *Basic Interpersonal Communication Skills (BICS)*.

Complex Sentence A sentence with at least one independent clause and one dependent clause (e.g., *I bought a jacket when I went to the mall*). An independent clause has its own subject and predicate and could stand alone if not part of the complex sentence (e.g., *I bought a jacket*). A dependent clause can not be a free-standing sentence (e.g., *when I went to the mall*). See *Compound Sentence, Simple Sentence*, and *Syntax*.

Compound Sentence A sentence with two or more independent clauses joined by a conjunction (e.g., *I went to the mall and I bought a jacket*). An independent clause has its own subject and predicate and could stand alone if not part of the compound sentence. See *Complex Sentence, Simple Sentence*, and *Syntax*.

Comprehensive Reading Program An approach to teaching reading to all children in an elementary school, including a scope and sequence of skills that will be taught at each grade level, materials that are to be read at each grade level, assessments to determine what children need to learn and to check whether they have learned what they have been taught, materials useful for reteaching when children demonstrate a need for it, and provisions for reading intervention.

Concept of Story A person's schema for story. A child's concept of story develops from very simple notions, such as that a story has a beginning, a middle, and an end, to the more complex notions embodied in story grammar. See *Story Grammar*.

Concept of Word Boundaries An aspect of Concept of Written Word. Children's knowledge that words in written text are bounded by the spaces between them. See *Concept of Written Word*.

Concept of Written Word Knowledge that words are composed of combinations of letters, that words in written text are bounded by the spaces between them, and that the sounds within them are related to alphabet letters. See *Metalinguistic Awareness* and *Phonemic Awareness*.

Concepts about Print (CAP) Understandings about how texts work, how they are configured, and how a reader approaches them, including that alphabet letters are a special category of visual symbols and that one reads the print rather than the pictures in a picture book. See *Bookhandling Skills*, *Book Orientation Concepts*, and *Directionality Concepts*.

Confusable Letters Alphabet letters that beginners easily mistake for one another. For example, *N* is easily mistaken for *Z*; they are alike except for orientation in space (*N* is a rotated *Z*).

Content-Specific Vocabulary Words that are unique to science, social studies, or another content area, or have meanings when used in those areas that are different from their meanings in everyday conversation.

Contextual Dependency A text's reliance on the situation of its composition for the conveying of its meaning. A mock cursive text, for example, cannot be read on its own. If, however, one was present when a child composed the text, then it is meaningful. For example, if during children's restaurant play, a teacher hears a child in the role of waiter repeat a customer's order for coffee and a doughnut, then the teacher can read the waiter's wavy lines on a pad of paper as *coffee* and *doughnut*. Another name for Contextual Dependency is *Sign Concept*.

Contextualized Language Language that occurs amid people, objects, actions, and events, and along with facial expression, gesture, and other forms of body language (e.g., head nodding, head shaking, and body leaning). Spoken language is almost always contextualized in this way, so in addition to information conveyed by words, information is also available from these sources in the context. In contrast, written language usually lacks these sources, and so the written words must do more of the work of conveying meaning. See *Decontextualized Language*.

Continuants Consonant phonemes whose pronunciations can be prolonged or stretched out. For example, one can say /s/ for as long as one has enough breath. In contrast, noncontinuants can be spoken only in an instant; one cannot, for example, stretch out the pronunciation of /b/. It is difficult to pronounce noncontinuants in isolation; one almost always adds a vowel sound, usually /u/. This sometimes causes teachers mistakenly to pronounce noncontinuants as continuants by adding the phoneme /u/. They say, for example, that the sound of the letter *B* is /bu/, and they stretch out the /u/ part of /bu/. This can confuse students; what they are hearing and paying attention to is not the phoneme /b/ but the teacher's prolonged pronunciation of the phoneme /u/.

Conventional Readers and Writers Children in the fourth of the four broad phases of literacy development described in this book (see Chapter 5). Their reading and writing increasingly resemble what adults in their language community would call "really reading and writing." See *Beginners*, *Novices*, and *Experimenters*.

Conventions of Written Language The characteristics of texts and the practices and processes for understanding and producing it that are accepted, expected, and used by accomplished readers and writers in a written language community. All writers and readers of English, for example, accept, expect, and use the convention of associating the letters *ph* with the phoneme /f/. Writers and readers of fairy tales accept, expect, and often use the convention of beginning a fairy tale with the phrase *Once upon a time*. Writers and readers of newspaper reporting accept, expect, and often use the convention of an opening paragraph that tells *who*, *what*, *when*, and *where*.

Core Reading Programs Commercial products promoted as having all that teachers and students need for the students to achieve grade-level expectations through daily instruction and practice in phonics and phonemic awareness, vocabulary, comprehension, and fluency.

Critical Interpretation A reader's appreciation of how literary forces interact with nonliterary (e.g., political, economical) forces in society and culture, especially of how a story might affect a reader's position in society and culture.

Culturally Authentic Literature Fiction and nonfiction that portray the people and the values, customs, and beliefs of a cultural group in ways recognized by members of that group as valid and truthful. See *Multicultural Literature*.

Culturally Responsive Instruction Instruction that is "consistent with the values of students' own cultures and aimed at improving academic learning."*

Curriculum What teachers plan to teach and expect that children will learn.

---

*Quoted from *Literacy Instruction in Multicultural Settings* (p. 13) by K. Au, 1993, New York, Harcourt.

Curriculum Integration Involving students in learning from more than one subject area at a time.

Decodable Word A word that a reader can identify by applying phonics generalizations. For example, *pin* is decodable as /pin/, using the phonics generalization that the vowel in a CVC word is short; and *pine* is decodable as /pIn/, using the phonics generalization that in a CVCe word, the final *e* is silent and the first vowel is long. Not all words are decodable, for example, *put*, which is an exception to the CVC generalization (it is pronounced /poot/, not the predicted /put/), and *love*, which is an exception to the CVCe generalization (it is pronounced /luv/, not the predicted /lOv/). See *Phonics*.

Decoding The ability to look at an unknown word—that is, a word that is not a sight word, that the reader cannot identify automatically on sight—and to produce a pronunciation that is accurate—that is, a pronunciation that identifies the word as one that the reader knows from his or her spoken vocabulary. See *Phonics*.

Decontextualized Language Language that greatly depends on itself for meaning. Spoken language usually occurs amid people, objects, actions, and events, and along with facial expression, gesture, and other forms of body language, and so it is contextualized by those co-occurrences. Written language, however, lacks those means of reinforcing its message; so, compared to spoken language, it is relatively decontextualized. When making meaning, readers' only resources are the text's words and the related understandings that the readers had before beginning to read. See *Contextualized Language*.

Developmental Spelling Inventory A list of words that children are asked to spell. Their spellings are then analyzed to determine which spelling patterns and spelling strategies—characteristic of various stages of spelling development—they use.

Direct Instruction Teaching by modeling how to perform a task and thinking aloud during performance of the task in order to provide explicit explanations of mental activities. Outcomes, that is, what children show they know and can do, are determined ahead of time by the teacher's choices of a task and criteria for children's successful completion of that task. See *Indirect Instruction* and *Explicit Instruction*.

Directionality Concepts Understandings that print is read from top to bottom and from left to right. Directionality Concepts are a subcategory of Concepts about Print. See *Concepts about Print* (*CAP*).

Drafting A writing process in which a writer first commits ideas to paper in a first draft. The purpose of a first draft is to begin preserving thoughts in print, without concern for structure, coherence, or correctness of punctuation or spelling. Later in the writing process, revising will result in better structured, more coherent drafts and editing will produce a final draft that meets a writer's current standards for punctuation and spelling (less stringent standards for beginners and higher standards for accomplished writers). See *Prewriting, Revising, Editing*, and *Publishing*.

Dramatic-Play-with-Print Centers Dramatic play centers that contain reading and writing materials relevant to the theme of the dramatic play (e.g., an appointment book and pen next to a telephone in a doctor's office play center). Availability of such materials and teacher modeling promote children's reading and writing as part of their dramatic play.

Dynamic Ability Grouping Forming small groups for reading and writing instruction based on students' similar abilities and needs and using texts carefully matched to those abilities and needs.

Early Production The second of four phases of children's second language acquisition, notable for children's attempting to speak but still using very limited language, drawing on the words and gestures learned in vocabulary games or other interactions during the first, mostly silent phase. See *Preproduction, Speech Emergence*, and *Intermediate Fluency*.

Early Readers and Writers The first of three phases of conventional reading and writing (see Chapter 5). Early readers and writers can produce simple texts that others can read. They can read with accuracy their own compositions and other simple texts, such as storybooks. See *Conventional Readers and Writers, Transitional Readers and Writers*, and *Self-Generative Readers and Writers*.

Editing A writing process in which a writer produces a final draft that meets his or her current standards for punctuation and spelling. Those standards depend on what a writer has already learned about punctuation and spelling. They are less stringent for beginners, who know fewer correct spellings and know less about punctuation, and higher for accomplished writers, who have learned more from reading and writing experience, minilessons, and other instruction in writing workshop. See *Prewriting, Drafting, Revising*, and *Publishing*.

Elements of Informational Texts The components of a well-crafted exposition. One way to characterize a well-crafted exposition is in terms of its topic presentation, description of attributes, characteristic events, category comparison, and final summary. Another way is in terms of its consistency, ordered relationships, and hierarchical relationships. See *Exposition*.

Elkonin Boxes An array with framed spaces for each sound segment of a word. Children move a poker chip or other token into the spaces as they segment a word by its sounds. At first, children might use this activity while attending to syllables, later to phonemes. If they are learning phonemic awareness, for example, they have a pile of poker chips and a laminated sheet of paper at the top of which are drawn three boxes in a horizontal array. Then as they say each phoneme of *mop*, they slide a chip to one of the boxes: one chip to the left-most box for /m/, then another chip to the middle box for /o/, and finally a third chip to the right-most box for /p/. When the tokens are letter tiles, "say it and move it" can be used to teach spelling. For example, moving *m, o,* and *p* letter tiles into the left, middle, and right boxes would teach associating those letters with the corresponding phonemes in *mop*.

ELL Interactive Read-Aloud Procedure A technique that teaches vocabulary and comprehension to English language learners, using longer, more complex picture books, both narrative and informational, than they can read on their own. Students read only a third or a fourth of a book each day for three or four successive days, with rereadings and with concentrated instruction about selected vocabulary.

English Language Learner (ELL) One whose home language is other than English and who is learning English in a school setting. English language learners are expected also to learn all the usual subjects taught in school and often with most of the teaching of those subjects being in English.

Environmental Print Text found in everyday settings, such as print on signs, clothing, and storefronts, and in logos.

Experimenters Children in the third of the four broad phases of literacy development described in this book (see Chapter 4). Experimenters understand the alphabetic principle; with their reading and writing, they investigate the power and the implications of sound-letter correspondences.

See *Alphabetic Principle, Beginners, Novices*, and *Conventional Readers and Writers*.

Explicit Instruction Teaching that includes specifying of learning outcomes, modeling of processes, thinking aloud, and explaining. Deliberately and clearly stating what students are to learn. Explicit instruction has much in common with Direct Instruction and is usually part of an instructional sequence called *Gradual Release of Responsibility*.

Exposition Nonnarrative, nonfictional text. Expositions serve such purposes as making arguments, persuading, explaining, describing, and instructing. The forms they take include essay, article, how-to text, thesis, biography, textbook, documentary, and exposé. Also called *expository text*.

Feature A component of a schema. A schema for the concept of *house* contains such features as *walls, windows, doors, roof, chimney*.

Finger-Point Reading Putting a finger or other pointer such as a ruler onto a discrete part of a text for each spoken part of a reading, using left-to-right directionality, but without necessarily correctly matching spoken and written words and without being able to correctly identify the same written words in other contexts. For example, a child may point one by one, from left to right to the words of the written text *Old Mother Hubbard went to the cupboard* while saying "Old Moth -er Hub -bard went to" and perhaps stop there or perhaps continue with "the cup -board" while pointing to the first three words of the next line of text. Finger-point reading is developmental. Eventually, the child will correctly match saying the seven words of that line of the nursery rhyme with pointing to the seven written words. And finger-point reading can lead to "real reading." The child who can correctly match his or her spoken words with the words of the text may eventually use what he or she notices about that matching to identify those words in print even outside of the context of the memorized nursery rhyme.

Fluent Reading Reading with quick and accurate word recognition and appropriate prosody (voicing and phrasing). Fluent reading includes a component of comprehension because readers cannot read with appropriate phrasing if they do not understand what they are reading.

Formulaic Speech Words or phrases that occur repeatedly and predictably in routine social situations. Their meanings are usually nonliteral; they serve instead to indicate the nature or boundaries of the situation. For example, *How are you?* is not usually intended as a request for information about a person's health. Instead, it is a ritual greeting and often marks the beginning of a conversation, equivalent to *Hi* or *Hello*. When formulaic speech occurs as a phrase rather than a single word, for example, *What's up?* instead of *Hello*, that phrase nonetheless conveys meaning as a single unit rather than as a combination of the usual meanings of the words. As such, it works as if it were a single word and the rules of syntax (which is about building meanings from combinations of individually meaningful words) are irrelevant. This is especially apparent when, as often happens, the phrase is contracted to a single word, as, for example, when *What's up?* becomes *'Tsup?* Another example of a formulaic expression is *So long*, which functions as an expression of goodwill on the occasion of a departure. The meanings of *so* and *long*, even if relevant to the expression when it originated long ago, no longer have in this expression either their usual meanings or any syntactic roles; *so long* works as a single semantic unit. Formulaic expressions in children's speech almost always work in this way. For example, a child can use *Give me* (usually pronounced "Gimme") as a formulaic request for an object without necessarily knowing the individual meanings of *Give* and *me* or being able to use those separate words meaningfully in other contexts. (It is likely a child will know the meaning of *me* and use it in other situations long before doing so with *give*.) See *Semantics* and *Syntax*.

Free Morpheme A morpheme that can stand alone is not required to be attached to another morpheme. See *Morpheme* and *Bound Morpheme*.

Functions of Written Language Purposes served by reading and writing. These include the functions of spoken language (instrumental, regulatory, interactional, personal, heuristic, imaginative, and representational) and additional writing-specific functions, such as recording and reminding.

Gradual Release of Responsibility An instructional sequence that begins with the teacher's explicit instruction about a single concept or strategy, one that can be expressed in the performance of a discrete task, and then proceeds with the teacher's gradually facilitating students' performance of that task, until students can perform it independently. See *Explicit Instruction*.

Grand Conversation A book discussion prompted by a teacher's open-ended question, such as "What do you think?" but guided by children's comments and questions rather than by the teacher's continued questioning.

Grapho-Semantics One of three interrelated systems for linking the forms of written language to its meanings. Grapho-semantics is the use of meanings of words and word parts (morphemes) to make effective use of written forms. Consider, for example, the written sentence *The artist is sculpting a statue*. And suppose a reader does not recognize the word *sculpting*. Knowing the meanings of *artist* and *statue* predisposes the reader to expect the written word *sculpting* to name something having to do with artists and statues, that some artists make statues through the process of sculpting. Efficient readers will use grapho-semantics in conjunction with the other two systems for linking forms and meanings. For example, they will use phonics to determine the sounds in the initial consonant blend (*sc*) and the final consonant blend (*lpt*) of *sculpt* and will use grapho-syntax to determine that *sculpt* is part of this sentence's verb. In fact, they will see that it is part of the present progressive verb form *is sculpting*, and so it names a continuing action that is taking place in the present. See *Morpheme, Semantics, Phonics*, and *Grapho-Syntax*.

Grapho-Syntax One of three interrelated systems for linking the forms of written language to its meanings. Grapho-syntax is the use of sentence structure knowledge to make effective use of written forms. Consider, for example, the written sentence *The artist is sculpting a statue*. And suppose a reader does not recognize the word *sculpting*. The syntactic knowledge of the present progressive verb tense—that in English it takes the form *is _____ing*—predisposes the reader to expect a verb after the word *is* and before the suffix *ing*. Efficient readers will use grapho-syntax in conjunction with the other two systems for linking forms and meanings. For example, they will use phonics to determine the sounds in the initial consonant blend (*sc*) and the final consonant blend (*lpt*) of sculpt, and will use grapho-semantics to determine that the action named by the verb form *sculpt* is something that artists do to statues. See *Syntax, Phonics*, and *Grapho-Semantics*.

Guided Drawing The teacher's demonstrating basic strokes and shapes used in drawing and writing, such as vertical, horizontal, and slanting lines and circles, squares, triangles, and dots.

Guided Reading Instruction in which the teacher selects a particular text for children to read and then directs and supports children as they read that text.

Guided Spelling Spelling instruction for small groups of children with similar abilities. Instruction is about spelling patterns the members of a group are just beginning to recognize and use.

High-Frequency Words Words that appear often in just about any text that is longer than a few sentences. High-frequency words usually are grammatical words, that is, words that create sentence structure and coherence, such as articles (*the, a, an*), prepositions (e.g., *of, from, with*), conjunctions (*and, or, but*), pronouns (e.g., *I, she, us*), auxiliary verbs (e.g., *have, been*), and all forms of the verb *to be* (e.g., *am, were, is*) rather than content words that name objects, actions, and qualities (e.g., *house, run, big*). Experts have compiled lists of high-frequency words (e.g., *The Dolch word list*), which if learned as sight words, enable a reader to read a large proportion of words in almost any text automatically, thus freeing him or her to devote conscious attention to other reading processes, such as identifying unfamiliar words and comprehending the text. See *Sight Words* and *Orchestration*.

Homographs Words that are spelled the same but do not sound alike, such as *bow* in *bow and arrow* and *bow* in *bow to the king*. See *Homophones*.

Homophones Words that sound alike but are not spelled the same, such as *bare* and *bear*. See *Homographs*.

Independent Reading Level The level of text that a child can read on his or her own, without a teacher's support, determined from 96–100 percent word reading accuracy and 91–100 percent correct responses to comprehension questions. See *Individualized Reading Inventory* and *Instructional Reading Level*.

Indirect Instruction Teaching by providing materials and opportunities for children to learn from doing and from watching others. The teacher plans activities to allow children to respond in their own ways, with multiple acceptable responses. See *Direct Instruction*.

Individualized Reading Inventory A commercially published collection of grade-leveled texts (from preprimer to middle school, or even high school), used to determine a child's instructional

and independent reading levels. See *Instructional Reading Level, Independent Reading Level*, and *Running Record*.

Inquiry Unit Study of a particular topic for which children observe, participate in experiments or other hands-on experiences, read from a variety of texts, and communicate their findings, often through writing.

Instructional Reading Level The level of text that a child can read with a teacher's support, determined from 90–95 percent word reading accuracy and 70–90 percent correct responses to comprehension questions. See *Individualized Reading Inventory* and *Independent Reading Level*.

Interactive Bookreading A booksharing experience by a child and a more knowledgeable other person, usually an adult, to which both contribute. During interactive bookreading, for example, the adult invites the child to participate in the making of meanings from the book's texts and illustrations and responds to the child's gestures, facial expressions, statements, questions, and reading attempts by validating, elaborating, and clarifying.

Interactive Read-Aloud Reading aloud a storybook or information book to a group of children, allowing them, during the reading, to ask and answer questions, predict outcomes, and make other comments. Interactive read-alouds have many of the features of interactive bookreading, but they are done with groups rather than individual children. See *Interactive Bookreading*.

Interactive Writing Instruction in which the teacher and students write on chart paper. The teacher helps the children to determine what will be written and then selects children to step up to the chart and write words or parts of words. During interactive writing, teachers model for children how to write texts that serve a variety of purposes. See *Shared Writing*.

Intermediate Fluency The fourth of four phases of children's second language acquisition, notable for children's having acquired sufficient vocabulary and fluency with a variety of sentence structures that they are ready to acquire academic concepts in reading, writing, math, and science. See *Preproduction, Early Production*, and *Speech Emergence*.

Internet Workshop An approach to teaching about the Internet that includes regularly scheduled time for children to work online ("workshop time"). Teachers teach mini-lessons about using the Internet, students and teachers hold conferences to review and plan Internet research around a topic of inquiry, and students share results of Internet research. See *Inquiry Unit*.

Invented Spelling Children's systematic but not conventional matching of sounds in words (phonemes) with letters. Invented spelling is developmental, that is, it moves from less to more sophisticated representations. Early invented spellings may be single letters for beginning sounds of words (for example, *M* for *mouse*) and often rely on children's knowledge of letter names and attention to sounds in those names (for example, /m/ in *em*, the name of the letter *M*, which is also the sound at the beginning of the word *mouse*). Later invented spellings, though still not conventional, combine visual and auditory strategies. The visual strategies come from what children have seen in books and environmental print. For example, in the spelling *MOSS* for *mouse*, the choices of the letters *M, O,* and *S* show awareness of the phonemes /m/, /ow/, and /s/ in beginning, middle, and final positions of *mouse* and awareness of the same or similar phonemes in the names of those letters, but the use of the double *SS* shows also the inventive speller's familiarity with final double consonants in English—from seeing such words as *grass* and *kiss*. See *Phoneme, Phonemic Awareness, Meaning-Form Links,* and *Orthography*.

Journal Writing Children's daily independent writing about personal topics.

K-W-L Chart A chart on which a teacher lists, before students read a text, what they *know* about the text's topic and what they *want* to learn, and, after they have read the text, what they have *learned*.

Kid Writing A teacher-supported activity in which children decide on a short message, make lines to indicate each word that will be needed to write that message, listen to the sounds in each word, and write the sounds they hear.

Language Experience Approach A method for teaching reading and writing in which teachers engage children in discussion of an activity they have participated in (e.g., an art or cooking activity), invite children to dictate sentences about the activity, and then lead the children in the reading and rereading of the resulting text.

Language Scaffold A teacher's intentional sustaining of conversation to provide children with models of new vocabulary and sentence structures, for example, by repeating but expanding on a child's utterance. When a child says, "Milk!" an adult might say, "Oh, would you like some milk? Just a minute. I'll get you some milk. . . . Here's your milk. Drink up!" Scaffolding of talk supports children's understanding even when they know very little of the vocabulary included in the talk. The term *scaffolding* implies not just support but also that the support is removable. As children show greater competence, their need for language scaffolding decreases.

Letter and Word Concepts Understandings about letters and words and how they are related, for example, that words are comprised of letters, that words have first and last letters, and that there are first and last words on a page.

Letter Features The lines from which letters of the alphabet are composed. These include straight lines and curves, horizontals, verticals, and diagonals.

Leveled Books A series of books used for reading instruction that are calibrated and labeled by degree of difficulty. Low-level texts, which are repetitive and use few words, are easier than high-level texts, which use more words, convey more information, and use more complex and more literary language.

Lexile Book Measure A metric for determining a book's difficulty based on word frequency and sentence length.

List, Group, and Label Activity A vocabulary development activity in which children choose words from a Word Wall and tell how they are related. See *Word Wall*.

Literacy and Language Environment Rating Scale An instrument for documenting the quality of a classroom literacy environment, taking into account the physical arrangement, materials, displays, and the quality of the interactions between children and teachers.

Literary Interpretation An understanding of a story at a personal, often abstract, level. Literary interpretations often result in understanding one's self and the world, not just the events of the story.

Literature Text Set A selection of books with a common theme (e.g., that friends are often found in unusual places), author or illustrator (e.g., books illustrated by Jerry Pinkney), literary element (e.g., tricksters or dynamic characters), or genre (e.g., poetry or animal fantasy).

Make-a-Rhyming-Word Activity A process by which children build word families, using phonogram cards and beginning consonant cards in response to a teacher's prompts. For example, the teacher says, "I have the word *all;* now what do we need to make the word *tall?* Who can show me?" The teacher repeats the /t/ sound, and children place the *t* letter card before the *all* phonogram card.

Making Big Words An approach to advanced word study in which teachers help students to build and discuss meanings of words composed from the letters of a multisyllable target word. First they build one-syllable words using subsets of the letters, then multisyllable words other than the target word, and finally the target word using all of the letters. See *Making Words.*

Making Words A word-work activity, using alphabet cards to construct new words from old words by changing or adding just one letter in a word at a time. For example, children begin with *slip* and exchange the *l* for a *k* to make *skip;* then they may change *skip* to *skin* by exchanging the *p* for an *n.*

Meaning-Form Links Connections between understanding of language and the processing of visual characteristics of text. Children use meaning-form links, for example, when they write with invented spelling (connecting what they know about the sounds of spoken language with what they know about the names and shapes of alphabet letters) or when they connect what they know about the functions of a list (to help you organize and remember information) with what they know about how a list looks (words or phrases arranged vertically, without the punctuation and paragraph structure of a story or a letter from Grandma).

Message Concept The idea that writing can preserve exactly the meanings that a writer wants to convey. Marie Clay* identified the discovery of this concept as a significant achievement in emergent literacy. Without it, children must see writing as random and purposeless and so have little reason to write or to read others' writing. Of course, in reality, no writer can exactly convey an intended message; all writing is open to interpretation by readers, sometimes interpretations quite divergent from what writers intend. Fortunately, the discovery of writing's

*Clay, M.M. (1975). *What did I write? Beginning writing behavior.* Exeter, NH: Heinemann.

subtleties and inexactness comes later, after the message concept has served to ignite children's writing development.

Metacognitive Awareness Consciousness of mental processes, including those for word identification and reading comprehension. Children who read with metacognitive awareness are conscious of how well or poorly they are understanding a text and choose appropriate strategies for maintaining or improving their understanding as they continue to read.

Metalinguistic Awareness Conscious attention to properties of language. This includes not only phonological awareness but also awareness of other aspects of language, such as concept of written word, sentence structure, and concept of story. Children demonstrate metalinguistic awareness when they can finger-point read a familiar text, when they correctly use such words as *question* and *statement,* and when they can retell a story including important information from the beginning, middle, and end of the story. See *Phonological Awareness, Concept of Written Word, Syntax,* and *Concept of Story.*

Mini-Lesson A component of writing instruction in which a teacher provides to a whole-class group a short period of focused instruction about some small part of the writing process. The purpose of a mini-lesson is merely to raise students' awareness, sometimes as a reminder of what they already know and sometimes as an introduction to a new topic. More individualized writing instruction occurs in small groups and during individual writing conferences.

Miscue Analysis A profiling of a child's use and misuse of grapho-phonic, grapho-semantic, and grapho-syntactic cuing systems, determined from an examination of mistakes documented on a running record. See *Running Record, Phonics, Grapho-Semantics,* and *Grapho-Syntax.*

Mock Cursive Horizontally arranged wavy lines. These are also called *linear scribble writing.*

Mock Letters Symbols that look like conventional letters of the alphabet because they are composed of letter features, but are not conventional letters. These are also called *letter-like forms.*

Modeled Writing Instruction in which teachers compose a text as children watch. The teacher first thinks aloud about what he or she might write, then talks through the composition process. The teacher then thinks aloud while rereading and revising the text.

Modern Folktale Variants. Folktales retold by contemporary authors with different settings and/or with transformed characters (e.g., people changed to animals).

Monitoring Assessments Assessments to track children's progress and to identify those who need adjustments in instruction, such as placement in a different reading instruction group. These contrast with screening assessments. See *Screening Assessments.*

Morning Message A short text written by the teacher on a topic that is relevant to students' classroom lives and posted for children's easy access, for example, written on a special part of the chalkboard or written on chart paper and hung on an easel.

Morpheme The smallest unit of meaning. *Hose* is one morpheme; it means "a flexible tube through which gases or fluids can move." *Toes* is two morphemes; it means "*toe* plus plural" or "more than one terminal digit on a vertebrate foot." The /z/ at the end of *hose* is just part of the single unit of meaning pronounced /hOz/; the /z/ at the end of *toes* is an extra unit of meaning, a sound added to /tO/ to make it plural, to give it the extra meaning of *more than one.*

Morphological Awareness Conscious attention to a language's morphemes, what they mean, and how they work. For example, readers and writers need to know that adding the prefix *dis-* negates the meaning of a base word (e.g., *dissatisfied* means "not satisfied"). See *Morpheme, Affix, Prefix,* and *Suffix.*

Motif A kind of character, event, or other story element recurring across many folktales or fairy tales.

Multicultural Literature Fiction and nonfiction that, in addition to representing the lives and concerns of a nation's own majority, also represent the lives and concerns of cultural, ethnic, and religious minorities and peoples living beyond its borders. These representations include minority races and members of minority religions within a nation and other national cultures beyond a nation's borders (even those that are the majority in another nation). Among minority ethnic groups in the United States are African Americans, Asian Americans, Hispanic Americans, and Native Americans. None of these groups is homogeneous; all contain their own cultural diversity. See *Culturally Authentic Literature.*

Multiliteracy Using and honoring in both print and speech students' home languages and English.

Multiple-Character-Perspective Approach A story discussion technique that calls for children to understand the story from different characters' points of view and to compare and contrast those different perspectives.

Multiple Literacies Knowledge of and abilities to make meaning from more than one print medium (for example, from print on computer screens as well as from print in books) or from more than one symbol system (for example, from the visual features of paintings as well as from the graphemes used in reading and writing).

Novices Children in the second of the four broad phases of literacy development described in this book (see Chapter 3). Novices write with an intention to communicate, and their pretend reading is based on their understanding that reading must be meaningful. See *Beginners, Experimenters,* and *Conventional Readers and Writers.*

Onset The initial consonant, consonant blend, or consonant digraph of a syllable. For example, the onsets in *pan, plan,* and *than* are *p, pl,* and *th.* See *Rime.*

Orchestration The ability to coordinate many literacy processes at one time. As some literacy processes become automatic and unconscious, readers and writers are able to give their conscious attention to others.

Orthographic Reading Identifying an unknown word by using familiar word parts and knowledge of orthographic patterns, such as phonograms, suffixes, and affixes. For example, familiarity with the phonogram *-it* and the prefix *un-* helps a reader to identify the word *unfit* by recognizing in it the base word *fit* (from the *-it* word family with the consonant *f* added) and the prefix *un* (a morpheme meaning "not"). This is decoding by analogy because it involves seeing that *unfit* is like other words in the *-it* word family and other words with the prefix *un-*. See *Phonogram, Orthography,* and *Morpheme.*

Orthography A system for associating word parts (individual sounds or larger chunks of spoken words) with individual letters or combinations of letters. Orthography is always systematic and often abstract. It is systematic in that it is not random. A writer can't use any string of letters he or she wants when spelling a particular word; there are sound-based and meaning-based reasons for the letter combinations used in a particular written language. For example, in English, associating the letter *t* with the sound /t/

enables us to spell the final sound of the word *pit* but also the sound /t/ in literally thousands of other words in which it occurs, sometimes in the final position but also at the beginning or middle of a word. That is being systematic based on sounds. It is equally important that the /t/ sound be allowed to be associated with the *-ed* at the end of the word *walked*, even though *-ed* looks nothing like *t*. We always associate *-ed* at the end of a verb with the meaning *past tense* even though that *-ed* is sometimes pronounced /d/ (as in *played*), sometimes /ud/ (as in *wanted*), and, yes, sometimes /t/ (as in *walked*). That is being systematic based on meaning. Orthography is abstract when it ignores some sounds in favor of others (for example, ignoring the /ch/ sound between the /t/ and /r/ sounds in *train*). *Orthography* is synonymous with *Spelling*.

Pattern Innovation Composing a new text based on manipulation of salient features of an existing text. For example, a teacher and students in a shared writing activity may write an extension of the story of the Gingerbread Boy by using the story's frequently repeated language about the boy's running away and his saying "You can't catch me. I'm the Gingerbread Boy," but creating a new character for him to run from.

Perspective An illustrating technique that gives a viewer a particular viewpoint, for example, straight on, below the horizon line, or bird's-eye.

Phoneme Repertoire The collection of sounds that a language uses in meaningful ways. In each language, approximately forty sounds are phonemic, that is, they are combined and contrasted in meaningful ways in that language's words. However, one language's repertoire of forty or so phonemes seldom exactly matches another language's repertoire of forty or so phonemes. For example, some languages have phonemes not found in English (e.g., the rolled *r* sound in Spanish that is absent in English), and English has phonemes not found in some other languages (e.g., the /ng/ sound in English that is absent in Spanish). See *Phonemes*.

Phoneme Scaffolding A systematic approach to teaching students to isolate or segment beginning phonemes. Teachers decrease the amount of support as students demonstrate greater ability. See *Phonemic Awareness* and *Scaffolding*.

Phonemes The smallest units of sound that are combined and contrasted in meaningful ways in a language's words. For example, in English, the phonemes /p/, /i/, and /t/ are combined to make the word *pit*, and the phonemes /p/ and /b/ are contrasted when distinguishing the words *pit* and *bit* (thus, the difference between /p/ and /b/ is meaningful; it allows us to distinguish between the large seed in the middle of a peach and what you did when you sunk your teeth into a peach). But the difference between the phoneme /p/ in *pit* and the phoneme /p/ in *spit* (the /p/ in *pit* is breathy or pronounced with a burst of air, enough to move a piece of paper held before the mouth; the /p/ in *spit* isn't breathy) is not a difference between phonemes (both pronunciations fall within the category of sounds we call the phoneme /p/). That's because the breathy /p/ versus the breathless /p/ difference is not by itself meaningful. *Pit* and *spit* convey two different meanings (the large seed in the middle of a peach and what you do if you expel from your mouth the worm that was in the peach) not by virtue of contrasting breathy /p/ and breathless /p/ but rather by virtue of contrasting /p/ alone and /p/ combined with another phoneme, /s/. English has no pair of words that is different only because one has a breathy /p/ where the other has a breathless /p/. If there were such a pair, then that difference would be meaningful. Then it could not remain a difference within the /p/ category; we would then have to create two different phonemes and give them different symbols, perhaps /p/ for the breathy one and /ꝑ/ for the breathless one, just as we already have two different symbols, /p/ and /b/, for the different phonemes—that is, the meaningfully different sounds—at the beginnings of *pit* and *bit*.

Phonemic Awareness The aspect of phonological awareness that involves conscious attention to the phonemes of a spoken language. Children demonstrate phonemic awareness, for example, when they can segment phonemes (e.g., separately pronounce /d/, /aw/, and /g/ after hearing and saying the word *dog*), blend phonemes (e.g., hear /d/, /aw/, and /g/ separately pronounced and combine them to say *dog*), or write with invented spelling (e.g., write *chair* as *HAR*, because they hear the three phonemes in *chair*—/ch/, /A/, and /r/—and represent them with *H, A,* and *R* due to hearing those sounds in the letters' names, the /ch/ in *aitch*, the /A/ in *ay*, and the /r/ in *ar*).

Phonics One of three interrelated systems for linking the forms of written language to its meanings. Phonics is the more or less regular linking of letters and combinations of letters with sounds (phonemes) and combinations of sounds. Also called *graphophonics*. When particular letters and combinations of letters (phonograms) frequently—even if not always—stand for particular sounds or combinations of sounds, then those relationships merit teaching as part of the academic subject known as phonics. For example, the letter *b* has a very high frequency of association with the phoneme /b/ (as in *bit, rub, alphabet*); the combination of letters *ch* has a very high frequency of association with the phoneme /ch/ (as in *chin, such, teacher*); the phonogram *ine* has a very high frequency of association with the combination of sounds /In/ (as in *fine, twine, vine*). These relationships do not always hold; that is why our definition includes the words *more or less regular*. For example, *b* does not stand for the sound /b/ in the word *comb*, *ch* does not stand for the sound /ch/ in the word *machine*, and *ine* does not stand for /In/ in *machine*. Nonetheless, they hold frequently enough to warrant teaching them, especially in conjunction with the other two systems for linking the forms of written language to its meanings, grapho-syntax and grapho-semantics. See *Meaning-Form Links, Phoneme, Phonogram, Grapho-Syntax* and *Grapho-Semantics*.

Phonogram A combination of letters that is reliably associated with a particular pronunciation, especially in the middle and final positions of a word. For example, *-an* is pronounced /an/ in the middle and final positions of *ban, can, fan, pan, plan, tan*, and *van*.

Phonological Awareness Conscious attention to the sounds of spoken language. This includes not only awareness of phonemes but also awareness of other units of language, such as syllables, onsets, and rimes, and other aspects of the sounds of a language, such as intonation patterns. Children demonstrate phonological awareness, for example, when they can provide a rhyming word (e.g., *dog* when given *log*) or when they can tell the difference between the question *Sandy can skip rope?* (with end-rising intonation) and the statement *Sandy can skip rope* (with end-falling intonation). See *Phonemic Awareness, Onset*, and *Rime*.

Phonology Of the four linguistic systems, the one that has to do with sounds. This includes a wide range, from phonemes (e.g., that *night* is composed of three phonemes, /n/, /I/, /t/) to inflections (e.g., *SANDY can whistle* versus *Sandy can WHISTLE*, where the first emphasizes who can whistle, that of Sandy and her friend Patty, only Sandy can; the second emphasizes what Sandy can do, that she can whistle but perhaps not perform a handstand).

Portfolio A large folder in which a teacher keeps samples of a child's work.

Pragmatics Of the four linguistic systems, the one that has to do with how language is used in everyday life to get done that which would be difficult or impossible without language. Pragmatics includes, for example, requests for action and forms of politeness, such that a child who says, "May I have a cookie?" or better yet, "Please, may I have a cookie?" is more effective than a child who only points in the general direction of the cookie jar and grunts.

Prefix An affix attached to the beginning of a base word, for example, *un-* in *unbelievable*. See *Affix*.

Preproduction The first of four phases of children's second language acquisition, most notable for children's speaking very little in the second language. Although they are silent, English language learners in this phase are actively listening to the sounds of English spoken around them and trying to connect the actions they see with the sounds they hear. They intuitively acquire information about English intonation, speed, pausing, loudness, and pitch. See *Early Production, Speech Emergence*, and *Intermediate Fluency*.

Pretend Reading A telling of the content of a book, rather than an actual reading of the text, but performed as if it were an actual reading (with reading intonation and often with remembered words and phrases), by a child who cannot read conventionally, usually of a very familiar or favorite book, one that the child frequently has heard read to him or her.

Prewriting A writing process in which a writer searches for a topic, identifies his or her audience and purpose, and collects ideas about which to write. See *Drafting, Revising, Editing*, and *Publishing*.

Process Approach to Writing See *Writing Workshop*.

Project Approach Children's construction of simulations of real-world settings for literacy activity. For example, they may build a shoe store. They bring shoe boxes, shopping bags, and old shoes from home; collect newspaper and magazine advertising for shoes; make signs; set up shelves, benches, and floor-length mirrors; and make a checkout counter with a toy cash register, a pretend credit card machine, and child-made coupons and receipt forms. Once established, these function like dramatic-play-with-print centers. See *Dramatic-Play-with-Print Center*.

Prosody Use of pace, pitch, and stress in speech.

Publishing A writing process in which a writer shares his or her work with an audience. See *Prewriting, Drafting, Revising,* and *Editing.*

Readers' Theater A simple form of dramatization in which players read their lines rather than memorize them. Readers' theater scripts can be composed by the performers as they revise the text of a story they wish to perform, selecting important events and dialogue, and creating descriptive lines for a narrator.

Referential Dimension The range of a writer's possible relationship to the subject matter of the text she or he is composing, from the personal and immediate to the abstract and imaginative. A writer of autobiography works at the personal and immediate end of the referential dimension; a writer of science fiction works at the abstract and imaginative end.

Response Journal A journal in which readers record their reactions to and thoughts about books they read.

Response to Intervention (RTI) An approach to identifying struggling students who may need extra support and instruction and, later, students who may need special education. RTI includes up to five steps: identification of good literacy practices, screening assessment, extra instructional support for those identified by screening, monitoring assessment, and referral for special education for those identified by monitoring. See *Screening Assessments* and *Monitoring Assessments.*

Retelling Checklist A list of the important events in a story and a story's important and sophisticated vocabulary. Teachers use a retelling checklist to record which of those a child includes in his or her retelling of the story. See *Pretend Reading.*

Revising A writing process in which a writer rereads a current draft of a writing piece; rethinks what he or she has written; and improves word choice, phrasing, sentence structure, sentence order, and the overall structure of the piece. The goal is greater clarity and coherence. The purpose is to make a piece better communicate what the author intends; those intentions can become clearer to the writer himself or herself as a result of the rereading and rethinking that are part of revision. Final corrections of punctuation and spelling do not occur until the editing process. See *Prewriting, Drafting, Editing,* and *Publishing.*

Rime The part of a syllable from its vowel though its end. For example, the rimes in *pan, pen,* and *pie* are *-an, -en,* and *-ie.* Rhyming words have identical rimes, for example, *-an* in *can, fan, pan, plan, tan,* and *than.* See *Onset.*

Rubric An assessment tool that identifies required elements of a work sample and provides a range of descriptions of possible achievements of each element. Teachers compare students' work with the rubric to determine what levels of performance the work represents. Some rubrics assign numerical values to the descriptions, yielding a total numerical score for the work sample.

Running Record A real-time documentation of a child's reading performance, made by observing the child read a grade-leveled text and marking a copy of the text or using checks and other symbols on a separate sheet of paper to show accurate readings, substitutions, omissions, insertions, repetitions, self-corrections, and teacher prompts. A running record provides information about the child's instructional and independent reading levels and his or her use of cuing systems during reading. See *Instructional Reading Level, Independent Reading Level, Phonics, Grapho-Semantics,* and *Grapho-Syntax.*

Scaffolding An adult's or an older child's assisting a child to perform within his or her zone of proximal development. See *Zone of Proximal Development.*

Schema A mental structure in which one stores information necessary for the understanding of a concept. A schema for the game of football contains such information as how to play football, how a football field is configured, what positions football players play (e.g., quarterback, center, tight end) and how many points are awarded for scoring plays (e.g., a touchdown, a field goal, a touchback).

School Literacy Perspective A view of reading and writing as ends in themselves, skills to be learned, rather than as tools for genuine communication. This view contrasts with a situated literacy perspective. See *Situated Literacy Perspective.*

Screening Assessments Assessments given at the beginning of the school year to support teachers' decisions about initial instruction, such as in which reading group to place a student so as to best match what the student knows and is ready to learn with what will be taught to a particular group. These contrast with monitoring assessments. See *Monitoring Assessments.*

Scribbling Marks made on a page without control, that is, without any intention of making a particular representation, neither drawing nor text.

Self-Generative Readers and Writers The third of three phases of conventional reading and writing (see Chapter 5). Self-generative readers and writers are highly skilled, control many reading and writing strategies, and write and read a variety of complex texts. See *Conventional Readers and Writers*, *Early Readers and Writers*, and *Transitional Readers and Writers*.

Self-Regulation Ability to inhibit one's own behaviors that are not condoned, focus attention on others including the teacher, willingly take on roles directed by others, and monitor one's own behavior in varied settings.

Semantics Of the four linguistic systems, the one that has to do with meanings. Semantics includes vocabulary knowledge (a *ball* is a round object that can be rolled, thrown, caught, and sometimes bounced), knowledge of word parts (*to roll* means to move end over end along a plane, and *rolled* is *roll* plus *ed* and so it means *roll* plus *past tense* or *roll* plus *already happened*), and knowledge of how words work together (*The ball rolled down the___* can end with *hill* or *hallway* but not with *toothpick*).

Shared Language Language that English language learners and their teachers use easily when communicating about reading and writing tasks. Repeated use of a few key words or phrases in instructional routines makes them accessible to students when they can as yet speak and understand very little other English.

Shared Reading A form of reading aloud to children in which, in addition to reading for enjoyment and understanding, the teacher and children read for teaching and learning literacy concepts and strategies. The text (for example, a big book) is large enough so that the children can read the text along with the teacher.

Shared Writing Instruction in which the teacher writes on chart paper so that students can see and contribute ideas for the content of the piece. During shared writing, teachers model for children how to write texts that serve a variety of purposes. See *Interactive Writing*.

Shared Writing with Write On An instructional activity that combines shared writing and write-on charts. Teachers compose a text on chart paper so that students can see and teachers can explain writing processes, and then the chart-paper text is available for students to write on during choice time. Children may, for example, copy letters, words, or phrases. They write directly on the chart paper above the teacher's writing. See *Shared Writing*.

Sheltered Instructional Observation Protocol (SIOP) A model of instruction for English language learners that includes joint productive activity, focused language instruction, conversations, contextualized instruction, and a rigorous curriculum.

Sight Words Words that one can read immediately upon seeing them, automatically, and without sounding them out. Sight-word vocabularies are personal; their composition varies from one learner to another. They depend on the learning of the individual reader. The words that one reader has learned to read on sight may not be the same as those that another reader has learned to read that way. Eventually, as readers become more skilled, their sight-word vocabularies become large and overlapping. That is, all good readers know a great number of sight words, many of them the same words as in other good readers' sight-word vocabularies, including all high-frequency words. See *High-Frequency Words*.

Sign Concept See *Contextual Dependency*.

Sign-In Procedure A classroom routine in which children begin their day by writing their names on a special form, the sign-in sheet. This serves an attendance-taking function and gives children practice writing their names. Variations include, for very young children, finding their name card and depositing it in a special box and, for older children, in addition to writing their names, writing an answer to a question of the day.

Simple Sentence A sentence composed of a subject and its predicate (e.g., *Chris joined Angela at the piano*, in which *Chris* is the subject and *joined Angela at the piano* is the predicate). See *Compound Sentence*, *Complex Sentence*, and *Syntax*.

Sit and Stay Teachers' remaining in a center for an extended period of time in order to engage children in authentic conversation.

Situated Literacy Perspective A view of reading and writing as activities taking place in the real world for the purpose of achieving real-life goals. This view contrasts with a school literacy perspective. See *School Literacy Perspective*.

Sounding Literate Children's use of literary language, reading intonation, and dialogue markers (such as *he said*) as they compose their own stories, read their compositions, and pretend to read familiar storybooks.

Speech Emergence The third of four phases of children's second language acquisition, notable for children's continuing to acquire vocabulary and developing a wider range of sentence structures. See *Preproduction, Early Production*, and *Intermediate Fluency*.

Spelling See *Orthography*.

Story Grammar A representation of the structure of a typical narrative, including the required elements of a main character or characters; a setting; a problem-setting action or event; a goal; an attempt or attempts to solve the problem or attain the goal; resolution (solution of the problem or attainment of the goal); and the main character's or characters' reaction to the resolution. *Story grammar* is also called *story structure*.

Subtractive Approaches Instructional methods that attempt to replace children's home languages and cultures with English and mainstream culture. These contrast with additive approaches that build on students' home languages and cultures. See *Additive Approaches*.

Suffix An affix attached to the end of a base word, for example, *able* in *unbelievable*. See *Affix*.

Syntax Of the four linguistic systems, the one that has to do with sentence structure. In English, syntax mostly uses word order. For example, noun-verb-noun signifies subject-verb-object: With *The goat kicked the boy*, the goat is the kicker and the boy is the one who was kicked; with *The boy kicked the goat*, the boy is the kicker and the goat is the one who was kicked.

Systematic Phonics Instruction Teaching of phonics by following a sequence of skills considered necessary for efficient word decoding and spelling. Most sequences are arranged from those skills considered easiest to those considered most difficult.

Tabula Rasa Literally, "blank slate." According to the Tabula Rasa theory, a newborn child's mind is a blank slate; it is empty of knowledge or schemas.

Talk-Through Activity A teacher's preview of a text in order to orient children to its overall meaning, repetitive language patterns, particular new and important words, and unusual language structures.

Telegraphic Speech Two- or three-word combinations that signal such semantic content as subject-verb, verb-object, or subject-verb-object without the structural morphemes that are found in mature speech. *Mommy pull, Pull wagon*, and *Mommy pull wagon* are examples of subject-verb, verb-object, and subject-verb-object utterances in telegraphic speech. *Mommy is pulling the wagon* is an example of an utterance in mature speech; it contains the structural morphemes (*is, ing*, and *the*) that are missing in the examples of telegraphic speech.

Text and Toy Sets A storybook and related, realistic, small-scale toys and other props. These are used to stimulate dramatic play about books. During free-choice time, for example, children might tell a story they have heard in an earlier read-aloud and dramatize it using the toys and props.

Tier 2 Words Words that are more sophisticated than everyday words. For example, the everyday word *car* is related to the more sophisticated tier 2 word *automobile*.

Total Physical Response (TPR) A vocabulary development activity for English language learners in which teachers hold up an object or a picture of an object and say its name, and children respond physically rather than verbally to indicate their understanding.

Transaction A unique interaction between a reader and a text, founded on prior knowledge and resulting in personal understandings and interpretations.

Transitional Readers and Writers The second of three phases of conventional reading and writing (see Chapter 5). Transitional readers and writers use multiple sophisticated decoding and comprehension strategies to read fluently and to understand complicated informational texts and stories, including chapter books. They become conventional spellers and write in several genres. See *Conventional Readers and Writers, Early Readers and Writers*, and *Self-Generative Readers and Writers*.

Utterance Complexity How many and what kinds of phrases and clauses a child uses to make a number of different kinds of sentences.

Utterance Length The number of morphemes a child uses, on average, in a turn at talking. Also called *mean length of utterance*. Utterance length is computed by sampling a child's language, counting the number of morphemes in the whole sample, and dividing by the number of the child's turns at talking in the sample.

Vocabulary Prop Box A box of objects that are mentioned in a storybook or information book. Teachers display and talk about the items in connection with reading the books aloud, in order to enhance children's vocabularies.

Vocabulary Variety The number of different words, especially rare words, that a child understands and uses.

Vowel Markers Letters whose function is not to represent their own sounds but instead to indicate the long quality or other nonshort quality of a neighboring vowel. Without vowel markers, vowels often have the default, that is, short, quality. For example, the final *e* in *bite* is silent, but it nonetheless has the important role of marking the *i* as long (*i* in *bite* has the sound /I/). In contrast, *bit* does not need a vowel marker; its vowel is short (/i/). Similarly, the *w* in *fawn* marks the *a* as having a nonshort quality, in this case, /aw/. Without the vowel marker *w*, the *a* would be, by default, short (/a/); the word would be *fan*, pronounced /fan/. Of course, as with most phonics generalizations, this one does not always apply. That is why we said "often" about default short vowels. It's often the case that unmarked vowels are short, but not always. The greatest number of exceptions is the case of open vowels that are often long without having markers (e.g., the *e* in *be* and the *o* in *so*), but there are many other exceptions (e.g., the *o* in *dog*, which in most dialects is /aw/, not the short /o/).

"What-Can-You-Show-Us?" Activity An activity in which a teacher displays a new text and, before reading it, invites children to demonstrate what they know about it. Children with a wide range of reading abilities can participate successfully. For example, some may identify individual letters, some may point out punctuation, some may read sight words, some may show how they decode a decodable word, and some may read whole phrases or sentences. The teacher uses children's demonstrated knowledge when they later read the text together.

Word Consciousness Awareness of words and interest in their meanings.

Word Hunt A word-study activity in which children search for words with particular spelling patterns in books, magazines, and newspapers.

Word-Sort Activity A word-study activity in which children collect words by making word cards for them, and then, after several days of collecting, arrange the cards according to the words' spelling patterns.

Word Wall A display on a classroom wall or large bulletin board of word cards for children's reference when reading and writing, usually of undecodable and high-frequency words, grouped by initial letter.

Writing the Room An activity in which children walk around their classroom in search of print—usually carrying pencils and paper on clipboards—and then copy words that interest them.

Writing Workshop An approach to teaching writing that includes regularly scheduled time for children to work as writers ("workshop time") by using the processes of drafting, revising, editing, and sharing. Teachers teach mini-lessons about writing processes, and students and teachers hold writing conferences and celebrate students' published writing.

Written Language Assessment Any activity to determine a person's state of knowledge of, understanding about, or ability with reading and writing.

Written Language Forms All aspects of how written language looks. These cover a wide range. At the small end of that range are the features of which individual alphabet letters are composed (such as two vertical lines and two diagonal lines for *M* and a vertical line and part of a circle for *P*). At the large end are the organizational features of whole texts (such as the rows of words and phrases that make a list or the collection of chapters that make a novel). See *Letter Features* and *Text Format*.

Written Language Meanings Messages conveyed by texts. These include implied as well as literal meanings. Children have acquired the most important insight about written language when they understand that texts are not randomly occurring, haphazard marks on a page, but rather represent a writer's encoded message that is decodable by a reader.

Zone of Proximal Development Vygotsky's* notion of a space between what a child can do on his or her own and what he or she can do with the help of a more knowledgeable other person, usually an adult. A four-year-old girl who can put on her shoes but can't tie them operates in the zone of proximal development when she makes the first knot with the help of her mother and then holds down that knot with her finger while her mother forms loops and makes of them the second, finishing knot.

---

*Vygotsky, L.S. (1978). *Mind in society: The development of higher psychological processes* (Michael Cole, Translator). Cambridge: Harvard University Press.

Name Index

Subject Index